United States
and
Africa Relations,
1400s to the Present

UNITED STATES AND AFRICA RELATIONS, 1400S TO THE PRESENT

Toyin Falola and
Raphael Chijioke Njoku

Yale
UNIVERSITY
PRESS
New Haven & London

Published with assistance from the Louis Stern Memorial Fund.

Yale University Press books may be purchased in quantity for educational, business, or
promotional use. For information, please e-mail sales.press@yale.edu (U.S. office) or
sales@yaleup.co.uk (U.K. office).

Set in Electra type by Newgen North America.
Printed in the United States of America.

Library of Congress Control Number: 2019956877
ISBN 978-0-300-23483-1 (paper : alk. paper)

A catalogue record for this book is available from the British Library.

This paper meets the requirements of ANSI/NISO Z39.48-1992 (Permanence of Paper).

10 9 8 7 6 5 4 3 2 1

To
Prof. John E. McLeod
and
Dr. Mary McLeod

CONTENTS

PREFACE

The idea of this book materialized from deep contemplation of the momentous election of Barack Obama to the presidency in November 2008 and all it tells us about African Americans' six-century-long journey in the Americas. As Obama's second term was ending, the authors compiled a plan for an account of the long-running United States-Africa relationship that paved his road to the White House. The story of United States-Africa relations is rooted in the trans-Atlantic slave trade beginning in the mid-fifteenth century. The relationship gradually developed with Black struggles for emancipation, enfranchisement, and empowerment. The struggle spanned several centuries and is in certain respects ongoing. In other words, the Black odyssey was the mother of the unique relationship between Africa and the United States of America.

In an academic field that has witnessed a profusion of literature reflecting diverse disciplinary perspectives, this account of United States-Africa relations from the fifteenth century to the present is complex and challenging. Given the overflow of events from one historical period to another, it was sometimes difficult to impose a neat chronological structure. In terms of methodology, it was unavoidable now and then to use social science theories to shed light on some ideas in the historical narrative. Yet, we acknowledge that a discourse of this nature, located at the intersection of race, oppression, religious creed, and nationalist ethos, has the potential to stir up a wide range of human emotions, misconceptions, and agitated debates. Our intent is purely academic: to provide scholars, graduate and undergraduate students interested in Africana studies, African American studies, African studies, Atlantic history, world history, and international relations with a one-stop account of Africa's bonding with the United States.

The process of economic, cultural, and political bonding began long before the official founding of Britain's American colonies, and its geographical spread encompasses the entire Atlantic world. Our emphasis on the United States is amply justified. The United States represents the most successful and powerful of all the colonies the Europeans built in the age of imperialism. Despite the difficult circumstances in which they strived, the Black population occupies a central position in the American success story. African Americans now constitute the most potent Black community in the world.

Considering the length of time this book covers, prioritizing the African American experience is the most suitable but not the only model for historicizing United States-Africa relations. The manner in which Whites treated Blacks in America shaped the nature and substance of the United States-Africa relationship. The African American experience was the most notable life force that produced the trans-Atlantic exchanges and continued to drive them until 1900. This process will likely continue to affect the future of United States-Africa relations.

We therefore delineate the foundations of United States-Africa relations through the prisms of slavery, emancipation, colonization, American missionary evangelism, and Pan-Africanism. If the African American perspective is dominant in the various foundational themes so explored, it is because the United States-Africa relationship, over these historical eras, was more about the enslaved people and how their fate in the Americas affected the future of Africa than anything else. The trials and pains of the men and women in bondage reverberated across the Atlantic world and impacted sociopolitical and economic developments in the African continent, including the abolitionist movement that led to the founding of Sierra Leone and Liberian colonies.

The emphasis on the African American connection tapers as Africa emerged from European colonial rule after World War II. It was in the context of the Cold War that the United States began to implement a more articulate foreign policy toward Africa. As a result, the tone of the book's narrative changes from a primarily historical account to a more contemporary approach to foreign policy.

In the process of writing this book, we consulted numerous libraries, archives, depositories, and museums, and borrowed materials from many colleagues. We owe immense gratitude to several friends, colleagues, and anonymous referees who read several drafts of this book and provided insightful comments. Special thanks to Erika Kuhlman, Kevin Marsh, John Gribas, and Kandi Turley-Ames for organizing a forum (with funds from the Idaho Humanities Council) at which the first draft of this book was presented. The participation of the Red Hill Band and the entire audience at that Café added an extra flavor to the discussion. We owe immense gratitude to King Yik for his generosity with ideas and materials for this research. The final product of the book, therefore, is a composite of our original designs and thoughts from our readers, audience, and colleagues.

We thank Yale University Press's acquisitions editor and faculty Publications Committee for supporting this ambitious project. Together, they provided the motivation and enthusiasm that have seen to the successful completion of *United States and Africa Relations, 1400s to the Present.*

INTRODUCTION

This multilayered study of the history of relations between Africa and the Americas focuses on the United States from the colonial era to the present. The relationship began with the dawn of the trans-Atlantic slave trade, which preceded the official founding of the United States. As a result, the early stage of United States-Africa relations is situated within the history of slavery and African American struggles for survival, emancipation, and reconnection with the African ancestral homeland. The Black struggle in America intersects with economic exchanges and wealth production, race relations, cultural invention, colonialism, revolutionary movements in the Atlantic world, religion, politics, and intellectual ideas.

In a discourse involving two entities where one is an old continent (Africa) and the other (the United States) did not declare itself a sovereign state until July 4, 1776, one may wonder why going back to the 1400s matters. Before the founding of the American Colonization Society (ACS) and Liberia in the second decade of the nineteenth century, direct contact between America and Africa was limited. The justification for extending our history of the relationship back to the fifteenth century is to account for shifting concepts, geographical spaces, and peoples.[1] Africa, Pan-Africanism, and the United States have meant different things at different times to different peoples.

For most of the sixteenth century, North America, as a distinct space in the developing Atlantic relationship, was a symbol of the Spanish power that encompassed several parts of what is now the United States. The Spanish conquistadors and speculators at one point or another laid claim to Florida (1513), Upper New York Bay (1525), South Carolina (1526), Arkansas (1539), Kansas (1540), the California coast (1542), and so on. What in time became the United

States of America, the most successful colony in the entire European imperial project, started to take its present form in 1607, when the English Pilgrims arrived at Jamestown, Virginia. By 1650, the North Atlantic coastal expanse had turned into a solid part of the British imperial presence, with the thirteen original colonies standing as the precursor of the modern United States.

The African presence was integral to early American colonial history. In August 1619, the *White Lion*, an English ship, brought to Jamestown the first documented group of twenty Africans, most of whom were indentured laborers.[2] The Africans acquired by the Portuguese from West and Central Africa were heading to Mexico when a British squadron intercepted and removed them from the Portuguese ship *San Juan Bautista*. However, the discovery of the *Farrar Papers* reveals that by March 1619, residents of the Virginia colony already included fifteen Black men and seventeen Black women.[3] This revelation means either that there were other Africans in Virginia prior to the arrival of the twenty slaves, or that there is a severe error in the historical record. Though it is evident that most, if not all, of the other captive Africans arrived as indentured laborers, a considerable number of them, like Anthony and Mary Johnson, either purchased their freedom in Virginia or were freed soon after arriving in the colony.[4] Whether servant, slave, or free, these Africans appropriated most of the same rights and duties as other Virginians—English, Spanish, Portuguese, Dutch, and Turkish.

Before 1662, when slavery was enshrined in Virginia's legal corpus, the Africans could use the courts to seek redress for wrongs, reserved the right to a legitimate enterprise such as land ownership and farming business, and observed atonement in parish churches for common human follies, including breeding illegitimate children.[5] For the Europeans who lived side by side with Blacks in the colony, it was difficult to comprehend Africa at this time as an immense and polysemous entity. Like the first Portuguese visitors to the continent, the Virginia residents came to understand the African continent from the nature of their acquaintance and interaction with the West and Central Africans who represented a fraction of the continent's immense ethnic and cultural diversity.

The story of United States-Africa relations is one of globalization. On one side of the Atlantic, the context of the relationship evolved in a centripetal fashion—from the Grand American space to the British-owned North American empire. On the other side of the Atlantic, the concepts of Africa and Pan-Africanism developed centrifugally. In the perception of the early European colonists in America, West and Central Africans were apparently identical to the other ethnicities found in the continent. Over time, this narrow concept of Africa in the Atlantic world expanded to denote first sub-Saharan Africa, then continental Africa and its diasporas, including the Caribbean, Latin America, and North America.

Thus, tracing the history of United States-Africa relations back to the fifteenth century allows us to appreciate how the relationship has changed from the very beginning. Considering the evolving meanings of the concepts from the fifteenth century, "Africa" and "the United States," as used in the early period of this relationship, serve more as identifiers in shifting Atlantic relations. In reality, the focus is on the complex social engineering and cultural hybridities the Europeans created in the American setting. The cross-Atlantic exchanges that led to the birth of the United States involved diverse spaces, actors, and peoples — Europeans, Africans, Native Americans, and other races. As a result, the United States-Africa relationship is as fluid and multifaceted as the historical arcs. Sometimes the story we tell in this book assumes a predominantly economic dimension, with a chain of players drawn from different regions of the Atlantic world. At other times it accentuates the political and cultural elements, with multiple geographical boundaries.

To be clear, *United States and Africa Relations* is not a conventional study of international relations that focuses on state actors and the consequences of their actions. In our view, United States-Africa relations are analogous to a marital relationship. They share all the suspense, resolution, love, and hate that go with every connubial relationship, especially a forced marriage. They further denote the allure of creolization, trust and betrayal, patriarchal authority and defiance, the sublimity of rights and wrongs associated with kinship belonging, the consequences of the actions, inactions, and indulgences of members in a common union, and of course the rigors of hubris, abuses, diplomacy, and the throes of conflict and peacemaking.

The broad range of subjects we treat in the following chapters includes the trans-Atlantic slave trade, the making of the African diasporas in the Americas, African influences on agriculture in North America, the Back-to-Africa movement, and the founding of the colonies of Sierra Leone and Liberia. Other themes explored are the American missionary enterprise in Africa and African influences on American culture, particularly blues and jazz music, family rituals, and religions. Also covered are more recent events, from the rise of Pan-Africanism around 1900 through the presidency of Barack Obama.

Other subjects highlighted include the careers of Black thinkers in both the Americas and the African continent. Through their writings and speeches, these individuals shaped and reshaped the African question in line with the ideologies they espoused. We also examine the intersection between the U.S. civil rights movement of the 1950s and 1960s and decolonization in Africa in the same period. A more formal U.S. African policy emerged through these processes, especially during the interwar years and the Cold War as the United States fought to blunt the ideological warfare waged by the Communist bloc. Other topics explored are the more recent presence of African-born immigrants in the United States, the foreign policy interests that drove the U.S. engagement with Africa on issues related to human rights, the democratization of state institutions and governance, globalization and neoliberalism, and the war against terrorism. Additionally, we highlight China's recent foreign policy and its ongoing massive economic investments in Africa. We present the new Sino-African partnership not just as a counterhegemonic influence to Western interests in the region, but also as a manifest outcome of America's often ad hoc and hesitant African policies.

This account of the long relationship between the United States and Africa reveals a mix of intrigue and complexities. The early era (ca. 1440s–1800) was the age of slavocrats, the global elite of the period, engrossed in aggressive and exploitative economic and political practices. The need for survival in an interdependent world prompted trans-Atlantic collaboration; hence, a frantic quest by the European colonists in the Americas for African labor and products drove large commercial transactions, long-distance crossings, and forced migrations. Africans embraced the stimulus for sociocultural, economic, and political exchanges that this trans-Atlantic commerce engendered. Perhaps no region of the world reveals the contradictions that characterized the Atlantic world during this period more clearly than Africa.

By outsourcing an estimated 9 to 12 million slaves to the New World, Africans bore the enormous weight of the labor that was crucial for the British American colonies' survival and subsequent growth as a nation. Rev. Peter Fontaine, an Anglican minister and English resident of colonial Virginia, offered a realistic, if rather relativist, justification for the existence of slavery in Virginia when he stated that "to live in Virginia without slaves is morally impossible."[6] It is not clear what Reverend Fontaine meant by the phrase "morally impossible," but one may deduce that the physical survival of his race in this era was heavily dependent on the labor of African slaves. Indeed, a state of interdependency at both the individual and group levels bonded the lives of peoples throughout the Atlantic world.

Reverend Fontaine's statement necessitates a review of the trans-Atlantic slave trade not only from the socioeconomic perspective that characterizes most extant studies but also through the lenses of international relations and psychology. David Brion Davis reminds us that "from the very beginnings of American history, the lives of blacks and whites had been intertwined on the most complex social, cultural, economic and psychological levels."[7] The pertinent question becomes how these various levels of interactions and their density structured a pattern of trans-Atlantic relations, and how those relations have evolved over time. These diverse and multifaceted linkages, beginning with the slave trade, laid the foundation on which present-day United States-Africa ties were established.

The beginning of the twentieth century marked the dawn of a new era in Africa-United States relations, as people of African descent championed an ideology of "We Africans," or what a commentator has identified as a pragmatic ideology for self-preservation.[8] For Blacks, this was the age of self-reinvention. As a catalyst for uplifting the Black race led by such pioneers of modern Pan-African thought as Alexander Crummell and W. E. B. Du Bois, collective political and ideological leadership in a transnational framework became the most sensible option for a race and a continent constantly threatened by predatory alien actors. Pan-Africanism, therefore, offered a survivalist toolkit for the global community of races.[9]

Perhaps at no other time did Pan-Africanism better serve as an inoculation against a depredatory inter-race association than in the two centuries before 2000. While American society of the nineteenth and early twentieth centuries transitioned from the pangs of emancipation and the Jim Crow laws to the era of the civil rights movement, the African continent fought to end European colonial domination and exploitation. In the 1960s, Africans experienced a wide range of emotions as they moved from the exuberance of nationalist movements and decolonization, through the political turmoil of postcolonialism and the politics of the Cold War, to the economic challenges of the 1970s and 1980s. The fiscal chaos that threatened the postcolonial African state was provoked by the collapse of commodity markets and the Structural Adjustment Programs (SAPs) sponsored by the International Monetary Fund (IMF) and mediated by the United States and its Western allies. This period offers a host of African triumphs and setbacks. It was also the age of hastened cultural exchanges on the global stage, as Africans took advantage of transnational connections and new forms of communication to engage with other regions of the world, including the United States, in a variety of ways.

As exchanges between the United States and Africa transitioned from an ad hoc commitment to a more regularized relationship in the late twentieth and early twenty-first centuries, international and diplomatic relations became increasingly essential. Recognizing the necessity for a more productive engagement with the African postcolonial states, the U.S. State Department in 1958 created the Bureau of African Affairs under President Dwight D. Eisenhower to provide informed advice to the Secretary of State on issues related to sub-Saharan Africa. In 1961, President John F. Kennedy founded the United States

Agency for International Development (USAID). The primary purpose of the agency was to allow for closer and mutually beneficial foreign assistance, with the Peace Corps volunteers program serving as the cornerstone of this initiative. In March 1978, President Jimmy Carter made a trip to Nigeria and Liberia during which he declared that the United States "has now turned in an unprecedented way toward Africa."[10]

While the agencies created to advance the U.S. presence in Africa have achieved tremendous successes in furthering United States-Africa relations, there is room for improvement. A drawback evident in the trans-Atlantic exchanges remains the manner in which the United States administers its development aid to the continent. *United States and Africa Relations* reveals that a deeper appreciation of the underlying history that bonded the peoples on both sides of the Atlantic is central to more mutually beneficial U.S.-African foreign policy goals.

The value of this volume lies in its concise presentation of a broad perspective and the addition of new themes to a variety of well-studied topics. Previous works have focused on aspects of the trans-Atlantic linkages, but none treats the six centuries of unbroken relationship starting in the 1400s. Curtis Keim's *Mistaking Africa: Curiosities and Inventions of the American Mind* attempts to persuade the average American not to imagine Africa as merely a space for wildlife and barbarism. Joseph Holloway's edited volume *Africanisms in American Culture* explores the impact of African cultural traits on White America.[11] Peter Duignan and L. H. Gann's *The United States and Africa: A History*, published in 1987 and critiqued by Peter J. Schraeder as a defense of America's Cold War–era foreign policy, also focuses on the slave trade and commerce, and therefore cannot deal with other diverse nuances of United States-Africa relations, especially developments since the 1960s.[12] As if picking up where Duignan and Gann stop, the volume edited by G. Macharia Munene and others entitled *The United States and Africa* surveys the themes of war, democratization, trade, and security from the 1960s to the end of the Cold War in the early 1990s.[13] The authors do not pretend to offer broad coverage of the several centuries of trans-Atlantic relations, and since the 1990s new developments have emerged in both Africa and the United States.

Several other African diaspora studies focus on the slave trade and the planting of African cultural practices in the Americas. Examples include Toyin Falola's *The African Diaspora* and the volume edited by Linda Haywood, *Central Africans and Cultural Transformations in the American Diaspora*.[14] Other studies converging on related themes are Ibrahim Sundiata's *Brothers and Strangers: Black Zion, Black Slavery*, a sterling treatment of the founding of Liberia, and James Meriwether's *Proudly We Can Be Africans: Black Americans and Africa,*

1935–1961.[15] While these and many other works provide excellent accounts of specific ethnic groups in the Americas and their contributions to the rise of culture, they do not give a concise treatment of the long history of United States-Africa relations that this book offers. In *Between Homeland and Motherland*, Alvin B. Tillery, Jr., reflects on the history of U.S. engagement with Africa from the African American perspective, from Paul Cuffee's Back-to-Africa movement in the nineteenth century to the recent struggle by the congressional Black Caucus to come to a consensus on the African Growth and Opportunity Act of 2000. Tillery's work is essential because it recognizes the critical role of America's domestic politics and how issues within the African American community shape U.S.-African foreign relations.

Among other things, *United States and Africa Relations* centralizes the role of American domestic issues, mainly as they have affected Americans of African descent. Our study offers an important update on United States-Africa relations by addressing such themes as African immigration to the United States, the U.S. human rights agenda, global Africa, and Obama and Africa. These themes constitute a valuable update to such seminal works as Peter Schraeder's *United States Foreign Policy toward Africa*; Elliot P. Skinner's *African Americans and U.S. Policy toward Africa, 1850–1924: In Defense of Black Nationality*, or even shorter and more narrowly focused studies such as Raymond Copson's *The United States and Africa: Bush Policy and Beyond* and David Gordon, David Miller, and Gordon Wolpe's *The United States and Africa: A Post–Cold War Perspective.*[16]

The present study stresses that states and regions tend to enter into international dealings from a position of either strength or weakness. Judicious use of the theories of international relations, including those of realism, liberalism, constructivism, critical approaches, and institutionalism, elucidates our interpretation of the dynamics of slavery and post-slavery and its implications for United States-Africa relations in both the early and later periods. The study of international relations embraces a broad range of theoretical approaches, drawing from disciplines such as economics, history, religion, sociology, and even psychology. Notwithstanding the interdisciplinary nature of the field, there are different schools of thought with different areas of emphasis such as coercive capabilities, economic power, or ideological inclinations.[17]

CHAPTER OUTLINES

The book, comprising fourteen chapters, is organized into three parts with overlapping periodization. Part I, "The Age of Slavocrats: Labor, Culture, and Power Relations," contains four chapters covering events from early American colonial history to the era of emancipation. The narrative proceeds from the understanding that a seed must die for it to grow.

In Chapter 1, "African Labor and the British American Colony," we identify the seed as the American Dream embodied by the United States, and the planters as the Europeans and Africans. The focus is on one of the most transformative features of the early modern period — the trans-Atlantic commercial system. Slave labor enabled the Europeans to harness the abundant natural resources in their American colonies. By 1865, when the Thirteenth Amendment to the U.S. Constitution prohibited slavery in the United States, both enslaved and free had helped build a solid economic foundation in America.[18] Without retelling the history of the slave trade already covered in the extant literature,[19] we emphasize the role of enslaved Africans in the building of the U.S. economy and society from the original colonies dependent on slavery to an industrialized and prosperous nation-state.[20]

In Chapter 2, "The African Diaspora: Memory, Survival, and Longing for Africa," we recount the dynamics of survival and how Africa was remembered among the enslaved Africans. The emphasis is on the practices, memories, institutions, coping strategies, and structures that provided succor and identity for those in bondage. This understanding resonates with a long-lasting debate in African diaspora studies over whether the African slaves arrived in the New World devoid of their African heritage. For instance, Albert Raboteau claims that the "African religious heritage was lost" among slaves in British North America and that "the gods of Africa gave way to the God of Christianity."[21] Rather than dwelling on this old debate, we focus on how the survival of African religions and other items of culture contributed to the development of African American culture.

Chapter 3, "From Land of Freedom to Crown Colony of Sierra Leone," is about the British colony of Sierra Leone and its historical connection with slaves and the Black race in the United States. The British philanthropists and abolitionists who founded the "Freetown colony," established on August 22, 1788, conceived of it as a home for emancipated African slaves in England and other parts of the British Empire. The emancipation movement received a big boost when émigrés from the United States (through Nova Scotia, Canada) joined the first settlers of the colony.[22] This dynamic positioned the Black émigrés as symbols and conductors of United States-Africa cooperation.

In Chapter 4, "President James Monroe and the Colonization Society: From Monrovia to Liberia," we observe the attempt to equate African American settlers in Liberia with the British founders of Jamestown and Plymouth. This supposed similarity rested on the new settlers' recreation of certain aspects of U.S.-style sociopolitical, cultural, and legal systems in West Africa. The nineteenth-century supporters of colonization anticipated a role for settlers in Liberia in "civilizing" Africa and building a new society that would be as attractive to American Blacks as the United States had proved to be for European immigrants. Liberia was envisaged, as John Winthrop imagined Puritan settlements, as "a city on a hill" that would tower above others.[23] Under President Monroe, promoters of Black immigration to Liberia framed the discourse within the biblical Exodus narrative as a journey to the Promised Land. Its exponents (including the American founding fathers) endorsed Liberia as an answer to the crime rampant among emancipated Blacks.[24]

Although the enslaved Africans had long nursed the idea of African regeneration, a more pragmatic sense of this notion of rebirth materialized with the Liberian colony scheme. The Christian missionary enterprises in Africa went hand in hand with the Back-to-Africa movement sponsored by a rainbow coalition of politicians, abolitionists, missionaries, and philanthropists with diverse agendas. This is the theme of Part II, "The Age of Ideas: Pragmatism, Self-Preservation, and African Regenerations."

Chapter 5, "American Missionaries in Africa," highlights a recurring theme in Adrian Hastings's magisterial study of the church in Africa: people of African descent played a central role in evangelizing the continent. According to Hastings, by the 1780s the small Black elite in London, which included men such as Olaudah Equiano and Ottobah Cugoano, "appear[ed] already conscious of constituting something of a cultural, linguistic, and religious bridge with Africa."[25] A further group to whom he refers, although fleetingly, is African American missionaries. Over a period of 150 years, starting in the 1870s, African American missionaries led by White American and European boards sought to spread the Christian gospel in the Black Atlantic.[26] Despite attempts by the White missionaries to limit their works in Africa, by the 1920s, the African American missionaries had bequeathed to Africa a Black theology that set the continent on the road to spiritual and political emancipation from European colonial domination.

Chapter 6, "The Back-to-Africa Movement/Black Zionism," extends the discussion on colonization. In the twentieth century, Marcus Garvey emerged as the flagbearer of colonization. To breathe new life into the movement, he likened the Liberia project to the Jewish Zionist movement. In the words of Martin Luther King, Jr., Garvey was the first man "on a mass scale and level to give millions of Negroes a sense of dignity and destiny and make the Negro feel he was somebody."[27] One can question Garvey's private intentions as the "Provisional President of Africa." Garvey's critics say that his ulterior motive was to gain power as the spokesperson and leader of the entire continent. However, he fell victim to the race supremacists who concocted colonization with the intention of ridding the United States of free and emancipated Blacks.

Chapter 7, "The Pan-Africanist Idea," treats the ideology in depth as a Black movement in a transnational context. Although talked about a great deal, Pan-Africanism deserves more attention as a political movement or concept. While often identified with the first Pan-African Conference held in London in July 1900, the ideology reaches back to 1787, when significant developments occurred across the Atlantic world: in the United States, the effective beginning of organized abolitionism and of organized activities by free African Americans; in Britain, the beginning of abolitionist agitation; and in West Africa, as an indirect result of abolitionism, the foundation of Sierra Leone, which was to make a significant contribution to the formation of the modern intellectual elites in British West Africa. Thus, abolitionism on both sides of the Atlantic helped to produce those modern (educated) elites in the New World and Africa who alone could articulate the concept of Pan-Africanism and translate it into political agitation and action in the twentieth century. As authors, ministers, and activists, they provided some glimpses of the political evolution of Pan-Africanism in African identities.

Chapter 8, "Cultural Exchanges and Trans-Atlantic Bonds: African Music and the Evolution of Blues and Jazz," discusses the evolution of jazz from the musical traditions of Blacks in the Mississippi Delta in the 1920s, when the blues came to be seen as a standard of authenticity for jazz musicians. We remind the reader that American blues and jazz did not emerge in a vacuum. They are not just relics of slavery and ancient musical instruments but also an expression of sentiments, an expression of African and Creole identity and emotions, a form of American mannerism, and even a collective history. The multiple forms of Black music in the United States, including blues, jazz, and rock and roll, have fueled waves of musical innovation, such as hip-hop and Afrobeat, particularly in West Africa. African American music may have African origins (and we easily demonstrate these linkages with jazz and the blues), but hip-hop (a *cultural* transmitter) marks an African Americanized form that has migrated *back* to Africa. Music, Africa's gift to humanity, has been the most potent force in cross-cultural exchange within the Atlantic world.

If enslaved Africans played a considerable role in the American success story, Parrt III, "African Colonial Freedom and the Modern Experience," acknowledges the U.S. involvement in Africa's colonial economies in the nineteenth and twentieth centuries. However, modern Pan-Africanist agitation, nurtured in the United States, prepared the ground for the final face-off between Black freedoms in the United States and Africa on the one hand, and race suprema-cists and colonial subjugation on the other.

Chapter 9, "The Civil Rights Movement Meets Decolonization," demon-strates how people of African descent on both sides of the Atlantic drew inspira-tion and support from one another in their quest for Black freedom from cen-turies of alien domination and exploitation. The post–World War II era offers a unique opportunity for a comparative study of social and political movements in the United States and Africa. Liberation movements in the form of civil rights and women's rights movements changed the calculus of social dynamics in the West, and decolonization transformed the non-Western world and global poli-tics. Other movements, such as the struggle against apartheid in South Africa and Pan-Arabism, helped establish linkages across the borders of new states and with the African diaspora.[28] Of particular interest is how the various movements in the Atlantic world informed one another and interacted. Specific examples include the collaboration between African nationalist leaders living or study-ing in the United States from the 1940s to the 1960s and their shared visions of freedom for the Black race and African development.

Chapter 10, "The Cold War: U.S. African Policy Reset," identifies the inter-war years as the beginning of a more focused and deliberate U.S. African policy. Before this, America's engagement with Africa in the realm of international re-lations was ad hoc, hesitant, and inconsistent. This chapter highlights the ways that the ideological duel between the capitalist West and the communist East played out in Africa, and its deep-seated consequences.

Chapter 11, "African-Born Immigrants in the United States," underscores the roots of the recent arrival of the African-born immigrants in the United States and how this immigration parallels a continuum of the United States-African dialogue. Although a handful of Africans studied in the United States between the 1940s and the 1960s, the labor needs for building the postcolonial state stimulated considerable growth in university-level education for Africans. Thus, the 1970s and 1980s saw an increased desire for American higher edu-cation among the new generation of Africans. Often these Africans returned to apply the knowledge and benefits of their sojourns in the United States to the socioeconomic and political developmental needs of their home countries. However, not all of these students and their families went back to Africa. The chief reasons for this were the increasing incidence of conflict on the conti-nent and the attractions of an American lifestyle. As civil crises increased in the 1990s, Africa witnessed a brain drain.[29] Whether Africans who emigrated were engineers, doctors, teachers, nurses, or writers, their presence in the United States refreshed the long history of United States-Africa relations and enriched cultural exchanges. There are now hundreds of African ethnic unions in the United States observing a myriad of ethnic cultural events and "national days."[30] Through these events, African foods, plays, music, religious adaptations, moonlight songs (or folktales), films, new religious ideas, and so on are imported and transmitted to the new generation of African Americans with African parents.

In Chapter 12, "U.S. Pressures: Human Rights and Recent Democratization Movements in Africa," we see a progression of the Cold War–era foreign policy strategy toward institution building and liberal values. Over the past two decades, the United States' effective foreign policy approach on human rights and democratization in Africa has resulted in fewer incidents of military coups and a rise in democratic transitions across the continent. One explanation for these development stands out: namely, the dread of the United States that seized the hearts of African dictators and would-be coup plotters soon after the U.S. military invaded Saddam Hussein's Iraq, first in 1991 and then in 2003. In early April 1986, President Ronald Reagan ordered the bombing of Col. Muammar Gaddafi's Libya, accusing him of sponsoring terrorism. Even more shocking was the killing of the Libyan dictator in October 2011 at the hands of insurgents supported by U.S. and French aerial assaults under the NATO banner. Through these forms of pressures, often accompanied by threats of economic sanctions, the United States has helped advance democratic transitions in Africa even as dictators and their cronies have been trying to impose their wills.

Chapter 13, "Africa and the New Global Age: China's Giant Strides," holds some of the most important lessons for contemporary American politicians and policymakers. This message is implicit in Africa's manifest gravitation toward China in the past two decades. While many African states faced economic declines in the 1970s and 1980s, others saw boom periods resulting from the discovery and exploitation of vast petroleum reserves or mineral deposits. This recent growth reflects earlier booms (and busts), but it has also been accompanied by infrastructure development. From our standpoint, it has been driven less by U.S. policies than by other "global" dynamics, especially the rise of China. In other words, China's recent involvement in Africa can be viewed in relation to U.S. actions (and inactions) toward the postcolonial states in Africa over the years.

Chapter 14, "The Obama Presidency and Africa: Opportunities and Disappointments," caps our account of centuries of United States-Africa relations in a positive light, though with paradoxical and complex results. The rise of Barack Obama, the son of a Kenyan immigrant father and a White American woman from Kansas, perhaps epitomizes one of the most substantial outcomes of the long history of United States-Africa exchanges. The focus here is on the points of connection that Obama represented for Africa and the United States, and what this may say about the strength of the United States-Africa relationship, especially in the minds of many Africans, even despite centuries of inequality.

In sum, this book features the strength of United States-Africa partnerships as globalization simultaneously expands and constricts national and regional borders. Situating the United States-Africa experience in a global context allows for a better appreciation of how the European colonists in the Americas initially conceived Africa as a reservoir of labor. Though Americans have not always considered Africans as equal partners in Atlantic exchanges, the subtleties of interdependency have persisted despite the physical separation imposed by the Atlantic Ocean. The enslaved people's survival of their American experience remains one of the wonders of the modern world. It shows that African Americans in the United States have earned a rightful place in the American Dream. To paraphrase Martin Luther King, Jr., Blacks have seen the mountaintop.[31] This is to say that the collective heritage of the United States and Africa is more relevant than ever in the new global age.

Part I

THE AGE OF SLAVOCRATS

Labor, Culture, and Power Relations

1

AFRICAN LABOR AND THE BRITISH AMERICAN COLONY, 1619–1865

One of the most transformative episodes of the early modern period in world history is the trans-Atlantic slave trade, a commercial system involving Europe, Africa, and the Americas. Before the first boatload of enslaved Africans made the trans-Atlantic voyage to the Americas, the Portuguese had already started putting African slaves to work on their sugar plantations located on the islands of Madeira, off the northwest coast of Africa, and São Tomé in the Gulf of Guinea. The four centuries of the Atlantic slave trade turned Africa into a labor farm for European business holdings in the Americas. In the early sixteenth century, both Africa and the Americas became lands of immense opportunity and possibility, and therefore favored destinations for European speculators and fortune seekers. The Europeans scoured Africa in search of slave labor, which enabled them to harness the abundant natural resources of their American colonies. Motivated by a common interest in profit making, African slave dealers supplied captive people for the ocean-borne trade, which lasted from around 1501 to 1875 (Table 1.1.).[1]

By 1865, when the Thirteenth Amendment in the United States abolished slavery, millions of enslaved Africans had rendered the crucial labor that not only sustained the everyday existence of the American colonists but also erected a solid economic foundation for the United States' economic future.[2] The focus here is not to recount the history of the trans-Atlantic slave trade already covered in the extant literature.[3] Rather, the emphasis is on the role of African labor, handicraft, and technology in the development of the U.S. economy from the original thirteen trading colonies to a robust plantation economy to an industrialized nation-state. The ensuing discussion asserts the early bonds between Africa and the United States, notwithstanding the flaws and imbalances

Table 1.1 Numbers of Enslaved Africans Transported by European and U.S. Slavers, 1501–1875

Year	Spain/Uruguay	Portugal/Brazil	Great Britain	Netherlands	USA	France	Denmark/Baltic	Totals
1501–1525	6,363	7,000	0	0	0	0	0	13,363
1526–1550	25,375	25,387	0	0	0	0	0	50,762
1551–1575	28,167	31,089	1,685	0	0	66	0	61,007
1576–1600	60,056	90,715	237	1,365	0	0	0	152,373
1601–1625	83,496	267,519	0	1,829	0	0	0	352,844
1626–1650	44,313	201,609	33,695	31,729	824	1,827	1,053	315,050
1651–1675	12,601	244,793	122,367	100,526	0	7,125	653	488,065
1676–1700	5,860	297,272	272,200	85,847	3,327	29,484	25,685	719,675
1701–1725	0	474,447	410,597	73,816	3,277	120,939	5,833	1,088,909
1726–1750	0	536,696	554,042	83,095	34,004	259,095	4,793	1,471,725
1751–1775	4,239	528,693	832,047	132,330	84,580	325,918	17,508	1,925,315
1776–1800	6,415	673,167	748,612	40,773	67,443	433,061	39,199	2,008,670
1801–1825	168,087	1,160,601	283,959	2,669	109,545	135,815	16,316	1,876,992
1826–1850	400,728	1,299,969	0	357	1,850	68,074	0	1,770,978
1851–1875	215,824	9,309	0	0	476	0	0	225,609
Totals	1,061524	5,848,266	3,259,441	554,336	305,326	1,381,404	111,040	12,521,337

Source: Voyages: The Trans-Atlantic Slave Trade Database (www.slavevoyages.org/).

in this relation. On the African side of the Atlantic, the trans-Atlantic exchanges extracted skilled labor and depopulated the African continent, resulting in political and economic insecurity and the establishment of a new elite who built their wealth on the slave trade on the continent of Africa (Fig. 1.1).

On the American side, enslaved Africans engaged in diverse tasks, chief among them plantation agriculture (Fig. 1.2). The Africans, for example, deployed their skills in Virginia and Maryland (where tobacco was grown) and in South Carolina (where indigo and rice were grown), primarily by the so-called Gullah from the Windward Coast or Rice Coast of Guinea, Senegambia, and Sierra Leone in West Africa. Cotton, grown primarily in the U.S. southern states, became a major economic crop in the early 1800s and further implicated the entire country in slavery. Though all the northern states had outlawed slavery by 1804, the North continued to benefit financially from the practice, providing transportation, financing, and other services that supported slavery. In essence, this is a synthesis of the economies of slavery, described here as "slavocracy." The profits the system generated linked the fates of Africa and the United States in what one can describe in modern economic parlance as an unequal exchange. A proper account of the trans-Atlantic exchanges requires an understanding of the ideological convictions that drove the slaveholders and their businesses.

THE IDEOLOGY OF SLAVOCRACY: REALISM AND MORAL RELATIVISM

Given that the prevalent political orders reinforced the practice in the Atlantic world, the period from the 1460s to the 1880s was the age of slavocracy, with changing phases and regional variations. Slavocracy is an oligarchic system operated by majority plantation owners and slaveholders, who used slave labor as a mode of economic production. The system backed by political power placed profit and exploitation above all else.[4] In Africa, Europe, and the Americas, slavocrats bonded together in their practice of slavery for power and profit making. Under the guise of political realism, this generation of global elites had no cause to worry about the moral implications of servitude and all that it entailed. A handful of slaveholders—among them the American founding fathers, including Thomas Jefferson—who were sober enough to contemplate the conditions of the slaves did not match their verbal commitment to liberty with actions.

Born wealthy, well educated, and respected by Abigail Adams (wife of President John Quincy Adams) as "one of the choice ones of the earth,"[5] Jefferson, in

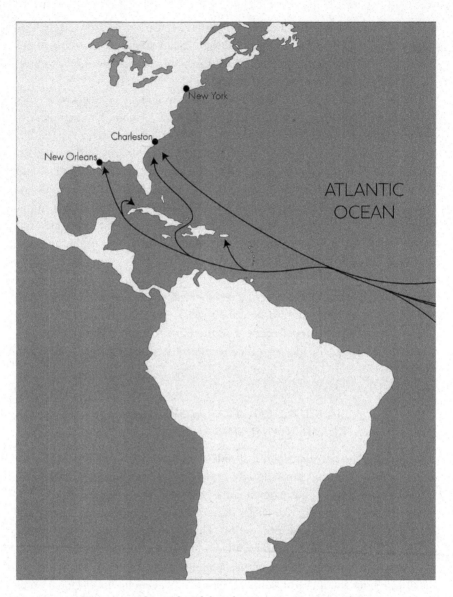

Figure 1.1. African slave labor shipments to North America.
Toyin Falola and Nathan McCormack.

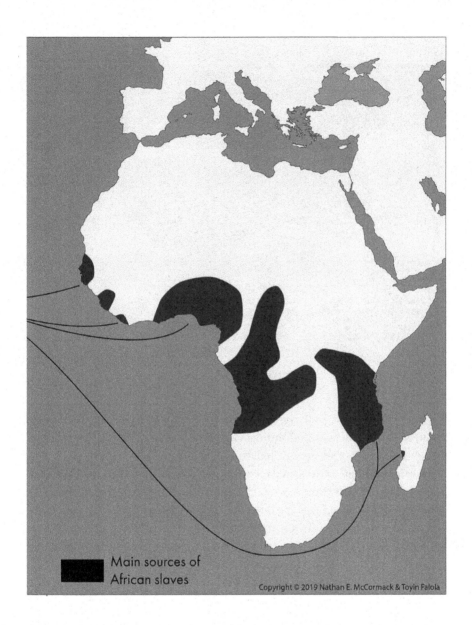

Main sources of
African slaves

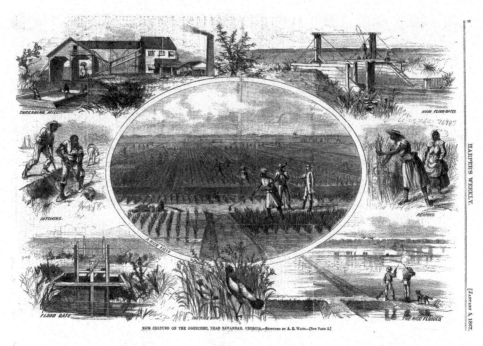

Figure 1.2. African slaves working on a rice plantation. *Library of Congress.*

the same manner as the other slavocrats in the period, approached slavery with a pattern of self-interests that mirrors economic realism. Despite his political thoughts and pronouncements, Jefferson's handling of his slaves parallels that of the most obstinate slavery apologists in the United States, who used *Watson's Jefferson Magazine* as a forum to spread propaganda justifying the practice. For example, in an editorial that appeared in October 1909, publisher Theo E. Watson, a white supremacist whose grandfather was a slaveholder, quoted a verse from the Bible that supported slavery and master–servant relations: "Paul commanded slaves to obey their masters as they would Christ." The editorial goes on to say: "The seven wonders of the world were the work of slave-holders: the glory that was Greece and the grandeur that was Rome were the triumphs of slave-owners."[6]

In retrospect, the spirit of unbridled economic realism resonates with modern social scientific theories. Hans J. Morgenthau reminds us that the fact that a theory of politics is new or old is not enough to reject or accept its soundness. He reasons, "A theory of politics must be subjected to the dual test of reason and experience. . . . [Otherwise, to] dismiss such a theory because it had its flowering in centuries past is to present not a rational argument but a modernistic prejudice that takes for granted the superiority of the present over the past."[7]

Morgenthau identifies six basic principles that govern political realism, which together provide insight into the mainly unexplored political economy of the slavocracy. First, fair or neutral laws with roots in human nature govern politics. Second, defining interest in relation to authority permeates coherent order "into the subject matter (i.e., politics), and thus makes the theoretical understanding of politics possible." The third point is that defining interest in terms of power relations "is an objective category, which is universally valid," although it does not provide us with a fixed implication. Power is the domination of man by fellow man. Fourth, Morgenthau argues that universal moral principles do not apply "to the actions of states in their abstract universal formulation but rather filtered through the existing circumstances of time and place." The fifth point, and perhaps the most controversial, is the idea that "moral aspirations of a particular nation are not identifiable with the moral laws that govern the universe." Morgenthau sees power as appropriated in terms of self-interest or national interest, which in the second case protects the people from individual or collective excesses and human follies. Sixth, the pluralistic conception of human nature is also a factor—that is, the understanding that there are multiple factors (economic, social, emotions, psychological, health, and so on) that contribute to human perceptions and actions. To this regard, Morgenthau submits that a man who was nothing but "political man would be a beast, completely lacking in moral restraints." However, to develop an autonomous theory of political behavior, "political man" must ignore other aspects of human nature.[8]

From the preceding, it is evident that slavocrats of the early modern era recognized only neutral or disinterested laws rather than moral/religious laws in matters of international relations. By implication, the same contagious principles governed their attitudes toward wealth accumulation and interhuman/interclass relations. Indeed, the slavocrats conducted their economic pursuits with real coercive power. Similar to political realists, who made states the center of their analysis, the slavocrats treated their financial investments in plantation slavery as paramount. An observant Chauncey Boucher noted that from the antebellum period (ca. 1789–1861) the obvious dominant factor controlling the course of events in the United States was "a powerful, united, well-organized, aggressive slavocracy."[9] This group, after the War of 1812 between the United States and Britain, became nervous about its future possibilities. In 1909 the publisher of *Watson's Jefferson Magazine* observed, "I am not the least ashamed of the fact that the South owned slaves: if we had treated them with the brutality that Northern corporations inflicted upon white slaves under the wage system, I would be ashamed."[10]

It was not only in the United States that the slavocrats reacted aggressively to the abolitionist and emancipation movements. In East Africa, for instance, the dominant Arab slavocrats in the island enclave of Zanzibar, where slaves produced cloves for the global market, vehemently rejected the global emancipation crusade led by the British government from 1807. Frustrated by their responses in 1872, the British government sent a special mission to the rulers of the island in an attempt to negotiate "a new treaty for the immediate abolition."[11] In West Africa, the Aro slaving oligarchy of southeastern Nigeria, who were directly responsible for the export of nearly 1.4 million people from the Bight of Biafra, stubbornly rejected the British antislavery crusade. The Aro slavers chose instead war with the British forces in 1901–1902.[12]

Novelist Adaobi Tricia Nwaubani of Umujieze, Nigeria, provides an accurate and horrid account of her "most celebrated ancestor: my great-grandfather Nwaubani Ogogo Oriaku," an Igbo slave trader who held a slave-trading license from the British-owned Royal Niger Company, which once exercised political control over southern Nigeria on behalf of the British monarchy. Nwaubani was among a long list of African slavocrats who accumulated wealth and influence by selling other Africans to the New World. "He was a renowned trader," wrote Erasmus, who was Nwaubani's son and Adaobi's father. "He dealt in palm produce and human beings." In a traditional community where funeral rites for a notable Igbo man often involved the slaughter of cows, goats, and chickens, Nwaubani Ogogo's funeral was marked by the killing of a leopard and six slaves who were "buried alive with him."[13]

As in the conduct of international relations, where states view power in military terms and the military influence of other countries presents the most significant potential danger to an individual state,[14] so slaveholders, as Adam Smith noted in a 1766 lecture, perceived the relative freedom of persons as dangerous.[15] A realist approach to international diplomacy conceives economic advantage as a critical part of national power, and in this context, commercial exchanges in the global platform take it as a given that political and economic configurations are constructed by hegemonic actors. This mindset remained the basis of U.S. international relations for centuries. Joshua Goldstein and others have summarized it as an interplay of three principles: dominance, reciprocity, and identity.[16] Just as the Euro-American slavocrats perceived the commercial exchanges with their African cohorts as a function of domination, reciprocity, and identity, slaveholders, in general, saw their relationship with subordinates and the rest of society as a function of power relations.

Practitioners of political realism have strongly objected to the idea that systematic advancement and unhindered trade ensure peace and cooperation within and across states simply because those in power made a profit from chaos and long-term order may not be suitable for their selfish interests.[17] A similar position held by slavocrats led them to consider emancipation negotiated on terms of long-term compensation a dangerous fantasy. As the history of the U.S. southern states reveals, slavocrats neither believed in liberty nor considered a negotiated long-term settlement an option, perhaps because there was little incentive for freed slaves to comply with the financial bargain in exchange for gaining their freedom. In other words, as in realism, slavocrats believed that free labor was detrimental to their business and privileges. They were not concerned about the "normative and ethical concerns" expressed by abolitionists that persistent slavery inevitably led to relentless rivalry and the risk of open conflicts.[18] In this sense, slavocrats are purveyors of a zero-sum game; they think in terms of relative advantage (relativism) — that is, power positions and domination — rather than the size of their net worth. For slavocrats, oligarchic control is more important than the promotion of human liberty and collective security that emancipation would install.[19]

Thus, a defining attribute of a slavocracy is the principle of moral relativism. This controversial value system stresses the dissimilarities in ethical decisions among peoples and cultures. Scholars like James Kellenberger argue that "the phenomenon of moral diversity is connected with moral relativism," such as virtue, moral goods, and moral rights, but these are too generic to help clarify the matter.[20] Perhaps one may argue that in a choice between universal moral actions and relative moral actions, virtues are difficult to observe when there is substantial material advantage involved. Along with this line of thought, Neil Levy has argued that moral facts, unlike scientific facts, "are in some way importantly dependent upon us, upon our beliefs, and our interests."[21] In other words, what we choose to observe as morality may be subject to personal interests rather than what is best for individuals and society. In ninth-century Igbo society, as Thurstan Shaw's archaeological excavations at Igbo-Ukwu, Nigeria, show, a chief was interred with at least five slaves as sacrificial victims.[22] These trends mirror what one may describe as the pathologies of slaveholding, appropriated with graveyard humor — a common culture observed among slavocrats on both sides of the Atlantic world.

In the United States, slavocrats and plantation owners, like their African and Asian counterparts, continued to demonstrate a disinterest in the moral implications of servitude — whether relating to Black, White, or Native American slaves. This behavior troubled the classical economist Adam Smith (1723–1790); hence, he provided a couple of assumptions why plantation owners were adamant about slavery in the context of developing economies. Smith first observes that "slavery economies" are highly inefficient and that the volume of economic production under freedom is twelve times larger than under slavery. Despite that fact, as Smith noted, slavery persisted in most of the eighteenth-century world. The central question then is why the slaveholding elites in precolonial Africa, early modern Europe, and colonial America—all of whom also controlled political power in their different societies—negated economic modernization by rejecting emancipation.

Smith alleges that humans have a fundamental desire to dominate others. Slavery provided slavocrats an outlet to appropriate that natural proclivity to domination. Some critics have rejected this view as ad hoc, favoring instead Smith's second argument, which postulates that plantation owners were reluctant to accept emancipation because to them, freeing the slaves without adequate compensation would deprive them of their property rights.[23] It was for this reason, following the British Emancipation Act of 1833, which took effect on August 1, 1834, that the British government offered slave owners (not traders) a compensation fund of £20 million.[24] The British government obtained a loan worth about £1 billion today from the Rothschild banking family. The British proceeded with the plan even though Liverpool's leading members of Parliament, Bamber Gascoyne and Col. Banastre Tarleton, protested that the city would die if slavery ceased.[25] Liverpool—the British city that invested most heavily in mercantilism in general, and in the slave trade in particular—supported the rebellious Confederate states during the American Civil War. This intervention occurred despite the policy of neutrality the British government adopted. Liverpool built and supplied vessels, ammunition, and funds to the slave-holding southern states.[26]

As a result of Liverpool's resistance to the emancipation struggle, the slave trade persisted. Liverpool traders and merchants continued to trade in guns, gunpowder, and other goods, while bankers and shipbuilders continued to participate in the illegal trade. Because of this fact, critics like Marvin Brown have charged that Adam Smith condoned the British practice of slavery and tended to place a premium on property rights over freedom for the enslaved. Such charges emanate from a misrepresentation of Smith's thoughts: Brown is confusing Smith's classical economic theory with the more recent neoclassicism developed by Alfred Marshall, which was built on the foundation erected by Smith and David Ricardo.[27] This parody is evident in Brown's false claim that the model of economics projected by Smith was responsible for slavery.[28] Thomas Wells debunks Brown's reading of Smith, asserting that his distortion of facts is "particularly unfortunate since Adam Smith was certainly a real-world economist" and, to that end, an abolitionist campaigner.[29] Indeed, Smith was among the very few in the European society of his time who risked their prestige and respect in society by encouraging a humanistic approach to wealth accumulation in an age of slavery and cut-throat mercantilism.

Whether one embraces Smith's argument that the psychological satisfaction accruing from domination was the cause of slavery, or the argument that there was a lack of incentive for emancipation, the elite in the age of slavocracy placed self-interest over everything else. The pursuit of self-interest has been part of human history and occupies a central place in America's own "Manifest Destiny."[30] While this thinking might not be in alignment with what is moral, American slavocrats, like their counterparts elsewhere, were rational actors. They espoused economic realism in an age of transition from the slumbering economies of feudalism to full-blown capitalism. Because of weak incentives and high risk of default, slaveholders rejected the long-term compensation scheme. In other words, the idea that free labor would be a better option was for slavocrats inconceivable; hence, they shunned emancipation notwithstanding the high investment risks associated with the econometrics of slavery.

ENSLAVED AFRICANS IN THE AMERICAN ECONOMY

Considering the ideological drivers of slavery—that is, realists' practices of self-interest, struggle for wealth accumulation, and the attractions of power and privilege—one must now reconsider the history of enslaved Africans in the American economy. Notwithstanding the historical importance of the cargo of African slaves comprising twenty people from Angola who landed in Virginia in 1619,[31] one of the earliest known Africans to set foot in the Americas was Juan Garrido (1487–1547), who was part of a 1502 Spanish expedition. Garrido did not come to the New World as a slave but as an economic investor and adventurer. Garrido's career, like those of other Africans who collaborated with the Europeans in the slave trade business, provides insight into how the pursuit of profit (rather than race) structured the history of the period from 1607, when the colony of Jamestown in Virginia was founded, to 1865 when the Thirteenth Amendment abolished slavery. We agree with David Olusoga that slavery was a principal cause of the European propagation of scientific racism, and Benjamin Bower concludes that scientific racism emerged as putative justification for Black slavery and oppression. In other words, profit, science, race, and religion were inextricably tied.[32]

The pertinent questions are: How did the realist approach adopted in this book relate to the trans-Atlantic slave trade? How does it differ from existing works on the subject? How did slavery lay the foundation of United States-Africa relations, and what are the consequences? What are the differences between being Black, people of African descent, African Americans, and diaspora Africans in the period of the trans-Atlantic slave trade? Our reexamination of the trans-Atlantic slave trade in the context of international relations proceeds from the standpoint of state actors and businesspersons from both sides of the Atlantic. The motivation for the European slave dealers and their patrons in the Americas was profit, just as African rulers and chiefs, along with kidnappers and others who procured the victims of the trans-Atlantic exchanges, were driven by profit and exercise of power. The American planters needed slaves to cultivate their crops, and the African slave dealers needed European-made goods such as mirrors, guns, clothes, cigarettes, umbrellas, and other consumable items to quench their egotistical appetites for the esoteric life of luxury. Therefore, the econometrics of want and supply determined the trans-Atlantic exchanges. One side of the Atlantic societies needed a vast pool of labor; the African side had an excess pool of workers capable of performing the tasks of which the colonists were incapable and in desperate need.

The realization is not lost that the victims of the human trade had no control over their fates, yet on both sides of the Atlantic, those private profiteers and governments involved in the commercial exchanges conducted their businesses from a position of either strength or weakness. International negotiations and bilateral trades are what modern nations do in international relations. Thus, the pros and cons of these negotiations and trades touch on theories related to realism, complex interdependence theory, liberalism, relativism, constructivism, and so on. Geoffrey Gertz of the Brookings Institution notes that the U.S. government's "embrace of bilateral negotiations is borne [sic] out of [the] understanding of the global economy as a zero-sum conflict. From this starting point, it follows that the key question in assessing any trade deal is not whether it creates overall economic gains, but how its benefits are distributed between countries—who's getting the biggest slice of the pie."[33] This contemporary paradigm to bilateral trade relations best describes the conundrum of United States-Africa relations in the era of the slave trade.

A brief consideration of the concept of complex interdependence theory and its relation to the practice of Atlantic slavery is necessary, but first, we need to further flesh out the principle of relativism in both the conduct of international relations and the practice of slavery. Garrido's career in the Americas is illuminating. Born in West Africa around 1480, Garrido came to the Americas as a free man of color and a business speculator. In an affidavit (*probanza*) dated 1538, he categorically submitted that his decision to move from Africa to Lisbon, Portugal, was a personal choice. It is not entirely clear to historians what brought

Garrido to Portugal or what kind of life he lived there. Some estimates have noted that nearly 10 percent (44,000) of the population of the archbishopric of Lisbon, one of the largest cities in Europe in the sixteenth century, were Africans.[34] After seven years in Portugal, Garrido joined the earliest conquistadors in Seville. In 1502, he departed to the New World and landed on the island of Española or Hispaniola (today the Dominican Republic and Haiti) in search of fortune and fame.[35] In his insightful study, which focused heavily on the conquistadors in Mexico and Peru, Matthew Restall noted that Garrido, who once sojourned in San Juan, Puerto Rico, finally settled in Mexico City between 1524 and 1528.[36]

The part of Garrido's resumé that intersects with this study is his mission to Baja California in 1533 as a member of the notorious Hernán Cortés expedition. During the mission, Garrido was in command of a band composed of enslaved Africans and Native American slaves commissioned for mining in California. His life history shows that in the age of slavocracy, the utmost motive of the fortune hunters and businesspersons was profit making rather than race or morality. In his affidavit of 1538, Garrido declared that he was "the first to have the inspiration to sow maize here in New Spain and to see if it took; I did this and experimented at my own expense."[37] Other Black conquistadors included Francisco de Eguiá, Sebastien Toral, and Estebanillo or "Black Stephen," some of whom had limited freedom and rights in early Spanish America.[38]

With the systematic decimation of the indigenous population through acts of war and diseases, the necessity for African slaves to work on the fast-growing plantations and mines became urgent. Therefore, plantation owners needed to make the business decisions that prompted the trans-Atlantic exchanges. While the choice lacked what some religious-minded people would call morality, the action taken for the colonists' survival was predicated on full exploitation of the abundant economic resources in the Americas. The relationships among the peoples within the Atlantic world hinged on a complex interdependent system.

Proposed by Robert Keohane and Joseph Nye, complex interdependence theory in international relations asserts the strong bonds inseparably holding states and their fortunes.[39] The interdependencies or complex transnational connections are not new in the broader resonance of theoretical musing, and Keohane and Nye acknowledge this fact in their essay "Globalization: What's New and What's Not? (And So What?)."[40] However, the popularization of the concept came earlier in 1968 when Richard Cooper published his influential book *The Economics of Interdependence: Economic Policy in the Atlantic Community*.[41] The theory projects the central argument that the dominance of one

nation-state in the international arena, and the constant danger of military conflict it poses, entails the loss of power for another. The theory recognizes that
no one nation can lord it over all the others, and the survival of each country is
correlated to the well-being and durability of the others. Thus, complex interdependence theory is a juxtaposition of the political realist and contemporary
neoliberal thoughts mirroring "today's multidimensional economic, social and
ecological interdependence."[42]

By the 1860s, the slavocrats in the Western Hemisphere in collaboration
with their African partners had forcibly transported an estimated 10–12.5 million Africans to the Americas (Table 1.2). Of this number, the 388,747 slaves
who disembarked in mainland North America came from West Central Africa,
Senegambia, the Bight of Biafra, the Bight of Benin, Gold Coast, Sierra Leone,
the Windward Coast, and Southeast Africa. About 305,326 landed in the North
American region that is now known as the United States between 1620 and
1860.[43] Although this represents about 2.43 percent of the overall number of
enslaved Africans in the Americas, the rather small fraction of the enslaved men
and women multiplied to over 2.5 million by the start of the Civil War on April
12, 1861. Federal census data shows that in 1790, about 680,000 slaves cultivated
rice, indigo, and tobacco on plantations, and by 1880, about 1.8 million slaves
worked in the cotton industry, which grew exponentially following the 1793
invention of the cotton gin by Eli Whitney.[44]

Several factors contributed to the quick increase in the slave population.
Despite poor health conditions and nutrition, the African slaves had higher
birth rates and lower mortality rates than the European or Native American
populations. The semitropical climate in the southern parts of the country, with
its associated pathogens, favored the health of enslaved Africans who were accustomed to a similar environment in West and Central Africa. Additional slave
imports from the Caribbean and South America further increased the slave
population in North America (Tables 1.3 and 1.4).

Before elaborating on the impact of African labor and agriculture in the development of United States, we should reflect briefly on the differences between being Black, people of African descent, African Americans, and diaspora
Africans in the period of slavery. These categories emerged in various historical
contexts.[45] In broad terms, being Black in the Americas is synonymous with
the totality of heritage resulting from the dispersal of people of African descent
in the diaspora. With revolutions in the Atlantic world, such as the Haitian
Revolution of 1791–1804 and the Islamic revolutions in West Africa that started
in the seventeenth century and gained currency in 1804 with the Sokoto jihad
led by Usman Dan Fodio (1754–1817), the African heritage acquired a complex

Table 1.2 Africa Departures / Disembarkations by Region (1501–1866)

Disembarkations	Senegambia	Sierra Leone	Windward Coast	Gold Coast	Bight of Benin	Bight of Biafra	West Central Africa	Southeast Africa	Totals
Europe	4,889	152	380	576	356	968	1,539	0	8,860
Mainland North America	92,030	44,893	21,781	56,248	9,231	64,782	92,191	7,591	388,747
British Caribbean	124,720	115,169	146,684	601,243	268,060	712,623	329,688	20,663	2,318,251
French Caribbean	97,024	42,919	21,442	108,669	281,596	116,042	425,688	26,835	1,120,215
Dutch Americas	5,495	8,349	70,446	98,330	86,173	20,631	154,763	540	444,727
Danish West Indies	5,867	3,707	1,465	48,016	17,070	16,641	16,208	25	108,727
Spanish Americas	170,179	98,740	16,238	51,198	138,406	223,520	502,586	92,050	1,292,912
Brazil	109,108	8,835	6,161	64,478	877,034	122,617	3,396,909	279,232	4,864,374
Africa	1,706	16,020	2,770	2,165	46,909	39,951	36,457	9,591	436,527
Totals	611,018	338,784	287,367	1,030,918	1,724,835	1,317,775	4,955,430	436,527	10,702,654

Source: Voyages: The Trans-Atlantic Slave Trade Database (www.slavevoyages.org/).

Table 1.3 Africans Transported to North America, 1626–1822

Year	Northern Region	Chesapeake	Carolinas and Georgia	Gulf States	Unspecified	Total
1626–1650	114	239	0	0	0	353
1651–1675	1,177	3,355	0	0	0	4,532
1676–1700	1,246	8,436	21	0	174	9,876
1701–1725	1,245	55,552	3,220	4,076	0	64,093
1726–1750	8,817	87,619	58,118	5,804	537	160,895
1751–1775	9,100	35,362	93,733	1,490	0	139,686
1776–1800	312	0	44,946	2,827	0	48,085
1801–1822	515	0	97,588	9,989	1,278	109,370
Total	22,527	190,564	297,625	24,186	1,989	536,891
Percent	4.3	35.6	55.5	4.5	0.4	

Source: Voyages: The Trans-Atlantic Slave Trade Database (www.slavevoyages.org/).

Table 1.4 Estimated Slave Imports to North America, 1619–1810

U.S. States	Direct Imports from Africa	Imports from the Caribbean	Total Estimates of Slaves Imported	Percentage of Slaves Imported from the Caribbean by State
Virginia	101,842	12,060	113,902	10.6
South Carolina	188,114	21,122	209,236	10.1
Maryland	25,826	5,010	30,836	16.2
North Carolina	2,180	2,130	4,310	49.4
Georgia	19,785	5,414	25,199	21.5
Louisiana	13,033	11,869	24,199	47.7
Florida	3,378	1,647	5,025	32.5
New York	14,680	4,250	18,930	22.3
Pennsylvania and New Jersey	2,461	4,282	6,743	63.5
New England	9,813	3,870	13,683	28.8
Totals	381,112	71,654	452,766	15.8
Percent	84.2	15.8	100	100

Note: These figures are not inclusive of U.S. domestic slave trade shipments.
Source: Voyages: The Trans-Atlantic Slave Trade Database (www.slavevoyages.org/).

meaning. Being Black is also about those who self-identified as Black, adopted a globalized notion of blackness, and conceived of a relation between themselves and others in the African diaspora. Some distinctions are, however, found in individuals born in Africa and those born on American soil. While the African-born nurtured the African American subtype, not all African Americans were of pure African blood. Some were creoles or products of relationships between Whites, Native Americans, and so on. Gwendolyn Midlo Hall reminds us that "the most precise definition of Creole is a person of non-American ancestry," though the term sometimes applies to Native Americans who were born into slavery.[46] As a result, the African-born may be the custodians of the indigenous African ways of life; African Americans have served and continue to serve as the bridge between the African-born and all other Americans.

The U.S. legal and political systems reinforced the practices of slavery. From about the mid-seventeenth century, the status of Blacks, irrespective of whether they were free or bonded, was dependent on their mothers' status. While Africans and Native Americans could be slaves, as a rule, a person identified as "White" could not be a slave. In some instances, the offspring of a free White woman and a slave were consigned to servitude for as long as thirty-one years. In the early colonial period, conversion to Christianity could set a slave free, but this escape route was soon reversed. In the South, skin color was a marker of social status. Blacks or people of African origin were usually recognized as slaves. In Virginia, where a law classified people by race, those with one-quarter or more African ancestry were considered Black. Other states arbitrarily determined blackness by use of informal tests in addition to visual inspection. In 1838, a Kentucky court ruled in *Turner v. Johnson* that "slaves are property and must, under our present institutions, be treated as such."[47] However, the same Kentucky court ruling acknowledged that slaves are also "human beings, with like passions, sympathies, and affections with ourselves. And while we must treat them as property, we should not entirely overlook the obligation due to them as human beings."[48] The result of the court ruling was some rules that entrenched specific ways of life in the U.S. South. In 1857, Chief Justice Roger Taney, writing for the majority in the Supreme Court's *Dred Scott v. Sanford* ruling, denied Black people citizenship, adding that the mere presence of Blacks in a free state or a sovereign territory could not ensure their emancipation. "The plaintiff himself acquired no title to freedom by being taken, by his owner, to Rock Island, in Illinois, and brought back to Missouri. This court has heretofore decided that the status or condition of a person of African descent depended on the laws of the State in which he resided."[49]

The primary intent of the laws and practices that supported slavery was to keep the enslaved Africans and their offspring on the farms. The African-born and the African American together provided the free labor the European settlers leveraged for wealth creation and the United States' economic foundation. Some of the enslaved Africans were engaged in carpentry, road construction, holstering, blacksmithing, carriage driving, weaving, coopering, spinning, butchering, and preserving. Others performed domestic chores for their owners such as laundry, janitorial duties, cooking, cleaning, tailoring, stonemasonry, milling, and so on. Enslaved men and women of African ancestry, visual artists and craftsmen, laid the foundation of today's African American visual arts tradition. Slave artisans fashioned tables, chairs, and other useful items, some of which revealed distinctive New World African visual arts expressions. These carvers and stone sculptors left utilitarian objects and artworks of aesthetic quality. Quilt makers made objects of beauty from scraps of cloth, and milliners and tailors were among the first American fashion stylists. Slave owners sexually exploited enslaved women, but some female slaves acted as mistresses for slavocrats and their subordinates.[50]

Approximately 10 percent of the enslaved Africans in the United States lived and worked in urban areas such as Richmond, Mobile, Charleston, Savannah, New Orleans, New York, and Philadelphia. In the eighteenth century, an estimated 65 percent of enslaved Africans lived in southern U.S. cities. In the urban centers, the vast majority of the enslaved people worked directly for their masters. However, the slave owners also hired out skilled laborers to those who needed their skills. A small minority of the enslaved Africans had the opportunity to make themselves available for paid jobs, and they used part of their wages to pay their owners. Overall, the cities offered more opportunities for the enslaved. While work as domestic servants was often the norm in the industrializing urban centers like New York, slaves also worked as anglers, sailors, bakers, tailors, painters, coopers, porters, draymen, peddlers, bricklayers, and blacksmiths. In 1819, the Augusta, Georgia, *Chronicle* declared that "these there are gainful occupations of free persons of color."[51] The majority of enslaved Africans worked countless hours on plantations as cultivators and harvesters of food and cash crops in the United States.

AFRICAN SLAVE LABOR AND AGRICULTURE

Scholars quarrel over the impact of slave labor on the United States' economic ascendancy. While some vehemently deny that slaves had any role in the process, others merely contend that their impact was insignificant. Rev.

Peter Fontaine, an English resident of colonial Virginia, best captured the crucial relevance of slave labor in the United States to the original settlers in a controversial letter written in 1757 to his brother, Moses Fontaine, in England. In this memo, Reverend Fontaine, an Anglican minister, struggled to address a legitimate moral question his brother had raised in a previous letter concerning the compatibility between the colonists' practice of slavery and the Christian religion that individuals like his brother represented. Writing during the Seven Years' War (1756–1763) that pitted France against England, which ravaged the economy of the British colonies, Fontaine instead described the conditions in Virginia that justified slavery, absolving himself of blame.

Perceptively, Reverend Fontaine provided a rather relativist/realist explanation to the critical question about slavery in Virginia when he categorically stated that it would have been practically impossible for Whites to survive physically in Virginia without slaves.[52] Fontaine reminded his brother that slavery was already in existence in Africa before the trans-Atlantic slave trade. "The Negroes are enslaved by the Negroes themselves before they are purchased by the masters of the ships who bring them here."[53] He meant to explain that the institution of slavery was indigenous to Africa and that the Africans were collaborators in the import of human cargoes from across the ocean. But it is also worthy of note that an Afro-Arab slave trade preceded the trans-Atlantic slave trade. Some scholars estimate that 14 million enslaved Africans, the majority of them women, were in the Arab world over a period of 1,300 years. Ronald Segal has tried to differentiate between the trans-Atlantic slave trade and the Arab slave trade by arguing that the conditions of the enslaved under Islam were very different from the conditions imposed by Europeans, the fundamental difference being that under Islam the subjugated were still human beings with some rights.[54] In reality, labor needs in the Americas were bigger and the conditions of slavery more gruesome than in the Arab world.

In the same letter, Fontaine disclosed that the colonies were under constant pressure from England to maintain the chain of demand and supply for slaves. His view is a discourse on complex interdependence: those in need of slaves are interdependent with those responsible for the supply, and the network runs from the African suppliers, through the European shippers, to the British government, to the Virginia/American planters and households. In other words, the African slave trade was a business with diverse stakeholders, including the Liverpool slavocrats who were hostile to emancipation. It is notable that after the British Parliament abolished slavery in 1807 and passed the Emancipation Act in 1833, the slave business lingered in England as part of a coordinated effort by slavocrats around the world to safeguard their investments.

The indulgent did not miss the eyes of Fontaine, who saw the persistent pressure for more slaves as "part of the mercantilist system." He explained that the British Crown, embodied by the Board of Trade and the African Company, aimed to sell "as many slaves as possible to the colonies."[55] He stressed the amount of pressure from England as overbearing on the colonists of Virginia: "By this means they are forced upon us, whether we will or will not."[56]

Having stated the connection between slavery in Virginia in particular and the original colonies in general, Fontaine addressed the paramount need for African slaves. He made it clear that without the services provided by the African slaves, the Virginia residents would not have survived. Without slaves, he underscored, the colonists and their families either would have starved to death or or would have had to assume the role of servants themselves. "Before our troubles, you could not hire a servant or slave for love or money, so that, unless robust enough to cut wood, to go to the mill, to work at the hoe, etc., you must starve or board in some family where they both fleece and half starve you."[57] The type of chores and services the enslaved rendered to the colonists is perhaps the most revealing part of Fontaine's letter. Cutting down forests, working the land, and going to the mills reveal the nature of slavocracy and the interdependence of the free and the bonded. In this system, slaves and servants were indispensable. It is apparent that there was a survivalist mentality in play for every group. Alluding to this, Fontaine observed that even slaves and servants "take advantage of the necessities of strangers, who are thus obliged to purchase some slaves and land." It was easier to become a planter than a merchant in Virginia; indeed, there were "no merchants, traders, or artificers of any sort but what become planters in a short time."[58]

Nonetheless, Fontaine recognized the colonists' responsibility when he wrote that it was "our choice whether we buy them or not, so this then is our crime, folly, or whatever you will please to call it." He acknowledged that slavery was the country's "original sin and curse" and that the Virginia colonists would have to learn to live without it.[59] As the war between England and France raged, it depleted the British economy and increased poverty among the colonists. David Kennedy has noted that it was not only the war with the French that depleted the economic resources of the colonists but also the conflict with the Native Americans in Virginia and elsewhere. Consequently, the importation of slaves stopped shortly, prompting Reverend Fontaine to declare, "Our poverty then is our best security."[60]

Besides the variety of labor rendered by the enslaved, the internal redistribution of African slaves from the northern slavocracies of New York, New Jersey, Massachusetts, and Pennsylvania to the southern regions of South Carolina and other colonies was a crucial part of the North and Middle Atlantic colonies' economy. In the 1760s, Massachusetts, New York, Pennsylvania, and New Jersey sold enslaved Africans to the southern colonies. Advertisements for African slaves were standard in southern newspapers such as the *South Carolina City Gazette*. The ads referenced numerous men and women brought from the northern colonies.[61] In the 1770s, slavocrats, slaveholders, and dealers or speculators routinely advertised their captives in the *Boston Gazette and Country Journal*. One advertisement on July 22, 1776, informed potential buyers of the availability of "a stout, strong, healthy negro man, about twenty years of age" for sale.[62] Similar ads offered healthy slaves of all genders to buyers, telling them that these slaves had been in the country for some years and that they were under twenty years of age.[63] When the practice of slavery began to decline in the Middle Atlantic and northern colonies, slave dealers from the North started targeting traders who were selling them off in markets further south.

The 1780s were pivotal in the history of both the international slave trade and the U.S. domestic slave trade. In colonial America, tobacco was the main commodity slaves produced, primarily in Virginia and Maryland. In the period preceding the American Revolution, the tobacco industry utilized a considerable number of enslaved Africans brought into the British American colonies. In South Carolina, a large percentage of the enslaved toiled on rice and indigo estates. The tobacco trade suffered heavy losses during the uprising against colonial domination that took place between 1765 and 1783. In the immediate aftermath of the Revolution, it appeared that slavery would soon end in the United States. The majority of northern states outlawed the institution, and even Virginia's Assembly debated abolition.

At the Constitutional Convention of 1787, former U.S. senator Charles C. Pinckney argued that Virginia stood to gain more economic benefits by ending the importation of slaves from Africa. Reiterating the simple economic logic of supply and demand, he explained that the value of domestic slaves would increase and that Virginia had a surplus of slaves to dispose of. While Virginia, Maryland, and Delaware basked in what one may regard as a slave glut, planters and slavocrats in South Carolina and Georgia demanded more slaves. Dealers in Richmond, Virginia, and the surrounding areas, such as Austin Moses, responded with advertisements in 1787 offering "one hundred Negroes from 20 to 30 years old for which a good price will be given. They are to be sent out of state, therefore we shall not be particular respecting the character of any of them—hearty and well-made is all that is necessary."[64]

In 1793, slavery regained its prominence following new demands resulting from the invention of the cotton gin in the United States. By the late eighteenth

century, the slave population reproduced itself on the basis of birth and importations. Rather than continued reliance on importation, slaveholders could rely
on enslaved people to reproduce the slave population. As a result of the massive
number of people available for disposal, the sale of Black slaves grew exponentially in volume as part of the U.S. economy.

In the next six decades, from 1800 to 1860, the cotton industry expanded from
South Carolina and Georgia to newly occupied territories west of the Mississippi. The new settlers brought slaves with them. The transition witnessed in
the slave economy moving from the Upper South (Maryland and Virginia) to
the Lower South ran concurrently with an equal movement of the population
of enslaved Africans to the Lower South and western part of the country. Following passage of the Act to Prohibit the Importation of Slaves in 1807, the Upper
South became the primary supply source of the slaves streaming into the Lower
South. By 1850, about 72 percent of the 2.5 million enslaved Africans engaged
in the agriculture sector of the U.S. economy worked on cotton plantations.
Wilma Dunaway has calculated that the slave trade in the mountain South
amounted to about half of the total: "In the Appalachian counties of South
Carolina and Virginia, slave trading was more economically significant than all
local and external sales of agricultural commodities. . . . Even though the Appalachian counties of Maryland and North Carolina were exporting tobacco,
slave trading generated about $1 for every $3 accrued from marketing the crops.
For every $4 collected from the marketing of agricultural commodities, the Ap-
palachian counties of Tennessee generated a dollar from slave trading."[65]

The second issue arising in the late 1780s was a troubling tendency toward
tyranny and the unbridled waste of human lives among slaveholders and planters. Although one may argue that not all slaveholders were cruel to the enslaved people, there was undoubtedly no happiness in slavery. In the late 1790s,
the economies of Virginia, Delaware, and Maryland became so dependent on
slaves as a commodity that the abolitionist Alvan Stewart (1790–1849), a former slave apologist who became an antislavery campaigner and successful New
York lawyer, asserted that ending the slave trade would break open "the great
door to the slave Bastille."[66] Stewart argued that without the internal slave market, the growing numbers of African slaves in Virginia and Maryland "would
eat up their masters, and the masters must emancipate in self-defense to save
themselves from destruction."[67]

The volume of African slaves moved from North to South was so high that
residents of South Carolina expressed fears that newly arrived Blacks would
undermine the discipline of the local enslaved population. In 1792, for example, White residents of Beaufort, South Carolina, petitioned the state legisla-

ture, complaining about the "notorious" practice of Northerners, who "have for a number of years past been in the habit of shipping to these Southern states slaves who are scandalously infamous and incorrigible."[68] Despite such fears, the agriculture-based economy of the Carolinas depended heavily on slave labor. This dependency reminds us of the debate about recognizing the roles of African slaves on the development of agriculture in the New World. Ulrich B. Phillips and others have explained the intricate relationship between the enslaved Africans and the culture of rice farming in the Carolinas and Georgia.[69] Phillips elaborately explains the engagement of the enslaved Africans on tobacco, cotton, rice, and sugar plantations.[70] Indeed, some observers admitted that when rice growers in South Carolina and Georgia realized that rice cultivation would yield an abundant harvest in the region, they also understood that they could not prosper without the help of enslaved Africans who were skilled in planting, tending, harvesting, and processing this crop.

In *Seed from Madagascar*, Gov. Duncan Heyward, a former South Carolina rice planter, vehemently denied any suggestion that African slaves deserved credit for turning the state's agro-based economy into one of the wealthiest economies among the original Confederate states. Heyward represents the mainstream claim that Europeans were primarily responsible for the extraordinary success of South Carolina's prosperous economy in the eighteenth century. He claimed that the system of rice cultivation in China, rather than the experience of the planters from Africa, was the source of South Carolina's agricultural success.[71] Judith Ann Carney has challenged this view with the contention that African slaves brought with them from Africa their expertise in agronomics as well as skilled labor, which significantly affected the success story of the American plantation economy.[72] The available evidence shows that enslaved Africans, especially those from the West African rice region of Senegambia and Sierra Leone, were the only people in Carolina who possessed the knowledge of rice planting, since the crop was not indigenous to America. Although this debate is not entirely settled, it corroborates Walter Rodney's position on Europe's critical role in the problem of Africa's underdevelopment in modern times because of the systematic drainage of African skilled labor to the Americas.[73]

Rice cultivation required special skills because of the hardship involved. Given the level of technology in the eighteenth century, Daniel Littlefield notes that in the Carolina low country, which also comprised coastal Georgia, planters specialized in rice by taking advantage of the technology and farming skills brought over by enslaved Africans from rice-growing regions of West Africa. Agricultural labor was harsh work, since getting the land ready for farming typically entailed rescuing wetlands that were more favorable for rice growing.

Slaves built drains to ensure not just the availability of water but also its removal. The water channels took substantial effort to develop and maintain, and they were ridden with reptiles and other dangers. The crude hand tools available to the enslaved people, such as axes and shovels, made the tasks extremely miserable. Also, they planted, weeded, and harvested the crops in soggy, pest-infested fields. Near the end of the eighteenth century, planters adapted rice farming to the tide flow, thereby making it possible to inundate fields with fresh water. However, rice cultivation remained a risky occupation. For instance, the slaves continued to deal with the problem of stagnant water, which bred mosquitoes that carried diseases. Compared to tobacco, the kind of labor required for rice cultivation was more complex and difficult. The slaveholders enacted the task system, which allowed laborers time off to attend to some personal and family matters on the farm after they completed the assigned tasks.[74]

The bulk of slave shipments from Virginia and Maryland went to the Carolinas and the so-called tobacco belt: Tennessee, Kentucky, and Georgia. Other slaves were shipped to sugar-growing Louisiana. By the 1820s, the oversupply of slaves had grown to the point that Kentucky and the Carolinas were selling more slaves than they were buying. The slave glut reveals that trafficking in humans had become so pervasive that despite the saturation in supply, prices remained high and the Upper South slavocrats kept pushing the trade to sustain the interest of professional slave traffickers despite the effects on its victims. Alvan Stewart noted that in places like Louisiana, Alabama, and Mississippi, slave deaths on the plantations were at epidemic levels. Yet, instead of calling for an end to slavery, he expressed concern about potential economic consequences, warning that if planters continued to accept that many deaths, "in less than seven years, if no slave could be imported into those southern regions, one half of the plantations would lie uncultivated for want of slaves."[75]

The enslaved Africans engaged on the plantations prepared the farms for cultivation and planted, tended, and harvested the crops. In general, their duties as field hands were not limited to agricultural work; they worked in other capacities as domestic servants and seamstresses as part of their plantation duties. A proud South Carolina slavocrat/planter named Langdon Chevas, Sr. referred to his rice plantations on the Savannah River as "gold mines." Indeed, some plantations raked in a profit as high as 26 percent for their White owners. The slaves who labored reaped nothing but pain, suffering, and death. A representative South Carolina plantation was the Gowrie, purchased by Charles Manigault in 1833. Described as a "gentleman capitalist" and "cosmopolitan," Manigault invested $49,500 in Gowrie when he bought it. By 1861, the plantation was worth $266,000. This profit margin, more than anything, proved that the plantation system was indeed a gold mine. A record of sales of slaves in 1863 at an unspecified "Lower Market House" in Virginia stated that "prices of negroes . . . were quite high." The report continued with the prices of those offered for sale as follows: "Man Len, 26 years old, $1970; man Bill, 35 years old, unsold, $735; Lila, age 14, $2050; woman and two children, $2720."[76]

The national U.S. economy was an essential part of the broader international political economy. Each plantation constituted a vital part of the global exchanges. For example, a study of tobacco plantations shows that the slaves on the plantations in Alabama, Tennessee, Kentucky, and South Carolina "were horizontally integrated into the world economy and while West Virginia produced cloth from about two-fifths of its wool, the Appalachian counties of North Carolina and Tennessee manufactured one-third to one-half of their cotton before export. The greatest vertical integration characterized western Virginia and Maryland, where most of the local wool was manufactured into cloth before export."[77]

The economy of the U.S. South relied heavily on the cotton industry. By the 1830s, "cotton was king," not only in the South but also in the United States. In fact, by the mid-eighteenth century, the southern states produced two-thirds of the global cotton supply. The country vied for control of the global economy and the power that came with it. The cotton produced by enslaved Africans remained the cornerstone of the South's economic strength in the period before the Civil War.

Cotton produced by the enslaved Africans not only supported the U.S. financial and shipping sectors but also formed the basis of the booming textile industry in Britain. There was no direct shipment of cotton from the southern states to Europe. Instead, it was sent from New York depots to centers of cotton manufacturing in Europe. Expansion in the U.S. cotton industry proceeded along with the growth of the financial sector in New York, which provided the funds with which investors and speculators secured additional lands and slaves. The slaves further served as political and economic fodder for the U.S. sociopolitical and economic system. Slaveholders used the Africans as collateral in all kinds of trade, including the trade for goods and services; for securing business loans such as the purchase of agricultural land; and even for paying off debts. Values of estates also included the estimated cost of each slave belonging to the property owner, and the accrued taxes were calculated for the state revenue.

Until the Civil War, the U.S. Constitution integrated a feature that recognized the enslaved Africans as political capital—especially to the advantage of the southern slavocrats. The three-fifths clause gave southern slavocrats the legal leeway to count a slave as no more than three-fifths of a person. Enacted for the purpose of determining congressional representations in Washington, this law upended the power equation between the slaveholding South and the nonslaveholding states.[78] Although the policy ensured that taxes levied on slaves did not go into the national treasury, the three-fifths formula also determined the percentage of taxes paid by slave owners. In sum, the institution of slavery pervaded society to the very core and substantially shaped the country's political, legal, psychological, and socioeconomic values.[79]

Historian George Woolfolk studied slavery as a mode of production, analyzing what he called "planter capitalism" from the perspective of the "labor thesis." He echoed Adam Smith's conclusion that slavery was more harmful to the economy than profitable.[80] Frederic Bancroft similarly noted that American "planters were proverbially impatient to mortgage their crops to buy more slaves to make more cotton to buy more slaves."[81] Early on, Phillips criticized slaveholding as a regime that "kept money scarce, population sparse and land values accordingly low." He argued that slavery "restricted the opportunities of many men of both races, and it kept many of the natural resources of the southern country neglected." He concluded that slavery "was the worst feature of the regime from an economic point of view."[82]

However, slavery apologists like Lewis Gray and Esther Thompson completely disagreed with the notion that slavery was a hindrance to economic development: "Far from being a decrepit institution, the economic motives for a continuance of slavery from the standpoint of the employer were never as strong as in the years just preceding the Civil War."[83] Such assertions chime with the views of Henry Bolingbroke, who in 1813 supported the slave trade and everything it represented "as an agency for distributing labor." According to Bolingbroke, "The great use of selling a man by auction is this, that he is thereby beckoned immediately into the form of employment for which there is the greatest call. The carpenter, the blacksmith, outbid the planter if their labor is most in demand. The planter outbids them when agriculture is the most thriving employment. Thus, without waiting for the lesson of observation, a man finds out at once the most productive form of industry; without paying for instructions, he is at once apprenticed to the most expedient department of labor."[84]

THE ANTEBELLUM PERIOD TO THE END
OF THE CIVIL WAR (1812–1865)

In the antebellum period, the reformer Solon Robinson published an observation based on the plantation business owned by Col. L. M. Williams of Society Hill, South Carolina. Robinson concluded that the profit margin on investment based on slave labor was meager; at one point, cotton fetched as low as $4.03, a roughly 3 percent profit margin.[85] Robinson, a committed abolitionist campaigner, may have understated the margin: the editor of the *South Carolinian* estimated that cotton planters made a profit of over 13 percent on investment per annum.[86] Nevertheless, it is evident that planter capitalism did not yield as much profit as was the case before the antebellum era. In a study purposely conducted to resolve this debate, historian Thomas Govan found that from 1827 to 1840, profit margins, whether high or low, did not represent the entire story. Other factors, such as experimentation with new crops and selling lands at a loss, usually accounted for profits or losses. In this light, Govan wrote, "the students who have stated that slavery was profitable are more nearly correct than those who deny its profitability."[87] This conclusion corroborates a related study by George Woolfolk in Texas. According to Woolfolk, "The Texas experience provides a partial but significant answer to the question. Investigation of planter capitalism in the long river counties of East Texas suggests that slavery also served the important function of providing both producer's and liquid capital in an economy where the value of land and the unpredictability of entrepreneurial skill made hazardous the risk of capital."[88] As Woolfolk argues, it is inconceivable to reduce "economic efficiency" to simply "how much the planter-capitalist made." Instead, the most pertinent question is whether planter capitalism built on the institution of slavery facilitated and successfully supported an orderly production of economic existence. The answer he arrived at is that "the Texas experience answers these questions in the affirmative."[89]

Additionally, Kenneth Stampp has critically surveyed what he calls the inherent biases associated with history and historians. Considering various arguments, some borrowing from "scientific" treatises and others from the so-called subjective-presentist-relativist school, Stampp concludes that slavery "was the inevitable product of neither the weather nor some irresistible force in the South's economic evolution. Southern planters employed slaves in agriculture because men sought greater returns than they could obtain from their own labor alone. It was a man-made institution. It was inevitable only insofar as everything that has happened in history was inevitable, not in terms of immutable or naturalistic laws."[90]

We have tried to highlight the impact of enslaved African labor on the development of the U.S. economy from an agriculture-based economy to an industrial capitalist economy. The discussion corroborates recent studies of the relationship between slavery and capitalism—such as those by Walter Johnson and Edward E. Baptist—and their impact on the making of modern American capitalism.[91] Of particular interest is the inherent attitude with which slaveholders, who owned the plantation businesses, from tobacco to cotton and rice, conducted their activities. The planters did everything within their powers to maintain the master-slave status quo to protect their investments. The U.S. political and legal system reinforced slavery because the slaveholders were often the same as the political and the economic elites.

Through their free labor, the enslaved people laid the foundation on which the U.S. economy was constructed. Yet, the most significant contribution of enslaved Africans to the flowering of the U.S. economy is not reflected in the statistical representations of net profits accruing from slave labor and agricultural productivity, the gains made from the exports and imports of goods and service, or the free labor worth an estimated $100 trillion that the slaves provided.[92] Instead, their most crucial contribution resides in the strong spirit that survived the cruelty of slavery. That survival is the foundation of the resilient bonds between Africa and the United States.

2

THE AFRICAN DIASPORA: MEMORY, SURVIVAL, AND LONGING FOR AFRICA

On September 22, 1735, a Boston-area newspaper carried a story about a free Black couple residing in Rhode Island who had saved "two or three thousand Pounds, having a Desire to return to their own Country."[1] While it remains uncertain if the couple actualized their desire, intents like this are central in the story of *survival* and all it connotes among the enslaved Africans in the Americas and the forging of what we know today as African American culture, a binding force in the United States-Africa relationship. The survival question was not lost on government officials throughout the colonial period as an assortment of diseases ravaged the inhabitants of the British North American colony. The problem persisted into the late nineteenth century, with poor sanitation and acute shortages of medical supplies and qualified health personnel compounding an already grave situation. In 1860, a frustrated Boston-based physician, Oliver Wendell Holmes, Jr. (1809–1894), drove home the obvious point when he declared: "I firmly believe that if the whole materia medica, as now used, could be sunk to the bottom of the sea, it would be all the better for mankind,—and all the worse for the fishes."[2]

While Holmes spoke to the overall poor state of healthcare in the United States in that period, the condition of African Americans was frightful. In 1860, N. A. Apollonio, the City of Boston's registrar, noted that among the African American population in Boston, the annual death rate exceeded the annual birth rate. Thus, Apollonio concluded, "it is manifest . . . that the [Black] race among us is doomed to a speedy extinction unless sustained by accessions from without."[3] Fourteen years later, the same office issued a similar gloomy prediction with a comment that "the African race is an exotic one in northern latitudes."[4] A careful observer, however, will notice that before the 1860s, the population of Blacks in the United States had increased substantially, leading to hysteria among specific segments of the White elite. Because of the panic, there was a noticeable and perhaps systematic effort to curb the rising population of Blacks in a society where racial malevolence was rife.

Boston city officials were not alone in observing the troubling decline in the African American population, which was common across the Deep South states of Louisiana, Alabama, and Mississippi.[5] During the 1865 census in Rhode Island, Edwin Snow, the census superintendent, stated that "the colored population of New England is not self-sustaining as to numbers." Snow went on to say that the climate and other influences suggested that the Black population would continue to decline "unless renewed by immigration, [and] would, in a comparatively brief period, become extinct."[6]

The trends in Black mortality over the period of slavery and in the post–Civil War era highlight the fact that the enslaved Africans' survival of their ordeal was the cornerstone of the historic United States-Africa relationship. Survival, the evasion of death, typifies the strength to absorb and overcome life-threatening circumstances. Studies on African survival in the Americas are not in short supply, but what the history implies is more than the abstract and cursory attention it often receives in the literature. Among other things, many of the extant works adopt the creolization paradigm and center on resistance, which was either violent or nonviolent. These studies have treated strategies through which the enslaved people overcame the perils of plantation life, including physical escape from the plantations. Explicitly, the previous studies have covered those cultural practices, memories, institutions, coping plans, and structures that provided succor and identity for those in bondage.[7] Also highlighted in the scholarship are personal experiences of slaves as they relate to their sufferings and emotions.[8]

Among the exponents of the creolization paradigm are Sidney Mintz and Richard Price, who postulate that the "randomizing" nature of slavery prevented the recreation of specific African cultures in the Americas. They therefore see cultural models as a hybrid of African, European, and Native American ideas. In other words, for the paradigm's proponents, creolization or cultural mixing ensured African survival in the Americas.[9] Vicente Diaz, another prominent champion of the creolization model, equates cultural mixing with slave survival. Diaz argues that through the process of creolization, the enslaved people have "come to make a privileged claim to the New World space-place."[10] This understanding validates Viranjini Munasinghe's earlier work, which suggested that for the enslaved Africans, creolization was a process of incorporation into indigeneity or native status in the Caribbean.[11]

Critics of the creolization paradigm, among them Daniel Segal, have argued that its supporters willfully or otherwise push forward an image of the "Africans" as persons devoid of an ancestral "civilization," who by way of "mixing" became partially White "West Indian," and as such gained some measure of "respectability."[12] Implicit in this line of thought is the notion that there was no alternative pathway to African survivals in the Americas other than through creolization. In the face of the slave owners' efforts to strip slaves of every vestige of humanity, especially family and inherited African culture, it is pertinent to treat in whole the dynamics of survival and longing for Africa among the enslaved Africans in the United States. A multipronged approach allows for a better understanding of the complex ways through which the enslaved Africans evaded a complete emasculation and helped lay the foundation of United States-Africa relations.

Building on the prior studies, we maintain that the idioms of African American survival under enslavement connote more than the ordinary conjectural musings. Theorizing bondage as a metaphor for death and survival enables us to represent adequately the enslaved people's physical evasion of death, their African cultural adaptations and continuities in the New World, and the freedom these symbolize. It is futile to study the African cultural survivals in the Americas apart from the struggle for the continued physical existence of the Black genus in the Americas. This reasoning aligns with the principle of natural selection, a process whereby living organisms must successfully adapt to their environment to survive and reproduce their kind. Scholars now agree that this theory, first expounded by Charles Darwin, is the primary process that brings about evolution.[13]

Throughout the period of enslavement, Africans had two options: survive or perish. They responded with diverse strategies that ensured their existence. The life and death alternatives presented to the slaves do not preclude the incidental benefits of creolization and rare acts of pity some slaveholders demonstrated toward those under their care. For example, in 1791, his owner manumitted Newport Gardner, an enslaved African from Sierra Leone, along with his wife and children, after overhearing him praying for his liberation. Reflecting on this, Newport commented that "the all-wise Disposer had signally answered his request before he had finished his supplication."[14] Nonetheless, survival and death operated in tandem as two sides of the same coin because, under slavery, the desire to live on was harder to achieve than the option to exit by death. The threat of death that persistently stalked those held in captivity pushed their survival instincts beyond the usual techniques individuals and groups in danger found helpful for self-preservation. The slaves struggled with such perennial problems as the erosion of confidence and hope, assaults on their religious faiths, shaming, family disruption, and sexual exploitation. These issues defied the enslaved people's humanity and their will to live.

Perhaps nothing best captures the metaphor of bondage as death than the story of "Igbo landing," an episode that purportedly happened in May 1803. According to the story, soon after a group of captive Igbo (also Ibo, Ebo) disembarked at Dunbar Creek, Georgia, the slave handlers prepared them for reloading and shipment to St. Simon's Island. However, the enslaved Africans quickly surveyed their environment and spontaneously resolved to regain freedom by first drowning the crew of the smaller ship and then themselves.[15] This tale of mass suicide shows that these Africans dreaded captivity more than "freedom" in captivity. Novelist Paula Marshall argues that mass death by drowning represented a unified act of indomitable spirituality:

> They turned . . . and looked at the white folks what brought 'em here. Took their time again and gived them the same long look. . . . [Then they] walked on back to the edge of the river here. . . . They just kept walking right on out over the river. Now you wouldna thought they'd of got very far seeing as it was water they was walking on. Besides they has all that iron on 'em. Iron on they ankles and they wrists and fastened 'round they necks like a dog collar. . . . And chains hooking up the iron. But chains didn't stop those Igbos none. Neither iron. . . . [T]hey just kept on walking like the water was solid ground. And they was singing by then. . . . When they realized there wasn't nothing between them and home but some water and that wasn't giving 'em no trouble they got so tickled they started into singing.[16]

Some doubt remains as to whether the event at Dunbar Creek happened or if it is part of the folklore, myths, and epic tales about "flying Africans" that have formed the archives of memory in the history of the enslavement of Africans in the Americas. Real or fictional, as Victor Turner has noted, "symbols may operate on several levels and in polarized dimensions, being at once 'sensory' (effective, easily recognized, and physiological) and at the same time, 'ideological' ([abstracted but] stressing a larger societal value)."[17]

For the enslaved community, stories such as the "Igbo landing" and "flying Africans," which conjures more than the apparent fantasy inherent in the use of aerial flight to escape bondage, are essential parts of the struggle between death and survival. In 1735, a Boston-area newspaper reported that a free Black couple living in Rhode Island nursed a strong desire to return back to Africa and had saved money for that purpose.[18] These stories are representative of the nostalgia or longing among the enslaved for freedom or a return to Africa, a desire they could not easily accomplish because of the nearly insurmountable barrier imposed by the Atlantic Ocean. Nevertheless, an ex-slave named Jack Tannali believed that such acts not only were possible but were actually executed by the enslaved Africans in the struggle for survival and freedom. As Tannali told his interviewers in the 1930s, "Lots of slaves what was brung over from Africa could fly. There was a crowd of them working in the field. They don't like it here and they think they go back to Africa. One by one they fly up in the air and all fly off and gone back to Africa."[19] In his study of Carriacou music, Andrew Pearse calls attention to such expressions of nostalgia preserved in slave music and odes as the "Oyo, Mama." The slaves sang about their desired wish to go to Africa to meet their parents but regretted that the Great Atlantic Sea hindered them.[20]

Throughout the United States, similar engagements in the dialectics of death and survival were common among the slaves, particularly the southern slaves of the antebellum period. However, scholars have somehow ignored suicide. Terri Snyder attributes this in part to "the problematic nature of [identifying] evidence for suicide." Therefore, it is difficult to know how many enslaved persons—or even free people—chose suicide in early modern America. This lack of data is because, as Terri Snyder has noted, "no systematic public accounting of deaths was undertaken when slaves were domestically dispersed, traded, and resold on the North American mainland." Snyder goes on to assert that "suicide figures for disembarkation are difficult to ascertain."[21]

If uncertainty obscures the fate of Africans arriving the New World, the autobiographies of those individuals who went through ordeals on the plantations provide clearer ideas about their emotions. In its sullen tone and persistent focus on bereavement, the autobiography of Harriet Ann Jacobs (1813–1897), *Incidents in the Life of a Slave Girl*, further reminds the reader that death was real in a slave's life and the plantations were enclosures where cruelty troubled the practice of capitalism and barbarism haunted slave lives.[22] In her careful study of Harriet Jacobs, Georgia Krieger argues that Jacobs's life history resonates with the message of abolitionists and, by implication, the slaves who had the opportunity to narrate their personal ordeals. Among these categories of people, death and resurrection stand out as the central events in the narrative. Thus, Krieger concludes that Jacobs created "a text that points out the extent to which resistance both to slavery and to ideologies of ideal womanhood and motherhood may involve, paradoxically, a submission to both."[23] In other words, survival for the enslaved Africans involved self-preservation in both the physical and ideological senses as slaveholders peddled paternalism in the midst of what Jeffrey Young, who has studied the Gowrie plantation in South Carolina (owned by the Manigault family), describes as "a good supply of disease and pain."[24] Thus, some thoughts need to be devoted to survival as a concept and a fundamental reality in American slavery.

MORTALITY AND DIFFERENTIAL SURVIVAL

Some of the literature on mortality and differential survival approaches the mortality gap among racial, ethnic, or social classes as a function of wealth, income, and inequality.[25] Others focus on occupational status or broader measures of socioeconomic status.[26] No matter the approach or terminology used in these studies, they all converge in their arguments for a strong association between mortality and economic status. In relation to the experience of enslaved Africans in the United States, accurate data is required "to produce the most reliable estimates of differential survival . . . [with consistent observations of] socioeconomic status over time, [one needs] a sufficient sample size, minimal attrition, and observations of actual deaths. But such ideal conditions are quite data-intensive."[27] Such statistics are poorly preserved, and it is, therefore, problematic to estimate the comparative survival rates of Black and White people. A starting point is an investigation of the role of institutional settings, policy, and social factors in explaining health inequalities within slave communities as compared to free Whites. Also, this method demonstrates the potential of subjective probabilities of survival to enable researchers to study the effects of mortality on behavior or to construct alternative life tables as indicators of morbidity within an age cohort.[28]

The data in Tables 2.1 and 2.2 show that although the mortality rate of adult slaves was close to that of the free adult Black population, it was not because the adult African slaves received adequate nutrition, as Clifton Bryant claims.[29] Slaves, more particularly the infants, struggled with an extraordinarily high death rate. Some scholars estimate that 50 percent of slave infants died within a year after birth. While this figure might be typical of the colonial period, the available historical demographic data does not permit a definitive conclusion. However, in 1850, 183 Black infants died before the first year in every 1,000 births, compared to 146 for Whites. This fact translates to 25 percent more Black deaths compared to the rate of White babies. The plantation owners often subjected slave children to harsh treatments in what Robert Fogel and Stanley Engerman have referred to as "the strange paradox of planters who treated pregnant women and new mothers quite well while abusing their offspring."[30] Such contradiction implicates the idiom of death and survival, as no mother is psychologically alive while her infant child passes through suffering. Although

Table 2.1 White and Black Populations, 1620–1860

	1620	1660	1700	1760	1790	1860
Total Population	2,302	75,058	250,888	1,593,625	3,929,214	31,443,876
White (%)	2,282	72,138	223,071	1,267,819	3,172,006	26,922,537
	99.1%	96.8%	88.9%	79.5%	80.7%	85.6%
Black (%)	20	2,920	27,817	325,806	459,822	4,441,830
	0.9%	3.9%	11.1%	20.4%	19.3%	14.1%

Note: These figures are only for the continental United States and may vary from the actual numbers.
Source: U.S. Bureau of the Census, *Historical Statistics of the United States from Colonial Times to 1957* (Washington, DC: Government Printing Office, 1970), 1–16.

Table 2.2 Death Rate (DR) of Blacks as an Index of Whites in Nine Cities, 1765–1860

City	Period	Population	DR-Black	DR-White	B/W
Boston	1765–1774	17,314	66.76	28.15	2.37
Newport	1774	9,163	37.72	23.49	1.61
Philadelphia	1821–1830	153,546	44.52	23.65	1.88
Baltimore	1817–1865	132,537	32.03	24.13	1.33
New York	1820–1865	391,348	43.9	31.3	1.40
Philadelphia	1821–1830	153,546	44.52	23.65	1.88
Charleston	1822–1848	28,929	26.17	26.08	1.00
Mobile	1843–1850	17,770	25.66	39.98	0.64
New Orleans	1850	116,407	16.5	30.11	0.55
Boston	1854–1875	212,862	34.48	24.08	1.43
Savannah	1855–1860	16,589	34.67	37.05	0.94

Note: The column on the far right is determined by dividing the Black index by the White index.
Sources: Christian Warren, "Northern Chills, Southern Fevers: Race-Specific Mortality in American Cities, 1730–1900," *Journal of Southern History* 63, no. 1 (1997): 23–56, here 27, 35; and Susan E. Klepp, "Seasoning and Society: Racial Differences in Mortality in Eighteenth-Century Philadelphia," *William and Mary Quarterly* 51, no. 3 (1994): 473–506, here 476–77, 479–80, 488–89.

the death rate tended to drop for the slave children who survived their first year, Mintz reminds us that "it remained twice the white rate through age 14."[31] The estimate for the colonial period is that "the average life expectancy of a slave at birth was just 21 or 22 years, compared to 40 to 43 years for antebellum whites. Compared to whites, relatively few slaves lived into old age."[32]

Studies by Richard H. Steckel and others have identified rampant disease and malnourishment as significant causes of the high infant and child death rate among the enslaved people.[33] According to Fogel and Engerman, the prenatal care accorded to slaves was dismal.[34] This view corroborates John Campbell's study, which correlated higher infant mortality rates to the level of excessive work assigned to pregnant mothers before delivery. "If slave women enjoyed little or no respite from their normal field duties during and immediately after pregnancy, the potential for infant and/or mother mortality would be heightened."[35]

Steckel probed deeper into the problem of prenatal illnesses and premature delivery and death by looking at other connected variables, including the age of pregnant mothers, environmental conditions like the size of the plantation region, and the historical period in question. Steckel concluded that the level of slave mortality during pregnancy varied from plantation to plantation and was dependent on the specific time during the slavery era (Table 2.3).[36] The results of other studies by scholars such as Kenneth F. Kiple and Virginia H. King further show that diet, acts of racism, and the cold climate contributed to the poor health of and morbidity among slave children of African ancestry.[37]

Table 2.3 Infant Death Rates Based on Plantation
Period and Occurring within 28 Days

Period	Number of Births	Infant Death Rate per 1,000
1786–1799	113	319
1800–1809	197	223
1810–1819	134	291
1820–1829	225	276
1830–1839	69	275
1840–1849	135	252
1850–1863	454	249
1786–1863	1,327	261

Source: Richard H. Steckel, "Slave Mortality: Analysis of Evidence from Plantation Records," *Social Science History* 3, nos. 2 and 3 (1979): 86–114, here 100.

Together, the various studies point to the fact that while slaves, in general, lacked adequate nutrition, the lives of slave mothers and their infants were more in danger because slave owners showed little concern for their well-being. Pregnant slave mothers were neither allowed the extra measure of food nor given the healthy diet their bodies required in the period of pregnancy. Rather, plantation owners subjected slave mothers to the usual intensive work until the very last week before delivery. Mintz's study reveals that fetal miscarriages and maternal deaths were common among slave mothers. A disproportionate percentage of slave infants were underweight, averaging about 5.5 pounds at birth, and often mothers had no choice but to wean their infants as early as three to four weeks after birth.[38] Instead of the regular diets for babies that White babies of their time lived on, slave children lived on cornmeal. Mintz concludes that "around the age of three, they began to eat vegetables, soups, potatoes, molasses, grits, hominy, and cornbread. This diet lacked protein, thiamine, niacin, calcium, magnesium, and vitamin D, and as a result, slave children often suffered from night blindness, abdominal swellings, swollen muscles, bowed legs, skin lesions, and convulsions."[39]

The Gowrie plantation on the Savannah River, purchased by business tycoon and slavocrat Charles Izard Manigault (1795–1874) in 1833, was notorious for its high child mortality rate. Through Manigault's papers, students of slavery studies see what life was like for slaves on the plantations. While slaveholders like Manigault presented themselves as humane and caring, the difference between the slave masters' families and their captives was often that of life and death. In 1848, for instance, Manigault told his estate overseer, "I allow no strange Negro to take a wife to my place, & none of [my slaves] to keep a boat."[40] Clearly, he would rather monopolize the slave children's attention and obedience, rather than see them turn to their biological parents, through whom they would have access to other slave communities.[41] At the Gowrie plantation, slave morbidity among young people below age sixteen rose up to 90 percent, meaning that most of them did not survive. This estimate is not inclusive of deaths through stillbirths or miscarriages. The records show that at Gowrie between 1846 and 1854, for every fifty-two newborns, 144 slaves died. In other words, the number of deaths surpassed the number of births by a ratio of 1:2.8.[42]

The simple explanations for high slave infant mortality are poor health, inadequate shelter, mediocre food, and brutal work. Water- and food-borne epidemics such as measles, dysentery, and cholera at the Gowrie plantation in 1848, 1850, 1852, 1853, and 1854 claimed the lives of hundreds of slaves. In addition, chronic diseases like malaria and pleurisy remained perennial. In 1849 during the cholera scare, one of Manigault's White overseers at Gowrie complained that water was seeping "through the bank and keeping the ground under the Negro Houses soft and wet, which emits a very poisonous effluvium. I have kept the weeds cut down and have small gutters cut to get all the water into the large ditch, but I cant begin to get the ground dry under the houses."[43] Because of the persistence of these poor conditions on the plantations, slave deaths at Gowrie rose as high as 50 percent of the population.

Soon after Christmas 1854, co-owner Louis Manigault (1828–1899), who persistently declined to acknowledge the local slave patrol's jurisdiction over the Savannah River estate, wrote to his father Charles: "it is now my painful duty to return You a list of the dead, and here they are in the order in which they died.—Hester, Flora, Cain, George, Sam, Eve, Cuffy, Will, Amos, Ellen, Rebecca,—Eleven from Cholera, and two Children viz.: Francis and Jane not from Cholera.—In all Thirteen names no longer on the Plantation Books."[44] It is altogether revealing that Louis Manigault, the so-called Gentleman Capitalist, who was reputed to have treated his slaves humanely, exhibited a laissez-faire attitude, if not an inhuman outlook, toward the deceased slaves. His primary concern was not the lives lost, but rather the apparent reduction in the plantation's labor force and its economic implications.

COPING TECHNIQUES AND SURVIVAL

How did the Africans survive the morbid, traumatic conditions of plantation slavery in America? The answer resides in the networks the enslaved people established within the limitations of servitude. To start with housing, the slaves lived in their own section of the plantation. While some planters provided housing for their slaves, others charged them to build their own homes. In this case, the slaves' houses tended to replicate those they were accustomed to in Africa, with thatched roofs, and they often lived in cramped conditions with as many as ten people sharing a hut, which they mended when they had their rest days. This fact aligns with Jay Edwards's study of the linear cottage in the Atlantic world, which reveals an archaeological landscape modeled after European, African, and American traditions.[45]

At times the slaves received pots and pans for cooking, but more often they had to make their own. Constrained by the long hours of work in the plantation fields, the slaves had limited free time to improve their living conditions. Some prepared their food with utensils fashioned from a woody gourd called calabash, which was common in precolonial West and Central Africa. The enslaved people spent their free time making pots and pans and growing food on the land that some plantation owners set aside for them. In the process, the enslaved Africans created a hybrid gastronomy of African, American, and European traditions, such as the southern cuisine and "soul food" retained today from the time of slavery.[46]

On a more serious note, separating family members was one of the strategies slavocrats found useful in their attempt to control the lives and bodies of the bonded people they held as private properties.[47] Since slave owners forbade the Africans to marry, many slaves contracted secret marriages in familial ceremonies. Those forcibly separated couples within the same locations visited their spouses under the darkness of night. Therefore, the beginning of survival started with the fear of separation. However, in the antebellum period, slaves in the South resided in family units. Marie Schwartz, who has studied family life and survival strategies in the slave quarters, notes that slave owners housed each slave family in the one- to two-room log cabins located in the slave quarters, and sometimes several families shared a single cabin (Fig. 2.1). "Here in the small, cramped indoor spaces, in the yards surrounding each cabin, and in the unpaved streets, slave families tried to fashion a private life for themselves that

Figure 2.1. Slave quarters inside a plantation. *Library of Congress.*

allowed each member to be more than a slave. They courted and married, bore babies and raised children, all actions that imparted meaning to their lives."[48]

Schwartz notes that in 1860, on the eve of the Civil War, about half of all slaves were younger than age sixteen. The most interesting dynamic of the period is that these slaves eluded acting merely in the role of slave. Rather, slaves defined themselves as mothers and fathers, brothers and sisters, aunts and uncles. This proclivity demonstrates that they were individuals within families, notwithstanding the unimaginable agonies of enslavement. In other words, for their survival, the enslaved people turned to the psychological security their ethnic and cultural belongingness provided to the individual. Time together with family within the slave residences provided significant opportunities for transmitting African-themed knowledge about different life lessons and practices, among them those connected with health, well-being, and ancestors. The enslaved Africans persevered by keeping some forms of family and ethnic networks through their oral traditions and folktales, religion, and personality.[49] Through these means, extended families established networks that spread information, helped groups to impart knowledge, and taught both the younger and older members ways to deal with the severe stresses of slave life. Schwartz adds that "families engaged in a variety of economic activities in an attempt to improve the material conditions under which each member lived. For example, some cultivated food for their consumption. They raised chickens and ate the eggs; grew rice, corn, and vegetables; kept bees and harvested the honey; and hunted and trapped small animals, which were cleaned and cooked for the table."[50]

In *My Bondage and My Freedom*, published in 1857, Frederick Douglass provides a vivid insight into how slave owners used starvation as an instrument of coercion. "I suffered little from the treatment I received, except from hunger and cold. These were my two great physical troubles. I could neither get a sufficiency of food nor of clothing."[51] Through this form of punishment and control mechanism, the slaveholder hoped that the recalcitrant slave would resist temptations to rebel or evade hard work.[52] In response, slave families strived to secure an alternative source of food outside the control of their owners. "For [enslaved] parents, this meant that work continued well into the night after they had left their owners' fields or other work sites."[53] In some instances, slaves stole necessities such as food from their owners. "I hated everything like stealing, as such, I nevertheless did not hesitate to take food, when I was hungry, whenever I could find it," Douglass wrote. "Nor was this practice the mere result of an unreasonable instinct; it was, in my case, the result of a clear apprehension of the claims of mortality. I weighed and considered the matter closely, before I ventured to satisfy my hunger by all means."[54]

From the early nineteenth century onwards, following passage of the Act to Prohibit the Importation of Slaves, children born to African slaves on American soil adapted more easily to specifically American ways of life. This provided the African slave community with new survival skills. Their ability to understand American regional dialects and customs improved their capacities to communicate, strategize, and escape from the oppressive forms of servitude. Despite the dangers of escaping, slaves in the nineteenth-century southern states began to flee to the northern parts of the United States in higher numbers than ever before.

The Fugitive Slave Law of 1850, which highlighted the evils of slavery to the more significant number of Americans in a manner previously unknown, emboldened many slave escapees.[55] Aided by Calvinists, Scotch Covenanters, Quakers, and Wesleyan Methodists, 100,000 slaves escaped from the South between 1810 and 1850 via the Underground Railroad, according to one estimate. In 1850, the District of Columbia complained that "underground railroads and felonious abductions" had reduced its slave population from 4,694 to 640.[56] Wilbur Siebert's *The Mysteries of Ohio's Underground Railroad*, first published in 1891, details the operations of the escape routes used by the abolitionists.[57] With data collected mainly from individuals who personally drove wagons from station to station in aid of the so-called fugitive slaves, Siebert reveals that the slaves showed up along the Ohio River from Cincinnati, Ripley, Portsmouth, Athens, and other places. At each of these well-identified collection stations, the slaves found friends. The rapidly expanding railroad transportation from the Ohio River northwards, in addition to the steamboats on Lake Erie, made escape easier for the enslaved Blacks.[58] Even after emancipation, throughout the late nineteenth century Quakers, free Blacks, and other antislavery groups continued to support individuals desirous of escape from the lingering form of bondage in the southern states.[59] In 1885, for instance, a fifteen-year-old slave girl named Anna Maria Weems from Rockville, Maryland, disguised as a boy, escaped to freedom in Chatham, Canada, with the help of the conductors of the Underground Railroad in Montgomery County.[60]

Another crucial survival tool for slaves was music, which goes with dancing. Coming from Africa, where music was a system of education and singing and dancing suffused every aspect of African lives, the enslaved people and their African American descendants reenacted familiar African forms of song and dance. In the ancestral homeland, singing and dancing remained shared undertakings that brought everyone together, which uplifted human spirits. Africans sang as they worked and on important occasions in life, including death, marriage, birth, puberty, and other rites of passage and maturity. The indigenous culture demanded that everyone in the kindred community come together to sing and dance in celebration as people passed through every stage of life. This cultural thinking led the enslaved people to rally around one another in celebration of the little cultural space they could find.

Sporadic songs and dances provided one foundation for the African-based expressive culture in the Americas. The rhythms and dances conserved "during the Middle Passage became the roots of New World African music and dances."[61] Eventually, when the slaves converted to Christianity and began to understand the Bible, they found inspiration from liberation stories such as the Israelites' escape from ancient Egypt. Additionally,

> the Pan-African synthesis started on the slave ships evolved into even greater syntheses in the Americas. In places where there were heavy concentrations of enslaved Africans from a single ethnic or national group, the music and dances of these peoples would come to dominate the musical and dancing practices of their community. Even in such settings, however, Africans from other ethnic and national groups made their contributions to the developing new cultural form. More typically, Africans from several different ethnicities and nationalities created something new out of the cultural and material resources found in their new environment. They built their religious and secular rituals, festivals, and social gatherings on the foundations of the song, dances, and rhythms they invented to cope with and express their New World realities.[62]

While the slave owners forbade the slaves to read and write, they allowed them to attend church on Sundays. However, neo-African religions—Santeria, Shango, Umbanda, Voodoo, and others—continued to be modes of religious identity and expression among the enslaved Africans. It is noteworthy that these indigenous African religions rely on African-based rhythms, music, and dances. One of the long-lasting debates in African diaspora studies is the question of whether the African slaves arrived in the New World devoid of their African heritage. In 1978, Albert Raboteau fired the first cannon of controversy with the argument that African traditional religious systems did not come to North America with the enslaved people. Raboteau contended that, unlike other New World slave societies, slaves in what became the United States constituted a small fraction of the overall population and that indigenous African gods yielded prominence to the Christian God. Raboteau and others have argued that the traumatic experience of the Middle Passage from Africa to the Americas was so intense that much of the slave's "past had been annihilated" or erased.[63]

However, Melville Herskovits and Sterling Stuckey vigorously argue that the African slaves migrated with their inherited cultures and tried to recreate them wherever they found themselves in the New World.[64] Both scholars emphasize the continuation of vestiges of African religion and other elements of culture in the United States, arguing that African religious belief systems and ritual practices furnished African Americans a social identity. Corroborating this view, Walter Rucker adds that a prevalent body of beliefs in death, reincarnation, and transmigration of souls in the afterlife was central in the development of slave resistance and revolt in the United States. Religious convictions held the enslaved people together for social actions, including widespread slave revolts.[65]

The fundamental problem with scholars like Raboteau is that they approach their study of African cultural artifacts in the New World from the anthropological present. They forget that cultures mutate as they pass through diverse geographical boundaries and social milieus. The intention here is not to dwell much on this old idea about cultural retention or lack of it among the slaves. Instead, we focus on how African religions and other items of culture were of consequence in the survival of African elements in the United States, as well as the subsequent development of African American culture. In separate studies, Sylviane A. Diouf, Yvonne P. Chireau, and Allan D. Austin concluded that enslaved African Americans used a broad spectrum of spiritual resources derived from African traditional religions, Christianity, and Islam. African traditional religious practices such as Conjure, Voodoo, and Santeria were invoked to heal, protect, and, when the occasion demanded, hurt or destroy an enemy or the opposition. Islam, too, contributed to the African American religion and cultural artifacts in the antebellum American South. Though the comparatively small Muslim population strived to preserve their religious and communal identity, individuals such as Omar ibn Said, captured from West Africa and enslaved in North Carolina in the early 1800s, were among the handful of enslaved African Muslims.[66] Christianity undoubtedly buttressed Nat Turner's appeal for organizing one of the most massive slave revolts in American history. In 1831, the slave preacher turned rebel claimed that he received a divine instruction to lead the rebellion.[67]

Together, this wide range of religious ideas—drawn from African indigenous religions, Islam, and Christianity—offered the enslaved people assets to reclaim some measure of their personhood, forge a collective identity, and develop common cultural traditions. Oratorical skills reinforced religious sermons and other forms of African American oral literature with roots to genres developed by

enslaved Africans in the period of slavery. This truth runs contrary to Jon Butler's *Awash in a Sea of Faith*, which claims "that between 1680 and 1760 'African
slaves in the British mainland colonies experienced a spiritual holocaust that
effectively destroyed traditional African religious *systems*.'"[68] The corrective is
that the enslaved Africans reenacted, with varied successes, African indigenous
forms of religion, like music, carnivals, and dances, in diverse styles as a body
of historical memory, cultural adaptation, and survival in the United States and
elsewhere.

Scholars who have explored a plethora of slave cultural ideas and traditions conclude that the roots of the musical and dancing performances that
characterize American carnivals and junkanoo festivals lie in Africa, or rather
represent the heritage of enslaved Africans' ancestors. For example, Robert
Nicholls's nuanced work links Igbo cultural forms (specifically, masquerades,
music, and dance) with their African diaspora antecedents in the U.S. Virgin
Islands.[69] Ivor Miller connects the Ékpè masquerade lodges among the Efik and
Ibibio of southeastern Nigeria with the Ábákuá secret society in Cuba.[70] As we
discuss in Chapter 8, the tropes of music and dance styles that are associated
with America's pop culture today started in the era of slavery. Howard Dodson
observes that African American artistic successes occurred even though many
slave owners disallowed the use of drums and some genres of African music and
dance. "When slave 'masters' and overseers in the United States discovered that
drums could be used as a secret means of communication, they were banned."
Nevertheless, the enslaved people did not give up. To reproduce the intricate
percussive rhythms of African drums, the enslaved Africans in the United States
improvised with hand clapping and foot tapping.[71]

Congo Square in New Orleans was one of the rare places where slave owners
allowed the enslaved Africans to use drums in music plays. Every Sunday in the
city's French Quarter, French culture encountered Africa's rumbling drums
as the enslaved gathered to shake off the drudgery of servitude.[72] The Congo
Square dance participants entertained their audiences with the strut, jigs, shuf-
fles, breakdowns, and the ring shout. They used the fiddle, the banjo, bows,
gourds, bells, and other instruments to create sound bites that would come to
represent the material cultural inventions of the African American dialogue.[73]
From these beginnings, the enslaved Africans emerged as the favorite artists not
just for Black-themed festivities but also for White celebrations. In the context
of survival, slave music not only provided succor for the enslaved people but
also won them widespread acclaim and admiration among the White population. It is no surprise that in colonial-era New York, the midwestern area that

later became Chicago, and the southern parts that became New Orleans in 1803, most fugitive slaves perceived themselves as professional musicians.[74]

In Rhode Island, one enslaved African musician known as Newport Gardner (1746–1826) was sought after by appreciative White and Black audiences. Writing in 1846, George Mason disclosed that Newport was the son of a wealthy trader from Sierra Leone "who was brought here directly from the coast of Africa when about fourteen years of age, and that he was entrusted to the captain of the vessel, who, having pledged himself to see that the boy was properly instructed, sold him into slavery."[75]

The story goes that Newport ended up as the property of Mrs. Caleb Gardner, from whom he took his name. However, the crooked Rhode Island slave trader was most likely Capt. William Gardner, who sailed to West Africa in 1774 to acquire slaves. While there is no way to ascertain the validity of this story, it is clear that Newport was the first enslaved African or African American to be duly acknowledged as a professional musician. Later on he served as a singing-school master within the community.[76] Newport "read and wrote music with ease, and his voice was remarkably strong and clear. Sacred music alone claimed his attention." According to Mason, Newport used the money he earned giving music lessons to "men and women who had better schooling" to purchase his freedom. Along with members of his band, John Quamine, Salmar Nubia (a.k.a. Jack Mason), and Bristol Yamma, Newport strove to retain his native tongue even as Blacks in the region tried to speak the English language.[77] Newport's effort to keep his African tongue suggests not only resistance to full acculturation but also the hope that one day he was going to return to Africa. Although he won his freedom in 1773, Newport Gardner, who "won the confidence and merited the respect of everyone, and about the year 1823 was ordained a deacon in the Congressional Church in Newport," never fulfilled his desire to return to Africa. He died of old age on board the *Brig Vine* bound for Liberia on February 6, 1825.[78]

This account of the survival techniques and strategies adopted by the enslaved Africans and their African Americans descendants in the United States reveals a complex intersection among the physical, spiritual, cultural, and psychological factors with which Blacks contended. Whichever approach or technique scholars may prefer to emphasize—music, food, religion, escape or running away, creolization, and so on—there was no single pathway to African survival under slavery. Instead, self-preservation involved diverse strategies. The end result of the slaves' exertions, as the example of Newport Gardner in Rhode Island reveals, was that those in bondage and their descendants succeeded in integrating African humanity and the culture it conveyed into the fabric of their American host society. Through integration, the enslaved served as a conduit between the new American community and African religion, music, dance, architecture, dress, food, and other ways of life. More important, individuals like Newport Gardner, Bristol Yamma, and Salmar Nubia (Jack Mason) were "zealous to go" back to Africa as early as 1773 despite their successes in Rhode Island. This longing for home remained a potent metaphor for survival among the enslaved people. It motivated their readiness to listen to ideas such as the Freetown colony that British philanthropists established in Sierra Leone in 1787 and was formally ratified in 1788 by the Temne chief. The Freetown colony served as a blueprint for the Liberia colony founded by the United States. Thus, it is essential to examine the connection between the two colonies in the context of United States-Africa relations.

3

FROM LAND OF FREEDOM TO CROWN
COLONY OF SIERRA LEONE

Scholars have yet to fully untangle the motives behind the founding of the freedom colony in Sierra Leone, West Africa, in 1787 (Fig. 3.1). It was championed by the British Committee for the Relief of the Black Poor (CRBP), which initially named its African project the Province of Freedom, then Granville Town, and later Freetown. Christopher Fyfe, the doyen of Sierra Leone history, has, among other things, covered the extreme challenges and social stratifications that confronted the inhabitants of the early colony.[1] Tara Helfman ably detailed how the deployment of a vice-admiralty court (1807) and a commission (1817) led by Chief Justice Robert Thorpe to adjudicate on the captured slave ships turned out to be the cornerstone of the early corpus of international human rights law, as well as the law governing world maritime exchanges.[2] Focusing on the fast development of missionary works led by the Wesleyan and Episcopal churches, Joseph Tracey further explains that Charles McCarthy, who first served as the colony's acting governor in 1814, had conceived Sierra Leone as a base for extending the advantages of civilization into the interior of Africa.[3] V. E. J. Buckle offers insight into the evolution of the Creole language in the colony as a complex mixture of the various patois of the émigré Nova Scotians, Maroons from the Caribbean, the African recaptives, and the indigenous ethnic groups in Sierra Leone.[4]

The founding of the colony and its reestablishment in 1791 not only marked a momentous turn of events in the history of the Atlantic slave trade but also bound the United States and Africa to each other.[5] Zachary Macaulay (who served as the colony's governor between 1790 and 1799) underlined the imperative in his journal entry of September 23, 1793, by narrating his encounter with the captain of a U.S. slave vessel from Boston. After he remonstrated with the

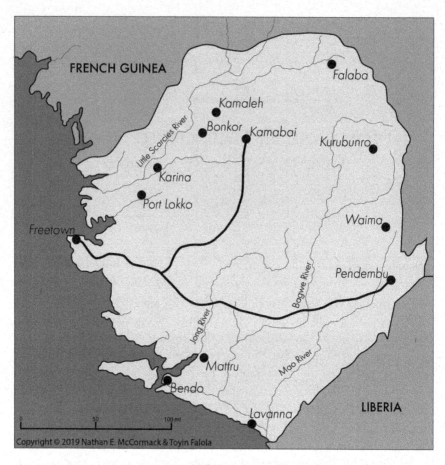

Figure 3.1. Sierra Leone. *Toyin Falola and Nathan McCormack.*

American slaver about the evil trade, the American offered "us his cargo of slaves, observing he could take nothing else, and that he hopes we should be able to dispatch him in a few days."[6] It is remarkable that this encounter took place fifteen years prior to the U.S. outlawing of slave importation from Africa.

For over three centuries, one pattern of mass movement of people had defined the trans-Atlantic exchanges: shipping of Africans to the Americas. The colony of Freetown was not just symbolic of the dramatic inverse movement; it was the first sociopolitical space solely dedicated to building a new Afro-American culture on African soil and based on the principles of freedom, liberty, and egalitarianism. Freetown provided a laboratory for a deeper understanding of the challenges that confronted the enslaved Africans in the Americas. The Nova Scotians, the Maroons, the various ethnic and vernacular recaptives, and the British rulers all met in a quite alien environment despite its African setting.

The new settlers in the colony faced pressures analogous to those applied to the enslaved Africans in the New World. In the settlement, the émigré communities along with the indigenous people of Sierra Leone either re-experienced or encountered for the first time Western-style education and the habituation of Protestant Christianity with indigenous forms of religiosity. The new settlers further dealt with monogamous marriages, European styles of dressing, work ethics, and wealth accumulation through commerce. Also in play was a propensity toward racial and ethnic categories as the Nova Scotians, when provoked, assumed social superiority over the recaptive Africans, whom they called "Willyfoss niggers" in reference to the role of William Wilberforce in the abolition movement. When quarrels broke out, the U.S. Civil War veterans also called the children of the recaptives "niggers."[7] These dynamics corroborate K. L. Little's observation that "it is possible that the Sierra Leone phenomena afford an opportunity of appreciating certain methodological aspects of the Afro-American problem in sharper perspective."[8]

In 1847, Freetown gained endorsement as a model for the United States' African colony of Monrovia, Liberia, founded during the administration of President James Monroe.[9] Thus, the place of Sierra Leone in the advancement of United States-Africa relations deserves more than casual attention. The development reinforces the critical fact that at every significant turn in its evolution, the elaborate connection between the United States and Africa endures. The unfolding discussion reveals that when the original thirteen colonies locked horns with the British colonial overlords, the American struggle for independence became inseparable from the rise and survival of the Sierra Leone Freedom colony in West Africa.

At the level of political discourses, Sierra Leone became synonymous with the American independence struggle. It is more ironic than coincidental that the very slavocrats and political elite who supported the institution of slavery also drove the events that led to the rise of Freetown. The plan for the colony in West Africa materialized at a time when political leaders in the United States and Britain were using metaphors of slavery to underscore political points. Until the outbreak of the American Revolution in 1775, thoughts of a potential colony for free Blacks were a seemingly unrealistic dream considering the unparalleled volume of slaves still being hauled away from Africa in the late eighteenth century. From 1771 to 1775, for example, the number of enslaved Africans shipped to the Americas stood at 1.9 million. The number increased to a little over 2 million in the ensuing twenty-four years from 1776 to 1800.[10] This reality prompted Ottobah Cugoano, the former slave and legendary abolitionist of African descent, to wonder whether the government of Britain was actually going to create an unhindered territory adjacent to the very location "[where] it supports its forts and garrisons, to ensnare, merchandise, and to carry others into captivity and slavery."[11] In his appraisal of Cugoano's views, Isaac Land notes that his cautious reaction reminds the reader that there was little reason to believe that in the late eighteenth century Freetown would grow "as part of a coherent, well-financed plan, backed by military force, to end the slave trade and transform West Africa."[12] Given this circumstance, it is remarkable that within a decade of its conception, the Freetown project had become a reality, offering the emancipated poor slaves from different parts of the British Empire an auspicious occasion to return to Africa.

Among the new settlers in Sierra Leone, the Black Nova Scotians from the thirteen colonies stood out both in the immediate nourishment of the idea of the colony and in its future development and stability. As explained here, the strength of their presence in Sierra Leone manifested in both the rise of new cultural tropes and, more important, in protecting the moral implication of freedom that the colony symbolized. To better account for this, it is critical to highlight how the trajectory of U.S. history in the 1770s had far-reaching consequences across the Atlantic world. Because slavery shaped the very foundation of U.S. society, the slavery metaphor compelled both the American patriots and the British colonists to devise a lucid and robust antislavery argument in order to smear the image of the opposition in the courts of local and international public opinion.

Positioning the servitude versus freedom argument as an instrument of the political contest allowed both sides in the American revolutionary struggle to rationalize their actions and inactions toward a wide range of issues relating to ideology, slavery, capitalist acquisition, colonialism, human rights, international law, and political power. In 1774, for example, George Washington complained to the loyalist George William Fairfax of Virginia, a member of the landed gentry and planter, former mentor, and neighbor who had newly relocated to England: "those from whom we have a right to seek protection are endeavoring by every piece of Art and despotism to fix the Shackles of Slavery upon us."[13] Washington's insipid and hypocritical words belie his status as a die-hard slavocrat who retained slaves throughout his life.[14] With those words, Washington, the man Henry Wiencek describes as "an imperfect God" and known today as the father of the nation, jolted an audience unfamiliar with the contentious issues surrounding the war of independence.[15] Those familiar with revolutionary texts, however, understood that White Americans expressed their displeasure with Great Britain in terms of an institution they practiced themselves. Corroborating this view, Peter Dorsey notes, "The use of the metaphor of slavery to foster colonial and national interests was so widespread that it quickly became a rhetorical commonplace, but the persistence with which it was used indicates it had a major impact on the way American revolutionaries thought and acted."[16]

Dorsey's observation implicates two critical issues with the abolitionist movement and the founding of Sierra Leone. First, it remains the fact that Enlightenment ideals inspired the anticolonial movement in the British American colony. Thomas Jefferson (1743–1826) wrote explicitly about Americans' natural rights in the Declaration of Independence as rights to life, liberty, and the pursuit of happiness. It is paradoxical that Jefferson, the United States' third president and the chief writer of the Declaration of Independence, entertained different ideas of freedom — one for Whites and another for slaves in the emergent nation. As Jefferson's *Notes on the State of Virginia* (1785) reveals, he wanted the offspring of slaves to undergo an apprenticeship education starting from 1800. In his view, this training must be completed before emancipation.[17] Since nearly half of Virginia's residents at this time were slaves, Jefferson's proposal was revolutionary in thought but fell short of expectation. Because he anticipated social upheaval following emancipation, Jefferson believed that it would be best for society for the freed Blacks to move out of Virginia. He decried the apparently hypothetical scenario in which ex-slaves and their former masters might coexist as equals.[18]

The second issue related to the Freetown cause is that the American colonists who fought British domination highlighted the damage slavery did to the ideals of human rights, morality, and freedom. Jefferson accurately assessed the problem when he proclaimed: "There must doubtless be an unhappy influence on the manners of our people produced by the existence of slavery among us. The whole commerce between master and slave is a perpetual exercise of the most boisterous passions, the most unremitting despotism on the one part, and degrading submissions on the other." Perhaps the most critical part of his take on slavery remains what Jefferson perceived as the long-term problems of social relations between the races: "Our children see this, and learn to imitate it; for man is an imitative animal. This quality is the germ of all education in him. From his cradle to his grave he is learning to do what he sees others do. If a parent could find no motive either in his philanthropy or his self-love, for restraining the intemperance of passion towards his slave, it should always be a sufficient one that his child is present. But generally it is not sufficient."[19]

Soon after the end of the American Revolution, George Washington and his comrades suppressed their inner feelings about slavery. However, slavery and abolition debates remained at the center of American society for most of the nineteenth century. Throughout this period slavocrats in Africa, Western Europe, and the Americas struggled against their conscience to ignore calls for abolition. Again, Jefferson observed correctly when he wrote: "I think a change already perceptible since the origin of the present revolution. The spirit of the master is abating, that of the slave rising from the dust, his condition mollifying, the way I hope preparing, under the auspices of heaven, for a total emancipation, and that this is disposed, in the order of events, to be with the consent of the masters, rather than by their extirpation."[20]

FREEDOM COLONY IN AN AGE OF REASON

Above all else, the Sierra Leone freedom colony was emblematic of a new moral compass in the entire Atlantic world. In an informative study of Freetown and the development of legitimate commerce in the adjoining West African areas, E. A. Ijagbemi extols the essence of the Enlightenment movement in Europe by stating that the colony of Freetown materialized solely as a late eighteenth-century Enlightenment project in Western Europe. He argues further that the era's revolutionary outlook and philosophical radicalism may have sought, in the light of reason, to build life anew for humankind in general. Ijagbemi contends that the intention of the English humanitarians—among them William Wilberforce, Granville Sharp, Thomas Clarkson, Henry Thornton, and others who belonged to the so-called Clapham Sect (unique for their dedicated attention to Africa)—was to extend the torch of the Enlightenment to the African continent. In so doing, Ijagbemi concludes, the humanitarians desired to reconstruct a perfect society out of the chaos and confusion that (to them) was the Africa of their day.[21] Without a doubt, the intent of this group of European humanitarians and abolitionists was not merely to dump the Black poor back in their ancestral continent but also to secure a settlement planned to provide a basis for a purposeful and profitable future.[22]

Along this line, the Europeans who led the movement sought to make the émigrés (who had witnessed the ideals of the Enlightenment in Europe) into their partners in the project of spreading the "blessings of industry and civilization" in Africa.[23] The familiar narrative that often privileges the Europeans while silencing the African voices leaves the reader with a lot to desire. If we understand the Enlightenment in the Western world as a period of intellectual ferment marked by constructive thoughts, liberal ideas, and humanistic thinking, then it is evident that there are liberals and humanists in every corner of the world across all ages. The difference between the European Enlightenment thinkers and their African counterparts, for instance, is that the former received more publicity than the latter.

In the extant literature on slavery and abolition, scholars have tended to portray the Enlightenment as something unknown to Africa; hence the role of African chiefs and other individuals who decried slavery and supported abolition has received no consideration. For instance, T. C. McCaskie describes Granville Sharp's novel idea for the colony as a gift "from the morally enlightened to the spiritually impoverished."[24] This form of historiography tends to ignore the morally superior action taken by the regent Tom (or Tham), who in 1787 initiated the grant of land bordering the north shore of the Freetown peninsula to Capt. John Taylor of the Sierra Leone Company (the former St. George's Bay Company). The humanitarian action taken by the Temne (Timni in the colonial records) chieftain has yet to receive a critical reflection. Instead, leading scholars of Sierra Leone studies tend to categorize the indigenous rulers as disingenuous enablers of colonial rule.[25] It is imperative to accentuate that both the Temne regent and King Harry Naimbanna of Robana, who at last signed the document now known as Treaty No. 1 of August 22, 1788, upheld liberal values of emancipation and freedom similar to those of the British abolitionists. If the British philanthropists, as Ijagbemi reminds us, launched the Freetown scheme to improve the lives of the emancipated slaves in England, it is critical to add that many African rulers along with ordinary people, particularly the African mothers and women who lost their children and siblings to slavers, profoundly shared this sentiment. Besides Naimbanna, whom Macaulay described as "an African native of uncommon intelligence," his son, Henry Naimbanna, was also an abolitionist. On his way to England in 1793, Henry requested his brother, Bartolome, "to oppose the Slave Trade" so that "nothing injurious may be imputed to Sierra Leone Company by evil-minded men whose interest may be in opposition to the worthy Company."[26]

The scholarly literature is replete with ideas and counterviews on the institution of slavery in the Atlantic world. The absorptionist analysis, promoted by Suzanne Miers and Igor Kopytoff, sees slavery as a process of absorbing the enslaved and marginalized people into society and kinship groups. The argument thus ascribes absorptiveness to the character of African slavery while it adjudges its American counterpart as a pattern of economic exploitation and social degradation.[27] A. G. Hopkins, an economist, sees the use of slaves as a rational economic choice in a system where the incentives brought by market forces demand engagement of slave labor to expand production and profit.[28] Unlike the economic and anthropological approaches that reify either the market or kinship, the Marxist analysis of Claude Meillassoux and others focuses on the capacity of privileged groups to control and use slaves, and the consequences of this power on cultural values, ideology, and social organizations.[29] This understanding is the context, one supposes, in which Henry Louis Gates conceived the precolonial Africans as no more than collaborative, exploitative, and miserable slave dealers, who compromised their sense of morality with the whiskey and gunpowder they received from the Europeans in exchange for slaves.[30]

Because the practice of slavery, for whatever purpose and manner, is cruel, Frederick Cooper has argued that it is also crucial to understand the institution in the Atlantic world as an "interactive process, shaped by slaves as well as by slave-holders."[31] Otherwise, the temptation is ubiquitous to give credence to such wild assumption that the precolonial African societies were devoid of humanists and antislavery exponents. Writing with this wrongful conviction, Anselma Guezo argues, "If the recollection of the selfless crusade of the abolitionists against the Atlantic slave trade has a soothing effect on the guilty conscience of the European perpetrators the same is not true for their West African counterparts."[32] The truth of the matter is that not all precolonial African rulers shared the same values or approved of the actions of King Adandozan of Dahomey, an unapologetic slavocrat who purportedly practiced slavery with uncommon impunity.[33]

The point we want to emphasize is that beyond Black abolitionists such as Olaudah Equiano, enlightened Africans in positions both high and low cooperated with European and American abolitionists to achieve the common goal of freedom and resettlement for emancipated poor slaves. Joseph Bangura's recent study *The Temne of Sierra Leone: African Agency in the Making of a British Colony* attests to this point. The study reveals that for Naimbanna, as the self-styled "King of Sierra Leone," money did not appear to be the primary motive for the lease of the original piece of land measuring about twenty square miles to the British philanthropists.[34] Instead, the Temne indigenous rulers received cloth, gold earrings, smoking pipes, beads, two pairs of pistols, and other cheap products as gifts.[35] Roy Lewis and others have observed that King Naimbanna publicized his liberal and "cosmopolitan character" when he strongly denounced the slave trade in 1788: "Many of us African rulers are not happy about the slave trade going on in our country. It brings to our country and people a lot of destruction and unhappiness. But we have found out that we cannot stop it on our own unless the white people cooperate with us."[36] King Naimbanna's confession misaligns with Henry Louis Gates' s controversial 2010 op-ed, which threw a blanket indictment on all African rulers as evil and individuals who acted in concert to sell fellow Africans into slavery for personal profit.[37]

So far, the argument underscores that specific individuals and groups spread across the Atlantic world worked in tandem in pursuit of the ideals and goals of the Enlightenment and abolitionist movements. As the nature of political discourses on the eve of the American Revolution indicates, the postwar events cohere through an understanding of the dialectics of patriots versus colonizers and slaves versus abolitionists. To start with, although the American patriots projected the confidence their antislavery proclamations substituted for emancipatory deeds, they left difficult political choices not only to succeeding generations of Americans but also to the British. In other words, in both the United States and other parts of the British Empire, the practice of slavery reached a crossroads from the late eighteenth century. Hence the cardinal importance of Sierra Leone as a symbol. From this moment, it became a matter of time before the very underlying ideology around which Atlantic-world slavocracy revolved broke apart.

Meanwhile within the broader resonance of revolutionary ferment, including the Enlightenment movement in Europe, the practice of applying revolutionary rhetoric and its favorite trope to new crises and partisan causes continued to remind White Americans that chattel slavery conflicted with their political ideals in both theoretical and normative terms. The postwar developments in the period represented one of the epiphanies that came with the Enlightenment—or, rather, an accident of conscience that met the times. Perhaps nothing better illustrates this than John Newton's "Amazing Grace" hymn. Born into a Puritan family, the former slave trader wrote the famous religious hymn in 1772 after he survived a violent storm on a return voyage from Africa.

> Amazing grace! (how sweet the sound)
> That sav'd a wretch like me!
> I once was lost, but now am found,
> Was blind, but now I see. . . .[38]

Newton's life history is reminiscent of the exemplary exertions of the American Quakers who led the way toward emancipation. In fact, "the Quaker majority welcomed runaway and freed slaves to the [Massachusetts] area as early as 1716."[39] With the support of the Quakers, emancipated slaves originally "from continental Africa and Cabo Verde (then a Portuguese colony) became part of the African-American heritage of New Bedford" in Massachusetts.[40]

Another significant way in which the currents of United States history helped promote the Freetown colony needs attention. By 1775, the predominantly enslaved African American population in the thirteen colonies was about half a million. Early in the eighteenth century, only a small number of New England ministers and concerned Quakers, among them John Woolman and George Keith, had questioned, along with other social ills, the morality of slavery, but few paid attention to their concerns.[41]

By the 1760s, however, as the settlers started to voice their concerns about British tyranny, more Americans, notably the affable Abigail Adams, wife of John Adams, the future second U.S. president, pointed out the apparent contradiction inherent in advocating liberty on the one hand and owning slaves on the other. Along with her commitment to women's rights and education, Abigail Adams (1744–1818) was ardent and forthright in her disapproval of slavery. Discontented with living in the White House due to the presence of slaves, Mrs. Adams decried what she perceived as the citizens' hypocrisy in a letter to her husband dated September 22, 1774. "It always appeared a most iniquitous scheme to me—to fight ourselves for what we are daily robbing and plundering from those who have as good a right to freedom as we have—you know my mind on this subject."[42] Adams was one of the first to warn political leaders that slavery was a hazard to the nascent American democracy and that by the practice of slavery in Virginia, free and privileged Whites were "depriving their fellow Creatures of freedom."[43]

If we are to question the primary motivation of Temne chiefs who gave up their lands to the founders of the Freetown colony, it needs to be reiterated that the spirit of philanthropy was not the sole driving force that moved the British government to act in support of the African colony. In 1893, Maj. J. J. Crooks corroborated this view when he noted that one of the primary motives of British government's support for the territory was to establish "an outlet for Great Britain's surplus population, such as other colonies."[44] This revelation contradicts the notion held by scholars like Ijagbemi, who touts only the humanitarian and philanthropic reasons often repeated in the mainstream literature.[45] It is fair to say that while the English humanitarians had genuinely Christian intentions, the British government had other designs. Indeed, the Anglican Church and the British state found common ground in the physical relocation of an unwanted section of the population to Africa. Thus, the intent was not solely to reconstruct "a perfect society out of the chaos and confusion that (to them) was the Africa of their day," as Ijagbemi claims.[46] Rather, the British government played along with the church for different motives: to reconstruct the chaos created by slavery not only in the English society of the time but also in the entire British Empire. The implication for West Africa was that the Europeans would expand the size of the Freetown colony to accommodate the demand for space as the number of emancipated slaves and other interest groups coming from the

Atlantic world continued to rise. Among these groups, the Black Nova Scotia loyalists occupied a prominent position in the history of the new settlement and the United States connection.

THE U.S. BLACK NOVA SCOTIANS AND FREETOWN

With the outbreak of the revolutionary war, a sizable group of Blacks (most of them enslaved) joined the ranks either of the American revolutionaries or of King George III and the British forces, as animated debates took place over the morality of slavery and emancipation. Although the British eventually lost the war, they attempted, with limited success, to make good their pledge to compensate both the Black and White loyalists from the original thirteen colonies with private land concessions in Nova Scotia, Canada.[47] As it turned out, most of the Black veterans were unable to cope with the poor soil and harsh weather of Birchtown, Nova Scotia, to say nothing of the daunting psychological impact of quasi-slavery and hostility from the European settlers including their former comrades, the White loyalists who also ended up in Nova Scotia after the war. When the founders of the Freetown colony presented the Black loyalists with the slogan "Freedom and Farm," their trials in Canada understandably convinced them that their best hope of survival was in Africa. As James Walker's *The Black Loyalists* recorded, Africa became "the promised land" for this group.[48] When the proposition came, 1,196 of the estimated 3,000 Blacks in Nova Scotia signed up for the journey to Sierra Leone. If the hopes of the enslaved Africans for freedom were on furlough in the late eighteenth century, the idea of a freedom colony somewhere on the African continent was a cause of optimism (Fig. 3.2).[49]

The readiness of the émigrés, led by David George, Boston King, and Moses Wilkinson, to relocate to Africa needs further attention.[50] In theory, the quest for African regeneration was one of the significant driving motifs behind the whole notion of the Freetown colony. In nonlinear order, this ideology and all it implied at this time—whether in terms of memory, remembering, reclamation of the Black man's dignity, repopulating the African continent, or the broad idea of cultural adaptation and continuities—were widely shared among generations of diaspora Africans. Christopher Fyfe captures this sentiment in his depiction of the Black loyalists' landing in Freetown on January 15, 1792: "Their pastors led them ashore, singing a hymn of praise. . . . Like the children of Israel, Israel which were come out again out of the captivity they rejoiced before the Lord, who had brought them from bondage to the land of their forefathers. When all had arrived, the whole colony assembled in worship, to proclaim to

Figure 3.2. Black Nova Scotians: Thomas Beals family, ca. 1930. *Nova Scotia Archives.*

the . . . continent whence they or their forbears had been carried in chains—
'The day of Jubilee comes; return ye ransomed sinners home.'"[51]

   In 1799, seven years after the Nova Scotia Blacks arrived at Freetown, a royal
charter granted to the Sierra Leone Company changed the name of the colony
to Sierra Leone. Subsequently, under Gov. Thomas Ludlam (1799–1800), the
Governor-in-Council (a legislative council comprising the American Colonization Society's fourteen agents and two governors) secured legislative powers.
Soon after, the abolitionists brought 550 Maroons from Jamaica to the colony.
The British Parliament finally abolished the slave trade in 1807, and Sierra
Leone became a British Crown Colony in 1808. Throughout the nineteenth
century, the size of the colony expanded through several "treaties of friendship"
and land grants secured from local African chiefs.[52] British squadrons turned the
entire Sierra Leone coast into a naval base, from which it sought to enforce the
abolition laws. Batches of slaves ranging in the hundreds, and sometimes a few
thousand who regained their freedom in the various British colonies around the
world, mostly resettled in Sierra Leone. British squadrons also policed the sea
to stop the trans-Atlantic slave trade as Portuguese and French traders continued to ship enslaved Africans to the Americas, particularly Brazil. By 1808, the
population of the new settlement was about 2,000, hailing from different parts
of West and Central Africa. The rule of allowing the recaptives a new beginning
there brought stability and coherence, with 50,000–70,000 slaves from different

ethnic groups and nationalities intercepted and liberated by the Royal Navy over the next six decades.[53]

HOPES AND IMPEDIMENTS

Scholars of Sierra Leone history tend to discuss the conflict between the settlers and the indigenous groups as a function of the latter's unwelcoming attitude toward the new arrivals. The extant literature often states that the greatest impediment confronting the émigrés was a fundamental lack of trust between them and the indigenous people. For instance, V. R. Dorjahn and Christopher Fyfe highlight this dynamic in their essay "Landlord and Stranger."[54] Colonial reports on the insistent conflicts in the colony also assigned the bulk of the blame to the indigenous people.[55] This narrow understanding of the enormous challenges involved is flawed and needs a better context.

In the eighteenth and early nineteenth centuries, Freetown was a quintessentially multiethnic, multiracial, cosmopolitan experiment in social engineering. Writing in 1863 after a visit to the colony, the British ethnologist Robert Clarke noted that "the negro population of Sierra Leone represents almost every tribe in West Africa, and the variety of spoken languages makes a perfect Babel of confusion. Fifty different languages are in use among the liberated Africans; many of these tribes differing greatly in their mode of life and progress in civilization."[56]

In terms of sheer size, the recaptives from different parts of the continent outstripped the settlers from Nova Scotia, who in turn outnumbered the Jamaican Maroons. The first batch of 411 (including sixty White female prostitutes and widows) from different parts of the British Empire made up the demographics.[57] To put this in perspective, the colony was a communal experiment in Anglo-American culture on African soil. The inclusion of the sixty White women (who were forcefully married off to the emancipated slaves) among the original settlers is akin to the Boko Haram extremists' kidnapping of and forceful marriage to the Chibok girls of northwestern Nigeria in 2014.[58] The White women who boarded the *Vernon* and *Atlantic* in December 1787—Sarah Whycuff (widow), Sarah Cambridge, Mary Sabb, Elizabeth Lemmon, Mary Tomlinson, Ann Thompson, Elizabeth Andrew, and others—represent more than mere "strumpets" or "women of lowest character," as J. J. Crooks called them in 1893.[59]

The problem of Sierra Leone, then, was not just about a division between émigrés and natives. Also in play were issues relating to gender. How both the British government and the abolitionists treated these destitute White women tells us more about the conditions of their gender in male-dominated societies before the twentieth century.[60] Falconbridge, who had a close encounter with some of the surviving White women a few years later, was informed that they had been drugged with alcohol and "inveigled" on board in what amounted to "a Gothic infringement on human Liberty."[61] Lucy Bland and her coauthors have noted that the entire passenger list reveals the "integrated lives that existed among the very poorest and marginalized in London as well as . . . the long migration histories of women, black and white, in the costly establishment of British colonies."[62]

More troubling is when we consider the vouchsafed character and reputation of the so-called philanthropists behind the Freetown project. Crooks stated the obvious when he observed that mere contemplation of such a thing "was nothing short of monstrous." According to Crooks, "that it was done will ever remain a blot, not only on the Government of the day that permitted it but on the memory of those men whose names will ever stand prominently in history as the leaders of one of the noblest movements ever made by man for his fellow-man."[63] The point, then, is that Sierra Leone harbored different strands of issues and cross-cutting cleavages that transcended African, European, and American identities. Making sense out of the chaos that confronted all the various stakeholders in the new society, particularly in its first forty years, mirrors the push and pull that described the new sociopolitical and economic institutions the colony's government put in place to arrest the rampant chaos of a new society in constant flux.

Perhaps the most significant problem that confronted the new colony was a lingering foreboding about enslavement and exploitation in a land of freedom. The unbridled quest for profit by the Sierra Leone Company in the colony exacerbated this concern among the Nova Scotia Blacks. In its first report to the shareholders, the company made it clear that "the leading object in the formation of the Sierra Leone Company may be briefly stated to have been to introduce just and honorable commerce with . . . Africa."[64] Thus, one surmises that the comfort of the new settlers was not of primary concern to the company. In a report published in *The Times* of London on October 14, 1793, the company informed the British public that it had shipped "Elephants Teeth, Frankincense, Bees Wax, Bum Coral, Guinea Grains, Rices in the Hair, 40 tons of wood and sponges" from Sierra Leone.[65]

The new settlers arriving in Freetown in the late eighteenth and early nineteenth centuries aspired to lives of freedom, liberty, and egalitarianism. They wanted rights to unhindered opportunities, not experiences as slaves or descendants of people held in servitude in the European dominions in the Americas.

The émigrés had backed freedom with their lives by fleeing to British army camps during the American War of Independence, and they desired to live their lives fully as citizens. These hopes and aspirations were the first steps toward an African renewal, the widely shared ambition to salvage the Black man's dignity, which had been severely impaired by centuries of slavery in the Americas.[66] As explained here, some of the émigrés' values and aspirations in Sierra Leone were quite attainable, while others were difficult to accomplish because of their formulation in cultures alien to Africa. In other words, the outcome of the mission of the émigrés in Africa was subject to the dialectics of hopes and impediments. These challenges reflect common human reactions to the dynamics of immigration, similar to the experiences of the Portuguese who returned to their European ancestral homeland after its African colonial posses-sions collapsed in the 1970s.[67]

Thus, contrary to the views of Dorjahn and Fyfe, which also echo official colonial reports,[68] the abolitionist Anna Maria Falconbridge, who worked with the new settlers in the early stages of the colony, observed that there was a severe problem of mistrust among the émigré communities toward their British over-lords. Aggravating this lack of trust among the Nova Scotians was the feeling that they had been "so often deceived by the white people."[69] As Lamin Sannah con-cluded, the climate of distrust between the Nova Scotia Blacks and the British officials was an outgrowth of the "officialdom which had twice let them down in the United States and in Nova Scotia, hardened with the severe privations suf-fered in the harsh climate of Sierra Leone where land was both scarce and filled with gravelstone."[70] This dynamic led to the emergence of individual preachers such as David George as advocates for the welfare of their communities.

The émigrés' resentment of the British officials in Sierra Leone pointed back to their American slave experience and reflected what they perceived as continuing White oppression. A quarrel between the colony's first British governor, John Clarkson, and the Nova Scotia Blacks community leader, ex-sergeant Thomas Peters (born Thomas Potters, 1738–1792), was documented in December 1793 when the settlers sent two delegates to England "in order to lay the various complaints of their constituents [against the governor] before the Court of [Sierra Leone Company] Directors."[71] The court, sitting in England, considered the evidence and ruled that "the petition of the Nova Scotians [was] hasty, and the facts herein mentioned [were] chiefly founded on mistake and misinformation."[72]

In 1793, when Beveshout[73]—a Black Nova Scotian and Methodist preacher whom Zachary describes as "a man of a restless turbulent spirit and immoderately fond of popularity"— declared "God in His good time will deliver Israel," he meant it to serve as a warning to the governor about a Black revolt in Freetown.[74] In the 1796 council elections, a group of Nova Scotian Blacks called on the voters to either ignore the eligible White candidates or face violent reprisal. "One white admitted [into the council] would prove too much for [our] liberty." A later governor, Zachary Macaulay, would complain that "there was something so unique in making a white face a civil disqualification."[75] Following a slave revolt in Virginia in 1800, a portion of the African settlers in Freetown, led by officers of the African American–controlled, newly established independent churches, rose in a violent agitation against Gov. Thomas Ludlam.[76]

Like the Nova Scotians, the indigenous people (Sherbro, Temne, Susu, Mende, Limba, and others) believed their concerns about the new settlements mattered little or not at all to British officials in Sierra Leone. Therefore, several sources of mistrust existed in the colony among the new settlers. In specific terms, for example, the émigré community wanted more land and less taxation to actualize their dreams of settlement in Africa, while the indigenous population of Sierra Leone strongly resented the taking of their lands to compensate the émigrés. This anger increased with Clarkson's unguarded declaration that he planned to secure the lands for the Nova Scotian Blacks as promised. "I promised to make it my business to see that their proper allotments of land were given them and declared I would never leave them till each individual assured me he was perfectly satisfied."[77]

On the positive side, African regeneration was a sentiment held by a more significant majority of the various actors involved in the Freetown project. As already alluded to, throughout its duration, Atlantic slavery was a somber source of grief for many African women and forward-thinking African precolonial elites who decried it.[78] By implication, African regeneration, at least in the eyes of both the various African groups and the émigrés, also meant uprooting those sociopolitical and economic practices that encouraged the rise and expansion of African slavery, including the mindsets among Atlantic-world slavocrats that sustained the commerce in human beings. As P. E. H. Hair observed, "The incoherent, unsystematic, and sometimes unreasonable complaints of the Nova Scotia settlers at Freetown were the beginning of African political nationalism, of Négritude in Africa—in sum, of conscious Africanism."[79] This important task required a collaborative effort in multiethnic and multiracial settings. Sierra Leone served as a symbol of this joint project.

With its foundation in the slave trade, Freetown faced many obstacles in constructing a stable and thriving society. The persistence of slavery (though not the slave trade) enabled the European officers and merchants in Africa to abuse their powers and conduct business as they pleased in the colony. Rampant corruption caused outrage among the original abolitionist founders of the colony, but they were unable to steady the order of things because the ruling powers sometimes sabotaged their efforts. However, through the persistence of individuals such as Clarkson in protecting the freed slaves' civil rights and liberty, the Europeans, Americans, and Africans laid the foundation for a more positive future for the inhabitants of Sierra Leone.

The survival of the colony in the late eighteenth and first half of the nineteenth centuries became possible by the combined efforts of missionaries from America and Britain, Black loyalists from the original thirteen American colonies, and the African recaptives from different parts of West and Central Africa. The establishment of the Church Missionary Society's Fourah Bay College in 1827 provided an extra incentive.[80] Fourah Bay College offered the émigrés and recaptives the rare opportunity to imbibe Western education, which comes with reading and writing skills. It is because of what Freetown symbolized for these different categories of peoples from its inception that it became a model colony, a prototype for the colony of Liberia officially established by U.S. president James Monroe in 1822. From the late eighteenth century, Sierra Leone emerged as the nursery for Atlantic ideas and culture in an age of reason.

The recaptives constituted the largest subgroup in nineteenth-century Sierra Leone, but they initially lacked the confidence to articulate a stronger claim to the freedom and opportunities the colony promised. The Nova Scotian contingent filled this critical need. As the settlement grew, the émigrés fell out of favor with the British authorities, who outlawed them and confiscated most of their property. After the deployment of colonial soldiers against the insubordinate Maroons, most of the survivors returned to Jamaica in 1841.[81] Meanwhile, the émigrés from the United States led the community to imbibe Anglo-American culture and lifestyles, which the early Freetonians attempted to pass on to their African neighbors. This form of enculturation was especially true for the recaptives, known as *Saros* in the coastal cities of Lagos and Port Harcourt (Nigeria) and as *Amuros* in Banjul, Gambia. One may identify the institutions facilitating and promoting Anglo-American-African relations as the "three Cs"—that is, the doctrines of Christianity, civilization, and commerce.

CHRISTIANITY, CIVILIZATION, AND COMMERCE

Diverse notions and practices of Christianity and commerce imagined as synonymous with the progress of civilizations marked the history of Atlantic slavery. These three doctrines resonated with the various subgroups of settlers who populated the Sierra Leone colony. The inchoate and spontaneous Black congregations that David George and others put together mirrored the Black religious communities that sprouted among the enslaved people on American plantations. The Nova Scotians fashioned these small congregations into precious and reputable churches in early Freetown. The most distinct character of the Black churches remained their assumption of independent initiative in West Africa, where conditions encouraged separation from the official church. In other words, the Nova Scotian Blacks laid the foundation of African independent churches. In an eyewitness account of the religious zeal associated with the émigrés from North America, Falconbridge noted, "Each sect has one or more preachers attached to it, who alternately preach throughout the whole night; indeed, I never met with, heard, or read of, any set of people observing the same appearance of godliness."[82]

Beside those emancipated Africans who voluntarily and permanently resettled in Sierra Leone, other groups launched spirited projects aimed at rescuing Africa from the centuries of pillages occasioned by the slave trade. Among them were the Friendly Society of Sierra Leone (FSSL), founded by Paul Cuffee, the affable African American New England mariner, merchant, and shipowner who first visited Sierra Leone in 1811 in his *Traveller*. No account of American influence in Africa in the eighteenth and nineteenth centuries would be complete without consideration of Cuffee. Under the aegis of the FSSL, he worked with the Black Nova Scotia settlers in Sierra Leone to put together a petition that he took to the British government in 1811.[83] Cuffee also campaigned for support from the "African Institution," founded in Britain in 1807 to help secure a safe colony for the freed slaves in Sierra Leone. With the support of the Institute, Cuffee formed an American branch of it in Philadelphia and Boston 1812 to help coordinate Black emigration to Africa. Through his initiatives, more African Americans took a keen interest in the affairs of the Sierra Leone colony.

From Cuffee's personal memoir as well as the 1856 *Maryland Colonization Journal*, scholars have gained insight into Cuffee's impressive career and activities in relation to the colonies of Sierra Leone and Liberia. His philanthropic work in promoting the welfare of the settlers in Sierra Leone indicates increasing American influence in the Sierra Leone colony. Like millions of enslaved Africans, Cuffee's father Kofi, who was born in Africa, was known as Cuffee and given the surname of his owner, a Massachusetts resident. As a slave in the United States, Kofi Slocum, Cuffee's father, married an Indian woman named Ruth Moses. His father was granted the privilege (rare in the era) of acquiring personal property because of his proven industry and diligence in the business of his master. Slocum bought his freedom. The Slocums raised ten children — among them Paul, who was born in 1759. After his father's death, the burden of supporting his mother and sisters fell on the shoulders of the fourteen-year-old and his brothers. Paul refused the name Slocum and changed his last name to his father's first name, Cuffee (Kofi).[84]

Because the land left behind by his father yielded poor harvests, Paul Cuffee conceived the idea that commerce brought ampler rewards than agriculture. He believed he had the skills that, properly cultivated, would enable him to successfully pursue commercial exploits. At the age of sixteen, Cuffee moved into the business as a servant on a fishing vessel going to the Bay of Mexico. During his third voyage in 1776, a British squadron took him captive and held him for three months in a New York prison. On his release, Cuffee returned home to Westport, Massachusetts, where he spent about two years trying his hand again at working the land.

During this interval, Cuffee and his brother John owed taxes to the local district of their residence. In response to the aggressive enforcement of the law by the tax collector, Cuffee noted that according to the Massachusetts constitution, taxation was ordinarily an obligation of those who enjoyed the full rights of citizenship. Thus, the Cuffees challenged the U.S. government for requiring them to pay taxes, while the same constitution failed to invest them with the rights of representation in the state legislature. Their sentiments echoed the American rebels' complaint of "taxation without representation."[85] After paying their taxes, the brothers were resolute in fighting for equal rights not just for themselves but also for all people of color, a resolution that informed Cuffee's commitment to the Sierra Leone project.

Cuffee progressed in his business and eventually came to be a prosperous merchant and shipbuilder. On his journey back from Sierra Leone, Cuffee docked at the seaport of Liverpool in 1811. The historic visit attracted the attention of the *Edinburgh Review*, whose editorial of August 1, 1811, paid a well-deserved tribute to Cuffee: "On the first of the present month of August, 1811, a vessel arrived at Liverpool, with a cargo from Sierra Leone, the owner, master, mate, and whole crew of which are free Negroes. The master, who is also the owner, is the son of an American Slave and is said to be very well skilled both in trade and navigation, as well as to be of a very pious and moral character. It must have been a strange and animating spectacle to see this free and enlightened African entering, as an independent trader, with his black crew, into that port which was so lately the nidus of the Slave Trade."[86]

Back in the United States in 1812, Cuffee sought an audience with President James Madison to discuss questions related to a cargo confiscated from one of his merchant ships by U.S. officials as the vessel approached Newport, Rhode Island. This incident happened during the War of 1812. Mr. Cuffee continued to devote his life to fighting for civil rights and liberties for the oppressed, including widows, for whose sake he funded an integrated community school so that children of the underprivileged could have access to basic education. His "heart grieved for the degraded state of his race."[87] In 1815, Cuffee transported thirty-eight African Americans back to Africa. Cuffee considered the expedition so vital that, in the absence of adequate funding for the families who moved to the new Freetown colony, he paid for all the costs from his account.

As the preceding discussion reveals, while most abolitionists intended Sierra Leone to serve as something like a glorified plantation colony, though apparently devoid of slave labor, Paul Cuffee envisioned a very different future for the West African freedom colony. His life and letters form an essential chapter in the history of United States-Africa relations. Through his initiatives, the movement of Black people in the Atlantic world continued to characterize Sierra Leone throughout the nineteenth and twentieth centuries. Starting in the 1810s, African Americans embraced the idea of going to Freetown in their quest to support the colony through Christianization, which was conceived as identical to civilization. Under the umbrella of the FSSL, American notions of education, Christianity, civilization, and commerce expanded and infiltrated the colony. Meanwhile, Africans of Sierra Leone traveled to Europe and the United States in search of a Western-style education.

Those trained by the missionaries contributed to changing the Freetown colony into an epicenter of civilization in the region. The same was true of various other early mission outposts located along the Upper Guinea coast of West Africa, including those at Bullon Shore. Through the various participating Christian missions, new schools were built for young people residing in the unique enclave, including the recaptives who would constitute the backbone of the new nation. Nonetheless, it is essential to note that before the colony, the Africans had an indigenous system of education based on the apprentice system. Also, Africans who had embraced the Islamic faith, the majority of them in the Futa Jalon (the highland region of modern Guinea, Sierra Leone, Senegal, and Gambia), attended Quranic school. Besides, as separate studies remind us, the Poro (Purroh) and Sande secret societies ran initiations into these societies, which served as a branch of the educational system.[88] Additionally, the youngsters of privileged merchants and local officials occasionally sent their wards to Europe to acquire Western-style education. The schools opened by the Christian missionaries, notably the Church Missionary Society (CMS), including those from Germany and the United States, increased access to education and presented an entirely new and innovatory approach to socialization and skills development for the region. The early CMS, Lutheran, and Friends of the Sierra Leone Colony schools turned Freetown into a colony of diversity and learning.

Among the Nova Scotian Black settlers in Sierra Leone were a handful of teachers who established schools in the settlement. In fact, authorities chose

Methodist preachers such as Luke Jordan, Henry Beverhout, and Boston King (1760–1802) to become schoolmasters.[89] Despite the difficulty of "finding decent teachers," as Governor Macaulay reported, education remained a crucial factor in the life and survival of the colony in the first few decades of the colonial leadership.[90] Several reports by missionaries lamented the unceasing pressure to remain in Freetown as teachers. As should be expected, a good number of the early schoolmasters had no formal education. Governor Macaulay sent King to England to be educated.[91]

Nova Scotian preachers of all three significant sects often doubled as schoolmasters, as described by the Sierra Leone Company in its 1794 report, which notes (with implicit criticism) the presence of teachers among the religious Black Nova Scotians: "Whatever education or instruction any of them have received, appears to have been chiefly, if not entirely, got since the era of their emancipation. A few of them with a part of their earnings put themselves to school, with the view either of increasing their religious knowledge or of laying the ground for some future improvement in their condition: and these are now the preachers and schoolmasters of the Sierra Leone colony."[92] The knowledge and skills exhibited by the mission-trained graduates ensured the dramatic and often rapid impact of mission education on African societies. Many of the mission school graduates became missionaries, teachers, or merchants who provided leadership not just in the consolidation of Freetown as a center of education and cultural plurality but also in the various coastal cities of West Africa, including Liberia, established in 1841.

Sierra Leone played an important role in the founding of Liberia, and both colonies stimulated the flowering of Anglo-American culture in West Africa. Nineteenth-century Freetown was a cradle for political nationalism and conscious Africanism. One central figure who personified this global movement and the early Pan-African discourses was Edward Wilmot Blyden. A native of St. Thomas who was born in 1832 to Igbo parents, Blyden first moved to Liberia in 1851 and in 1871 moved to Sierra Leone.[93] His place in the history of Liberia began with the United States and the establishment of the Monrovia colony.

In sum, the Sierra Leone model colony informed the founding of the colony of Liberia established during the presidency of President Monroe. Also, several African American émigrés, including Alexander Crummell, a New Yorker and an ordained minister, lived and operated in Liberia. Sierra Leone offers a background to Liberia and its history of progress and reversals.

4

PRESIDENT JAMES MONROE AND THE COLONIZATION SOCIETY: FROM MONROVIA TO LIBERIA

It is hoped that these vigorous measures supported by
like acts of other nations will soon terminate a commerce
so disgraceful to the civilized world.
—*President James Monroe (December 7, 1819)*[1]

Imagined after the British colony of Sierra Leone, and sited next to its eastern borders, the American colony of Liberia in West Africa happened during the presidency of James Monroe (1817–1825). Prior to his White House tenure, Monroe had been governor of Virginia from 1799 to 1802. Since the state retained the most significant number of slaves in the country until 1860, it is not entirely surprising that Monroe, who owned more than 250 slaves in his lifetime and brought some of them to serve his family at the White House, made Liberia one of the centerpieces of his foreign policy. In 1819, an act of Congress empowered the president to provide in Africa a suitable place for the projected colony.[2] Monrovia, the capital of this country, which the United States found expeditious in the termination of the trans-Atlantic slave trade and its enduring effects in America, was named in President Monroe's honor (Fig. 4.1).

Looking back today, one cannot but see the Liberia colony as a daring and calculated, if not desperate, move to rid the United States of what its founders (like President Monroe) and financiers considered an ominous threat: a rising population of denigrated free Blacks after the War of Independence and the War of 1812.[3] Despite the implicitly racist agenda behind the move, the Liberia colony broke new ground in the advancement of United States-Africa relations as the emergent American republic projected its rising global power toward Africa—the fountainhead of the global slave trade for 400 years. If the repatria-

Figure 4.1. President James Monroe. *National
Portrait Gallery, Washington, D.C.*

tion of Nova Scotia Black loyalists to Sierra Leone in 1791 served as a forerunner
of the Liberia scheme, the experience accruing from the British abolitionists'
invention of Freetown provided the U.S. government a helpful guide in the
planning and execution of the new colony. The government used the American Colonization Society (ACS) founded in December 1816 by Rev. Robert
Finley, a Baskin Ridge, New Jersey, Presbyterian preacher, as the facilitator of
this project.

But Liberia was neither a mere re-creation of the Sierra Leone effort nor a result of the European scramble for colonial dominions in Africa. Robert Brown
has noted that Liberia was more than a geographical expression. "It was also an
idea, a symbolic expression of the racial, religious, political and psychological
views of the population of the United States."[4] The launch of the American colony in Africa was somewhat reminiscent of the coming of the English founders

of Jamestown, Virginia (1607), and Plymouth, Massachusetts (1620). Like the Pilgrims, the Black émigrés to Africa perceived their return to Africa as another Exodus and carried with them an air of superiority similar to the attitude the British settlers propagated in the United States. In precise terms, the African American colonists in Liberia shared with the Pilgrims a belief that U.S.-style sociopolitical, cultural, and legal institutions and ideas were the sine qua non of the progress of civilization, not just in Africa but also elsewhere on earth.[5] In a similar spirit of thought propagated by the Pilgrims, the African American colonists described their claims over African lands, as the scholar-diplomat, theologian, and editor of the *Liberian Herald* William Blyden put it, as arising from the "superiority of civilization over barbarism."[6] In other words, the entire resettlement plan was a complex imperialistic mission in theory, but in reality, the deportation of an unwanted population.

The government pursued its policy of deportation in a makeshift diplomatic fashion. Yet the founding of Liberia was a significant development in furthering United States-Africa relations even as influential political figures and powerful groups in America would have instead favored turning away from this irreversible trans-Atlantic linkage. Olive Taylor reminds us that Chief Justice John Marshall of Virginia, a slavocrat and member of the Richmond Chapter of the ACS, embodied this sentiment prevalent among his peers with the proclamation that "America had a destiny. It was to be a beacon, a haven for white people to fulfill their desire for freedom and self-determination. Blacks had no place in it—except of course, as slaves. And if by chance blacks should fall through the cracks of slave law and become free, they would be sent back to Africa, through the Colonization Society."[7]

George W. Ellis later tried either to disguise the avowals of Justice Marshall or to sugarcoat the motives behind the colonization plan. In a report on political institutions in Liberia published in 1911, Ellis declared that "Liberia will long be a source of permanent interest to the government and people of the United States, not only because it was founded and fostered by American citizens, but because there is going on there in the interest of the African races one of the unique struggles in modern state-building, in an endeavor to perpetuate in West Africa a government fashioned after the American democracy in which liberty shall be limited and regulated by law."[8]

Ellis's allusion to democracy and liberty accorded with the guiding spirit of the American Revolution and the notion of citizenship it accentuated. However, the logistics and circumstances that led to the colony of Liberia on the one hand, and to the appropriation of citizenship in the original thirteen colonies on the other, were in some respects dissimilar. In 1823, Bushrod Washington, a slavocrat and prominent figure in the ACS from 1831, addressed the citizenship question by affirming that "the so-called free slaves were in no legal sense citizens of the United States and should, therefore, seize the opportunity to 'earn citizenship' in Africa."[9]

Extending this idea in a letter dated February 15, 1815, to John O. Mumford of New York City, Rev. Robert Finley, founder and first president of the ACS, passionately contended for the removal of the free Blacks from the republic. "Everything connected with their condition, including their color, is against them; nor is there [any prospect] that their state can ever be greatly ameliorated, while they shall continue among us."[10] Finley asked Mumford, "Could not the rich and benevolent *devise* means to form a colony on some part of the Coast of Africa, similar to the one at Sierra Leone, which might gradually *induce* many free blacks to go there and settle, devising for them the means of getting there, and of protection and support till they were established?"[11] Finley's specific disclosure that the entire colonization scheme was a "devise" to "induce" unwanted Blacks to depart from the United States remains a fitting epitaph for why the colony failed to prosper like other U.S. colonies, such as Panama or the Philippines. Thus, right from its conception, the Liberian colony effort was a subtle diplomatic maneuver to resolve what U.S. authorities considered a malignant problem. They predicted that the move would yield three major results: "We should be cleared of them; we should send to Africa a population partially civilized and christianized for its benefits; our blacks themselves would be put in better condition." Finley concluded his message to Mumford with a request to "think much on this subject, and then please write to me again when you have leisure."[12] The subsequent actions of Mumford and others of similar mind leaves no doubt that they got back to Finley and actively supported his plan.

Suffice it to say that while the English settlers of Jamestown and Plymouth took a daring leap of faith in coming to North America, an uncharted territory, Liberia (with its obvious risks for the new settlers) was planned, deliberated upon, and politically orchestrated to the letter. The scheme mirrored sociopolitical and economic currents in the early nineteenth-century United States, and the anxieties and hopes of both the low and the high in American society. It further reveals the subterfuge and contradictions of the colonization, missionary, and abolitionist movements that accompanied it, and how the linkages between Africa and the United States continued to deepen even as powerful political elites and slavocrats in the American republic struggled to scuttle the expansion of the slave trade.

The emerging evidence reveals that with no clear and well-articulated African foreign policy goal other than a self-defeatist intent to erase the African heritage in the United States, the founding fathers endorsed colonization to accomplish what the famous African American leader Booker T. Washington identified in 1909 as the "Negro peril"—that is, a hysteria shared mostly among the Southern White elite that free Blacks posed a threat to their existence.[13] Whether defined as the fear of the likely repercussions of slavery or apprehensions of biracial marriages, the Black peril was the whole point of Thomas Jefferson's insistence on the physical removal of freed Blacks: "The slave, when made free, might mix with, without staining the blood of his master. But with us, a second is necessary, unknown to history. When freed, he is to be removed beyond the reach of mixture."[14] In the antebellum period, political leaders and slavocrats like Jefferson used the Colonization Society as an anti-Black platform. In the mix, abolitionists and missionaries served as proxies of the government.[15] A more careful review of the key groups and figures that led the colonization idea further proves the fact.

POLITICIANS, ABOLITIONISTS, AND MISSIONARIES

For a proper understanding of the outcomes of the Liberia program, it is crucial to have a better grasp of politics in the antebellum United States. The period from 1789 to 1865 was characterized by a serious concern to stabilize the new nation in light of continuing British meddling in its affairs, particularly concerning slavery. We begin by examining the three key groups or classes of individuals involved in the planning and execution of the Liberia project—politicians, missionaries, and abolitionists. The three groups that dominated the activities of the Colonization Society harbored disparate intentions, all of which ultimately converged on a central goal: to relocate the increasing population of impoverished Blacks that emerged between the American Revolution and the War of 1812.[16] Leading the charge among the politicians were the nation's founding fathers like George Washington, Thomas Jefferson, and James Monroe. While the metaphors of slavery saturated political discourses throughout the revolutionary struggle, the founding fathers emerged from the war as conflicted individuals. This fact manifested in their unwillingness to promote freedom by merely supporting a mounting call by abolitionists for general emancipation. The opposition to emancipation arose from the fear that it would provoke serious social upheaval.[17] As the problem continued to haunt the young republic, the most audacious among the founding fathers began to float ideas for its possible resolution. In 1802, the U.S. government under President Thomas Jefferson (1801–1809) considered the idea of sending insurgent slaves to either Sierra Leone, Brazil, Columbia, or the Caribbean island of St. Croix. On March 2,

1807, federal lawmakers approved a law prohibiting slave importations, especially from Africa, to take effect in 1808.[18] Other thoughts and plans to deal with the slavery and emancipation conundrum continued with Jefferson, Monroe, and others exchanging ideas.

Monroe, as a private citizen, public official, and governor of Virginia, had a stake in the independence of the United States as he did with slaves. As governor of Virginia early in 1800, following the unsuccessful slave rebellion in the state led by Gabriel Prosser.[19] Monroe had considered sending the unruly slaves to Sierra Leone but quickly rescinded that plan after he found out that under the law of the Sierra Leone colony, the slaves would be free as soon as they arrived in West Africa. This revelation made Monroe cringe at the prospect of what he considered then a "mild and benevolent" policy.[20] Making his thoughts known two years later to Jefferson, after his friend and mentor had called for establishment of an overseas slave colony, Monroe responded, "Still I am persuaded that such was not the intention of the Legislature, as it would put culprits in a better condition than the deserving part of those people. . . . The ancestors of the present negroes were brought from Africa and sold here as slaves, they and their descendants forever."[21]

The reality of the Monroe "slave doctrine" is that the American leaders had won the military battle against the British colonists, but they sadly lost the peace of the time. This problem was because their noble quest for freedom was not in alignment with their continued practice and support of slavery. The U.S. elite interpreted the safety of White Americans in terms of continued subjugation of enslaved people. This despite the fact that Jefferson acknowledged in private that rebellious slaves "are not felons, or common malefactors, but persons guilty of what the safety of society, under actual circumstances, obliges us to treat as a crime, but which their feelings may represent in a far different shape."[22] Thus, the revolutionary rhetoric of freedom came into sharp conflict with the culture of slavocracy that threatened the peace of the republic. It was within this seemingly Manichean world of freedom and servitude that U.S. leaders searched for a possible balance.

In 1824, during Monroe's second administration, Jefferson wrote the Connecticut resident Jared Sparks (1789–1866), an educator and minister of the American Unitarian Association, iterating a similar plan he had outlined in his *Notes on the State of Virginia* of 1784, which was loaded with racist tirades.[23] In the 1824 letter, Jefferson admitted that as a "result of my reflections on the subject [under the] fourteenth query, I have never yet been able to conceive any other practicable plan."[24] Considering that "there are a million and a half of people of color in slavery," he argued that it would be neither expedient nor practicable for both the slave owners and the slaves to send off "the whole of these [people] at once." Jefferson proposed "emancipating the after-born [infant slaves], leaving them, on due compensation, with their mothers, until their services are worth their maintenance," and then "putting them to industrious occupations, until a proper age for deportation."[25]

Jefferson's ad hoc colonization plan was primarily targeted toward the slow but progressive disposal of older slaves from the continent and the deportation and colonization of younger slaves outside the United States. Although Jefferson realized that the physical separation of infants from their parents (as the Trump administration may attest to in dealing with migrants from Latin America) would cause serious "scruples of humanity," he asserted that gradual removal of Black slaves was a viable approach to end their presence from the union. Otherwise, Jefferson foresaw a possibility of the estimated six million slaves on the American continent launching a revolution similar to the one that upstaged the French slavocrats in Haiti in 1791. Given this threat, Jefferson counseled that the colonization plan should proceed despite its downsides. In Jefferson's view, considering anything else above the likelihood of a bloody slave revolt "would be straining at a gnat, and swallowing a camel."[26]

Appraising Jefferson and Monroe's ideas on colonization, Christa Dierksherida notes that the subject was only interesting to the founding fathers because they believed that it was a sine qua non of America's "happiness and safety." In this sense, Jefferson thought colonization would allow Americans to actualize the republican spirit of 1776—principles that they seemed to have nearly forgotten. Dierksherida, however, argues that the practice of slavery in the antebellum period "remained a remnant of tyranny, a state of war, and an impediment to civilization."[27]

One of the pressing problems of America remained the conscious choice of its leaders to retain the objectification of African slaves rather than treat them as humans. Like all the plantation owners and slavocrats of his time, Monroe depended for his wealth and fame on slave labor and the privileges it conferred on slave owners. With hundreds of slaves owned by him, Monroe was unapologetic about his convictions. At the same time, he expressed the belief in the need to abolish the institution and spoke out against it. In an 1829 letter to his friend John Mason, Monroe repeated a line from his earlier letter to Jefferson in which he labeled slavery "one of the evils still remaining, incident to our Colonial system."[28] Yet, like Jefferson, Monroe strongly maintained that abolition should be gradual to elude potential disorder in the social and economic order. Behind Monroe's colonization policy was a mindset nurtured on self-interest and predicated on fear. On the one hand, fear of the unknown led to his vigorous support for colonization, while on the other his economic interest predicated on slavery informed his gradualist emancipation stance. One cannot fail to note the contradiction underlying Jefferson's and Monroe's personal use of and dependency on slaves and their controverting political actions and pronouncement. This dualism is instructive of the fact that the cohort of slavocrats and public figures of this time had mixed feelings. They aspired to virtue and justice within the revolutionary rhetoric and yet they never entirely transcended the mainstream ideas and practices that defined the historical period. Because of their actions and inactions, Liberia became a gigantic foreign policy marred by a timid, hesitant, and lukewarm spirit.

The second group of key players in the Liberia project was the abolitionists within the American Colonization Society. Dominated by the political elite, the organization remained an influential part of American politics and society to the end of the Civil War in 1865. Contrary to popular belief, ACS members were the same as neither the abolitionists nor the missionaries who collaborated with them in the colonization scheme. Instead, the ACS was a platform for anti-Black sentiment. Abolitionists do not keep slaves. James Monroe, Andrew Jackson, and Henry Clay were active members of the American Colonization Society but were neither missionaries nor pious abolitionists like the Quakers. Many prominent members of the society, like the founding fathers, retained personal slaves and found common ground with some abolitionists who supported the colonization movement primarily because it aimed to transfer emancipated slaves outside the United States.[29] Politically minded abolitionists used the ACS as a platform to solicit and secure the financial and logistic support that deported thousands of African Americans to Liberia from 1816 to around 1845. Indeed, it was through their influence in government that the ACS secured $100,000 in federal grant money that paid for the piece of land in Cape Mesurado named Liberia, with its capital city Monrovia.[30]

In perspective, the Colonization Society seized a special place in the history of slavery and abolition in American society because it tackled head-on a complex problem that was, in reality, a citizenship question concerning the status of free Blacks in the American republic. This unresolved question under the American Constitution polarized the new nation and seriously threatened its stability. The ACS recognized that the seemingly irreversible position of the White race in America prohibited free and emancipated slaves from attaining full rights as citizens, but they were not concerned with fighting for the rights of Blacks in the country. They rather chose to advance the argument that Blacks freed from slavery would live a happier life in their ancestral land of Africa. Jane Ailes and Marie Tyler-McGraw have noted that the ACS presented

Liberia to the Black settlers as a place "where they could repeat the American experience of exploration and colonization and, through courage and sacrifice, build for themselves a republic like that of the United States. Furthermore, they could convert the Africans to Christianity and establish trade ties with the United States."[31]

A brief pause is in order here to consider the implications of the idealized vision of a Liberian-American republic that the Colonization Society peddled. In fact, pockets of emancipation without adequate restitution in the U.S. North in the antebellum period had trapped the Black population in abject poverty. Making the issue worse was the lack of opportunity for education for people of color who were deprived of civil rights and hope of meaningful improvement. Rather than address these social issues, the abolitionists and members of the ACS pursued a political agenda and ignored even a philanthropic cause they pretentiously advocated. The behavior demonstrated by some of the members also mitigated a genuine focus on the success of the African colony. Instead, the ACS wanted to make the practice of slavery less hazardous for the slave owners by reducing the potential danger already posed by idle and impoverished free Blacks in the light of discussions of general emancipation. In Virginia, the typical reaction mirrored that of Solomon Parker of Hampshire County, who signaled his disinclination to share the country with a freed Black slave. "I am not willing that the Man [the freed slave] or any of my Blacks shall ever be freed to remain . . . in our Country and do sincerely hope that the time is approaching when our Land shall be rid of them."[32] Despite the general disposition toward the deportation of emancipated Blacks in Virginia, some individuals such as William Johnson in Tyler County, who coincidentally was Solomon Parker's first cousin, argued for rewarding a family of slaves with the belief that God had directed him to this work.[33]

Genuine Christians like Tyler Johnson formed the third set of key players in the African colonization project. For missionaries such as Samson Caesar and Abraham Carper, the conversion of the Africans on the continent was a divine mandate. It follows that while the various key groups in the colonization effort had generally emphasized "civilization," with the Black settlers playing a central role in what was conceived as a mission to rescue Africa from centuries of barbarism, the Christian missionaries had a unique interpretation of the "civilizing" mission for Africa. They saw Liberia in the same way John Winthrop imagined the Puritan settlement in the seventeenth century. In other words, Liberia was to them "a city on a hill" from where they aimed "to save nations who now worshipped false gods."[34] Steeped in this ideology, one prominent leader of the church, Episcopal bishop William White (1748–1836), became a vice president of the ACS in 1819. Similarly, the Philadelphia Quaker Robert Vaux (1786–1836) emerged as an enthusiast of colonization in the 1820s. He believed that a Liberian settlement based on robust Christianity would help stop the African slave trade at its source.[35] Whether the evangelists fully understood the prejudices underlying the Liberia colonization scheme is open to debate. Obviously, their quest for new African converts took precedence over everything else, including potential threats to the lives of the individuals being shipped to a region about which they knew little or nothing.

Indeed, President Monroe likened Black emigration to Liberia to the Exodus story, much as the Pilgrims had fantasized of their migration as a journey to the Promised Land. Virginia's first English exponents of the colonization scheme advanced it as the perfect approach to bringing civilization and Christianity to the "savages" of North America and to remove from England the social problems of idleness and crime associated with the high rate of unemployment among the masses. In this manner, followers of colonization offered the Liberia settlement as a quick answer to the crime rampant among the emancipated Blacks. The U.S. government assisted the Americo-Liberians with funds with which they built educational institutions and places of worship. More important, this financial aid made it possible for the nascent nation to integrate enslaved Africans the U.S. Navy rescued from slave smugglers on the high seas, and to support the political parties that formed the foundation on which Liberia erected a constitutional republic modeled on the United States in 1847.

Writing in 1910, R. P. Falkner made an excellent point that further accentuates how British activities and slavery deeply affected American politics. "If the United States Government thus exhibited, as we have seen, a fatherly interest in the projected colony, it was because it was from the start a partner in the enterprise," he wrote. "The importation of slaves into the United States is forbidden, the United States joined with the other maritime powers, and especially Great Britain, in the effort to suppress this traffic at its source and employed its navy for this purpose." Falkner further argued that the United States had a moral responsibility to help the British Navy suppress the trans-Atlantic slave trade after the British Parliament outlawed it in 1807. "We could not, as did other nations, leave the matter largely to Great Britain. We had vigorously denied the right of search, and our flag protected American vessels off the coast."[36]

LIBERIA IN WORLD POLITICS

The tides of U.S. politics in the first half of the nineteenth century propelled Liberia (Fig. 4.2) into the center of world politics, but the struggles experienced

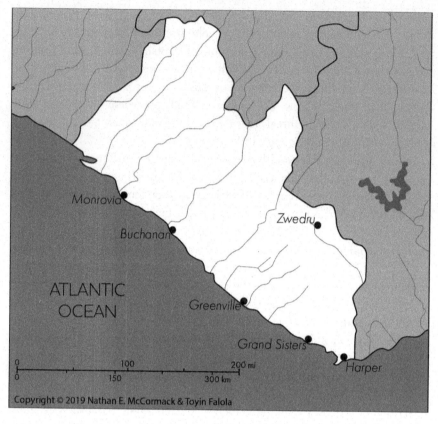

ATLANTIC
OCEAN

Monrovia

Buchanan

Zwedru

Greenville

Grand Sisters

Harper

0   100   200 mi
0   150   300 km

Figure 4.2. Liberia. *Toyin Falola and Nathan McCormack.*

by the African American colonists exposed the predictable dynamics that made
the early years of the colony unstable and hazardous. The initial arrangements
for the colony were made in 1817 when officials of the American Colonization
Society secured Sherbro Island in the British colony of Sierra Leone. In 1820,
a group of settlers arrived in West Africa on the U.S.S. *Cyane*—the warship the
U.S. forces had seized from the British Royal Navy in 1815.[37] The first group of
African American settlers met grave opposition from the local people mainly
because of lack of consultation with the Africans in the process of founding the
colony. The antagonism stemming from territorial and trade disputes forced
the leaders of the initial expedition to divert the migrants to Sierra Leone. The
second mission of 1821, which landed at Cape Mesurado, proved more successful. Lt. Robert F. Stockton, commander of the U.S. schooner *Alligator* (and
later a vice president of the ACS), compelled the representatives of Dei natives,
Long King Peter, and King Governor to sign a deed of land concession with

Dr. Eli Ayres, a Baltimore physician representing the American Colonization Society.[38] However, by 1822, when ACS officials returned to Liberia to take effective control of the land, the two chieftains had changed their mind, thereby vindicating Chief King Jimmy (Kai), the only Dei chief who was strongly opposed to the deal.

At different levels, the Liberia colony launched the United States on a deliberate African policy. Before this time, United States-Africa relations had been all about the purchase of enslaved Africans and the exploitation of their labor for various socioeconomic and political endeavors. But the revolutionary war and the abolitionist rhetoric it engendered forced the American government to accept its moral obligation to change its policy, as Falkner puts it, from denying British abolitionists "the right of search, and our flag protected American vessels off the coast of Africa as well as elsewhere. To maintain the principles in whose defense we had become involved in the war of 1812, it became necessary to take an active part in the suppression of the slave traffic."[39] Furthermore, strategic moves in Europe between 1814 and 1820 helped put in place some constraints on the slave trade. Britain's complete clamp-down on slavery in 1807 was followed by similar actions by France (1817), Portugal (1818), and Spain (1820). The dogmatic shift was the point of President Monroe's message of November 14, 1820. "In execution of the law of the last session, for the suppression of the slave trade, some of our public ships have also been employed on the coast of Africa, where several captures have already been made of vessels engaged in that disgraceful traffic."[40]

The new U.S. policy of collaboration in the suppression of the slave trade across the Atlantic did not address the question of what to do with the slaves captured on the slave ships. Nevertheless, British naval policy in this regard was available for the United States to emulate. The Americans embraced the idea of sending recaptives to Liberia. The first voyage to Liberia involved a return of newly captured Africans brought over to the United States. Additionally, the U.S. government declared its intention to assist free emigrants with the costs of emigration to Africa, with the advice of the Colonization Society. From these informal undertakings began regular coordination of resettling the victims of the slave traffic in Liberia. However, acute shortages of essential supplies troubled the colonization process, and settler complaints and riots became commonplace.

To consolidate the process of resettling the victims of the slave trade on the West African coast, the United States set up receiving stations there in 1824, with a manager charged with overseeing the operations and work of the Colonization Society.[41] Approving this move, Congress noted that "the evils of disaffection and insubordination had, at the commencement of the year 1824, attained such a growth, that the managers of the society represented strongly to the Executive of the United States the importance of sending an armed vessel to the colony, with some individual duly commissioned by the Government and society to examine the entire condition of the agency, the people, and the property of the United States and society."[42]

In Africa, the Liberia colonization project would follow a more violent path after 1828. First, the ACS chose Thomas Buchanan in 1829 to replace Ashmun.[43] The new governor launched a program of colonial territorial expansion beyond the forty-mile-wide coastal littoral or "constitutional zone" limit. In 1840, Governor Buchanan formed a rapacious militia made up of 300 fighters aged between sixteen and forty-five. The settler militias, who regarded the indigenous people as a "horde of blood-thirsty naked savages led by a noted cannibal, called Tecumseh of West Africa," were equipped with a number of field guns with which they subdued the poorly armed "native chiefs along the St. Paul River and made treaties with them."[44] Afterward, Buchanan turned his attention to the unabating trans-Atlantic slave trade perpetrated by Portuguese, Spanish, and American vessels sailing under the "Stars and Stripes."[45]

The death of Governor Buchanan in 1841 ended seventeen years of White overseers appointed by the ACS to run the Liberian colony. Buchanan's successor, Gen. Joseph Jenkins Roberts of Norfolk, Virginia, was the first African American to rule Liberia. He targeted the slave trade across Liberian waters and considerably increased the palm-oil business. Roberts's attempt to make British Sierra Leone pay trade tariffs to the colony led the ACS to call on the American government to intervene when the British government refused either to pay the customs duties or to recognize Liberia as a sovereign power. Instead, the British government recognized Liberia as "a mere commercial experiment of a philanthropic society."[46] The American government, continuing to demonstrate an ambivalent foreign policy toward Liberia, did not follow up its intervention, and the ACS felt compelled to give the colonists a freer hand to organize their own self-government and manage their foreign affairs. By a formal declaration in 1846, the ACS told the Liberia colonists to manage their own affairs. Subsequently, on July 25, 1847, a convention sitting in Liberia adopted a new republican constitution declaring Liberia a "free and independent state," with the motto "The Love of Liberty Brought Us Here." A section of the constitution said, "None but negroes or persons of negro descent shall be admitted to citizenship of this Republic." It also provided that no one but a citizen could own real estate.[47]

Until 1847, the colonization project was led by White Americans. However, thousands of Blacks eagerly sought autonomy and economic prospects outside North America. The functions and modus operandi of the African colonization movement provoked heated condemnation in some quarters. In Philadelphia, for example, where the idea to relocate free Blacks to Africa dated back to the 1770s, critics of colonization perceived the plan as a quasivoluntary banishment of people of African descent masked as a return to their homeland. Some honest abolitionists condemned the entire project as flawed. A Mother Bethel Church gathering of Black Philadelphians in 1817 decried the Liberia scheme "as an insult to African Americans and a forced removal hidden behind a thin veil of voluntary emigration."[48]

The Bethel Church position contradicted fervent colonization enthusiasts like Bishop Richard Allen and James Forten (early African American supporters of colonization). At the initial stage of the colonization movement, Forten had declared that Blacks "will never become a people until they come out from among the white people."[49] In a letter to Cuffee, Forten had declared that free people of color in the city of Richmond, Virginia "perfectly agree with the Society, that it is not only proper, but would ultimately tend to the benefit and advantage of a great portion of our suffering fellow creatures, to be colonized; but while we thus express our approbation of a measure laudable in its purposes, and beneficial in its designs, it may not be improper in us to say, that we prefer being colonized in the most remote corner of the land of our nativity, to being exiled to a foreign."[50]

After the Bethel Church's 1817 declaration, Forten and Allen began to show lukewarm support for colonization and often criticized the intentions behind it. Allen declared that the descendants of African slaves had watered the American soil "with our tears and our blood," and consequently the land "is now ours."[51] Likewise, Forten used the occasion provided by his address to White Pennsylvanians in 1818 to restate the wishes of the free Black majority to continue with their lives in America. He maintained that Blacks wanted to play a central role in the abolition of slavery and the improvement of their lives in the country. Forten's appeal soon caught the attention of the Pennsylvania Abolition Society, which in 1818 came out strongly against colonization. The society argued that the majority of emancipated and free Blacks desired to remain in the land of their birth and that they stood a better chance of improving their living conditions in the United States than elsewhere. Furthermore, the anticolonization crusaders in Pennsylvania pointed out that Sierra Leone, the British experiment that inspired Liberia, had failed to thrive, after two decades, as a home for Black emigrants from Canada and England. Notwithstanding this warning, the ACS held strongly to the idea that Blacks would benefit from relocation to the colony.

Nonetheless, the American Colonization Society enjoyed strong support across the nation. Through its agency, millions of Americans were brought to acquiesce in the logic that it was not right for Whites and descendants of slaves to live side by side as free men and women, and that if slavery was no longer a viable institution, then people of African descent should be sent back to their ancestral homeland.

RESULTS OF COLONIZATION AND
THE U.S. ODYSSEY IN AFRICA

Before proceeding to examine the mixed results of colonization, it is critical to highlight further the early problems the settlers encountered in Africa. The selections of Jamestown by its founders, the Virginia Company, and of Plymouth by the *Mayflower* Pilgrims, resonate in the choice of Monrovia by the American Colonization Society. The overriding factor in the selection of these locations on both sides of the Atlantic was their proximity to the sea. Access to the Atlantic Ocean offered enhanced odds for defense against physical attacks, the opportunity for agriculture, and access to trans-Atlantic commerce.[52] In Liberia, the African American settlers took over the seacoast in four principal provinces or counties: Montserrado, Basa, Sino, and Maryland. Monrovia, the capital city, is located in Montserrado County.

Yet, while nearly two and a half centuries separated the founding of the American and African colonies, Jamestown, Plymouth, and Liberia loom large as bloodlines in United States-Africa relations. The enormity of the problems confronting the early English settlers in Virginia and Massachusetts mirrors the experiences of the first African Americans in Liberia. In addition to malaria, which decimated the settlers, the African Americans fought bloody battles with the various indigenous groups present in West Africa.[53] As was the case with the Sierra Leone settlement, the indigenous inhabitants of the strip of land on which the Liberia colony was established were distraught by how the colonists took over their lands.

Information based on the memoir of Jehudi Ashmun, a White ACS agent in Liberia from 1822 to 1828, published in the *African Repository and Colonial Journal* (1825), reveals that the Dei chiefs, including King George and King Governor, saw the colonists as strangers who had lost a complete sense of their African roots. The African chieftains expected the colonists, rather than the White men who accompanied them, to seek their protection and blessings. The complaint made by the African chiefs represented an assertion of their right to sovereignty. Another source of grievance was what the local chiefs perceived as the threat of colonists' expansion into the hinterlands, which would entail the destruction of their ways of life. The local leaders pointed to Chief King George's removal from the cape as a sign of what to expect from the colonists.[54]

The conflictual relationship with the natives on the coast further implicated the Americo-Liberians' economic condition. Not only was their inclination to farming not supported by the slave labor that the British settlers in America exploited, the colonists needed some time to adapt to the African system of agriculture. Ralph Gurley, sent in 1824 to inquire into the matter, reported to the U.S. Congress that the African American settlers needed a little more time to be able to self-sustain in the colony. "We shall be obliged to allow them to draw rations longer than expected, owing to the great scarcity of country produce."[55] This problem suggests that there could have been no solid English foothold and influence in the United States as known today without the presence of the enslaved Africans, who started arriving with the twenty Africans who landed in Jamestown on August 20, 1619.[56] The African Americans expected that the indigenous people should provide them with access to labor, but it is not clear what kind of labor—free or paid. Yet, the economic development of a new colony predicated on trade in goods from the hinterland made the Americo-Liberians more reliant on making peace with the local people in order to survive. Despite a peace agreement concluded in December 1822, violence persisted mainly because the Dei chiefs refused to accept the colony as permanent, insisting that they did not fully understand the terms of the agreement they signed with the ACS.

In 1825, a breakthrough came as the Dei chiefs, for the first time, made genuine moves to cooperate with the colonists. This breakthrough happened by an act of good faith demonstrated to Ashmun by King Peter Bromley, who consented to give land and afford protection "to any good white man" who would settle and teach his people. Shortly afterward, the American colonists adopted about sixty Dei children so that they might obtain an education. According to Ashmun, there was suddenly a common desire among the locals to have "at least one of [their] sons fixed in some settlers' families."[57] This initiative led to a more trusting relationship between the colonists and the indigenous people, and on May 2, 1825, a proposal brought by Ashmun to buy some farmlands led to the "Treaty of Gourah." The treaty, formally signed on May 25, 1825, by Old King Peter, King James (Jimmy), King Long Peter, King Governor, and King Todo, marked the end of hostilities between colonists and the Dei people.[58] However, it did not eliminate continuing conflicts with non-Dei natives.[59]

By June 18, 1828, the relationship with the Dei chiefs and the ACS had progressed to the point that the local leaders came together to approve a deed of land concession to the settlers. The agreement defined the area of lands conceded as follows: "All that tract of Land on the north side of St. Paul's river, beginning at King James' line below the establishment called Millersburg Settlement, and . . . bounded as follows: by the St. Paul's river on the South, and thence running an East Northeast direction up the St. Paul's river, . . . and bounded on the West by King Jimmey's, and running thence a North direction as far as our power and influence extend."[60]

A dynamic similar to that which stimulated the rise in the population of the Freetown colony played out in Liberia. This dynamic related to the continuing slave trade in the region. While indigenous people outnumbered the African American population in Liberia, the recaptives resettled in the colony were swelling the population. A new spike in the slave trade from the mid-1830s to the end of 1837 translated into new populations for the Liberian settlement. More notably, the recaptives constituted the backbone of the Liberian Frontier Force that aided in the suppression of the slave trade. In the 1850s, an estimated 3,000 African Americans were already in Liberia. By 1866, more than 5,000 recaptive persons were added to the colony through the antislavery activities of the U.S. Navy off the coast of West Africa. Although African Americans in the Liberia colony remained a minority, they constituted a dominant political group over the indigenous African groups. Nonetheless, 3,000 Americo-Liberians was below the projected number ACS had planned to remove from the United States.

While Western-style education and Christianity defined the character of the African American settlers, the most visible way in which the colony resembled the United States remained its political system. As in the American democratic system, Liberia under the African American elite set forth the powers of the government in a written constitution that was approved in 1847. The document divided governmental authority into three branches, legislative, executive, and judicial. Under the constitution, the Liberian president and vice president were elected for terms of two years, the members of the House of Representatives for two years, and those of the Senate for four years. The legislature later raised the terms of service to four, four, and six years, respectively.

The president of the country appoints members of his cabinet with the approval of the Senate. Assisting the president is a council of seven advisers who hold their offices at the pleasure of the executive. Their removal may also come by a vote of two-thirds of the legislature. As in the U.S. system, the resident may face impeachment originating in the House of Representatives, with the senators acting as judges and the Chief Justice as the presiding officer. Also as practiced in the United States, where each state sends two senators to Congress, in the Liberian system, each county elects two senators and the number of representatives is determined by the population. The judiciary consists of a Supreme Court of three judges and quarterly, probate, and justice courts for each of the counties and territories. The constitution stipulates that no one can remove a judge except for just cause. The president has the power to suspend a judge, but this action, when necessary, is subject to the approval of the legislature.

The political structure the African Americans put in place in Liberia was alien to the Africans in terms of structure and modus operandi. A significant majority of the African chiefdoms operated a system of rule in which the elders served as representatives of the people, and the decision-making process was by popular vote. Today, some African countries—notably Nigeria and Ethiopia—have effectively adopted the American federal governmental system to address the multiethnic structures of their countries. This federal structure assumes superiority over the indigenous village structures, and in the hinterlands native Africans are subject to the Americanized courts, with only the right of appeal from the native courts of the interior to the Court of Quarter Sessions and Common Pleas of the county in which they reside.

In the early period, a governor (known as a superintendent), appointed by the executive, exercised the political authority of the Liberian presidential system in the counties and coastal territories. In the interior, a commissioner represented the president. The superintendent presided over each commissioner and the district under his control. The district commissioners supervised the native chiefs who were directly in control of the indigenous peoples of his district. In some instances, this commissioner had judicial functions from which an appeal could be made to the quarterly and supreme courts. A detachment of the Liberian Frontier Police Force, with headquarters at the Monrovia barracks, enforced the authority of the commissioner. The implication was the visible partition of Liberia into two republics. One was under the control of African Americans and directed from the capital city of Monrovia. The other comprised the subject population in the interior of the country, which leaned toward a native authority system—that is, the authority of the indigenous chiefs under colonial rule. It was therefore problematic that the Liberian government then was under a single-political-party system.

The lack of resources to operate a robust democratic system was the primary reason why Liberia could not manage a multiparty system during this period. Soon after the adoption of the Liberian constitution in 1847, the government instituted two political parties fashioned after those in the United States—the Republican and Whig parties. However, the abrogation of the party in opposition, the Republicans, left only the ruling Whig party. The excuse was that Liberia's coffee-based economy could not support a multiparty system. By 1910, the coffee planters in Liberia had sunk all their available capital into the industry, and soon after the crash of commodity prices at the turn of the century, the economy suffered massive paralysis that affected every aspect of life. "Disheartened and financially distressed, formerly strong, self-sustaining and independent Liberian planters, one after another, abandoned their plantations and transferred their time and attention from coffee culture and the farm to politics and office seeking." This set in motion a violent political culture that did not help Liberia's much sought-after unity.

The main thrust of the preceding discussion was to evaluate the United States' Liberian colony and its place in the United States-Africa linkages. All the partners in the colonization project—the U.S. government, the American Colonization Society, the abolitionists, and the missionaries—brought different goals to the table, but a single agenda bound them together. This bond was the physical deportation of the free Blacks to their ancestral continent. Because the U.S. government did not match its political rhetoric with financial and logistic resources, Liberia faltered on many fronts. Among other things, it did not turn out to be a fountainhead of the progress of civilization or the U.S. brand of democracy in Africa, as its founders planned. Nevertheless, Liberia's survival today as a bona fide nation stands as a symbol of the resilience of a relationship that was built on slavery and economic exploitation. Liberia, therefore, symbolizes an attempt, on the part of the American slavocrats, to make up for that historic exploitation, although the U.S. government never pursued this goal with zeal and commitment.

Indeed, an obvious problem of the colonization ideology promoted by the American founding fathers remained the indifference to the truth that "from the very beginnings of American history, the lives of blacks and whites had been intertwined on the most complex social, cultural, economic and psychological levels."[61] Whites were inseparably joined to the enslaved Africans whose labor they exploited: "The nation as a whole, modeled on ancient dreams of deliverance and fulfillment, could march no farther forward than all the victims of its self-betrayal."[62]

Despite its flaws, the U.S. colonization venture in West Africa helped build some measure of self-image and hope for the Black race on both sides of the Atlantic. On the African continent, Liberia and Sierra Leone emerged as centers of Western education and Christian culture. Western missionaries and other organizations found them willing allies in the attempt to cultivate the gospel of Jesus Christ in West Africa and beyond. For instance, a Philadelphia Ladies' Liberia School Association, established in 1832 by Quaker Beulah Biddle Sansom (1768–1837), started a fundraising effort to support new schools in the colony. In the 1830s, members funded the building of new schools and the recruitment of teachers in Liberia.[63] This enthusiasm waned in the 1840s in response to the diminishing of funds for the association's school projects in Liberia.[64] Ishmael

Locke, from the state of Massachusetts, who was employed by the American Colonization Society as a teacher in Liberia, quit his position in Liberia because of the abject condition of the schools. Upon returning to the United States in 1850, Locke—the grandfather of Alain Leroy Locke (1885–1954), a popular Harlem Renaissance figure—took up an appointment as principal of the Institute for Colored Youth in Philadelphia.

Meanwhile, on the American side of the Atlantic, the experience of African Americans in Liberia helped nourish Black nationalism and, in turn, the increasingly popular demand for equality and civil rights on the domestic front. In fact, the entire constitution of Liberia was a rebuke of White nationalism in the United States, which prevented African Americans "from participation in government" and denied them "the rights of man."[65] It is intriguing that while the colonization scheme prompted national debates about race and slavery beginning in the early nineteenth century, Liberia's status as a sovereign nation reshaped the relevance of the American Colonization Society's campaign. Brandon Mills observes that with Liberia's founding, public debate in the United States shifted toward grappling with the meaning of a Black republic in Africa at the same time that White citizens of "nonslaving states worked to exclude free African Americans from citizenship within their borders."[66] The debate exposed the United States' racialized notions of democracy, liberty, and nationalism to the view of the world, as several southern slavocrats supported a Black-led democratic government in Africa while at the same time endorsing the disenfranchisement of emancipated and free Blacks in America. The result would be gradual but eventual support of both African American suffrage and a belated formal U.S. recognition of Liberia's independence in 1862.

In the twentieth century, the dynamic Marcus Garvey championed a new wave of the colonization movement and compared emigration to Liberia to the Zionist Jews' goal of recovering their homeland in Palestine. In the words of Martin Luther King, Jr., Garvey was the first man "on a mass scale and level to give millions of Negroes a sense of dignity and destiny and make the Negro feel he was somebody."[67] The substance of this assertion needs due exploration, but for a chronological reason, the role of American missionary efforts in creating the contexts in which the Pan-African movement coheres comes first.

Part II

THE AGE OF IDEAS

*Pragmatism, Self-Preservation,
and African Regenerations*

5

American Missionaries in Africa, 1780–1920s

In the framework of United States-Africa relations, American missionary arrival in Africa did not emerge in a vacuum. Like the concept of pan-Negro consciousness, the American Colonization Society, the Back-to-Africa movement, and other similar ideological conduits that sustained the long-running trans-Atlantic exchanges, American missions to Africa further attest to the strong bonds between Africa and America. The late eighteenth century witnessed a sudden spike in Christian missionary interest in the Atlantic world as the fluxes and patterns of race relations in the United States continued to affect the African continent in radical ways.

The impetus for the American proselytizers (of whom African Americans were an important part) to connect with Africa paralleled other historical developments that had profound reverberations on both sides of the Atlantic world. Among them are the American Revolution (1775–1783), the discourses on slavery and freedom it engendered, and the dynamics that led to the founding of the colonies of Sierra Leone (1787) and Liberia (1822). These events, along with the Enlightenment ideals, moved some forward-thinking abolitionists and religious leaders to question the morality of slavery in particular and the oppression of the American poor in general.[1] William Kashatus observes that the Philadelphia Chapter of the American Quakers (or Society of Friends) emerged in the mid-eighteenth century as fervent advocates for the underprivileged, putting forth the view that Christianity was the answer to a more peaceful social order in a world in rapid flux.[2] This declaration prepared the stage for the gradual rise and expansion of the global American Christian evangelical enterprise, which encompassed Africa.

The American Christian missions to Africa are unique because of the African American factor. Whether pursued under the aegis of White boards or Black churches, African American missions to Africa came on the heels of those led by White Americans, which in turn followed European missions. Therefore, there can be no full discussion of the American missionary expansion overseas without situating it within its more extensive European heritage. Unlike the history of European Christian missions in Africa, the American effort has received only cursory scholarly attention from the African academe. The mainstream research on this subject is mostly the prerogative of Western scholars.[3]

A study of the United States-Africa missionary partnership is critical because it further highlights how Africans and Americans have planted common cultural trends on both sides of the Atlantic that no racial prejudices can break. In his study of the Black Atlantic missionary endeavors and Africa, David Killingray noted after Adrian Hastings's similar work that Africans themselves were pivotal in the evangelization of their native land.[4] This observation is important because Christian evangelism could not have prospered in the continent without African agency, of which American Blacks were a big part. With the hindsight of oppression in the Americas, the American Black missionary presence in Africa helped promote African agency not only in the spiritual domain but also in the elevation of cultural consciousness, socioeconomic awareness, and political liberation. In this sense, the African American turns out to be the proverbial rejected stone that became the chief cornerstone of Christian evangelism.

The argument then is that no account of American missionary successes in Africa will be complete without including the pivotal role of the Black missionary agent. The record shows that early attempts at spreading the Christian gospel by the Portuguese in West Africa (1420–1780) and East Africa (1560–1700) produced concrete results only among those communities where the intimacy and trust that came with African collaborators prevailed.[5] The fortunes of the sixteenth-century Portuguese missions in the Central African Kingdom of Kongo changed for good after it gained the patronage of the king's court. In *Africa and Africans in the Making of the Atlantic World*, John Thornton reminds us that the indigenous worldview modified the kingdom's brand of Catholicism. This alteration "provided a sort of lingua franca that joined various national religious traditions" together in the Americas.[6] In other words, local agency and the closeness it brings played an essential role in this history. Ann Stoler has noted that "intimate domains—sex, sentiment, domestic arrangement, and child rearing—figure in the making of racial categories and in the management of imperial rule."[7] Additionally, the early European missionary effort in Southern Africa showed more prospects from 1737 with the Moravian Church when the German missionary Georg Schmidt made the Khoi Khoi people the core of his local missionary team.[8]

In a similar dynamic, initial European missions on the West Coast of Africa from the eighteenth century relied profoundly on the patronage of Africans. In 1750, for instance, Thomas Thompson (1709–1773) of the Society for the Propagation of the Gospel (SPG), based in England, was the first Protestant agent in West Africa. For four years, Thompson—who had served as a minister in Monmouth County, New Jersey, from 1745 to 1751—concentrated his missionary activities on the coastal enclaves of modern Ghana. If not for the help of a native servant named Philip Quaque (ca. 1741–1816), the son of chief Cudjo, and two other local boys, Thompson's efforts in Africa would have been a complete failure. Before he departed from West Africa in 1754 due to persistent health problems, Thompson sent Quaque and his friends to England for formal pastoral education.[9] Quaque became the first African ordained preacher in the Anglican Church, commissioned by the Society for the Propagation of the Gospel on May 17, 1765, as a "Missionary Schoolmaster and Catechist to the Negroes on the Gold Coast in Africa."[10]

The preceding account provides a foreground to an appreciation of the central role of the African diaspora in the larger American missionary exertions in Africa starting in the late eighteenth century. The primary focus here is on a handful of Black men and women from the United States who joined forces with their cohorts from the Caribbean along with the indigenous African clergy, and on their role in spreading American influence in the religious domain and cultural production in Africa. However, until the latter part of the nineteenth century, it is difficult to differentiate the works of African Americans from those of the Euro-American missionary groups. Often, an American church running an overseas mission from the United States was in affiliation with the parent church in Europe.

Exceptional careers of individual Africans like Quaque who helped propagate the gospel among his African brethren reflect those by African American missionaries. Although introduced in a very problematic circumstance, African American missionaries in Africa served as a bridge, mitigating the racial distrust between White ministers and the indigenous African people. Religion, in general, was one of the forces that helped enslaved Africans cope with the ungodly plantation servitude in the Americas. Whereas the enslaved people brought to the Americas different shades of African traditional religions, a good number of them also brought an Africanized version of Portuguese Catholicism from Angola, Elmina, Warri, Benin, Gold Coast, and the Kongo. In the Americas, the enslaved people strategically sought membership in the various Christian denominations, the religion of the slave owners. Even though not always harnessed, a collective identity forged on Christianity between the enslaved and the enslaver offered a rare opportunity for empathy in a master–servant relationship. When White Christians were temperate enough to honor the teachings of the gospel they propagated, the enslaved people found some respite amid their oppression.

Katherine R. Gerbner's work on the Caribbean, which applies to the United States, shows that the slave owners and planters perceived slave conversion to Christianity as dangerous to slavocracy and therefore opposed the Anglican, Moravian, and Quaker advocates for slave Christianization. Notwithstanding the planters' obduracy in restricting slave conversion to Protestantism, Gerbner notes that "a small number of enslaved and free Africans advocated and won access to Protestant rites. As they did so, 'whiteness' emerged as a new way to separate enslaved and free black converts from Christian masters. Enslaved and free blacks who joined Protestant churches also forced Europeans to reinterpret critical points of Scripture and reconsider their ideas about 'true' Christian practice. As missionaries and slaves came to new agreements and interpretations, they remade Protestantism as an Atlantic institution."[11]

In their purist philosophy, the Quakers, who played a critical role in reshaping notions of slavery and its Christian receptivity in America, held that true Christianity equals universal priesthood through the savior Jesus Christ. This view persisted, although many Quakers retained slaves up to the 1730s. Three leading figures among them—Benjamin Lay, John Woolman, and Anthony Benezet—emerged with uncommon courage in 1754, challenging their brethren in Philadelphia to renounce the practice of slaveholding. This group of Christian abolitionists believed in the fatherhood of God and the unity of man.

Throughout the Atlantic world, three forces drove African Americans to engage with Africa in the religious sphere. First, the unabatingly delicate social conditions of deprivation and alienation in America based on slavery and race. Second, the impact of the African colonization movement that encouraged emigration to Sierra Leone and Liberia as a divine mission to salvage the souls of African barbarians. Third, the intent of some Black missionaries and educated elites to address the African question, which they conceived as a mission to remedy the continent's "primitive" state or lack of material and spiritual advancement along with Western ones. For these individuals and groups, Christianity, industrialization, and commerce, which developed the Western world, would also help build Africa.

The three forces so identified overlapped across time and space and carried a similar amount of importance. Demeaning racial conditions have always been present in America, and the attempt to deport free Blacks was in discussion long before the American Colonization Society finally put it into practice. Also, the bonds between the African diaspora and the African continent did not first appear in the eighteenth century. From the beginning of the trans-Atlantic slave trade in the fifteenth century, a collective kindred spirit had moved generations of Africans enslaved in the Americas to express interest in the affairs of Africa. For organizational purposes, we identify three overlapping stages of African American missionary activities in Africa.

STAGE 1: MISSIONS LED BY WHITE MISSIONARY BODIES, 1780s–1860s

This early stage of American Christian missions to Africa was the prerogative of White Christians who led the early endeavors to propagate the gospel of Jesus Christ not just in Africa but also in the entire Atlantic world and Asia. By the 1780s, Killingray notes, a small number of ex-slaves, Black educated elites, and abolitionist thinkers resident in London, among them Olaudah Equiano and Ottobah Cugoano, were "already conscious of constituting something of a cultural, linguistic, and religious bridge with Africa."[12]

Transitions and changes marked the period under review in the ecclesiastical, political, and socioeconomic domains. Because of space, we briefly highlight a couple of these dynamics. Andrew Porter's *Religion versus Empire,* a seminal account of more than two centuries of overseas Christian enterprise from colonial America to the end of the First World War (ca. 1700–1918), underscores the nuances of these transformations. The book gives the reader an important synopsis of the changing social and intellectual contexts within the European metropole and its implications for overseas Christian missionary evangelism. The changes were visible in the success of the Industrial Revolution and the manifest military strength and confidence it created in ordinary European Christians to approach non-European peoples with the Christian doctrine. One of Porter's important revelations is that the European missions were heavily dependent on their home governments for financial and material assistance and physical survival overseas. For example, Porter explains that as of March 1799, the London Missionary Society (LMS) had no option other than to depend on the British government for transportation to Cape Town, South Africa. Considering this, Porter underscores "the impossibility for missionaries of escaping the embrace of government, whatever illusions they might entertain as to the likelihood or desirability of independence."[13]

In other words, an alliance existed between the state and the church in ecclesiastical work and marketing Western values in the project of empire building.

Exploring this alliance further is essential. Lamin Sanneh notes that in the period between 1470 and 1785, the primary targets of Christian evangelical missions to Africa were the kings and chiefs. However, from the founding of the Sierra Leone colony in 1787, the main target shifted from the conversion of kings and chiefs to "the individual redeemed by God."[14] The career of David Livingston (1813–1873), the Scottish Christian Congregationalist, explorer, and missionary doctor who worked for the LMS in Southern and East Africa, represents the intricate connection between the church and the state. While Livingston helped further British colonial interests in the areas he "discovered," he also recognized the need for African agency in the propagation of the faith. In a letter to the London Missionary Society from Kuruman, South Africa, dated September 23, 1841, Livingston strongly recommended that the policy of the society be one of expansion, moving out everywhere "wherever there was an opening and making the utmost possible use of native agency in order to cultivate so wide a field."[15]

In the eighteenth century, Africans open to the Christian ideology propagated by missionaries like Livingston did not presuppose that potential converts would reject the White man's notion of a civilizing mission. Similarly, beginning in the late eighteenth century Black ministers from the Americas and Europe approached Africa strongly influenced by sociocultural and political trends in the United States. In other words, the missionaries, whether White or Black, shared these new cultural trends with the Africans, who processed and adapted them to the native culture.

While Whites largely staffed the overseas Christian missions to Africa in the eighteenth and most of the nineteenth centuries, a handful of people of African descent living in Europe at the time were also among the pioneers of this endeavor. Through their writings, these Black figures inserted their voices in the discourses that guided the policies and work of these early foreign Christian missions. For instance, the ex-slave of Igbo parentage Olaudah Equiano, first enslaved in South Carolina, as Vincent Coretta's research suggests, was a prominent voice in the call for African Christianization.[16] David Amponsah's study of the life and writings of Jacobus Elisa Capitein, the eighteenth-century ex-slave of mixed parentage, reveals that in the period from 1717 to 1747, these ex-slaves turned missionaries "were more preoccupied with the conversion of their fellow Africans than with the issue of slavery."[17] As a result, the Africans strove in diverse ways to accomplish the desired results.

However, Black participation in the Christian evangelical movements of this early period was very restricted for obvious reasons. White slave owners and planters in the United States and elsewhere in the Atlantic world intensely opposed slave conversion. In his study of religion in the United States, Martin Marty characterized the affiliation between religion and race as an "abyss," meaning that the race problem in the United States was so profoundly poisoned that there was no conceivable solution.[18] This venom permeated Christian ideology to the extent that the average White Christian saw nothing wrong in excluding Blacks from the mainstream churches. As a result, under slavery, there was an absence of a qualified pool of Black clergy to spearhead evangelical missions to Africa.

Annette Laing's study of Christianization and Anglicanism in South Carolina and Africa from 1700 to 1750 exposes the nonaccommodating attitude of the various parishioners toward the Black population.[19] The South Carolina elite was fearful that accepting Blacks into the Christian fold would cause serious harm to the slavocracy and its sociopolitical privileges. In 1710, Francis Le Jau, the Anglican minister of St. James Parish in South Carolina, reported that despite the longing of Blacks to embrace Christianity and receive the Holy Communion, White Anglican congregants were unwilling to accept them in the church.[20] Hence Le Jau found himself in the awkward position of delayed baptism to those Africans who approached him for the Christian sacrament. "I see no necessity," he replied, "to be too hasty, I stay till I have a proof of their good life by the testimony of their masters."[21]

By 1749, the inclination of White congregants to oppose the conversion of enslaved people into mainstream Christianity remained unchanged. William Cotes, who succeeded Francis Varnod as minister at another parish in South Carolina, noted in a letter that there were only a few baptized Africans among his parishioners: "And the few Negro communicants that I have heard of in my predecessors' times, upon enquiry, I found they were sold and dispersed into various parishes. Where once, in the 1720s, there had been almost an equal number of black and white communicants, now there were only whites."[22] In other words, the slave owners dissipated the nascent Black Christian community that showed interest in the Anglican Church in South Carolina to check its growth.

Laing curiously observes that the relationship between church officials and ordinary parishioners in British America was often so tense that "those who gave offense to the [White] laity were often humiliated with false charges of 'drunkenness, improper sexual conduct, or similarly scandalous accusations.'" Mostly, these pastors suffered such attacks in connection to "the ministers' encouragement of the proselytization of slaves."[23] White communicants would stop at nothing in keeping Blacks away from the church, even if it meant inventing an allegation against any minister who overtly showed friendship toward Africans.

The fact then is that resistance to slave Christianity hindered early preparation of African Americans for evangelical missions in the first half of the eighteenth century. Thus, enslaved Africans who were denied access to formal Anglican worship and leadership welcomed the overtures of George Whitefield
(1714–1770), one of the most renowned promoters of the Great Awakening and
a founder of the evangelical movement in America.[24] As an itinerant preacher,
Whitefield espoused Anglicanism with an uncommon passion and fervor. He
criticized church members who treated slaves unfairly and forcefully called for
Christianizing slaves. In a 1740 open letter addressed to slave owners in the Carolinas, Virginia, and Maryland, Whitefield decried the oppressive treatment of
Blacks in those areas.[25] He stressed that slaves should have access to the church,
arguing that this would spawn obedience rather than rebellion. His outspokenness attracted the attention of many slaves in South Carolina hitherto deprived
of access to the Anglican Church.

The opportunity for membership in the Christian community began to materialize for the enslaved people when Whitefield's efforts in South Carolina
and other parts of the Low Country captured the hearts of slave-owning brothers Jonathan Bryan and Hugh Bryan of St. Helen Parish. The Bryans accepted
Whitefield's appeal to open a school for slaves. Despite hostile opposition from
fellow slavocrats who complained to the SPG that these slaves were "taught
rather an Enthusiasm than religion," the example of the Bryans among their
own slaves had a profound effect in the region.[26] Gallay, Glasson, and others have underscored the crucial point that "the introduction of evangelism
to slaves on the Bryans' plantations was a seminal moment in the spread of
Christianity among Afro-Americans."[27] Through the Bryans, slave Christianity
spread beyond the narrow confines of the Bryan family's plantations empire in
Pocotaligo. In 1792, the Independent Presbyterian Chapel of Prince William
Parish, located in Stoney Creek, became an open place where Black and White
people worshipped together. The church, founded by Jonathan Bryan in 1843,
recorded 235 White members and 350 enslaved congregants, "many of whom
had not obtained the permission of their owners to be baptized."[28]

The goodwill of the Bryans—thanks to Whitefield—provided a new outlet
for the expression of Christian ideals among enslaved Africans in South Carolina and the adjoining areas. Hugh Bryan and his wife Katherine encouraged
African American preachers in their church and thus helped prepare Blacks
as evangelicals.[29] In 1852, Jonathan Bryan moved to Savannah, Georgia, where
he established the Bryan Baptist Church under the pastoral care of one of his
slaves named Andrew Bryan. The pioneering Black preacher was later tortured
to death by the master class.[30]

The examples of the Bryans bore lasting fruit with the rise of the Black church and other Black preachers and evangelicals within the broader American Baptist family. In Virginia, for example, Joseph Bishop was ordained a priest in 1792 along with William Leman of the Petworth or Gloucester Church, Virginia. Also, Joseph Willis, a mulatto and the first Baptist preacher in southwest Mississippi, was ordained a minister in 1798. Willis later became the founder of the early Baptist Church at Bayou Chicot, Ville Platte, Louisiana.[31] In 1815, William Crane established the Richmond Chapter of the African Baptist Missionary Society. In 1821, Lott Carey, a health officer and government inspector, founded the first Baptist Church in Sierra Leone and proceeded to establish the early Baptist Church in Monrovia, Liberia.[32] In his summation of the influence of the Bryans on the rise of the African American evangelical movement, Lawrence Rowland concluded that the Bryan brothers were altogether "responsible for initiating the evangelical missions to the growing slave population of the Beaufort District. The conversion of slaves to Christianity was one of the most important events in South Carolina history, and the particular form of evangelical Christianity practiced by many Black Americans to this day may have begun with George Whitefield, the Great Awakening, and the Bryan brothers of the Beaufort District."[33]

Yet, the era of the African American missionary journey to Africa remained limited. Slave Christianity continued to face stiff objections from American planters and slave owners, and this objection persisted until the late nineteenth century, when the African American missionary would finally emerge at the center stage of overseas Christian evangelism. The major breakthrough came with the emergence of *independent* Black Baptist churches in Virginia, Georgia, and South Carolina. While Black congregations were typical, they were dependent on the parent denominations under White American leadership. The independent Black Baptist churches of this era began several years before the first Black churches emerged from other denominations in America. In the U.S. North, where this trend was slower, the early African Baptist Church in Boston appeared in 1805, with Rev. Thomas Paul as rector.[34]

James A. Quirin has correctly observed that European and Euro-American missionary activities in Africa revived in the nineteenth century due to the abolitionist movement, the evangelistic "awakening," and later the growth of nationalism, colonialism, and their justifying ideologies.[35] The period between the 1870s and 1900 was the apogee of global Christian evangelism, with the number of individuals engaged in overseas missionary work rising from 2,000 to 15,000.[36] The surge in numbers reflected the needs of the time, which opened the door for the African American missionary to insert himself into the African evangelical vineyard.

Furthermore, the founding of the American colony of Liberia in 1822 by the American Colonization Society spurred the interest of African Americans in Christian missionary efforts. Liberia and all it symbolized attracted a good number of different African American emigration groups, prompting both Christian missionaries and lay groups to look toward Africa as a rich field for harvesting Christian souls. This development was part of the White man's self-appointed burden to "civilize" the African continent. As the need expanded, White church boards desperately courted the involvement of African American ministers, to the point that the latter acquiesced to the call for help. It is striking that the founding of the ACS in 1816 coincided with the inaugural ceremonies of the first historically Black denomination, the African Methodist Episcopal Church.[37] The underlying ideology for the recruitment of Black missionaries was the "Theory of Providential Design."[38] The theory purports that God pre-destined slavery as an apparatus for raising a new generation of African elite to civilize the continent through Christianity. Once enslaved Africans in the Americas had become civilized, the theory goes, it was their duty to bring Christ to Africa in order to overcome "the ignorance, the animalism, and the barbarism of the African tribes."[39]

STAGE 2: THE ERA OF TEMPORAL AND SPIRITUAL RECONSTRUCTION, 1860s–1900

Despite its inherent flaw as an ideology of imperial propaganda, the Theory of Providential Design captured the ears of many in the African diaspora. In his educative study *Black Americans and the Evangelization of Africa, 1877–1900*, Walter L. Williams emphasized that the response of African Americans to the Christian missionary work in Africa in the nineteenth century derived more from the writings of the Black intelligentsia, such as Henry Turner, W. E. B. Du Bois, and Marcus Garvey, than from any other factor. In chronicling the period from the end of Reconstruction in 1877 to the first Pan-African Congress in 1900 organized by Sylvester Williams, Walter Williams notes that about 116 African Americans served in mission works in Africa. Additionally, eighty individuals born in Africa were involved under mission sponsorships in missionary leadership training in the United States.[40] These figures do not tell the entire story, for there were hundreds of Black émigrés from the United States and several regions of the Americas who resettled in Liberia and Sierra Leone before the arrival of the African American missions in Africa.

The strengthening of the ecclesiastical foundation of the African American church in the second stage of global American Christian missionary work remains a crucial factor in the history of African Americans' involvement in evangelical work in Africa. Richard Allen, the African American minister who pioneered this effort, chartered a movement that would have even greater relevance to the nineteenth-century quest for a grand Black ecclesiastical separation. In this era, many African Americans continued to serve the missions under White boards, but a higher number of them worked for the emergent Black churches. It is essential to underline the distinctive modifications to the Christian faith that enabled this development and its connection to the African context. The early Black churches, which succeeded in separating from the mainstream White-controlled mission bodies, included the African Methodist Episcopal (AME) Church (first established in 1794 and officially granted independence in 1816 in Philadelphia) and the African Methodist Episcopal Zion (AMEZ) Church (founded in New York in 1796 and chartered in 1801). Both churches (now in serious merger discussions) sought to claim spiritual and temporal spheres for the survival of the Blacks in the broader American society.

Persistent incidents of racism in all spheres of American life in the Reconstruction era made it a self-fulfilling prophecy for many among the African American community that "there was a virtual religious devotion to racial injustice in the country."[41] Racially charged words and deeds of many White church leaders further encouraged and strengthened the growth of Black churches. A virulently White supremacist, Protestant discourse that claimed a "God-ordained" hierarchy of social ranks and spheres ensured that Blacks could no longer endure open disdain in the White churches. For example, Washington Chaffin, a nineteenth-century Methodist rector from North Carolina, contended that nature had "drawn lines of demarcation between [the races] "no physical, mental or religious cultivation can obliterate."[42] In a similar tone, James Thornwell, a notable Presbyterian clergyman from South Carolina, insisted that differences of authority along racial lines were not "artificial combinations to which men have been impelled by chance or choice" but were the "ordinance of God."[43]

Thus, to African American leaders who had endured the racist inclinations of White Americans, the first step toward survival was to appropriate black social space independent of White control. Efforts in this direction during the period materialized in migrations, mostly from the South to the North in the United States and also to Africa, and in Black community building inside the United States. Also, the formation of a diverse array of separate Black institutions, including Black-controlled churches, was prominent. In 1834, Rev. Peter Williams, Jr. (1780–1840), the first Black clergyman of St. Philips Episcopal Church in New York City and an abolitionist, had a bitter encounter with the White Episcopal leadership in New York over his pro-abolition speeches. After a group of anti-Black rioters and arsonists attacked the church where he preached, the bishop of New York, Benjamin T. Onderdonk, demanded Williams's resignation without any attempt to protect the Black congregants who were the target of this attack.[44] The resignation of Williams satisfied radical anti-abolitionist Whites, who wanted to perpetuate Black slavery in America. However, an enraged Black community attacked Williams for what they perceived as "complying with the counsel of his bishop," and of not having enough of the "moral stamina" to "renounce his connection with a church seeking to muzzle a man praying for the deliverance of his people."[45]

The divisive ideas propagated by the church reinforced earlier claims that social progress among the Black community was only feasible in life away from White-controlled spheres. By the end of the nineteenth century, the African Methodist Episcopal Zion (AMEZ) Church, the Colored Methodist Episcopal Church, and the National Baptists (most significant of the Black Baptist conventions) had all emerged as independent denominations. As with other civic, fraternal, and educational institutions owned by Blacks during the period, their primary purpose was to further African American interests and survival within the larger American society.

In separate studies, Walter Williams and Kenneth Barnes noted that beginning about the 1870s, many African American missionaries made the journey to Africa under White-led evangelical missions. Among the most notable was New York resident Alexander Crummell, who worked for twenty years in Liberia as an Episcopal missionary.[46] In the 1880s, when many independent Black Christian churches had come of age, they showed serious interest in African missions. Despite lacking the enormous financial resources enjoyed by mainstream White missions, quite a few African American ministers moved to Liberia in the 1870s and 1880s. Those who moved held worship among the African American settlers, but made little or no attempt to convert the indigenous Africans in the region. Leaders of the Black Baptist Church from some states—among them three delegates from Arkansas—met in Montgomery, Alabama, in 1880 to establish the Baptist Foreign Mission Convention (BFMC). Not discouraged by the dire shortage of funds, the BFMC sponsored a few missionaries to Liberia in the following decade. Some of these missionaries returned to the United States and spoke at the next BFMC meeting in Memphis in 1886. Some pastors from Arkansas attended the convention in Memphis, and the testimonies of the returned missionaries captured their interest.[47]

No account of African American missions to Africa would be complete without mentioning the historic role of Fisk University, founded by the American Missionary Association (AMA) in 1867. Like its parent organization, the Amistad

Committee, an antislavery organization devoted to the defense of Africans ille-
gally apprehended off the ship *Amistad*, the AMA came into existence in 1864
with a focus on advocating for total emancipation and rehabilitation of free
Blacks through vocational training. Between 1839 and 1841, the Amistad Committee—founded by abolitionists Lewis Tappan, Joshua Leavitt, and Simeon
Jocelyn—raised funds for the legal defense of captive Africans from the Mende
ethnic group in Sierra Leone. The committee had secured the services of lead
counsel Theodore Sedgwick, who saw the case through the district and circuit
courts until it reached the Supreme Court, where John Quincy Adams argued
the case. On March 9, 1841, Justice Joseph Story delivered the decision that
secured the release of thirty-five captives on the *Amistad*. Their journey back to
Sierra Leone began on November 27, 1841, accompanied by three White missionaries and two Black teachers. During the American Civil War, the AMA
continued its antislavery advocacy in the South and, as the first slaves regained
their freedom, the AMA turned to education and relief programs for the emancipated. Under the leadership of Erastus Milo Cravath, Edward P. Smith, and
John Ogden, who was then the Freedmen's Bureau school superintendent for
Tennessee and Kentucky, Fisk Colored School came into existence in 1866. In
1867, Ogden renamed this institution Fisk University.

Three years after the first college class of students graduated, Fisk University began to play a historic role in the missionary evangelization of Africa.[48] A
year later, the missionaries established a "Young People's Missionary Society"
to keep alive "interest in African missions."[49] In 1876, students formed a Society
for the Evangelization of Africa. In February 1878, Prof. Adam K. Spence read
a letter from Rev. G. D. Pike of the AMA calling on students to volunteer for
the Mendi Mission in Sierra Leone. The next day, the first responders were
two male students and two female students. The two men, Albert P. Miller and
Andrew E. Jackson, were ordained as ministers in preparation for the Mendi
Mission, and by 1907 a total of ten Fisk students had served as missionaries in
various locations in Africa, each spending an average of three years.

Some students, like Nancy Jones, moved on from Sierra Leone to Southern
Rhodesia (Zimbabwe), where she worked at Mt. Selinda. In 1901, John Jack-
son Pearce of Clinton, Mississippi, began his missionary career in Cape Town
(now part of South Africa), and in 1907, he moved to West Africa. A year later,
Pearce worked for the African Methodist Episcopal Zion Church in Kwitte,
Gold Coast, and by 1910, he was at the Brewerville African Methodist Episcopal
Church in Liberia. From 1902, Althea Maria Brown of Rolling Fork, Missis-
sippi, served at the mission station at Luebo in the Congo under the Congo
Presbyterian Mission, founded in 1891 by Samuel Norvell Lapsley and William

Henry Sheppard. Brown worked with eight other Blacks and two White missionaries in the area. In 1915, she wrote about her missionary work at a hospital and a school for thirty-five girls. She produced a book that doubled as both a dictionary and an introductory grammar text in Kuba languages and society in the nineteenth and early twentieth centuries.[50]

In the 1890s, as the study by Kenneth Barnes shows, several Black communities across Arkansas manifested an intense interest in African affairs. This development was in large part a response to the Arkansas General Assembly's disfranchisement/segregation policies. The Jim Crow laws of the early 1890s stimulated many African Americans to look to Africa for survival. These communities donated resources to support the African exodus, funding those willing to move to Liberia.[51] Barnes notes that of the 815 identified African American emigrants to Liberia in the 1890s alone, more than 50 percent departed from Arkansas.[52] The decision taken by these African Americans contributed to the broader efforts of the Black diaspora to plant Christianity on the continent. Other Black Arkansans, who either did not wish to move to Liberia or lacked the financial ability to actualize their dreams, helped organize missionary societies and raised money for the African American–led Christian missions to Africa. Several clergy and lay folks volunteered as missionary workers, and about a dozen Black Arkansans and their families made the trip to Africa to win the African soul for Jesus Christ. These foot soldiers of Christ from Arkansas constituted about 25 percent of the documented Black missionaries from the United States who went to Africa from 1890 to 1910.[53]

Also, the period under review witnessed a pronounced tension between African American cultural sensitivities and indigenous African practices as they related to colonial ideologies and Western cultural imperialism. Williams observes that "the mere fact that Africans were of the same skin color was not enough, by itself, to produce a feeling of identity with them by the black Americans."[54] Like most of the White missionaries, the African American missionaries saw themselves as conduits of civilization commissioned to redeem Africans from the life of darkness and savagery. As a result, Sylvia M. Jacobs concluded, "the relationship of Afro-American missionaries with Africa and Africans was both ambivalent and contradictory."[55]

Over time, the initial self-importance claimed by the African American missionaries in the continent gave way to a more positive interaction with the Africans. This new attitude was both a result of a better understanding of the indigenous African culture and a consequence of a persistent White racism toward all people of color. The development of closer contacts with Africans was especially exhibited in the emergence of West African and South African educated elites, through whose leadership the idea of a pan-African consciousness began to gain currency in the Atlantic world. These dynamics compelled Black American missionaries in Africa to reconsider the Providential Design Theory—this time in light of their perception of the African problem.[56] In other words, the African American missionaries began to process Africa's so-called problems through the lens of their own experiences in the United States. They came to terms with those discrete considerations of aptitudes of races and the idea that "restoration" of Africa could not succeed without an active role assigned to African Americans. This goal not only marked the beginning of African American philanthropic programs but also shaped some of the new partnerships between them and White American–led humanitarian organizations, as well as the manner in which European colonial governments conducted specific developmental programs in Africa.

To restate, the new collaboration between African American evangelists and Euro-American missionary boards materialized with the growth of the independent African American missionary movement in the second half of the nineteenth century. With the leadership of the AME Church, African America's first autonomous church, evangelical missions run by African Americans started to dispatch their members to overseas missions in West and South Africa. A vital component of this program was the idea of technical education. In line with Booker T. Washington's Tuskegee model, which primarily focused on vocational training for Blacks in the United States, African American mission schools incorporated training in crafts and agriculture as a core element of their curriculum. This emphasis was to aid Africans to improve their lives through entrepreneurship and the economic independence that comes with self-help.

Georgia's Henry McNeil Turner (1834–1915), a bishop in the AME Church, was one of the African Americans who immersed themselves in the programs of the AME churches in New York, Philadelphia, and other places in the U.S. North. Turner convinced AME officials to intensify their evangelical works in Africa and everywhere populated by Blacks. He called to mind how sermons delivered by Alexander Crummell of New York, who spent twenty years in Liberia as a missionary, convinced him that Africa was the rightful home of African Americans. Thus, the central aspect of his program for the AME Church was to urge emigration to Africa, particularly Liberia. Turner and his fellow abolitionist Martin R. Delany (1812–1885), like Marcus Garvey after them, actively worked to turn the Liberian exodus project around in 1877 because Africa was a symbol of identity and survival for the entire African diaspora. "I do not believe any race will ever be respected, or ought to be respected who do not show themselves capable of founding and maintaining a government of their own," Turner declared.[57]

Prominent Black missionaries of the nineteenth century such as Edward Wilmot Blyden and Alexander Crummell held a unique place among African Americans who labored in the African evangelization field. Born in the West Indies and the United States, respectively, Blyden and Crummell moved to Liberia, where their works connected the essence of bloodlines among Africa, the West Indies, and the United States. Unable to attend college in either St. Thomas or the United States because of racial oppression, Blyden seized the opportunity to study at Alexander High School in Monrovia. Once described by E. A. Ayandele as an African celebrity, Blyden made Liberia and Africa his home.[58] In 1862, he wrote: "My heart is in Liberia and longs for the welfare of Africa. . . . An African nationality is the great desire of my soul. I believe nationality to be an ordinance of nature, and no people can rise to an influential position among nations without a distinct and efficient nationality. . . . Could my voice reach every descendant of Africa in America, I would say to him: come away from the land of caste and oppression to the freedom of our young Republic. Come help us build a Nationality in Africa."[59]

To better put to use the economic, physical, and human resources of Africa, Blyden conceived of Liberia as a possible African power center from where to harness these strengths. He told Blacks in the United States that whatever gains they had made were at the cost of their manhood. Like Garvey, Blyden stressed that people of African descent must come together to build Africa. "We must build up Negro states; we must establish and maintain the various institutions; we must make and administer laws, erect and preserve churches; . . . we must build ships and navigate them; we must ply the trades, instruct the schools, control the press, and thus aid in shaping the opinions and guiding the destinies of mankind. Nationality is an ordinance of nature. The heart of every true [N]egro yearns after distinct and separate nationality."[60]

STAGE 3: THE ERA OF PAN-AFRICAN CONSCIOUSNESS, 1900–1945

While the works of African American missionaries in Africa attained significant growth in the latter half of the nineteenth century, the twentieth century witnessed a strong nationalist approach to missionary work constructed in the anticolonial fashion. The First World War briefly diverted the attention of both Africans and African American agitators against colonial rule. However, by the

1920s, it was evident that Black American missionaries had left a strong cultural mark on the new converts in Africa. Consequently, the colonial authorities began to express serious concerns that this trend was detrimental to prevailing racial ideas and social hierarchies in Africa. As a result, African colonial rulers began to prohibit them from most parts of their African dominions.

In East Africa, specifically in Kenya and Uganda, for example, there was a concerted effort by the British colonial governments to make African American missionaries feel uninvited. This ill feeling persisted even though in 1925, the Phelps-Stokes Fund's commission on African education recommended a Tuskegee approach to mission education in East Africa, and African American missionaries were strongly favored as partners in the project.[61] One of the reasons why several White Americans did not want to see African American missionaries in Africa was that they tended to draw followers in large numbers and their sermons encouraged the contagious rise of independent African church movements.

European imperialists scorned the presence of African American missionaries, suspecting that they promoted rebellion against European powers by encouraging African liberation or attracted Africans to the Pan-African movement that sprang up in the United States in the 1920s around the legendary Jamaican-born Pan-African nationalist and anticolonial agitator Marcus Garvey. Worries over the entrance of such theories into the colony—and, more particularly, into its schools—led Britain's Colonial Office to seek assurances in 1920 from Thomas Jesse Jones, head of the Phelps-Stokes Fund's commission on education in Africa. The colonial rulers wanted a guarantee that Jones would not send African Americans educated at the Tuskegee or Hampton Institutes to the Congo as tutors.[62] In a letter to Governor General Martin Rutten (1876–1944), minister Louis Franck wrote, "Nothing can guarantee us, in effect, that the blacks from Tuskegee or Hampton will not inculcate our natives with very advanced ideas, and that they are not affiliated to pan-African organizations whose infiltrations of our colony could be very dangerous."[63]

Nevertheless, White American missionaries and European colonial rulers acknowledged the potential inherent in the Black American missionary movement to facilitate the education of Africans for both imperial labor service and missionary expansion. This potential was identified in the Tuskegee system of education, and the assumption was that this model could help Africans improve their skills for colonial service.

By 1919, Christian missions were responsible for about 90 percent of Western education efforts in sub-Saharan Africa. In light of the number of young people in Africa who desired mission education, the resources available to the missionaries were far too little to meet the needs of the people. In response to this problem, Thomas Jesse Jones, director of the Phelps-Stokes Fund, notable for his studies of Black American education, led a commission on education in Africa.

Between 1920 and 1924, the Phelps-Stokes Fund sponsored two commissions to investigate schools in Africa and advise the British Colonial Office as to where the existing education needed adjustment. One of the distinguished members of the commission was the Gold Coast educator and missionary James Kwegyir Aggrey (1875–1927).[64] Aggrey was a graduate of Livingstone College in Salisbury, North Carolina, and his expertise resulted in the publication in 1922 of a significant report entitled *Education in Africa.* Another trip in 1924 resulted in a companion volume entitled *Education in East Africa.*[65] The commission's investigation revealed that with regard to method and content, education in Africa followed Western patterns. The curriculum of instruction was too European or American and contained little or nothing reflecting the realities of African life, needs, resources, environment, and experience. The report stressed that colonial educators prioritized rudimentary over lifelong educational skills. The Phelps-Stokes Fund commission's recommendations prompted many missionary teachers to adopt the philosophy of progressive education.[66] Over time, the commission's work resulted in a profound change of thought in African education.

The support of colonial governments emanated from a desire to streamline the part that African American evangelists played in their alliances with missionaries on the continent. Because the commission recommended the primacy of industrial and agricultural education over traditional literary education, the mission schools began to consider the philosophy of the Tuskegee Institute as a viable model for vocational training in Africa.

These efforts to enlist African Americans in a stronger partnership between the church and the colonial governments were the topic of a conference titled "The Christian Mission in Africa," held in Belgium in 1926. The organizer of the conference, the International Missionary Council (IMC), wanted to encourage teamwork among the various organizations and individuals working to achieve Africa's regeneration. The IMC recognized and commended the zeal demonstrated by the African American missionaries "to render unselfish service, and aiding in a natural and important way the cause of African evangelization, education and general welfare."[67] As a result, the conference participants drafted an official resolution to obligate missionary societies and colonial governments to encourage the involvement of the "educated Negro" in missionary efforts in Africa.

In the end, neither the Phelps-Stokes Fund's commission nor the resolution passed by the IMC resulted in broadening African American missionary work in Africa. A rough estimate by David Killingray, which covered the period from 1820 to 1970, suggests that there were 600 African Americans, or 11.6 percent of the 30,000 American missionaries in the continent over that period.[68] The idea of making the African American experience with technical education and ideas the cornerstone of missionary and humanitarian missions in Africa challenged White Christian missions and their colonial governments to reconsider their imperial agendas. The African American contribution to the spread of the Christian church in Africa is a theme that deserves a broader audience.

Writings of African American missionaries who led a Protestant mission to Galangue and Ovimbundu in Angola from about 1922 to 1940 reveal that the Black ministers had an evident appreciation of themselves and identified with Africans "through race and the legacy of the slave trade."[69] The Galangue missionaries attained remarkable success among the African converts because they engaged Africa as a symbol and a reality, following a circular from the Alabama-born Very Rev. Henry Curtis McDowell (1894–1989) in 1919 counseling the Black Congregationalists to better understand the African natives as the same as "American Negroes in that they have shades of color."[70] As for African geography, McDowell reminded his audience to think about Talladega, Florida, with its Iron Mountains and red soil, when they thought of Africa "as the Sahara Desert and jungles of coconuts and monkeys."[71] In another letter, McDowell acknowledged the dense culture of spirituality among the people of Umbundu, Angola, but added that without Jesus, "their very fine ideal and excellent culture have been as a ship without a rudder."[72]

The Ovimbundu people responded to the African American missionaries' cheerful attitude toward the Africans and their indigenous ways of life by embracing them as "natives" and part of their own extended families in some fictional sense. The Galangue mission ended in the late 1930s as a result of lack of finances. However, the Black Congregationalists left an enduring legacy among the Ovimbundu based on a vibrant family metaphor.

LEGACIES OF THE AFRICAN AMERICAN MISSIONARIES TO AFRICA

Central to African Americans' involvement in missionary work in Africa is the nationalist consciousness they implanted in the African mind. In South Africa in particular, where the history of Dutch colonialism and apartheid ideology parallel the African American experience with slavery and segregation, a real effect was evident. J. Mutero Chirenje's work on the evolution of the independent Black Christian churches in Southern Africa in the 1890s reminds us that "Ethiopianism" became a generic term to describe both secular and religious movements.[73]

In 1893, Rev. Mangena Maake Mokone pioneered African separation from White religious dominations by detaching his Wesleyan Methodist Church in Pretoria from the parent church. Three years later other clergymen followed his lead, when the Ethiopian Church of South Africa gained affiliation with the AME Church in the United States. A major catalyst in promoting the relationship between the two independent religious bodies was AME bishop Henry McNeil Turner, who remained an ardent advocate of Pan-Africanism and Black missionary activity throughout his life. In 1900, the AME denomination appointed Leroy J. Coppin as the first resident AME bishop in southern Africa. Although African Methodism exerted the greatest attraction for the leaders of the Ethiopian Church, the National Baptist Convention also attracted supporters, as did the various prophets and messianic leaders who embraced a millenarian approach to the Christian worship.

The rise of Ethiopianism frightened White leaders in southern Africa, prompting British officials in 1904 to deliberate about the emergence of a church in southern Africa that was "purely under Native management and control." They quickly concluded that the Ethiopian movement was "the work of the African Methodist Episcopal Church."[74] The authorities appointed a commission to investigate what they saw as a unified effort to oppose established White jurisdiction in the country. The commission's report following a two-year investigation produced mixed results. First, the commission concluded that Ethiopianism was not an underground movement. Instead, it noted that the campaign was the result of a genuine desire to show Black leadership. On the constructive side, the AME mission schools were endorsed by London. The Colonial Office in Britain registered the AME-run institutions "among those awarded government grants by local education departments with increasing regularity."[75] The rank and file of the leading European and American missionary organization operating in Africa comprised increasing numbers of members of the AME. The success of the African American–run missions led many among these missionary bodies to openly acknowledge the crucial role of the AME Church in the propagation of Christian gospel—precisely in winning "a really African church."[76] It is noteworthy that newspapers of various colonies now and then drew public attention to AME officials as having "brilliant careers" and espousing "wise words."[77]

On the negative side, the White settler minority government in the Union of South Africa enacted a new immigration law intended to prevent African Americans from entering the dominion.[78] This move was intended to break the tide of radicalization of the local population by their African American contacts. One positive result of the step was the creation of the South African Native College (later the University of Fort Hare) in 1916. Although the South African Union government created the college out of a fear shared with the White missionaries that South African Blacks were increasingly becoming radicalized by studying in the United States, the Western-educated Black South African elite also played a central role in founding the South African Native College. There were two competing college proposals, each championed by a prominent Black South African political leader, J. T. Jabavu and Walter Rubusana. Since the Union government officials and missionaries considered him more moderate and friendlier, Jabavu's scheme won out and his son, D. D. T. Jabavu, who had recently graduated from the University of London, became the first lecturer at the college. D. D. T. Jabavu was perhaps only the second Black South African to earn a university degree, after which he visited Booker T. Washington's Tuskegee Institute to learn some lessons from African American education. Ironically, the anti–African American immigration law instituted by the colonial government also stimulated Africans' quest for freedom and political determination, as symbolized by the formation of the South African National Congress in 1912. Indeed, J. Mutero Chirenje notes correctly that in Southern Africa, Ethiopianism was articulated as an ideology of freedom and self-determination.[79]

The most significant contribution of African American missions to Africa is, however, evident in their humanitarian deeds. Over the centuries, Christian missions to Africa, both Black and White, have become synonymous with philanthropic and humanitarian programs providing food aid, medical assistance, and education. The arrival of North American missionaries, including the African Americans, in the nineteenth century brought about a significant growth in this cause. The African Americans were a reliable conduit for American civilization in Africa, even as the European colonial presence continued to entrench Western cultural trends until the 1960s.

Overall, through missionary evangelical efforts in Africa, the Americans left a lasting impact on the native peoples' political, educational, and religious lives. Considering this, William Cohen was right when he noted that the Great Migration was a lever of social change in America. Indeed, the Great Migration, which extended to Africa, brought about significant social alterations in Africa.[80]

This exchange was not a one-directional flow of American cultural tropes to Africa, but rather a two-way exchange. Among other things, enslaved Africans in the Americas and their descendants adapted the Christian liturgy and worship to the African experience as encountered in the emergent Black churches. Du Bois emphasized the obvious when he wrote that "the Negro Church is the only social institution of the Negros which started in the African forest and survived slavery; under the leadership of priest or medicine man, afterward of the Christian pastor, the Church preserved in itself the remnants of African tribal life. So that today, the Negro population of the United States is virtually divided into church congregations which are the real units of race life."[81]

INDIGENOUS AGENCY IN AFRICAN CHRISTIANITY

It would amount to oversight to conclude this chapter without a few more words on African agency in Christian missionary successes in Africa. Not only in the Americas did Africans adapt the Christian religion to African symbols and rituals. Evidence from different parts of the continent shows that the Africans welcomed the new faith with caution. The practical benefits of Christianity, such as access to Western education, Western medicine, and employment opportunities in colonial service, were often the primary reasons why the indigenous people showed interest in the new religion. Felix Ekechi has argued that the Igbo accepted Christianity because of the calculated benefits and not "because they thought it was superior to their own religion."[82] Among the Fang of Gabon, James Fernandez observed that the new converts nursed a profound sense of deception and disappointment "where expectations of material advantages" fell short of their expectations.[83]

In the end, it was African reactions and perceptions that shaped the pattern of Christian missionary expansion—the extent to which evangelization was an achievement of the African clergy rather than their European counterparts. The brand of Christianity that eventually took root on the continent was determined by the elements in the alien religion that the Africans found relevant to the interpretations they assigned to them in the indigenous context.

6

THE BACK-TO-AFRICA MOVEMENT/
BLACK ZIONISM, 1916–1940

We of the Universal Negro Improvement Association are raising the
cry of "Africa for the Africans," those at home and those abroad.
— *Marcus Mosiah Garvey, 1922*[1]

With the above declarative, the Back-to-Africa movement, or Black Zionism
(denoting unity of race and redemption grounded in religion), struck a strong
chord, as a sequel both to Christian missionary evangelism in Africa and to
the African colonization enterprise hatched by the U.S. government and its
proxy, the American Colonization Society, in the nineteenth century. On a
closer look, however, the commitment to and philosophical underpinnings of
the colonization and Back-to-Africa ideologies are noticeably dissimilar. While
the U.S. political elite controlled the original colonization effort, with the overriding intent to rid the country of the emancipated Blacks whom most American Whites despised, the early twentieth-century Back-to-Africa movement was
the prerogative of Marcus Mosiah Garvey (1887–1940), who sought to restore
dignity to his race. The insistence of the Black Zionists that all people of African descent should return to Africa stood in sharp contradistinction to the view
held by the adversaries of colonization. The critics foresaw no commitment on
the part of the U.S. government to the success of the colony. As a result, they
contended that sending African Americans to the Liberia colony was not in
their best interest.

One may recall that after the launching of the African colonization mission
in 1816, many African Americans welcomed the idea, but as details began to
emerge, suspicion soon set in. Some groups and individuals, who viewed the
plan with distrust, started ripping it apart as a degenerative and spiteful idea. It

is conspicuous that the very first African American figures such as James Forten, a prominent business leader, and Richard Allen, bishop of the African Methodist Episcopal Church—who had initially welcomed the ACS's plan—would turn around to oppose it. In 1817, following the gathering of 3,000 emancipated African Americans in Philadelphia at the behest of Forten and Allen, the meeting decried the society's plans "as an outrage having no other object in view than the slaveholding interests of the country."[2] Despite acknowledging the pervading gross inequality between Whites and colored Americans, the members nonetheless insisted that America remained their home. The AME Church leaders contended that if indeed the colonization plan was for their interest and not their injury, as the ACS claimed, "we humbly and respectfully urge, that it is not asked for by us: nor will it be required by any circumstances, in our present or future condition."[3]

In 1830 the abolitionist Rev. Peter Williams, Jr. reminded the colonizationists in similar terms that African Americans "are natives of this country. We ask only to be treated as well as foreigners. Not a few of our fathers suffered and bled to purchase its independence; we ask only to be treated as those who fought against it. We ask only to share equal privileges with those who come from distant lands, to enjoy the fruits of our labor. . . . We cannot doubt the purity of the motives of persons who deny us those requests and would send us to Africa to gain what they might give us at home. Let these modest requests be granted, and we need not go to Africa or anywhere else to be improved and happy."[4] These and similar voices of opposition had risen exponentially to dull the first argument for colonization. Hence, nearly a century before Garvey's emergence, the Back-to-Africa scheme had become a divisive and conflictual topic among African Americans, and its relevance had become mired in severe doubts.

Still, Garvey and his followers maintained that White racial prejudice would remain intractable for generations, and that Black progress would be contingent upon unity among all Blacks and their willingness to work together as a group. Garvey emphasized that the quest for racial emancipation was integral to the imperative of securing a socioeconomic and political climate in which freed people could exercise their full capacities for human development.[5] In this sense, Black Zionism under Garvey became a renewal of the centuries-old call for an African renaissance, with the expectation that Blacks in the Americas should spearhead this new beginning.

Considering that Garvey founded the Universal Negro Improvement Association (UNIA) in his home country of Jamaica, the question arises as to why he chose the United States as the battleground to fight for the principles and goals he hoped to achieve for his race and himself. The simple answer is that the United States had already established the Liberia colony as a place of succor and freedom for African Americans. This development aligned with Garvey's plan to launch a country in Africa where Blacks from all parts of the Americas would be resettled and empowered to function as harbingers of African progress in the twentieth century. However, logistical reasons, including the potential to raise money for UNIA's ambitious projects, also made the United States a natural choice. New York, the new headquarters of UNIA from 1916, offered the best opportunity for shipping, business, employment opportunities, Black cultural renewal, and social action. The historic celebration of African American literary and artistic genius known as the Harlem Renaissance, or the New Negro Movement—starting around this time and picking up from 1920—provided natural support for Garveyism.[6] The Back-to-Africa discourse had been ongoing in the country long before Garvey. The ideology manifested in several debates connected with race, slavery, emancipation, citizenship, and freedom in the Americas.

In context, therefore, Black Zionism was a continuation of the African colonization project under the auspices of a revitalized and more aggressive Black racial consciousness. This Pan-Africanism encapsulated the conscious attempts of people of African descent in Africa and the African diaspora to unite and combat centuries of unending dehumanization structured by Atlantic slavery, the disrespect and racism it spurred, colonialism, and other oppression against peoples of African descent.[7] What made the Garvey movement and the racial consciousness it conjured unique was that Garvey, an outside arbiter in the U.S. colonization struggle, breathed new life into an idea that was then comatose. His ability to whip up a mass following among African Americans was unmatched until the time of Martin Luther King, Jr.

A closer look at the Garvey-led Black Zionism regarding its goals, successes, and failures offers an opportunity to test the honesty of the American government with regard to the success of Liberia as a Black colony, and to delineate the competing notions of colonization and their implications for Africa and its diaspora. While the American colonization initiative was more about deportation and occupation of a supposedly uncivilized part of Africa, Garveyism was, at least in theory, an effort to mobilize the people of African descent for self-help, racial advancement, and material progress on African soil. Making visible the racial fault lines demonstrates how the internal sociocultural and political cleavages inherent in U.S. culture truncated the ACS-led colonization effort and how this convolution intersected with the well-being of the global Black community vis-à-vis the rise of Garvey.

The available sources in the form of speeches, memoirs, and newspaper writings left behind by the exponents of the Back-to-Africa movement on both sides of the Atlantic provide insights into the real motivations, expected goals, and successes of the movement, as well as the challenges that confronted and stifled it. Of particular interest are the exchanges among W. E. B. Du Bois, the African American civil rights leader; Marcus Garvey, the leader of UNIA; and Booker T. Washington (1856–1915), the African American educator and principal of the Tuskegee Institute and Garvey's role model.[8] In 1921, prior to his imprisonment and eventual deportation from the United States in 1927, Garvey wrote one of the most revealing essays by a person of African descent, entitled "Objectives of the Universal Negro Improvement Association," in which he identified disunity as the most significant problem of the Negro in "the last 500 years."[9] The record provides a quick summary of the goals of the organization and its connection with the ACS's Liberia colony plan.

Other sources include the "Declaration of Rights of the Negro Peoples of the World," adopted by Garvey and his movement at their 1920 convention in New York; and "Negroes of the World, the Eternal Has Happened," a 1919 editorial in which Garvey announced the establishment of his shipping business, the Black Star Line. Additionally, attention is paid to "The Conspiracy of the East St. Louis Riots" (in which Garvey commented on the terrible race riots of 1917); "J. Edgar Hoover Memo" (evidence that the government watched Garvey very closely); "Garvey Must Go" (in which African American leaders called Garvey a menace); and "The Negro's Greatest Enemy" (Garvey's extensive autobiographical statement from 1923). These sources illuminate a complex mix of issues relating to slavery, race, politics, nation building, Pan-Africanism, leadership struggles among the Black elite, and African American survival in the post-emancipation United States. They further show not just why the émigrés resettled in Liberia, and why Sierra Leone failed to harness the original dreams for which the colonies were founded, but why the United States remained at the forefront of Africa's future, even as European colonial rule in Africa gained traction in the interwar years.

UNIA AND THE STRUGGLE FOR BLACK DIGNITY

Before proceeding to highlight the goals of UNIA and Garvey's strategies to rescue Africa and its descendants from centuries of economic plunder and racial abuse, it is necessary to provide a short account of Marcus Mosiah Garvey's career as a Pan-African leader and self-appointed "Provisional President of Africa."[10] Garvey was born on August 17, 1887, to Marcus and Sarah Garvey in Saint Ann's Bay, Jamaica. His parents considered themselves to be of pure African stock. Garvey claimed that his father, a teacher from whom he would acquire a fondness for books, descended from self-emancipated Maroons. David

Levering Lewis, in his biography of Du Bois, pointed out that this claim to Maroon ancestry could have been "fabricated" by one of Garvey's descendants "(probably by the son's second wife)."[11]

The question arises as to why Maroon ancestry matters. Jamaican Maroons were escaped African slaves and Jamaican Free Hill dwellers whose ancestors evaded slavery in the island region by fleeing to the hills, where they lived in free, self-governing communities. Their epic struggles in defense of their freedom remain an integral part of Jamaican history and folklore today. The prideful Jamaican Maroons claim a higher status among Black Jamaicans because of their strong resistance to British enslavement. In fact, they were instrumental in negotiating the 1739 treaty of independence from the British.[12] This background means that Garvey, unlike many Blacks in the Americas, including Booker T. Washington, never had to deal with the dual personality of mixed parentage and upbringing, which Du Bois described as two opposing ideas: being Black and American at the same time.[13] Garvey described his father as "severe, firm, determined, bold and strong, refusing to yield to superior forces if he believed he was right."[14]

As in the United States before the consummation of the civil rights struggles, the social system in which Garvey grew up placed Whites at the top, mixed-race people in the middle, and the majority Black populace at the bottom of the hierarchy.[15] Despite this disadvantage, Garvey later gloated about his Maroon African ancestry by labeling himself as a "full-blooded" Black man "without any taint of white blood" in his veins.[16] Later on, this view of himself would constitute one of the primary reasons he and Du Bois disliked each other.

In his autobiography, Garvey recounts that his education was possible first through the efforts of his private tutors. The tutors helped him navigate the murky waters of Anglican elementary or grammar schools, the town high school, and two colleges—one of which was Birkbeck College, University of London.[17] In their important study of Garvey, Tiki Sundiata and Phaon Sundiata noted that the institution's records show that Garvey was at Birkbeck from 1912 to 1913.[18]

Garvey further disclosed in his memoirs that he hardly understood the ramifications of the social distance that existed between the races until his early teens. For a people whose history is synonymous with scourging and other forms of humiliation on the plantations, Garvey was disinclined to the kind of indignity that came with flogging at British-style public schools. As he explained, humiliation and defeat always drove him to respond by mastering the offending person or situation. His early work experience starting at the age of fourteen was in the printing trade, and Garvey claimed that because of his superior aptitude and sturdy and virile strength he attained a managerial position in the business at the age of eighteen, "having under my control several men old enough to be my grandfathers."[19]

Similar to the experience of Blacks in the antebellum United States, Garvey was also a victim of racial chauvinism and snobbery. The living conditions of workers in Jamaica and the exploitation by White and mulatto supervisors worried Garvey. Several studies indicate that colorism has a sustained presence in the Black communities in the United States, Jamaica, and other societies of color.[20] Preoccupied with actual skin color, rather than racial or ethnic identity, colorism provokes prejudice or discrimination against darker-skinned individuals, typically by people within the same ethnic or racial group. Garvey's efforts to persuade Jamaican officials to intervene in this matter were in vain, triggering him to seek an active part in Jamaica's politics to confront the situation. He would write in his autobiography that during this time, "I saw the injustice done to my race because it was black, and I became dissatisfied on that account."[21]

As part of his preparation to assume the role of the Black spokesperson of his generation, Garvey trained himself in the art of public speaking by observing speakers at churches and other public forums in Jamaica. He also practiced reading and speaking privately and before fellow laborers. His involvement with workers' problems began in 1907, when at the age of twenty he helped organize the Printers' and Allied Workers' Union, the first union on the island. This early foray into the organized labor movement showed that Garvey was destined to inspire the oppressed and exploited in a transnational context. Throughout his days as a Pan-African crusader and Black race leader, public speaking would be one of his greatest strengths.

Garvey was also curious about the conditions of Black people on neighboring Caribbean islands and in Central and South America. In 1910, he toured Colombia, Costa Rica, Ecuador, Honduras, Nicaragua, Panama, and Venezuela to find out if Blacks in these countries shared the same social experience as those in Jamaica.[22] In 1912, the British colonial regime exiled Garvey to London.[23] During his sojourn in Europe in 1912–1913, Garvey continued to face color prejudice. As he explained in his personal life history, everywhere he went he was reminded, "You are black."[24]

It was in London that Garvey encountered Duse Mohamed Ali, the Pan-African editor of the *African Times and Orient Review*, who was Garvey's early mentor.[25] In his pugnacious biography of Garvey, *Negro with a Hat*, Colin Grant argues that it was "an extraordinary piece of good fortune [for Garvey] to have arrived at the birth of one of the most exciting journals to come out of London in decades."[26] While in London, Garvey read about the conditions of Blacks in the United States as depicted by Booker T. Washington in *Up from*

Slavery.[27] Garvey realized that he was going to be a global Black race agitator: "Then my doom—if I may so call it—of being a race leader dawned upon me in London after I had traveled through almost half of Europe. I asked, 'Where is the black man's Government?' . . . Becoming naturally restless for the opportunity of doing something [for] the advancement of my race, I was determined that the black man would not continue to be kicked about by all the other races and nations of the world, as I saw it in the West Indies, South and Central America and Europe, and as I read of it in America. My young and ambitious mind led me into flights of great imagination."[28]

In a letter to Booker T. Washington in 1914, Garvey noted that racial prejudice was commonplace everywhere in Europe, including England. "The Prejudice in these countries is far different from that of America. Here we have to face the prejudice of the hypocritical White men who nevertheless are our friends as also to fight down the prejudice of our race in shade colour. . . . Our organization [the Universal Negro Improvement Association and African Communities League] is marching steadily on and we hope to extend our scope all over the world within the next few years. I have just returned from a tour in Europe where I spent two years studying the Negro's place there."[29]

The picture of Garvey that emerges is that of a self-proclaimed leader of an oppressed race who was not intimidated by the task before him. Brimming with confidence, he saw that the best remedy for the Black race's problem was for Africans in the diaspora to join forces with the mother continent for the material and spiritual advancement of their race. Considering the enormous tests that Garvey contended with throughout the course of his work, perhaps one may look back today and conclude that he was somewhat too optimistic, if not delusional. Along this line, Eric Arnesen, in the *Chicago Tribune*, described Garvey as a "polarizing figure." While acknowledging Garvey's gifts as "charismatic and electrifying orator," Arnesen agrees with Grant that Garvey was "a flawed, occasionally delusional figure whose arrogance, incompetence, belligerence and combativeness, and inability to accept responsibility contributed substantially to his personal downfall as well as to the collapse of his movement."[30] As shown by his entire career, Garvey was not the type that turns away from challenges; he confronts obstacles in his way.

Returning to Jamaica in 1914, Garvey founded the Universal Negro Improvement Association. The articles of the association included: "To establish a Universal Confraternity among the race; to promote the spirit of pride and love; to reclaim the fallen; to administer to and assist the needy; to assist in civilizing the backward tribes of Africa; and to assist in the development of Independent Negro Nations and Communities." Other goals of the Association were "to establish a central nation for the race; to establish Commissaries or Agencies in the major countries and cities of the world for the representation of all Negroes. The group further aspired to promote conscientious Spiritual worship among the native tribes of Africa; to establish Universities, Colleges, Academies and Schools for the racial education and culture of the people; to work for better conditions among Negroes everywhere."[31]

Although conceived on a grander level, UNIA's philosophy of Black racial pride and self-improvement is reminiscent of Washington's diplomatic approach to Black–White relations in the United States, which he typified with the "Atlanta Exposition Address" or "Atlanta Compromise Speech" of 1895.[32] Just as some critics see Garveyism's advocacy for the separation of the races as a surrender to White chauvinism, so opponents of Booker T. Washington despise him for promoting Black subordination to the White race and thus betraying the core principles of the struggle for civil rights in the United States, which he branded an "extremist folly."[33] In his autobiography published in 1901, Washington defended his words by clarifying that "as I remember it now, the thing that was uppermost in my mind was the desire to say something that would cement the friendship of the races and bring about hearty cooperation between them."[34]

In light of the ideological kinship between Garvey and Washington, it is important to briefly highlight one of the institutions Washington used to promote racial peace: the Tuskegee Institute in Alabama, established in 1881. Tuskegee's brand of vocational education speaks to Washington's demonstrated social vision, political adroitness, and accommodative philosophy in antebellum America. In the literature, scholars often focus on Washington's collaboration with business owners and political leaders who provided much-needed funding for the institution. In return, Washington pledged to provide the vocational training that would keep Blacks "down on the farm" and in the trades.[35] What commentators often overlook is Washington's inclination to do or say anything in order to move forward with the more urgent imperative of helping a race that had been bereft of the benefits of education for centuries.[36]

Indeed, the Tuskegee Institute uplifted over a million southern Black farmers and expanded from just a few acres in 1882 to over 2,300 acres.[37] For Washington, Tuskegee was a new beginning for Blacks emerging from the devastations of southern slavery. It is striking that a similar idea was held for South Africa by both the local chiefs and colonial missionary officials.[38] It is not surprising that Washington's commitment to manpower training attracted the attention of millionaire patrons like John D. Rockefeller, Sr. (1839–1937) and Andrew Carnegie (1835–1919). Washington's pledge to inculcate the Protestant work ethic in his students made Tuskegee the wealthiest Black institution in the country in the late nineteenth and early twentieth centuries. Within the constrained space open to African Americans in the period, Washington upheld technical education as the answer to Black poverty in the short term, that is, the key to growing a Black middle class, increasing land ownership, and building small businesses.

While Washington was more of a refined diplomat and politician who skillfully avoided confrontation than his critics would be willing to admit, Garvey was a fearless, outspoken, and often antagonistic Pan-African ideologue. Garvey's recognition of and deference to the meaningful contribution of Washington to the education of African Americans in the post-Reconstruction era explain why he respected and admired the great African American educator, whom he called a mentor. Garvey's conflict with W. E. B. Du Bois was more personal than ideological. However, Alvin B. Tillery, in *Between Homeland and Motherland*, suggests precisely the opposite. Referring to the correspondence and exchanges between Garvey and Du Bois in 1915, Tillery concludes: "Given that Garvey had yet to make a name for himself in either the United States or his native Jamaica, it is not clear that these early dismissive contacts were more a function of his lack of stature than any animus that Du Bois had for the UNIA leader."[39] It is noteworthy that both Du Bois and Garvey, albeit in different ways, acknowledged similarities between Pan-Africanism and Zionism. Du Bois believed that it was foolhardy and illogical to endorse a mass exodus of African Americans to Africa after all their contributions to the economic development of American society. Yet, he believed that "the African movement [Pan-Africanism] must mean to us what the Zionist movement must mean to the Jews, the centralization of race effort and the recognition of a racial front."[40]

On both sides of the Atlantic, leaders of Black consciousness sought an effective response to the legacy of slavery in the New World, racial segregation in the United States, and colonial rule in Africa. Responses to these vexing issues are found in the monumental legacies of both Du Bois's Pan-Africanist ideology and Garvey's Back-to-Africa movement. In fact, Liberia was of central interest to both Black leaders. However, the two intellectuals expressed somewhat opposing views of how to move the Black race forward. On the one hand, Du Bois envisioned Liberia as a confirmation of the capability of Blacks to ably direct their affairs without Whites. Garvey, on the other hand, saw Liberia as the center of the African diaspora and the ultimate home base for the return-to-Africa dream. Both visions espoused by these leaders clashed in Liberia and seriously derailed Garvey's plans, including actualization of the proposed United States of Africa with Garvey as president.

Believing that White racism justified separate institutions such as the Tuskegee Institute, Garvey conceived industrialization and commerce as the keys to Africa's progress and therefore pushed for the development of worldwide Black-owned industries and shipping lines, while campaigning for the end of White colonialism in Africa. In a preamble to the UNIA's constitution, Garvey stated that the association sought "to the utmost to work for the general uplift of the Negro peoples of the world."[41] With the friendship of and words of encouragement from Washington, Garvey arrived in the United States in 1916, a year after the death of his mentor.

Garvey's original plan for coming to the United States was to promote his Back-to-Africa gospel and racial segregation and solicit for money for his organization. He soon decided to settle in New York City because of the opportunity it offered for fundraising, after Jamaica proved a dismal failure in this regard. In New York, where he opened a restaurant and started a newspaper, UNIA quickly gained popularity. Writing in 1923 as a prisoner in the Tombs, New York City's notorious jail, Garvey explained how his meeting with Du Bois at the National Association for the Advancement of Colored People (NAACP) office in 1916 helped shape his decision to remain in the United States. He was dumbfounded to find that apart from Augustus G. Dill, the business manager of the NAACP's magazine *Crisis*, Du Bois himself, and an office assistant, "the whole staff was either white or very nearly white, and thus Garvey got his first shock of the advancement of hypocrisy. There was no representation of race there that anyone could recognize. The advancement meant that you had to be as near white as possible . . . after a short talk with Du Bois, Garvey became so disgusted with the man and his principles that the thought he never contemplated entered his mind—that of remaining in America to teach Du Bois and his group what real race pride meant."[42]

Comments such as this, in which Garvey sees everything in either Black or White, did not augur well for the Pan-Africanist agenda. On June 23, 1919, Garvey incorporated the Black Star Line (BSL) in the state of Delaware. Modeled on the White Star Line, the BSL was the first commercial shipping business wholly owned and operated by Blacks in the United States.[43] The goal was to use the BSL to promote business and tourism between America, Africa, and the Caribbean. Paul Cuffee was the first shipbuilder and owner of African descent in the United States.[44] However, Garvey's BSL was the first shipping business set up to compete with established Western shipping conglomerates. Many African Americans enthusiastically embraced the BSL and purchased its stock. "Like Bishop Turner's shipping attempts, the Black Star Steamship Line stocks were sold to Blacks only and Garvey pledged to subscribers to the stocks that they would make profits while primarily helping restore dignity to their race. From 1919 to 1925, Garvey had raised enough money to procure three more used ships and to begin trade in the Caribbean."[45] Despite his many trials, in 1924 a determined Garvey announced the formation of another shipping line, the Black Cross Navigation and Trading Company, to complete his plans to resettle African Americans in Liberia. To this end, he bought the S.S. *Goethels* (which he renamed *Booker T. Washington*) and the S.S. *West Irmo*. The *Washington* toured various Caribbean ports in 1925, and the *West Irmo* took materials and supplies to Liberia in 1924.[46]

A year after the Black Star Line was established and four years after Garvey arrived in New York, more than 20,000 people flocked to the first UNIA convention in New York. The meeting produced a "Declaration of Negro Rights," which denounced lynching, segregated public transportation, job discrimination, and inferior Black public schools. In a pushback directed against European colonial rule, the document also demanded that Africa should be left for the Africans. It was also at this convention that Garvey proclaimed himself the "Provisional President of Africa" (Fig. 6.1).[47]

Figure 6.1. Marcus Mosiah Garvey,
photographed Aug. 5, 1924. *Library of Congress.*

In an address to the second convention of UNIA in New York in 1921, Garvey contended that "establishing a nation in Africa is where Negroes will have the opportunity to develop by themselves." In his view, this would prevent "creating the hatred and animosity that now exist in countries of the white race through Negroes rivaling them for the highest and best positions in government, politics, society, and industry."[48] Garvey further stated that UNIA accepted as real the rights of all people, no matter their race: "To us, the white race has a right to the peaceful possession and occupation of countries of its own and in like manner, the yellow and black races have their rights. It is only by an honest and liberal consideration of such rights can the world be blessed with the peace that is sought by Christian teachers and leaders [*sic*]."[49]

Deeply convinced that a dominant White society would never accept Black Americans as equals, Garvey advocated for an unhindered and independent environment where African Americans would appropriate the freedom to realize their potentials within the United States. Under the aegis of the UNIA, African Americans started small businesses, including children's toy companies, eating houses, grocery stores, and publishing businesses. It was Garvey's intent to carve out a separate business space controlled by African Americans. In other words, he fully realized Washington's approach and its implications. He desired to replicate it and build a world movement based on his economic philosophy of accommodation and separation from White America.

Garvey was persuaded that his friend Washington wanted to make the best of what the United States promised for African Americans and the rest of the Black diaspora. As we have seen, the Back-to-Africa movement was not a new idea; fellow travelers like Paul Cuffee, Chief Sam, Martin Robinson Delany, and Bishop Henry McNeil Turner, among others, had pursued similar aspirations in the past. Yet Garvey was unique in his strategies and his passion for strengthening Liberia, not as a colonial enclave, as the ACS intended, but as a foothold on the continent where the diaspora Africans would congregate to turn Africa around for the twentieth-century world. Unlike Du Bois, who promoted Pan-Africanism through academic congresses, Garvey created a populist message that resonated with the masses across the American and African continents.

GARVEYISM AND LIBERIA

Garvey designed elaborate plans for sending Black Americans to Liberia. Following the European scramble for and partition of Africa in the 1880s, Liberia and Ethiopia were the only African nations that had managed to evade European imperial control. Liberia was, for Garvey, a metaphor for independence and freedom, and a base for other projects aimed at securing the continent against outside pillage. His "Africa for Africans" slogan was, in reality, a declaration against colonial control, and his next plan was to plant his philosophy and missionary creed on the continent.

Garvey's elaborate blueprint for Liberia focused on building the African nation through the technical assistance of Blacks in the African diaspora. Other Black leaders, including Edward Wilmot Blyden, Delany (the abolitionist), and Washington, all dreamt of building a robust African nation. Washington actively worked to advance technical assistance to Africans by using the finance capital of the German imperialists to grow cotton in the West African country of Togo. As Washington explained the Togo mission later, "The instruction of black people in the principles of 'a higher moral life' involved showing the black Africans how to raise 'better sheep' or to create superior cotton cultivation methods."[50] What was innovative in the Garvey plan was the deployment of the UNIA's financial resources to commission projects and infrastructure such as roads, bridges, schools, and universities in the Republic of Liberia as symbols of freedom and strength in the African world.

In 1920, Garvey's plan met with the support of Liberia's president and secretary of state, both of West Indian background. Considering the country's economic woes at this time—including a debilitating foreign debt that threatened its sovereignty, rampant corruption, and misappropriation of public monies—Garvey could not have chosen a less likely base for his project.[51] UNIA earmarked $2 million to provide the initial 20,000–30,000 families with capital and appropriate professional skills in agriculture and industry. Each family was to have a minimum of $1,500 and every single person without a family at least $500. The settlers were to make a vow to abide by the laws and authority of Liberia as a sovereign nation.[52]

Additionally, Garvey offered to help defray Liberia's foreign debt, estimated at $5 million, in exchange for lands close to the River Cavalla, where he intended to settle the American émigrés. Liberia's president, Charles D. B. King, who was already negotiating with the U.S. government for a $5 million loan, welcomed the idea, and Garvey sent some of his officials to Liberia to examine the areas and prepare grounds for the settlers. Meanwhile, as a consequence of the U.S. Senate's decision to decline Liberia's loan request, Firestone Rubber Company provided a solution to the country's impending insolvency with a $15 million grant to Liberia.[53] In return, Firestone received generous concessions in 1926 to set up rubber plantations in Liberia, a move envisioned to upend British monopoly of the international rubber market. In other words,

Liberia would supply rubber to the expanding American automobile industry.[54] The growing permeation of U.S. financial capital in Liberia overlapped
with increasing interest among Pan-Africanists in Liberia's affairs. Du Bois, like
Garvey, watched keenly as the U.S. government failed to offer any meaningful
help to its African colony, while taking advantage of the financial crisis to exploit Liberia's few natural resources.

A document dated May 2, 1924, and credited to James J. Dossen, an official
of the UNIA, discloses that Du Bois had taken advantage of the presence of
Liberia's president in Washington, D.C., to secure an appointment as the U.S.
government's representative to President King's second-term inauguration,
planned for January 1, 1924. When the details of this development emerged, it
brought about an unforeseen consequence for UNIA. On the arrival of the experts and engineers of the UNIA in Liberia to execute the work of preparing for
the colonists, President King instructed his security officials to apprehend and
deport the team. The harrowing truth is that Du Bois was in collaboration with
the U.S. State Department to sabotage Garvey's efforts in Liberia. State Department records dated December 26, 1924, prove that Du Bois was empowered
to undermine Garvey's work as special representative and envoy of the U.S.
government.[55] In Liberia, Du Bois told everyone that UNIA was a serious threat
to the Americo-Liberian political elite and that Garvey had a secret agenda to
take over Liberia.[56]

At this point, it is not clear that the African American elite as a group was
jealous of Garvey, and even more intriguing is the reason behind Du Bois's
attempt to frustrate Garvey's UNIA from gaining a foothold in Liberia. The
campaign against Garvey also involved colorist attacks directed toward Garvey's
darker skin color. In an article entitled "The Madness of Marcus Garvey" in the
March 1923 issue of the *Messenger*, Robert Bagnall, the field secretary of the
NAACP, called for Garvey's deportation, depicting him as a "Jamaican Negro
of unmixed stock, squat, stocky, fat and sleek with protruding jaws, and heavy
jowls, small bright pig-like eyes and rather bull-dog like face. Boastful, egotistical, tyrannical, intolerant, cunning shifty, smooth and suave, avaricious and
devoid of intellectual argument."[57]

It is not as if everything Garvey did was pleasing to his audience; in fact,
some of his troubles were self-inflicted and stemmed from rash decisions. For
instance, after Garvey met with a leader of the Ku Klux Klan (KKK) named
Edward Young Clarke in Atlanta in June 1922, he declared that the UNIA and
KKK shared a common goal: to separate Black and White societies. Dana Johnson, who has studied incidents of strange alliances between White suprema-
cists and Black nationalists, notes, "With some logic, then, Garvey admired

the Ku Klux Klan for its explicit recognition of the incompatibility of the races. By joining forces, the two could quicken the polarization of America and the subsequent exodus of blacks to 'Motherland Africa.'"[58]

Garvey further lauded racial segregation laws because they were suitable for building Black-owned businesses.[59] Nothing good came out of this overreach except a growing criticism from his opponents as well as admirers. The NAACP spread the rumor that the KKK had commissioned Garvey to destroy the NAACP. Of course, one wonders why Garvey would agree to such a proposal with an organization that killed, raped, and hurt Black people. It is possible that the NAACP deliberately wanted to ruin Garvey's career, but the meeting provided the NAACP and Du Bois an opportunity to launch some of the most vicious attacks on Garvey. In an article published in *Crisis* magazine in May 1924, Du Bois branded Garvey "the worst enemy of the Black race." He also called Garvey a monumental and persistent liar: "Marcus Garvey is, without doubt, the most dangerous enemy of the Negro race in America and in the world. He is either lunatic or a traitor." With a note of finality, Du Bois declared that "the American Negroes have endured this wretch all too long with fine restraint and every effort at cooperation and understanding. But the end has come. Every man who apologizes for or defends Marcus Garvey from this date forth writes himself down as unworthy of the countenance of decent Americans."[60] In the February 1923 issue of *Century Magazine* Du Bois further compared Garvey to a character in Eugene O'Neill's 1920 play *The Emperor Jones*.[61] In the play, Brutus Jones came across as a confident Black man who went to jail for murdering a fellow Black in a dice game. Later, Jones escaped and took refuge on a small island in the Caribbean, where he amassed wealth and installed himself as "emperor." This was an interesting ridicule and characterization of Garvey by Du Bois.

A response from Garvey, in the form of an editorial published in the *Negro World* on February 17, 1923, described Du Bois as an "unfortunate mulatto who bewails every day the drop of Negro blood in his veins."[62] Garvey charged that Du Bois arrogated the privilege of "criticizing and condemning other people, but held himself up as the social unapproachable and the great I am of the Negro race."[63] He would go on to accuse Du Bois of being a self-hating Black founder of the NAACP who preferred the company of White people. He further alleged that Du Bois "likes to dance with white people and dine with them and sometimes sleep with them" because of his way of seeing all that was black as ugly and all that was white as beautiful. Garvey concluded that "very light-skinned Negroes" led by Du Bois were the enemies of colonization of Africa. He charged that his enemies, including "the black leadership and politicians, and those of the white race," wanted him to be discredited and imprisoned "to please their Negro political wards."[64]

In a study of Liberia as an ideological battleground between Du Bois and Garvey, the Sierra Leone historian Thamba E. M'bayo underlines the harsh reality with the observation that Pan-Africanism, as manifested in Liberia by both Garvey and Du Bois, "was a flawed and impractical project laden with Western cultural hierarchies. Consequently, the task of implementing it proved to be a botched project mainly because, as an ideological construct, Pan-Africanism misjudged the convolution of human situations when the politics of race, identity, and nationality all blended on a single stage."[65] To M'bayo's point, it is essential to reiterate that the fight between Garvey and Du Bois had little or nothing to do with their slight differences in ideology. Instead, the problem stemmed from a personality clash exacerbated by notions of prestige, self-interest, and ideas of superiority predicated on skin color. In other words, a lighter-skinned Du Bois assumed superiority over a darker-skinned Garvey.

One cannot but observe that the real victim of this fight between Garvey and Du Bois was the interests of the Black world they aspired to protect. It is a paradox that Du Bois led a small group of African American elite who worked with the U.S. government to truncate the visions Garvey held for Africa. The highly disappointed author of an editorial in the *Gold Coast Leader* of Cape Coast, Ghana, on July 19, 1924, sharply criticized Du Bois's attitude as follows: "We regret exceedingly that there should be this exhibition of ill-temper in the eyes of the whole world on the part of the distinguished, refined, and cultured editor of *The Crisis* upon one of the most vital issues that have ever engaged the attention of the race to which he belongs."[66]

It would be interesting to know whether Du Bois came to regret his tirade against Garvey, especially after he expressed severe bitterness against the government of the United States in a controversial speech in Peiping (now Beijing), China, in 1959: "in my own country for nearly a century I have been nothing but a nigger."[67] Two years later, Du Bois exiled himself to Ghana, where he died on August 27, 1963. While the Peiping speech summed up Du Bois's lifelong struggle for race emancipation, his self-exile to Ghana, at the age of ninety-three, was an unspoken validation of Garvey's Back-to-Africa campaign. It is telling that Du Bois's benefactor and friend, President Kwame Nkrumah, adopted Garvey's flag for the Black Star Line as Ghana's national emblem. Additionally, Garvey's slogans, including "Africa for Africans" and "one nation, one people," along with his other Pan-Africanist ideas, reflect his influence on a new generation of West Africans, who appreciated his thoughts and tried to recreate them across the continent.

TAKING STOCK OF GARVEY'S INFLUENCE IN AFRICA

In retrospect, one may conclude that the long list of problems that upended Garvey's Back-to-Africa movement was complex. The stark reality remains that if indeed the U.S. government was honest in its dealings with the colony of Liberia and the welfare of African Americans it encouraged to go there, it could not have missed an enormous opportunity to assist the province by supporting Garvey's UNIA with the materials and resources he needed to make the colony a success. Despite the affinity of his organization's goals with the African colonization effort, it is ironic that the government worked hard to sabotage and frustrate Garvey in Liberia. Also, UNIA's lack of critical support from the African American educated elite led to a lack of interest among Blacks in the United States in returning to Africa. A weak economy and the threat of bankruptcy for the Black Star Line forced Garvey to look for members who would pay membership dues to UNIA. His desperate flirtation with the Ku Klux Klan was primarily intended to help launch a recruitment campaign in the South, where he was unable to penetrate because of strong White resistance.

After several years of clandestine operations shadowing Garvey, in an attempt to deport him as an undesirable alien, the U.S. Department of Justice (which spawned the Federal Bureau of Investigation in 1908) arrested Garvey for mail fraud in 1922.[68] Details of the charges and their validity are unclear, but one of the charges was that Garvey broke the law by attempting to sell stock in the dying Black Star Line through the mail, referencing a vessel identified by its future name, S.S. *Phyllis Wheatley*, and another ship called S.S. *Orion*, which the BSL did not own. In his "Statement of Arrest" in January 1922, Garvey alleged, "Others of my race oppose me because they fear my influences among the people, and they judge me from their own corrupt, selfish consciences. There is an old adage that says, 'A thief does not like to see another man carrying a bag,' and thus the dishonest ones of our preachers and politicians believing that I am of their stamp, try to embarrass me by framing me up with the law."[69]

At his trial in 1923, the evidence showed that there was no strong case of fraud to warrant his imprisonment. Nonetheless, the jury found him guilty and sentenced Garvey to prison. In 1927, President Calvin Coolidge commuted his sentence, released him from jail, and subsequently deported him to Jamaica. Garvey died in London on June 10, 1940, but his message remained with the new African elite, to whom he was never a forgotten man. The *West African Pilot*—arguably one of the most influential nationalist mouthpieces in Africa, owned and edited by Nnamdi Azikiwe, the Nigerian nationalist leader and first president of the country—honored Garvey with a fitting tribute: "If Europe and America were made for the white races and Asia for the yellow races, then reasoned Marcus Garvey, Africa must have been made by God for the black races, hence he taught the religion of Pan-Africanism or the doctrine of 'Africa for the Africans.' Despite the fact that he was one of the few people in the world who suffered persecution from high and low, because of their opinion and beliefs, yet it is with pride that we remember Marcus Garvey because he was the fountain from which sprung other more scientific and effective ideas of Pan-Africanism. His memory should be revered by all who believe in the future of Africans."[70]

Various scholars have provided some assessment of Garvey's influence in Africa despite the difficulty in collecting materials related to the movement. In their separate studies, Hollis R. Lynch and J. A. Langley noted that the philosophy of racial consciousness starting with Edward Wilmot Blyden and Du Bois's book *The Negro in America* attained its apogee with the Garvey movement.[71] Despite his unbridled ambition to be known as the Provisional President of Africa, which casts his overall intentions in doubt, the truth is that Garvey made race consciousness a mass movement in the Atlantic world. He spoke a language with which the people could immediately identify. One critical lesson the Garvey movement taught the Africans was the imperative of "organizing an African Brotherhood," as noted by a *Times of Nigeria* editorial on March 1, 1920.[72] Garvey's "Africa for Africa" movement captured the imagination of Africans because, by the 1920s, the sociopolitical and psychological climate engendered by European imperialist aggression favored Garveyism. Rina L. Okonkwo's 1980 study "The Garvey Movement in British West Africa" notes that the Garveyist enthusiasts were many, and that often the movement and the rhetoric it conveyed found intricate bonding with preexisting cultural associations in Sierra Leone, Liberia, Nigeria, and the Gold Coast.[73]

In Nigeria, Garveyism attracted more supporters than in any other West African country. Along with S. M. Abiodun and Rev. W. E. Euba, one of the leaders of the movement in Nigeria was Akinbami Agbebi, who developed strong American ties after his visit to the United States in 1903.[74] Agbebi joined the Garvey movement as a student in America in 1919, and after his return to Lagos, he became an agent of the Black Star Line. After securing the license to register the BSL in Nigeria, Agbebi in 1921 announced the sale of over $100,000 of shares costing $5 each. Agbebi was skeptical about Garvey's one-African government, but fascinated by his industrialization plan for Africa. Unfortunately, Garvey never set foot on African soil. Celebrating her husband's ideology and its relation to Africa's freedom from colonial subjugation in 1960, Amy Jacques Garvey noted that Marcus Garvey "was always denied entry to any territory, and warned that he was an agitator and would suffer grave consequences if he were discovered there in disguise; so the dearest wish of his heart was not accomplished. . . . So it was with gratification and joy that I received a cabled invitation from the Nigerian government to attend the inaugural ceremonies of the installation of Nnamdi Azikiwe as Governor-General [of Nigeria] in November 1960."[75]

In Sierra Leone, Garveyism brought a group of Americans together to support the BSL in 1920. The group sponsored several fundraising events in Freetown, including a harvest sale and a concert held on July 11–12, 1920. Headed by President J. E. Casely Hayford's wife, Adelaide, the female group planned to build a technical school for girls in Freetown, but met with opposition from male members of UNIA because the organization had a gender-specific activity for young people that was supposed to lead them to adulthood. In fact, the Freetown branch of UNIA was strong enough to send a representative to a convention held in New York from August 1 to 30, 1920.[76]

With its racialist policies and practices modeled on those of the United States, South Africa was perhaps the most evident site of the Garveyite impact.[77] Here, American-educated leaders such as James Thaele, the president of the African National Congress (Cape Western Province) and a graduate of Lincoln University in Pennsylvania, adopted imageries of Black America and the Garveyist ideology as vital features of his war against racial segregation.[78] On May 24, 1921, the South African state police massacred more than 200 followers of Enoch Mgijima's religious sect known as the Israelites at Ntabelanga, a suburb about twenty-five miles from Queenstown, where they had been waiting for an approaching millennium as instructed by their leader.[79] The sect suspected of planning a rebellion against the oppressive White minority rule was an offshoot of the Church of God and the Saints of Christ, founded by African American missionaries in the Cape in the late nineteenth century. Bishop William Saunders Crowdy established the church in 1896, which was first known as the Black Hebrew Israelite religious group in Lawrence, Kansas. After the death of Crowdy, the church moved its headquarters to Belleville, Virginia, in 1921, claimed adherence to the tenets of Judaism, and heartily espoused a belief in the equality of all men and women. W. Oliphant, Johnson Plaatjie, and others led the Church of Christ expansion to Cape Town, South Africa, with the critical support of native South Africans such as Charles Sigxabayi and Bishop James Limba.[80]

As the economic powerhouse of the entire southern African region, South Africa became a regional base for the expansion of Garveyism through the presence of migrant laborers, students, and visitors from adjoining colonial territories. The developments in the region mostly piqued the U.S. government because of the strategic interest of the USSR in South Africa, as apartheid polarized African society along racial lines. It is interesting that Garveyism fared favorably in its aspiration to assume the leadership of the Black proletariat under the Pan-African Congress in the interwar years, despite the fact that the Communist International (Comintern, or Third International) was better organized and more extensive.[81] It could not match the UNIA in terms of mass appeal. As Michael West observed, the "race first" message propagated by the UNIA and "its insistence that racism and white supremacy were the principal sources of black misery" everywhere obviously struck a more significant chord in the heads of the Africans than the Comintern's anticapitalist propaganda.[82]

Through Cape Town, the epicenter of UNIA activities in the entire southern Africa subregion, Garveyism infiltrated colonial Zimbabwe (known as Southern Rhodesia until 1980). It was in Cape Town that migrant laborers from Southern Rhodesia formed several ethnic associations inspired by Garveyism, among them the African Universal Benefit Society. The society became a source of concern to the colonial officials in mid-1923, when one Southern Rhodesian official reported that it was working "in conjunction with the American Improvement Society and the Industrial Commercial Union at Cape Town." Garveyist agitation also provoked hysteria among European missionaries in colonial Zimbabwe. In 1930, for example, a Jesuit priest in Manicaland, Father Jerome O'Hea, complained to his superior that Manyika migrants in Johannesburg, "probably all rotten Christians," had sent "unsigned letters to boys about here [on the mission station] to stir up protests at the church on Sunday and to get the [African] teachers on their side against the use of Chizezuru books."[83] It is essential to point out that Manyika, Zezuru, Budya, Korekore, and Karanga dialects all belong to the Shona language and are therefore similar. However, the colonial officials promoted Zezuru, spoken widely around Salisbury (now Harare), over the supposedly marginal Manyika, Karenga, and Korekore. This intra-ethnic dynamic was the primary issue that led to the Manyika protest in 1930.

Indeed, the assertions of a member of the all-European Legislative Assembly in Southern Rhodesia toward Garveyism and other similar nationalist agitations in 1980 reveals the official approach of colonial authorities. In disparaging "the awakening of the native to race consciousness," the official described Garveyism as a "colour question" that could not be ignored because of Garvey's statement that the Blacks were waiting for an "opportunity to draw the sword for Africa's redemption."[84] "That is what Marcus Garvey said. We can say that he is a raving fanatic and that we ignore him. But every big movement of change in the world that has taken place has been the result of the ravings of a fanatic, as they were called, and ignored in their own day; but history has shown what the ravings of a so-called fanatic are capable of. The seed is sown and it develops."[85]

In the end, Garvey's legacies became a widespread source of inspiration for anticolonial agitators as colonial rule entrenched itself in Africa. New generations of Africans who read the *Negro World* as students began early to question the legitimacy of the European colonial presence in Africa. As a student in the United States in the 1920s, Nkrumah expressed his admiration of Garvey, and he would honor him in 1957 when he became the first postcolonial leader of the West African country.[86] Thus, although the African colonial rulers prevented the Garvey movement from ushering in an independence movement in the 1920s, Garveyism played a significant role in providing African nationalists and future postcolonial leaders with much-needed psychological preparation for waging the fight for independence. Among the African nationalists who embraced the Garveyist philosophy are Kwame Nkrumah of Ghana (president 1957), Jomo Kenyatta of Kenya (prime minister 1960, president 1964), Nnamdi Azikiwe of Nigeria (governor-general 1960), and Kenneth Kaunda of Zambia (president 1964).

7

THE PAN-AFRICANIST IDEA

Perhaps one of the greatest "gifts" the African diaspora bequeathed to the race is the Pan-Africanist idea. The construction of this philosophical heritage began the moment the first slave ship left the West African Coast in the fifteenth century and continues today. Given that every theme of the African and African diaspora exchanges reflects some element of Pan-Africanism, treating the subject as a separate chapter in a book of this nature may come across as repetitive or redundant, but it is also apposite. In a general sense, Pan-Africanism reflects the sentiment that as a race, African descendants have a great deal in common and that these commonalities are a source of unity, strength, survival, and pride, and are, therefore, worthy of celebration. Thus, a mutual concern for the welfare of the Black race is a common thread that connects all the different fabrics of the United States-Africa dialogue.

The forcible exploitation of African labor in the Americas, the rise of abolitionist agitations that led to the founding of the colonies of Sierra Leone and Liberia, the Back-to-Africa movement, the growth of the American missionary enterprise, and so on—all have serious implications for the condition of the Black race. These events also provide serious incentives to the evolutionary growth of different brands and stages of Pan-Africanism. In other words, every episode of sociocultural, economic, and political experience related to slavery, marginality, incorporation, and survival in the Americas depicts multiple layers and idioms of Pan-Africanism. The complexity and scope of what may be included in the broad subject of Pan-Africanist thinking explain why some scholars and practitioners see the concept as an idea, or a struggle and a process toward a goal that has come and gone, rather than a single historical episode often appropriated as a political or sociocultural movement. Colin Legum points out that Pan-Africanism may be conceived of as the "emotions of the Black people," but then adds that "although it is possible to talk about the way Pan-Africanism expresses itself, it is not so easy to give a concise definition of this relatively new recruit to the world's political vocabulary. Pan-Africanism has come to be used by both its protagonists and its antagonists as if it were a declaration of political principles. It is not."[1]

Other scholars have expressed similar ambivalence. In his insightful study of the phenomenon, P. Olisawuche Esedebe notes that no other movement has attracted more differing interpretations than Pan-Africanism. African thinkers have variously interpreted Pan-Africanism as synonymous with self-government, avoidance of internal conflicts, African personality, Négritude, continental African unity, and even an ideology of African foreign policy or engagement with the postcolonial global order.[2] In other words, Pan-Africanism is all of these things and more, depending on whom you ask. Its political idiom, as articulated by the chief Pan-Africanist purveyors such as W. E. B. Du Bois, Marcus Moriah Garvey, and Kwame Nkrumah, demonstrate that the heart of Pan-Africanism in the twentieth century was to claim a unified and robust territory where all people of African descent would pursue their dreams without alien hindrances.[3] In 1924, Garvey lucidly emphasized the imperative for Africa's self-determination in "Aims and Objectives of Movement for Solution of Negro Problem": to make the Black race better in every respect of life. To this regard, Garvey believed that creating "a Nation in Africa" for all people of African descent would be the right starting point. His sense was that emigration of the African diaspora back to Africa would resolve the race conflict inherent in the Americas and other places where Blacks had to compete with Whites for position and power.[4] Of course, this interpretation remained relevant across different eras and historical contexts, but not all Black leaders agreed with Garvey.

Pan-Africanism emerged as a natural response to slavery, racism, mental anguish, material exploitation, colonial domination, and the consequent state of arrested development these historical trends have left on African people wherever they may live. The pioneers of the ideology include Black patriots and thinkers like Paul Cuffee, Henry Turner, Lott Carey, Edward Blyden, Alexander Crummell, and W. E. B. Du Bois, along with their descendants such as Garvey, Nnamdi Azikiwe, Nkrumah, and Julius Nyerere. They all talked about Africa's regeneration as a step toward addressing the centuries of degradation brought upon Africa by alien activities. For example, on his way to Liberia in 1821, Rev. Lott Carey (1780–1828), who became the first African American missionary to Africa under the American Baptist Foreign Missions Society of Richmond, Virginia, declared that "I am an African and in this country, however meritorious my conduct and respectable my character, I cannot receive the credit due to either. I wish to go to a country where I shall be estimated by my merits not by my complexion, and I feel bound to labor for my suffering race."[5]

Carey's feeling resonates with similar Pan-Africanist thoughts expressed by John Kizzell (a South Carolina slave who returned to Sierra Leone to fight the evil trade), Turner, Crummell, Blyden, and many others who saw no bright future for Blacks in postemancipation America.[6] Writing in 1923 in *Philosophy and Opinions*, Garvey predicted that "with the rising ambition of the Negro, if a country is not provided for him in another 50 or 100 years, there will be a terrible clash that will end disastrously to him and disgrace our civilization."[7] While one may look back today and say that the fear harbored by most Black thinkers of this period was wrong, it is also true, as L. G. E. Edmondson observed, that "Americans, black and white, have yet to give a final answer to this prediction."[8]

Since the Pan-Africanist ideology permeates all facets of the United States-Africa exchanges, it is pertinent to highlight the concept further as a catalyst for Africa's survival in an international community of super-powerism and realpolitik, where military strength makes right and the weak are subject to the whims and caprices of the strong. Pan-Africanism was the cement that brought people of African descent to forge a strong web of an "imagined community": a platform on which the Africans advocated for an end to the common problems that afflicted the Black race.[9] The historian Nikhil Pal Singh has argued that the importance of Black intellectuals in the creation of this "black counter-public sphere," which brought a profound counterhegemonic discourse to imperialistic claims, "cannot be underestimated."[10] For instance, when King Leopold II's agents in the Congo oppressed the natives with all manner of affliction and death, it was the African American intellectual George Washington Williams who addressed the matter in an open letter to the Belgian monarch in 1890. Williams expressed his anxiety about the heinous crimes going on in the Congo as a colossal disappointment coming against the backdrop of "the fostering care" and "benevolent enterprise" the king had promised to bring to the Africans. "Instead of the natives of the Congo adopting the fostering care of your Majesty's Government, they everywhere complain that their land has been taken from them by force; that the Government is cruel and arbitrary, and declare that they neither love nor respect the Government and its flag. Your Majesty's Government has sequestered their land, burned their towns, stolen their property, enslaved their women and children, and committed other crimes too numerous to mention in detail."[11] Through their efforts, the Black intellectuals in the diaspora created "the web of disporan identities and concerns" that the historian Paul Gilroy identified as "the Black Atlantic."[12] The web, spanning several centuries and transcending the physical separation imposed by the ocean, "drew together the domestic and foreign theaters of the race revolution."[13]

The primary interest here is to highlight the role played by the Pan-Africanist idea in the emergence of anticolonial nationalist movements in Africa from 1900, when the first Pan-African Conference took place in London, to the 1960s, when most African countries regained independence from colonial rule. Although talked about a great deal, this role is still very vague, and its history is complicated. Some observers have been content with the exploratory if not cautious account by W. E. B. Du Bois.[14] Others, more inclined to socialist ideals, have applauded the more detailed work by George Padmore, who advocated for Pan-African Socialism in Africa.[15]

EARLY BEGINNINGS

Writing in the early twenty-first century, Cornell University scholar Don C. Ohadike argues that Pan-Africanism as an idea and a movement has its roots on board the first slave ships that departed from West Africa in the fifteenth century. Although this assertion may seem too optimistic, Ohadike insists that the language barrier that confronted the captive people and the threat of enslavement on foreign soil convinced them that forging a common unity was the only way to survive the Middle Passage and all that servitude on the other side of the Atlantic portended for them.[16] Yet, one is inclined to agree with Horace Campbell that at this early stage, it was impossible for Pan-Africanism "to have the same nationalist appeal embracing all classes and strata as did the appeal made in the constitutional decolonization and armed struggles."[17] Enslaved Africans in the early period responded to the Pan-Africanist message in a variety of ways, including riots, rebellions, escape, homicides, and suicides on and off the slave ships. Such responses continued throughout the period of slavery and led to the formation of the Maroon communities in the Caribbean and North, South, and Central America. In addition, the relentless plantation uprisings inculcated in the enslaved people the principal lessons of resistance and dignity.

The next stage in the evolutionary process of Pan-Africanism resides in historical developments in the Atlantic world starting in 1787. Among these is the founding of the Sierra Leone colony, which provided a strong incentive for a higher level of racial consciousness. In America, this period witnessed the effective beginning of organized abolitionism and organized activities by free African Americans as a direct response to the successes of abolitionists in Britain.

Among the influential abolitionists in England were emancipated slaves of African descent. This group included people who were initially enslaved in the Americas, those brought to Britain as slaves, and those who secured their freedom (either by paying for it or by being manumitted). These individuals availed themselves of Western education, and many were self-taught, including Ottobah Cugoano and Gustavus Vassa (also known as Olaudah Equiano). These educated Africans developed a body of ideas and an intellectual tradition that provided the basis for the later emergence of Pan-Africanism. After their generation had died out, free African Americans in the United States, most of them Christian ministers, carried on the struggle from about 1830.

In West Africa, the founding of Sierra Leone and Liberia prepared the stage for the rise of modern intellectual elites in British West Africa. Prominent among the West African educated elite were the recaptives who were rescued by the British Navy and resettled in Sierra Leone. The recaptives received education and Christianity as part of the resettlement program. The 1850s then saw the emergence of Edward W. Blyden, who, like George Padmore after him, was of West Indian origin. Blyden lived most of his life in Liberia and Sierra Leone, and it was there that he met the only African author of stature of that time: James Beale (better known as Africanus Beale Horton), a Sierra Leonean writer and physician of Igbo stock.[18]

In other words, abolitionist movements on both sides of the Atlantic in the late eighteenth century helped to produce those modern elites in the New World and Africa. Through the benefit of their Western-style education, these elites began articulating a Pan-Africanist ideology that also critiqued twentieth-century political currents and actions in the United States and Europe. This crop of Black intellectuals picked up the mantle in response to the opportunities offered by the founding of the Liberian colony and the Back-to-Africa movement of the nineteenth century to push for the ideals of Pan-African consciousness.[19]

Beside the West Indian Black celebrity Edward Blyden, Martin Robinson Delany (1812–1885) and Alexander Crummell were among the most notable early Pan-Africanist ideologues. Delany was proud of Black people's African ancestry. Frederick Douglass once said of Delany, "I have always thanked God for making me a Man, but Martin Delany always thanked God for making him a black man."[20] Delany and Crummell emphasized the commonalities between Africans and diaspora Blacks everywhere. The adverse racial climate of post–Civil War America led Delany and other prominent Black leaders to believe it was impossible for Blacks to cohabit with Whites and prosper among them. Thus, they called on African Americans to secede from the United States and establish their own nation.[21] In a similar tone, Crummell and Blyden, both contemporaries of Delany, perceived Africa as the right location for the new nation promoted by Delany. The nineteenth-century Christian missionary movement predicated on the Theory of Providential Design convinced the Black patriots to acquiesce in the idea that Africans in the Americas should return to their homelands and convert and civilize the inhabitants there.[22]

It was in the early twentieth century that Pan-Africanism took a well-defined form. Still under the tutelage of African descendants in the African diaspora, Henry Sylvester Williams (1869–1911), the respected Trinidadian lawyer, convened a conference in Westminster Hall, London, from July 23 to 25, 1900, to "protest stealing of lands in the colonies, racial discrimination and deal with other issues of interest to Blacks."[23] W. E. B. Du Bois, who was a primary facilitator of the London conference, played a significant role in drafting a letter to the British monarch and other European rulers appealing to them to fight racism and grant independence to their colonies.

It is uncertain to what extent the early nineteenth-century Pan-Africanist idea contributed to the First Universal Races Congress (FURC) of 1911 held in London, which was attended by Du Bois, John Tengo Jabavu (the legendary South African political activist and editor of the first newspaper published in Xhosa), and Walter Benson Rubusana (the first African elected to the Cape Council in 1909 and cofounder of the nationalist newspaper *Izwi Labantu*, also in Xhosa). The 1911 FURC was significant because it brought together people of all races to discuss ways of creating understanding between people of the East and the West and abridging inequality among peoples. Led by Philip Stanhope, the conveners of the meeting declared that its mission was:

> To discuss, in the light of science and modern conscience, the general relations between the peoples of the West and those of the East, between the so-called "white" and the so-called "colored" peoples, with a view to encouraging between them a fuller understanding, the most friendly feelings, and the heartier co-operation. . . . The interchange of material and other wealth between the races of mankind has of late years assumed such dimensions that the old attitude of distrust and aloofness is giving way to a genuine desire for a closer acquaintanceship. Out of this interesting situation has sprung the idea of holding a Congress where the representatives of the different races might meet each other face to face, and might, in friendly rivalry, further the cause of mutual trust and respect between the Occident and Orient, between the so-called "white" peoples and the so-called "colored" peoples.[24]

For the African American and South African delegates to the convention, the themes of understanding, racial friendship, trust, and respect resonated with the wider Pan-Africanist struggle.

Figure 7.1. W. E. B. Du Bois. *Special
Collections and University Archives, University
of Massachusetts Amherst Libraries.*

In 1919, Du Bois (Fig. 7.1) emerged as Pan-Africanism's most eloquent catalyst
and prolific propagandist. His leadership proved important because many of the
torchbearers from the first Pan-African Congress—convened by the Trinidadian
barrister Henry Sylvester Williams in Paris from July 23 to 25, 1900—had passed
away. Henry Sylvester Williams died in 1911, and Edward W. Blyden followed
1912. Then three Pan-Africanist giants—Henry McNeal Turner, Booker T. Washington, and Benito Sylvain—all died in 1915. James Johnson, a Nigerian nationalist, and Alexander Walters, an African American president of the Pan-African
Association of 1900, also passed away. The long list of deaths also included another Nigerian nationalist and friend of Du Bois, Rev. Majola Agbebi.[25]

THE AGE OF W. E. B. DU BOIS AND
ORGANIZED CONGRESSES

In this context, Du Bois emerged as the father of Pan-Africanism, primarily
through his ability to facilitate organized Pan-African congresses. He pressed on

with his first Pan-African Congress in Paris, France. The distinction between the 1900 conference and the 1919 meeting convened by Du Bois with the support of Blaise Diagne (1872–1934), a Senegalese native elected to the French Chamber of Deputies in 1914, is that African students in Europe had the privilege to collaborate with others in the African diaspora. The involvement of the West African students in London opened a channel for the emergence of the next generation of Pan-Africanists: the African-born nationalist figures who would lead the charge for decolonization on the continent. Among them were J. E. Casely Hayford and Rev. Attoh Ahuma, both from the Gold Coast.[26] Their followers included well-known figures as Nnamdi Azikiwe and Kwame Nkrumah. Authors and politicians from French-speaking African countries, such as Léopold Senghor, the first president of independent Senegal, also emerged, mainly as exponents of the concept of Négritude. Educated as a poet in Paris during the Great Depression, Senghor became disillusioned about many aspects of European life, including the Western practice of capitalism. More important, he began to make closer contacts with African American, West Indian, and African writers, who helped sharpen his ideology of Négritude. In a broad and general sense, the term denotes "the black world in its historical being, in opposition to the West, and in this way resumes the total consciousness of belonging to the black race, as well as an awareness of the objective historical and sociological implications of that fact."[27]

The interwar years were a watershed in the growth of Pan-Africanism. Students such as Azikiwe, Nkrumah, Nyerere, and Mboya, who also turned out to be successful writers and politicians, provide some glimpse of the political evolution of Pan-Africanism in Africa and the ideological rift between the Monrovia and Casablanca schools of thought. While the Casablanca group, led by Ghana and Guinea, wanted a United States of Africa with one standing army, the Monrovia group, led by Nigerians, believed in the unity of Africans but rejected the United States of Africa idea as utopian.[28]

Meanwhile, like the first Pan-African Conference, the conferees at the subsequent meeting led by Du Bois in 1919 called on the colonial powers to consider independence for African nations. The Pan-Africanists repeated this request at meetings held in 1921 in London, Brussels, and Paris. The Pan-Africanists held two more meetings in London and Lisbon in 1923, followed by a major summit in New York in 1927. During each of these meetings, the leaders repeated and refined the imperatives of human rights and political and cultural freedom for the Africans. They built an increasingly strong case for their cause based on universal ideals. As already discussed in the preceding chapters, the twentieth century was the apex of the Pan-Africanist movement. Starting in the 1920s in

New York, Black cultural pride intertwined with the political narrative in the rise of the Harlem Renaissance.

Garvey was among the crème de la crème of the Harlem Renaissance, with his persistent campaigning for pride in black skin color and call for a return to Africa. His bold ideas were sometimes antithetical to Du Bois's more moderate views related to race and citizenship. In 1924, Garvey categorically declared that "the time has come for the Negro to look homeward [to Africa]." Then, in an apparent attack on Du Bois, Garvey continued: "The very light element of Negroes do not want to go back to Africa. They believe that in time, through miscegenation, the American race will be of their type. This is a fallacy and in that respect the agitation of the mulatto leader, W. E. B. Du Bois and the National Association for the Advancement of Colored People is dangerous to both races."[29]

Appraising Garvey's impact on Pan-African consciousness and his "magnetic and compelling personality" in Harlem, John Henrik Clarke concluded that Du Bois "was the most seriously considered and the most colorful of the numerous black Manassehs who presented themselves and their grandiose programs to the people of Harlem. Marcus Garvey's reaction to color prejudice and his search for a way to rise above it and lead his people back to Africa, spiritually if not physically, was the all-consuming passion of his existence."[30] Indeed, Garvey's pride in blackness inspired the francophone philosophy of Négritude, the Afrocentrism of Diop, and the Rastafarianism popularized by the Jamaican singer Bob Marley. From Harlem, hip-hop musicians of African descent embraced the newly found inspiration the period provided to not only explore, discover, and appropriate their connections with the African continent but to press colonial overlords to relinquish their vile grip on the African people.

One may argue that the most momentous of the Pan-African congresses was the Fifth Congress convened in Manchester, United Kingdom, in 1945. This meeting was especially significant because for the first time, rather than a handful of African students studying in European universities, in attendance were many Africans nationalists and political forces from the African continent. Among the attendees were committed Garveyists as well as Marxist ideologues from Africa. The latter backed the brand of communism espoused by Padmore. In a sense, which was not evident in the previous congresses, the outcome at Manchester reflected the ideological preferences of the Pan-Africanists.

If the purpose of the Universal Negro Improvement Association (UNIA) delegates at the Manchester summit was to resurrect Garvey's back-to-Africa dream, they were disappointed at the outcome of the meeting. P. Kevin Tunteng observes that while the Garveyists lacked Garvey's flamboyant oratorical skills and vision," "the dominant themes at the Congress were Marxian socialism and the colonial world."[31] The gathering generated impetus and momentum for the various post–World War II independence movements. The conveners of the meeting also proclaimed that those under colonial domination reserved the right, if no peaceful decolonization was feasible, to use force as a legal recourse to advance their struggle for self-determination. Summing up what transpired at Manchester in 1962, Jon Kraus argued: "In the period from 1900 to 1945, the demands of the movement passed from ameliorating the conditions of the African to responsible government, from self-government and independence to a United States of Africa. Not able to unite what did not exist, Africans then turned to agitating actively for independence in the years that followed."[32]

In what may serve as a powerful and fitting tribute to Du Bois and other Black patriots who led the movement from the African diaspora, Jason Parker has noted that the legal-political victories accomplished under the umbrella of Pan-Africanism "were in a sense the formalization of identities explored earlier by such visionary nonstate actors as W. E. B. Du Bois, who rallied black intellectuals to a globally conceived freedom struggle."[33]

UNDER THE LEADERSHIP OF THE EMERGENT AFRICAN NATIONALISTS

Indeed, the Pan-Africanist movement that started in the African diaspora formed the basis on which not only the anticolonial movement and decolonization gained traction in Africa, but also the eventual founding of the Organization of African Unity (OAU). In December 1958, following a meeting in April of the same year, Kwame Nkrumah, Ghana's first postcolonial president and African nationalist, summoned all the independent African nations to a meeting in Accra, Ghana's capital. In attendance were delegates from Egypt, Ethiopia, Liberia, Libya, Morocco, and Sudan. Du Bois also attended. He was ninety-one years old when he gave the plenary address. Nkrumah explicitly stated the primary purpose of the meeting: for African leaders to recommit their political assets and resources to supporting independence for the rest of the continent. The conference, which attracted more than 300 delegates of different political affiliations from across the continent, had a tremendous influence on anticolonial agitation in Africa, and the representatives whose countries were still under colonial domination went home to step up their anticolonial agitation.

By 1963, there were thirty-one independent African nations. This more than anything else proved to political observers that Pan-Africanism had evolved from an idea to a reality. However, the new reality also implicated the problem of divisions and power struggle within the movement in the form of the Casablanca and Monrovia groups. The first group, championed by Nkrumah, agitated for immediate continental political union. Nkrumah's Garveyist idea was informed by the same thought held by a host of Black Pan-Africanist leaders: that "for Blacks worldwide to change the paradigm of disrespect and exploitation we face daily, Africans in the Diaspora and the continent had to find effective ways to re-connect and work toward the unification of the continent into a giant country. That Union of African States would have the leverage in international relations to change for the better how Africans see themselves and how Africans are seen."[34]

The other group, led by Nigeria and Liberia, favored slower steps toward unity. A compromise grew out of exchanges between the two camps. The result was the OAU, which was formally signed into law in Addis Ababa, the Ethiopian capital, in May 1963.[35]

In the postcolonial order, a new generation of African thinkers and writers, among them Chinua Achebe, Wole Soyinka, Wa Thiong'o, and Bessie Head, gave a literary voice to common issues that touched every life on the continent. The Sixth Pan-African Congress, held at the behest of Julius Nyerere, took place in Dar es Salaam, Tanzania, in 1974. The congress identified three key objectives: (1) Broadening the international African community's understanding of the issues involved in the struggle in southern Africa, and methods of increasing the concrete base of support for the liberation movements. (2) Economic dependency and exploitation, and how to end them—including questions of self-reliance, systems of economic production and distribution, purposes of development, applications of science and technology, and economic cooperation among African states and communities. (3) Fulfillment of the potential of political independence; including the issues of African unity, Federation of Caribbean states, broadening mass participation in African political life, and political cooperation between African states and communities.[36]

The congress also raised another critical question, which touched on the economic development of Africa as a means of sustaining its newly found political freedom: "We believe that the future of Africans lies in the fullest utilization of our own human resources instead of continued dependency on loans and gifts from abroad . . . if we do not control the means of survival and protection in the context of the twentieth century, we will continue to be colonized." Simply stated, Nyerere and others who organized the meeting were troubled by Africa's economic dependence on its former colonial masters. It felt good to denounce imperialism, but what was needed was a continent-wide commitment to building Africa's economy using its abundant human and material resources to guarantee its "future development as free people."[37]

Overall, the Sixth Pan-African Congress reflected the spirit of Black movements across the African diaspora, which promoted pride in everything Black and resistance to White domination with Black separatist organizations, including Christian churches. The Dar es Salaam gathering hosted fifty-two delegates from Africa, the Caribbean, the Americas, Britain, and the Pacific. Irked by the OAU's lack of engagement with the African diaspora, the delegates restated the imperative of liberation and freedom for all people of African descent from all forms of domination around the world. In other words, the principles of self-reliance being stressed by intellectuals like Julius Nyerere imagined African freedom from colonial subjugation, and the meeting resolved to support the new wave of independence movements in Angola, Guinea-Bissau, Mozambique, Zimbabwe, and South Africa. Unfortunately, the delegates at the conference were unable to determine clear structures and logistics to advance such action.

The Seventh Pan-African Congress, organized under the theme "Facing the Future in Unity, Social Progress and Democracy," was the last. It took place in Kampala, Uganda, in April 1994—twenty years after the Dar es Salaam summit. It is notable that this event coincided with the end of apartheid in South Africa: the last bastion of colonial domination to collapse. South Africa under the apartheid regime had brought together various regions of the Black Atlantic since at least 1945. The summit took up the challenge of creating the fundamental structures necessary for the realization of the goals of the Pan-Africanist movement. One of the steps was to set up a permanent organizational structure to carry forward decisions taken at the meetings. In total, more than 2,000 participants took part in all of the activities organized by the congress, including the 800 official delegates representing Pan-African organizations from the entire Atlantic world. One of the highlights included the Women's Pre-Congress Meeting.

The Women's Pre-Congress Meeting was a historic one designed to address past efforts to exclude women. Before the Kampala meeting, some argued that if Pan-Africanism was to be relevant in the twenty-first century, it must break out of the male-centered mold that stressed the achievements of male leaders such as Marcus Garvey, W. E. B. Du Bois, George Padmore, C. L. R. James, Kwame Nkrumah, and Julius Nyerere. It is striking that while African women played a central role in the independence struggle and had been at the forefront of Pan-Africanism since the 1880s, male Pan-African leaders, either by commission or oversight, failed to duly acknowledge women's contributions.[38]

Other significant events were the cultural expressions at the Uganda National Theatre, the African Art Exhibition, the opening of Africa Freedom Park, and the congress itself. Three significant features of the congress were the successful hosting of the meeting in spite of the internal and external contradictions of the movement; the inauguration of the Pan-African Women's Liberation Organization; and the formation of a permanent Pan-African Secretariat. The debates and actions of the congress signaled a firm commitment to the idea that the Pan-African struggle was "one struggle, many fronts."[39]

Unfortunately, divisions within the membership of the organization persisted, and futile ideological debates and leadership struggles truncated its core ideas. At this point, several questions arose as to the future of the movement. The question remains as to whether Pan-Africanism was still a people's movement or whether its political leaders, motivated by parochial political interests and self-interests, had taken over the movement, leaving it with a privileged minority in sub-Saharan Africa who lacked the vision and the clout to sustain its prestige and ideals.

Although this question is difficult to answer definitively, it is essential to note that the crisis that undermined the cohesion and ideals of Pan-Africanism is not unique to Africa. Other broad-based and passionate political movements, such as the Arab League, the European Union, and even the United Nations, have suffered severe leadership crises. These organizations harbor diverse and sometimes opposing interests. When it comes to realizing the collective goals of Pan-Africanism, the contention was about the most viable strategy to achieve self-determination and freedom for Africa and people of African descent wherever they may be. The inability of the Seventh Congress to reconcile the inherent differences in the movement and to create a broad and open coalition of all citizens of African countries and the African diaspora committed to African liberation became its most significant failure. There were Pan-Africanists of all persuasions and ideologies: discredited socialists, advocates of Afrocentricism, grassroots elements, workers, urban youth, the homeless, members of the Nation of Islam, Christians, atheists, and so on. This broad spectrum of groups symbolized the changes that had taken place on a global scale since 1900. In other words, the context and message of the Pan-African struggle had changed, and so did the actors.

Although there were no further congresses after the Kampala event, Pan-Africanism remains a vital force for survival within Africa and the African diaspora as people of the African continent continue to push their culture and politics to the center of the global agenda. One of the lessons of the civil rights struggle in the United States in relation to anticolonial agitations in Africa is that the dangers confronting people of African descent around the world may change their manifestations, but they never completely disappear. A resilient spirit of Pan-Africanism provided a powerful front that saw African Americans through the dangerous eras of Jim Crow and the civil rights movement led by Martin Luther King, Jr. and his compatriots.

8

CULTURAL EXCHANGES AND TRANS-ATLANTIC BONDS: AFRICAN MUSIC AND THE EVOLUTION OF BLUES AND JAZZ

The subject of Black music and its African cultural roots is arguably one of the most engaging topics in contemporary Africana studies, cultural anthropology, and ethnomusicology. It is compelling because the record of successes attained by Black music artists across the world is one of the best testaments of African genius. Music and dance in the African world constitute a unique cultural invention that racial prejudice and oppression cannot smother. Rather than destroying it, American plantation slavery and its culture of despoliation strengthened Black music. Under slavery, music was not just a coping mechanism amid coercion; it was also a repertoire of knowledge, an intellectual tradition, and an outlet for those suppressed thoughts and emotions that found alternative expressive outlets in the forms of blues and jazz.

Academic interest in Black music as a field of analysis goes back to the early twentieth century, following the works of pioneering Black intellectuals such as W. E. B. Du Bois in the United States and Fernando Ortiz in Cuba. These writers were interested in the importation of African praxes to the Americas. In *The Souls of Black Folk,* Du Bois presented an engaging disquisition on the aesthetic threads and religious ideas that Africans in the United States retained from their African roots.[1] Concurrently with Du Bois, Ortiz completed a study of the customs of Cuba's diverse African ethnicities, which culminated in the publication of his controversial work *Hampa afro-cubana: Los negros brujos, apuntes para un estudio de etnología criminal (Afro-Cuban Underworld: The Black Sorcerers, Notes for a Study of Criminal Ethnography)* in 1906.[2] Although the initial focus of Ortiz's research was on what he perceived as delinquent behaviors identified with people of African origins in the nineteenth-century Cuban society of his time, he soon realized that oppression, poverty, exploitation, and criminality have no skin color and, therefore, are not unique to Blacks. Ortiz then shifted his attention to more scholarly inquiries into African cultural and intellectual values, strengths, and other contributions of African descendants to Cuba's national identity and global cultures. One of his related works is *Los bailes y el teatro de los negros en el folklore de Cuba* (*The Dances and Theater of Blacks in Cuban Folklore*).[3]

On the strength of Du Bois, Ortiz, and others whose studies focused on cultural retentions, African American cultural pride and tractions culminated in the Harlem Renaissance, the golden age of Black cultural revivals that began in the 1920s. At the same time, the anthropological works launched by Melville Jean Herskovits in the late 1920s aimed to dispel wrong notions that being African was synonymous with subordination and cultural limitations. As African Americans unleashed their creativity in the performing arts in cities like New York and Chicago, Herskovits's works, synchronized with those of other anthropologists, offered a global philosophy and system of sacred beliefs that established and affirmed that a continuum existed among African practices reinvented in the Americas. A worldwide network of scholars, including Ortiz (Cuba), Nina Rodríguez (Brazil), Gonzalo Aguirre Beltrán (Mexico), and Herskovits (United States), investigated African cultures and African-descended people in the Americas.[4] They extended their findings to other locations and inspired others who started investigating African-themed cultural ideas in Asia and Europe. These pioneers followed the examples of Du Bois and Ortiz and ultimately instituted contexts in which they and others were able to carry out comparative research on African continuities in the Americas. Simply put, these pioneers "were important catalysts, nurturing future generations of researchers and promulgators of the importance of African diaspora studies."[5]

Above all, what made the new trends in academic and artistic production in the Harlem period exceptional was the complementarity of theory and practice. In other words, no discussion of Harlem Renaissance writers is complete without also considering the legendary jazz maestro Louis Armstrong.[6] Jazz, one of the most studied musical genres today, took a giant step forward in 1922 when a Chicago-based Creole jazz band led by Joseph Nathan "King" Oliver (1881–1931), the brothers Johnny and Baby Dodds, and pianist Lil Hardin requested that Armstrong play second cornet during one of the band's New York shows. The opportunity unleashed the creativity of the young Armstrong in New York, with his ingenious ensemble lead, second cornet lines, and solos. With the support of his wife, Lucille (Lil), whom he married in 1924, Armstrong (Fig. 8.1) broke out with his first solos as a member of the Oliver band in such pieces as "Chimes Blues" (April 1923) and "Tears" (December 24, 1923).[7]

Figure 8.1. Louis Armstrong. *Library of Congress.*

After his separation from King Oliver's band, Armstrong briefly played in New York–based Fletcher Henderson's band and made several recordings with other artists before going back to Chicago, where he played in large orchestras. In Chicago, Armstrong created his most important early work with the "Hot Five" and "Hot Seven" recordings of 1925 to 1928 on the Okeh label. These led to his emergence as the foremost jazz soloist of his time.[8] From this point on, the original New Orleans group style, which did not permit solo opportunities, became inappropriate for Armstrong's intense ingenuity. The jazz maestro retained elements of the style that distinguished "Hotter than That," "Struttin' with Some Barbecue," "Wild Man Blues," and "Potato Head Blues" as masterworks.[9] Altogether, Armstrong's trumpet skills and technique had emerged above those of his competitors. His grander and more versatile talent allowed him to produce vital melodies with a deft touch of timbre. His sense of harmony often involved complex musical synergies that only a genius could handle in a solo design. In short, Armstrong's expressive attack and articulations made his jazz recordings unique and innovative.[10]

The era between the late 1960s and the 1990s further saw a robust theoretical debate about diverse brands of African and African American traditions and practices, including music. This debate emerged because of increased levels of curiosity on the part of scholars to highlight what they perceived as interconnections between African American cultures and their African prototypes. The present contribution is not mainly about African diaspora cultural retentions, but rather about the role of music in the creation, sustenance, and expansion of the bonds between the United States and Africa. In examining diverse genres of African and African American music, it becomes clear how succeeding generations of Africans and African Americans have used music, particularly jazz and blues, as a conduit of kinship spirit and trans-Atlantic cultural styles.

THEORY AND THE BURDEN OF PROOF

It is important to outline in brief the historical and theoretical parameters for the rise of Black music in the Americas. Central in this debate is the African retentions paradigm endorsed by Melville Herskovits, David Evan, Sterling Stuckey, and others. This theory postulates that the enslaved Africans arrived in the Americas with their inherited African culture, which they reenacted in their various American host societies by way of retention, syncretism, reinterpretation, and cultural focus.[11] In this context, cultural anthropologists and ethnomusicologists have paid tribute to the indomitable spirit of the ancestors of African American musicians, performers, and singers who laid the foundation upon which modern American music, as a vehicle of enculturation, is constructed.[12]

Coming from Africa, where music is a system of education, and dance and oral traditions intersperse rituals, poetry, philosophy, identities, and aesthetics, Don C. Ohadike argues that the enslaved African exiles aboard the slave ships (ca. 1503–1875) brought with them diverse idioms of music that nurtured blues, rhythm and blues (R&B), soul, jazz, rock, hip-hop, rap, and other modern-day world musics.[13] Extending this claim, Fredrick Kaufman and John P. Guckin in *The African Roots of Jazz* assert that the blues, inspired by slave spirituals and field hollers, started to gain popularity in the era of emancipation and Reconstruction (ca. 1863–1877). Blues is the precursor of all Black American music genres.[14] In a review of Kaufman and Guckin's book, Eddie Meadows has noted what he sees as a lack of concrete evidence from scholars who assert an emotional connection between African and African diaspora music: "The unsubstantiated claims include: the musical acculturation that is presumed to have taken place during the 'Middle Passage' leading to the development of jazz in New Orleans, steel band in the Caribbean, and the samba in Brazil."[15] Thus, without disputing the idea of retention entirely, Meadows concludes that the subject of African roots of jazz—or any other musical genre, for that matter—is a vast subject that deserves closer attention than it usually receives.

Other works have tried to link the origin of blues to Africa. Among these studies are Paul Oliver's *Savannah Syncopators: African Retentions in the Blues*, published in 1970, which tried to link jazz with the Gullah African heritage in America.[16] While Oliver did not provide specific evidence in support of his conclusions, Samuel Charters in *The Roots of the Blues: An American Search* attempted to transcend Meadows's sharp methodological criticism of previous works related to jazz. The author's ethnographic fieldwork in Africa involved investigating whether rhythmic structures and singing styles of the blues shared connections with the musical traditions of the griots of Gambia and Senegal.[17] Predictably, Charters's fieldwork led him to conclude that a connection between the African and African American traditions did exist and that blues elements had been distilled in rock and roll and, ultimately, rock. In addition, rap music, which employs extensive use of percussion, began with Jamaican-style deejaying and spoken word. Over time, rap music would heavily rely on rhythms from R&B and soul.

Writing in 1959, Stanley Elkins countered the retention thesis by setting forth provocative claims about the vast dissimilarities between Africans and African Americans in the realm of culture, which of course includes religion and music.[18] In 1978, David Evans came out forcefully in support of Herskovits's retention paradigm by laying out an elaborate definition of the key concepts of retention, syncretism, reinterpretation, and cultural focus as follows: "*Retention:* An African musical concept is retained in America. *Syncretism:* A process whereby African and European elements are merged into a functioning unified entity of clear bi-cultural derivation. *Reinterpretation:* A process by which old meanings are ascribed to new elements or by which new values change the cultural significance of old forms. *Cultural Focus:* A phenomenon which gives a culture its particular emphasis; which permits the outsider to sense its special distinguishing flavor."[19]

Elsewhere, we have separately argued that the dynamics of tradition, adaptation, and continuity explain how Black musical genres and other cultural tropes in the Americas reflect elements of African cultures without necessarily being exact replicas of the African originals.[20] This perspective is further strengthened by the argument that cultures in motion are like rolling streams of water: they form an ecosystem in a specific environment. Cultures in motion need not re-create the original because they cannot be the same as their prototypes.

The historical context in which jazz music grew is a prime example of how cultures in motion assume a life of their own, even though they may have a dispersal point. Philip McGuire notes that the 1920s represented a watershed in the cultural history of African Americans. Indeed, the "Golden Age of the New Negro," freed from the shackles of bondage, "saw an explosion of African American creativity in both literature and the performing arts."[21] Following the evolution of jazz from the musical traditions of Blacks from the Mississippi Delta area back in the 1920s, the blues remains a standard of authenticity for jazz musicians. It is critical then to remind the reader that blues and jazz are not just relics and instruments but represent the expression of sentiments, a sense of identity, a genre of melodic rendition, a type of melody, a specific chord progression, a lyrical form, a form of mannerism, and, more important, a collective history and memory. Along this line, Frank Tirro asserts that "jazz is more than a historical style: it is a [piece of] living music that will continue to change."[22]

Starting from its modest crude-chord instrumentation to the urbane ensem-bles of contemporary jazz, the artists who produce jazz have evolved over time, and these genres of music have successfully planted African and African Ameri-can cultures and ideas across the globe. Tirro's study of jazz reminds us that it is an art form derived from some levels of collaborative efforts between Black and White musicians.[23] These efforts are evident in the post–Civil War develop-ments encountered in the technological advances in the recording industry, the emergence of star soloists, and big bands. In an insightful review of Tirro's *Jazz: A History*, Marjorie Richie concluded that the post–Civil War developments led to a "growing awareness of the public that jazz had legitimate roots, was capable of change, and could endure criticism."[24]

ATLANTIC WORLD EXCHANGES IN MUSICAL BEATS

Music remains the most potent force in cross-cultural exchanges within the Atlantic world. Black music in the United States, encountered in multiple forms including blues, jazz, hip-hop, and rock and roll, has provided the soundtrack for generational, social, and political revolutions not just in Africa, the Ameri-cas, and Europe but also across the globe. At the same time, the importation of rock, funk, psychedelic, and jazz forms into Africa fueled waves of musical innovation, such as Afrobeat, particularly in West Africa.

Jazz, the most stylish of all, came into vogue around 1913; however, no one can categorically pin down when it was born. While some date the birth of jazz to 1917, when the Original Dixieland Band led by Nick LaRocca recorded the first jazz number, entitled "Livery Stable Blues," others assert that it started in 1885 with Papa Jack Laine's band, or in 1895 with Buddy Bolden's band. In his 1995 book A *History of Jazz in America*, Barry Ulanov argued that the "spiritual reality" that gave rise to jazz as a distinct genre of music emerged "in the decade from 1870 to 1880." He linked this to the performances of the Fisk Jubilee Singers, who made their first concert tour in 1871. "Thereafter in their jaunts around America and in the concert tours of other Negro institutions like the Hampton Institute, such songs as 'Deep River,' 'Go Down, Moses,' 'Heaven,' 'Little David, Play on Your Harp,' 'Swing Low, Sweet Chariot,' and 'Sometimes I Feel Like a Motherless Child' were standard parts of a growing repertory."[25]

Whichever of these views is accepted, it is essential to note that jazz is to American music what the Mississippi River is to the American South. Just as many rivers feed into the Mississippi, so diverse genres of music (and musicians) from cultures around the world came together in the creation of jazz. What this tells us is that jazz was not born on a particular day but rather evolved over a period of time. To illustrate, jazz reminds us about gumbo (the traditional rice-based American dish), possibly derived from *ki ngombo* (the name of okra in the West African Bantu tongue). The recipe is a mixture of African, Native American, and European gastronomies. The Africans brought okra (the fertility crop among the Yorubas of Nigeria), the Native Americans contributed powdered sassafras leaves, and the Europeans offered dark French roux, which is a mixture of flour and oil.[26]

Jazz combines blues-style percussion, European musical traditions, Western military music, and African indigenous sacred beats. Jazz or *jazu* (in Japanese) spread so quickly that by 1929, it allowed societies even in Far East Asia, including China, to experience what Taylor Atkins describes as "authentic modernity." Jazz placed the Japanese "in the politically and culturally prestigious company of elite Western nations."[27] Although rock and roll and rap—an off-shoot of hip-hop—came into vogue only in 1954 and 1974, respectively, the latter has become a supercraze among music lovers, especially in the past two decades. Its continuing popularity overshadows the success of American country music and reggae—both of which share roots in blues and R&B.

One of the most interesting developments in Black music is the trans-Atlantic flow of modern jazz and hip-hop. Several experts, including John Collins, the

British-born guitarist, Highlife genius, and African neotraditional music expert, have provided glimpses into the extensive impact of African American music, particularly swing-era jazz, on African music beginning in the 1920s. This crossover or "double transformation brought about by leaving and returning home, has created a truly international music-style in Africa, and yet one that is doubly African."[28] African diaspora music captured the interest of Africans at the turn of the twentieth century, when African American foxtrots, quicksteps, and ragtimes (known as "coon-songs" in the Congo) arrived on the continent in the form of sheet music and wax cylinder recordings. In South Africa, the popular urban Marabi music of the 1920s and 1930s included ragtime and honky-tonk piano produced on pedal-organs. Local Zulu musician Reuben Caluzza merged ragtime with indigenous Zulu rhythms for choral groups.[29]

Succeeding the ragtime and Black minstrelsy craze (with its tap-dancing and plantation-based percussions) in Africa was "hot" or "traditional" jazz (also known as Dixieland jazz), which made history in the United States in 1917 and became especially popular in South Africa in the 1920s.[30] In South Africa, several local Dixie bands sprouted, including the Darktown Strutters and the Big Four of Johannesburg.[31] John Collins asserts that African Highlife music and swing jazz started their journeys in Africa with the introduction of European brass band music. "Basically the West Africans hijacked European brass band music and turned it in recreational music called Adaha [in Ghana], which is an early form of Highlife."[32] This conclusion is not entirely accurate because African musical genres are dispersed and vary as new ideas emerge. While the argument is not about the connection between brass band music and Adaha in Ghana, the roots of Africa's Highlife music lie in the Bongo music of Central Africa and the Igbo music of southeastern Nigeria.

However, to put Collins's ideas in perspective, it is essential to remember that long before the 1920s, when New World jazz music infiltrated the African continent, Jamaican Goombay (Gumbe) music had made its homecoming as the first genre of Black diaspora music to infiltrate Africa. Invented in the Americas as a composite of Bantu, Yoruba, Fon, Kongo, and other ethnic African sounds and a blend of French, English, Spanish, and Portuguese musical forms, in the coastal areas of West Africa Goombay music met with indigenous African music styles such as Ashiko, Timo, and Osibisaaba rhythms. Over time, the local musical styles merged into Highlife and Juju music.[33]

Goombay music returned to Africa accompanied by the Goombay drum, its principal percussion. Although Goombay music is native to Africa and was exported to the Americas with the slave trade, the Goombay drum is an eighteenth-century modified African original reinvented by enslaved Africans in the Caribbean. In 1800, after the founding of the Sierra Leone colony in 1792, the British transported the first group of 500 emancipated slaves or Ma-roons from Jamaica, who brought Goombay with them. From Sierra Leone, Goombay proliferated to other parts of West Africa.

Until the 1880s, West Africans could play brass band music only when they were allowed to by the Europeans. The idea was to dissuade the Africans from playing African drums and bugles, which the Europeans considered part of the indigenous command-and-logistic tools used for communication in warfare. Things began to change during the Ashanti Wars of 1873–1901, when the British colonists stationed about 6,000 West Indian soldiers in Elmina and Cape Coast to help defeat the Ashanti soldiers. It was over this period that the British and the Dutch introduced brass band music.

The presence of Caribbean military personnel enriched the repertoire of New World music in West Africa. The troops from the Caribbean "introduced early forms of Calypso, and they brought the 5 pulse (3–2) claves or bell rhythm played in 4/4 time." The new rhythm easily captured the attention of music lovers in Ghana because, as Samuel A. Floyd, Jr., has noted, "the 5 pulse rhythm" is not indigenous to Africa. Rather, it is a reinvention of the 6/8 polyrhythm African original in the New World. In the New World model, "the 5 pulse is grouped as 1, 2, 3–1, 2 and layered onto the various multiple rhythms of the polyrhythmic structure."[34]

As Ghanaian musicians began to adopt Caribbean rhythms and songs in the 1880s, they also incorporated brass band style. Consequently, what evolved was what we know today as Adaha—a form of brass band music developed in Africa. In the 1920s, when Adaha and other street songs entered the repertoire of the ballroom dance orchestras favored by the local elite, the name was changed to Highlife. Musical innovations heralded by the presence of African American artists continued to make their ways to Africa and increased tremendously during the Second World War with the presence of Allied soldiers in Africa and African soldiers who served overseas. In East Africa, for instance, African soldiers, known as the King's African Rifles, or KAR, returning from the war brought home with them the rumba and soon established such bands as the Rhino Boys. Another group led by Lucas Tututu made history with the famous song "Malaika," which Miriam Makeba performed in the 1960s. "Malaika" became a favorite song in both anglophone and francophone Africa, including French-speaking Central Africa and the Belgian Congo, where the greatest appeal was recorded.[35]

Meanwhile, the 1940s marked a watershed in the history of jazz in West Africa because it provided an opportunity for American and British soldiers to spread the popularity of swing music. Ghana, Nigeria, Sierra Leone, Liberia, and other African countries that contributed to the Allied war effort hosted the new musical emblem. In colonial Accra, Ghana, musicians entertained the urban elite, and their music attracted the interest of the American and British soldiers who patronized the bars at night. However, these soldiers also yearned for swing music. While they enjoyed recorded swing music, they further wanted to experience live swing music. As a result, in the early 1940s, American and British soldiers formed groups such as Sergeant Leopard, the Black and White Spots, and the Tempos band. These mixed bands based in Accra comprised White soldiers and skilled African musicians. Among the three significant bands, only the Tempos survived the departure of the British and Americans soldiers at the end of the Second World War in 1945.

With the exit of the American and British soldiers came an attempt to adopt the percussion to more African styles. The process was hastened because after the instruments bequeathed to the Africans began to age, it was difficult for African musicians to procure new ones. The only choice left was to use local African drums. One of the African musicians who helped in this process of Africanizing the Ghanaian dance bands was the percussionist Guy Warren, or Kofi Ghanaba (1923–2008), who was also a member of the Tempos dance band along with his countryman E. T. Mensah. Although his primary passion was jazz, Warren also showed remarkable interest in bebop, as well as Cuba's CuBop. Originally named Warren Gamaliel Kpakpo, the jazz maestro's strong interest and attraction to modern jazz took him to the United States in 1955. There, Warren met and played jazz with Charlie Parker, who died a short while after.[36]

Guy Warren produced quite a few Afro-jazz albums, including *Africa Speaks, America Answers*, released in the United States in early 1957. In other words, Warren had recorded his presence long before John Coltrane and others began to apply African musical ideas to modern jazz forms. Warren further collaborated with other American stars such as General Bey and Max Roach. He later moved from Highlife into jazz. Later still, after he came back to Ghana and changed his name to Kofi Ghanaba, he created an Afro-jazz kit comprising a collection of different African drums but also using foot pedals. Through this hybridization, Warren (respected by the older generation of American jazz musicians) masterfully turned African drums into a jazz toolkit. In the 1970s, jazz and rock musicians like Randy Western, Max Roach, and Ginger Baker from the United States, who acknowledged Warren as a jazz guru, visited him in Ghana.

Influenced by Warren's accomplishments in the worlds of jazz and Highlife music, Armstrong also saw Ghana as the homeland of his ancestors. He visited the West African country twice in 1956 (with his wife Lucille) and again during his tour of Africa in 1960–1961. In Ghana in 1956, Armstrong played jazz with

E. T. Mensah, the leader of the Tempos, and the Ghanaian *Daily Graphic* carried a headline announcing the presence of the "Old Man of Jazz" in the country. The paper later reported that "E. T. [Mensah] seems to have been inspired by the presence of the great Louis."[37] After the May 23 and May 25, 1956, shows at the Old Polo Ground and the Opera Cinema (located along Pagan Road in Accra), respectively, Armstrong and his wife were hosted by Kwame Nkrumah (in 1956 already the elected premier of an internally self-governing Gold Coast), who ultimately emerged as the first postcolonial president of independent Ghana in 1957.

As in South Africa in the apartheid era, most of the hundreds of Highlife bands in the 1950s and 1960s—such as the Tempos, Ramblers, Broadway, Uhuru, and Messengers—made it the most famous music in Ghana and elsewhere in West and Central Africa. These bands played Highlife tunes that incorporated elements of swing, Calypso styles, and Latin music. These music styles were enjoyed in Ghana as part of the emergent pop culture.

In a colonial social mélange, with its Victorian ethos, E. T. Mensah was one of the first artists who put women on an important dance-band stage. Among them were Julie Okine, who played with the Tempos from the mid-1950s. Courageous and bold, Julie Okine wrote for the Tempos "the first modern Ghanaian feminist song called *Nothing but a Man's Slave*," which came out in 1957. "If I die of a man's love / I'm nothing but a man's slave," she sang.[38] Significantly, this track appeared at the same time as the album *Ghana Freedom*, which Mensah produced to commemorate Ghana's independence on March 6, 1957.[39] Mensah's biographer, John Lewis, believed that American influence informed Mensah's decision to put women on stage at a time when the Ghanaian and colonial social ethos frowned on such ideas. In other words, Mensah saw Black American female artists such as Ella Fitzgerald, Lena Horn, and Sarah Vaughan as role models.

Female pioneers like Julie Okine, who ignored whispers of male chauvinism that considered them loose women, echo the careers of the celebrated South African musician Miriam Makeba, who married Stokely Carmichael, the legendary African American activist, in 1968. Makeba, who became the most popular female voice against apartheid, "started her career with the Manhattan Brothers, which was a South African swing band and her great heroine was Ella Fitzgerald. So basically black American women superstars created a space in Africa for women popular performers."[40]

In Lagos, Nigeria, the new or modernized Highlife under the spell of swing jazz was introduced by the Tempos from Ghana. There were diverse genres of music and bands in the post–World War II Nigerian urban centers. However, these groups did not perform a particular kind of rhythm that one might describe as swing jazz. Therefore, when E. T. Mensah and his Tempos arrived, Nigerian artists saw an opportunity to adapt the indigenous styles to a new structure.

One of those artists was the trumpeter Victor Abimbola Olaiya (a.k.a. Papingo Dalaya), whose Highlife band Cool Cats was formed in 1954 (it was renamed the All Stars Band in 1963). Fela Anikulapo-Kuti (1938–1997), the architect of Afrobeat music, started his career in Lagos, Nigeria, with the Olaiya-led band in the 1950s.[41] In the 1960s, his Koola Lobitos (Spanish for "Little Wolves") band played a genre of Highlife that incorporated jazz percussions.[42] Eventually, Fela moved to Ghana in 1967, where he turned his Highlife brand into his signature creation, the Afrobeat style, in 1969. Afrobeat is essentially a fusion of West African Highlife with jazz and soul music. The originality of Afrobeat music made Fela the most spectacular musical figure to come out of Africa in the 1970s, and his activist model of music making made him the Bob Dylan and Mick Jagger of Africa.[43]

The preceding demonstrates that African American music may have African origins (and we have so far shown linkages with jazz, blues, and other genres), but hip-hop marks one of the most popular African Americanized forms that has migrated *back* to Africa. It is also a *cultural* transmitter. By way of illustration, the triad of Nigerian-born Oladapo Daniel Oyebanjo (a.k.a. D'Banj), Senegalese-born Aliaune Damala Badara Thiam (a.k.a. Akon), and American-born Nigerian artist Olubowale Victor Akintimehin (a.k.a. Wale) embody the continuing flow of trans-Atlantic/African diasporic exchanges. As rap artists, these African musicians lend and borrow mixtapes, fashion, dance steps, punchlines, and polysyllabic lyrics to and from their African American counterparts.

Black music artists are active agents of globalization. The meeting between elements of indigenous African musical forms and those of the New World societies is a signpost in the history of globalization. The spirituals, blues, jazz, R&B, soul, hip-hop, and rap of Black artists on both sides of the Atlantic have claimed dominance in contemporary popular culture. Playing a central role in the ascendancy of Black music to global dominance is Western technology. While technology has helped in marketing Black artists worldwide, music created by American artists serves to spread a distinct form of Americanism across diverse cultural regions. Black artists sing about American cars, aircraft, electronics, politics, society, business, churches, schools, sex, family life, crime, fashion, and more. These musicians showcase, with spectacle and drama, American goods and inventions on music videos transmitted via satellite TVs into private and public domains across all geographical boundaries. The power of these images and tunes on the audiences' psyches makes them important agents in the continuing spread of American global influence, a subject that deserves more nuanced scholarly attention.

CULTURAL CARRIERS IN A GILDED AGE

Exponents of globalization describe the mobility and speed with which information is disseminated across the world as a revolutionary marker of the new global village. Indeed, from Los Angeles to Lagos and from Tokyo to Toronto, such innovations as films, satellite TV, cell phones, the internet, and the up-to-the-minute digital and multimedia culture of music streaming services have delivered familiar soundtracks that make Black hot lyrics the flagship of postmodern techno-culture. These late twentieth- and twenty-first-century inventions have enabled the youth of our global "cybervillage" to establish cross-cutting identities and new perceptions that blur racial and cultural barriers.

Thus, contrary to popular assumptions, Alexander Weheliye, a scholar of African American studies, observes that Black culture sometimes takes the lead in technological innovations, especially when they involve the improvement of musical soundtracks: "This has been the case since the beginning of sound recording at the end of the [nineteenth] century and still holds true in our current globalization era."[44] The contemporary trends of remixing in popular music and disc jockeying that turned the record player into an instrument illustrate the inventiveness of Black entertainers that gave birth to such genres as disco, hip-hop, and techno music. The success of Black musical entertainers as culture-carriers on the global stage corroborates the idea that music is a way of perceiving the world, and a vehicle through which human and material cultures flourish.

Apparently, what distinguishes popular culture from indigenous culture are the contexts and the range of the messages they communicate. This fact holds the key to an understanding of the power of Black popular music in the diffusion of global cultural trends. A better appreciation of blues, for instance, is to consider its historical and transnational development as an offshoot of West African traditional songs, or "work songs." Its rendition by slaves on the American plantations in the form of lamentations, spirituals, call-and-response, shouts, and hollers has received full scholarly attention. Iain Anderson's study of the stylistic traits of slave music in the antebellum South revealed that slaves usually sang a cappella work songs, such as "Pick a Bale of Cotton" or "Ho' Round the Corn, Sally," in groups while performing a common task. A solitary worker might engage in a more plaintive "cry" or "holler," possibly answered by another bondsman in a neighboring field. Slaves sang their religious music—songs like "Roll, Jordan, Roll" or "There's a Meeting Here Tonight"—at secret gatherings as well as camp meetings and churches. The music's overt use, needless to say, was for spiritual uplift.[45]

In his important study *Sinful Tunes and Spirituals*, Dena Epstein notes that eighteenth-century European and American visitors to Africa heard collective songs accompanying work, especially in West Africa.[46] Although these travelers did not provide enough details to enable their American audience to corroborate suspicions of a more or less direct cultural transfer, work songs and call-and-response patterns are indeed native to the African continent. As the plantation owners plowed on the backs of the enslaved people, these genres of music provided them with coping skills.

Additionally, James Weldon Johnson studied the stylistic aspects of plantation work songs, comparing them to their West African antecedents. One of these is the call-and-response style, in which a leader exchanges vocal lines with a chorus. An antiphonal song of the Bornou (that is, the Borno, of northern Nigeria) in praise of their sultan, published by Denham and Clapperton in 1826, provides insights:

Give flesh to the hyenas—
Oh, the broad spears!
The spear of the Sultan is the broadest—
Oh, the broad spears!
I behold to see none other—
Oh, the broad spears!
My horse is as tall as a high wall—
Oh, the broad spears! He will fight ten—he fears nothing—
Oh, the broad spears!
He has slain ten, the guns are yet behind—
Oh, the broad spears! . . .
Be brave, be brave my friends and kinsmen—
Oh, the broad spears![47]

Johnson then compares and contrasts it with one of the most famous of all the spirituals, which displays a similar structure:

LEADER: Swing low, sweet chariot,
CONGREGATION: Comin' for to carry me home.
LEADER: Swing low, sweet chariot,
CONGREGATION: Comin' for to carry me home.
LEADER: I look over Jordan, what do I see?
CONGREGATION: Comin' for to carry me home.
LEADER. A band of angels comin' after me,
CONGREGATION: Comin' for to carry me home.[48]

The plantation songs of this nature formed the foundations on which contemporary Black music emerged in the postemancipation period. After emancipation, blues transformed from "primitive" into "classical," or "city," blues. The tunes captured general moods of loneliness, confusion, and hardship among the Black population, as most of the master race found it challenging to accept the emancipated Blacks as equals in society. Because social discrimination against the African Americans was more intense in the American South, individuals and families embarked on the so-called Great Migration to evade the dehumanizing pains that racism perpetrates.[49]

In the decades leading to the early 1950s, the "blues bug" caught many non-Black soul composers, who now turned to the blues genre of music with all devotion. The Beatles, the Rolling Stones, the Animals, Eric Clapton, and other performers who emerged because of this conversion are still fresh in our memories. A straightforward explanation for why Black music quickly gained a popular audience may be its potential to lift the soul. What elevates the soul rules the world. Another answer is found in the society of their times. Musicologists agree that music, like other art forms, is a product of its social environment, history, memory, emotions, consciousness, and imagination.[50]

Black artists on both sides of the Atlantic are not only a reflection of their historical milieu but also active agents in this fluid sociopolitical space. The social ills that plagued America from the end of the slave trade in 1808 through the Civil War—namely, oppression, fear, open hatred, racism, unemployment, hunger, loneliness, and disillusionment—are common to all human societies. The experiences of colonialism (including the apartheid regime in South Africa) and the First and Second World Wars—as milestones of globalization—had, like the American experience, altered lives in the Americas, Africa, Asia, and Europe.

The anomalies, or rather disorders, of American society enabled blues, jazz, and other musical forms to expand globally as a therapy for broken lives and desolate souls. Ndiouga Benga, who has surveyed the meanings and challenges of modern urban music in colonial and postcolonial Senegal, concludes that until "the 1970s, most of the musical production [in Senegal] was influenced by the Afro-Cuban style."[51] For instance, Star Jazz, a local band from Saint Louis, adopted jazz from New Orleans as a model of its musical lyrics. In a similar move, the Dakar University Sextet (founded in 1964 by Ousmane Sow Huchard and the Dreyfus Brothers from Guinea) enhanced their popularity by accepting some elements of Western styles. This eclecticism implies that popular culture is encountered in different forms of expressions and symbols. It further demonstrates that although Black diaspora cultural tropes took life from Africa, African diaspora cultures have also *reversed sail* to the mother continent.

Popular culture spreads through the effects of charm and prestige. It enters into a new society in the company of alien language, architecture, science, sexual mores, fashion, and other cultural baggage. The youth tend to be the first to embrace the exotic lifestyles, dressing habits, and different mannerisms as they adopt foreign superstars as role models. Consequently, the recipient society is gripped in a "neo-imperial" mood, which soon converts the local society into an extension of the alien culture's spheres of the cultural empire.

Within this dynamism, Black artists, working with other Americans, have extended the United States' hegemonic position in music and performance art with more aggressive lyrics in the popular music known as hip-hop. Across the globe, music lovers packed discothèques, especially in the 1970s and 1980s, to enjoy the genius of legends like the Jacksons, Diana Ross, and the Commodores. In the same period, rap music emerged out of the frustrated expectations of urban youth to articulate new and hybrid cultural matrices. Cities, particularly New Orleans, New York, Los Angeles, Chicago, and Detroit, provided the melting pot for the new idiom in popular music called rap.

Rap music is an old West African tradition closely associated with praise singing and the social performances of oral historians known in Mali, for instance, as *griots*. While its primary functions included historical recording and entertainment, the Africans also used this medium to reproach and ridicule the oppressive elite and other social transgressions. Contemporary rap music remains a platform for social protest, or what Brian Cross perceives as "a way of delineating community and of communicating history."[52]

It is within this context of entertainment, aesthetics, identity formation, history keeping, protest, admonition, and ridicule (all issues that define our global age) that contemporary American rap music has won a big audience. By 1974, when Joseph Saddler (a.k.a. Grandmaster Flash) began playing his unique turntables in the Bronx area of New York City, rap was rapidly gaining a popular audience, and by 1979, when Sugar Hill Records (owned by Sylvia Robinson) released an album entitled *Rapper's Delight*, it became an instant success.[53]

From the Bronx and Brooklyn, rap acquired a distinct style, ethos, and sound, spreading across America and beyond. The first wave of rap artists, now known as the "old school" included Run-D.M.C., Queen Latifah, Big Daddy Kane, Salt-N-Pepa, Public Enemy, Afrika Bambaataa, KRS-One, MC Lyte, and of course, Grandmaster Flash. The musical stars who have together sold hundreds of millions of albums have won famous followers in Africa, Europe, and Asia.

The international pop revolution reached Africa in the early 1960s in the form of rock and roll, a commercialized version of rhythm and blues that emerged in the 1940s following the Great Migration of the 1920s to the 1940s. Although initially played by American Whites, rock and roll captured the interest and imaginations of African youth, who began "to play the music of Elvis Presley, Fats Domino, and Cliff Richard. One of the first African pop-bands was the Heartbeats of Sierra Leone, formed in 1961 by Geraldo Pino. This band was to change the face of the music scene."[54]

Everywhere in sub-Saharan Africa today, young people garbed in American attire frequent social clubs and public events as either professional or guest rappers. Hundreds of their Japanese counterparts perform in clubs and public drinking places every night. Perhaps the strongest impact of Black music on Europe manifests in the explosion of government-sponsored summer music festivals and expositions across Belgium, Germany, and France every year. In the summer of 1998, for instance, one of the writers of this book watched a pregnant woman dance herself into early labor at an open-air live music bash in Brussels. The event featured artists from different countries, including Femi Kuti, son of Fela Kuti, the legendary Afrobeat king.[55]

Today there are several varieties of rap and hip-hop music, each with its theme and style. Most of those who belong to the "new school" came into public view with the national and global rise of West Coast gangster rap culture. Heralding this new genre was Ice-T, the self-proclaimed "original gangster." Others include Talib Kweli, Lauryn Hill, the visionary Tupac Shakur, and the Notorious B.I.G. In 1987, a hit album by N.W.A. (Niggaz With Attitude), formed by the late Eazy-E, Dr. Dre, and Ice Cube and arguably the most feared group in the history of rap, featured the song "Straight Outta Compton" and announced the dawn of a more controversial version of rap that extols thuggery and hooliganism.

The new form of rap threatens to tarnish the honor that reggae and some visionary rap artists have achieved over the years. Dead Prez, a visionary rap duo, for example, are well-known Pan-Africanist ideologues. They continually remind all people of African descent to defend their African roots. In their highly socio-politically sensitive album *I'm a African*, Dead Prez declared pride in their African heritage and curiously disavowed the entire idea of being an African American. They emphasized that they are "Blacker than Black," alluding to the origin of humans in Africa.

Although not always consciously planned, such expressions of Black consciousness play a crucial role in forging the trans-Atlantic and transnational identities that have also extended the admiration held for African and African American cultures overseas. However, a discrete genre of rap music that glorifies sex, illicit drugs, and an ostentatious lifestyle is a source of concern not just in the African American community but also in Africa. In a 2002 article in *Ebony* magazine, Lerone Bennett, Jr. expressed a common anxiety about this modern trend in calling upon Black women to rise against this notorious group of rap musicians. The women were concerned about social values and gender roles, and had been portrayed as sex objects. They have "got to say that there's not going to be any 'ho-mongering.'"[56]

Nonetheless, rap continues to reign. Perhaps this is because it provides youth around the world with an escape from the usual storm and stress psychologists have identified as part of adolescent culture. Steven Best and Douglas Kellner have noted that the popular appeal of rap ranges "from the urban fury of gangster rap to the rural fusion of blues and rap in Arrested Development, to the educated raps about black history of Chuck D, to the poetic and political discourses of the Disposable Heroes of Hypocrisy, to the G-funk melodies of Snoop Doggy Dogg."[57]

In this context, American rap music has something for everyone, thus claiming a role as a powerful vehicle for cultural expression, "an informational medium" or a "satellite communication system."[58]

This discussion has explored the power of Black popular music as a central agency in continuing United States-Africa relations and as a major force in the globalization of cultures, mainly African and African American culture. Emily Gray aptly concludes that "popular art does not, cannot, reach us unmediated—it is labeled, packaged, marketed and sold."[59] In light of this hypothetical fact, one must appreciate the role of Black music as authentic mastery of the art form and modern technology, which has helped entrench some aspects of Americanism through music.

The legacy that African American musicians in particular, and American musicians in general, have bequeathed to the world is a dramatized vestige of what it meant to be American and their perceptions of both the world around them and the one afar. As Dead Prez contend in their album *Turn Off the Radio*, the lyrics on the airwaves serve as a mind control mechanism. Somehow, music has proved a more effective control mechanism in spreading American influence and culture than the weapons of warfare that politicians often extol. Black lyrics cheer the heart. What lifts the soul runs the mind.

Part III

AFRICAN COLONIAL FREEDOM AND THE MODERN EXPERIENCE

9

THE CIVIL RIGHTS MOVEMENT
MEETS DECOLONIZATION

"Daddy, why do white people treat colored people so mean?"
— *Martin Luther King, Jr., "Letter from Birmingham Jail"*[1]

The question above, posed by a five-year-old boy at the height of the civil rights movement in 1963, highlights the disturbing problem of race, ideology, social conscience, and even psychiatry in Jim Crow America (ca. 1870–1964). A related question with no precise answer defined Frantz Fanon's career in colonial Algeria as a medical psychiatrist in the French imperial army.[2] In fact, Theodore Rubin, a medical psychiatrist who studies anti-Semitism, argues that prejudiced people and race-haters suffer from an emotional disturbance, a deep-seated, nonorganic disease of the mind elevated to the level of "Symbol Sickness." At its extreme form, Rubin notes that the condition—which emanates from "anxiety, repressed anger, low self-esteem, insecurity, etc.—as well as neurotic defenses—displacement, projection, rationalization, alienation, compartmentalization—all provide fertile grounds for this kind of illness"— motivates individuals and groups to become psychotic and murderous.[3] The insight provided by Rubin corroborates ideas by philosopher Kwame Appiah, whose critical humanistic inquiry on race and racism, identity, and moral consciousness posits that people with racist inclination suffer from psychopathologies. They lack the basic heuristic and cerebral understanding of what goes on around them. Appiah concludes that such individuals deserve more pity than anger.[4]

Rubin and Appiah present an opening to examine further the argument by Mauricio Mazon, whose study of the "zoot-suit riots" of June 1943 in Los

Angeles focused on the violent relationship between U.S. service members and Mexican-American youths. The study concluded that minorities and people of color in the United States became victims of White mobs, politicians, police, the press, and military personnel who virtually suffered from symbol sickness and demonization of Blacks and Mexicans. Mazon contends that the dominant group in post–Civil War America viewed the minorities as subordinate ethnic and cultural groups under the United States' laws and practices.[5] Since the 1930s, scholars in Germany and the United States have documented incidents of state-sponsored repression and mob violence against Jews and Blacks by the dominant groups in these countries. The rationale behind their actions has remained subject to heated debates even in recent times.[6] As these studies reveal, religious and ethnic hatred ran so deep in both Nazi Germany and Jim Crow America that the visible minorities suffered acute dehumanization as the political elite in these countries systematically enacted laws and social practices that portrayed the victims as a symbol of everything antithetical to these societies.

The post–World War II era offers a unique opportunity for a comparative study of congruent sociopolitical and economic agitations in the United States and colonial Africa. Liberation movements in the forms of the civil rights and women's rights movements changed social dynamics in the West, and decolonization transformed the non-Western world and global politics. Other movements, such as Léopold Sédar Senghor's Négritude, struggles against the oppressive apartheid system in South Africa, and Pan-Arabism in the Arab world, helped establish cross-regional linkages. From the 1950s, the borders of the new postcolonial states virtually merged with those of the African diaspora. The primary interest, therefore, is on how the various liberation movements in the Atlantic world informed one another, interacting and converging on the same theme of freedom from oppression.

In the United States and colonial Africa in the 1950s and 1960s, specific issues of subjugation in the forms of segregation of public spaces, denial of citizenship rights, disenfranchisement, and colonial alienation increased the imperative of self-determination. The commonality of these social issues on both sides of the Atlantic engendered a historic collaboration between African American civil rights leaders and African nationalist leaders. Some of the emergent African political and educated elite, such as Keke Seme of South Africa, Nnamdi Azikiwe of Nigeria, and Kwame Nkrumah of Ghana, were either living/studying in the United States between the 1930s and 1960s or returned to their African homelands to spearhead Africa's liberation from European colonialism. The shared visions of freedom for the entire Black race and their material advancement held by these leaders on both sides of the Atlantic world echoed the essence of Pan-Africanism, which was, in the main, a call for unity among Blacks to confront and overcome the conditions of helplessness and degradation plaguing their race. It is crucial to understand the complementary and mutual influences of African independence on notions of Black Power in the United States and the ideals of the African American civil rights movement on African nationalism and decolonization.[7] An examination of debates over women's rights in independent African nations further highlights the complex and contentious interactions between these liberation movements taking place concurrently in national, transregional, and transnational contexts.

Within the transnational framework in which these mass movements were unfolding, one can assert the obvious that the civil rights movement in the United States and the Pan-African/anticolonial agitations in Africa shared close symbiotic relations. With the shift of leadership from the African American founding fathers to the emergent African political elite at the 1945 Manchester Congress, postwar Pan-Africanism gained traction by reinforcing that spirit of unity and purpose. Thus, people of African descent, wherever they may be, could strive to reclaim security and attain political, economic, as well as psychological empowerment and freedom.[8]

The connection between Pan-Africanism and the events of the 1950s and 1960s in the Atlantic world demonstrates that long before the events, Pan-Africanism prepared the African American's mind and psyche for the civil rights struggle in the United States just as it prepared the emergent African educated elite and nationalists for the fight to end imperialism in Africa. In his "Letter from Birmingham Jail" dated April 16, 1963, Martin Luther King underscored the apparent connection between Pan-Africanism and the 1960s civil rights struggle in the United States with his rejection of what he perceived as "the disease of segregation" and the slow pace of civil rights reforms in the United States. According to King, "the nations of Asia and Africa are moving with jetlike speed towards the goal of political independence, and we still creep at horse and buggy pace towards the gaining of a cup of coffee at a lunch counter."[9] In 1964, Malcolm X also called out the "old, tricky blue-eyed liberal who is supposed to be" a friend and supporter of the struggle, but "never tells you anything about human rights."[10]

The rhetoric of King and Malcolm X was embedded in the global human rights discourses that implicated the hypocrisy of the liberal agenda during the civil rights movement. In 1973, Steve Biko repeated similar words of frustration in the face of the delayed pace of sociopolitical reforms in apartheid South Africa while the Africans suffered under the hateful regime. In one of his scathing articles, entitled "I Write What I Like," Biko, the leader of the Black Consciousness movement, decried the lukewarm approach of White liberals in the country to resolve White oppression of the indigenes there: "No one is suggesting that it is not the business of liberal whites to oppose what is wrong. However, it appears to us too much of a coincidence that liberals—few as they are—should not only be determining the modus operandi of those blacks who oppose the system, but also be leading it, in spite of their involvement in the system."[11]

King and Biko shared a commitment to nonviolence. Their ideological affinity demonstrated the former's dedication to and promotion of Pan-African ideals. In a study of King's contributions to Pan-Africanism, Jeremy Levitt noted that some scholars had questioned the civil rights leader's commitment to the movement.[12] Perhaps the best response to this question, one that dispels any doubt about his commitment to Pan-Africanism, remains King's powerful tribute to W. E. B. Du Bois on February 23, 1968.[13] King wrote, "But he was an exile only to the land of his birth. He died at home in Africa among his cherished ancestors, and he was ignored by a pathetically ignorant America but not by history." King goes on to say that history cannot ignore Du Bois "because history has to reflect truth and Dr. Du Bois was a tireless explorer and a gifted discoverer of social truths. His singular greatness lay in his quest for the truth about his own people."[14]

King was not only a compelling personality in the Pan-Africanist movement but also a transcendent universal advocate of freedom and human rights. He saw it as necessary to speak for all peoples of the world encumbered by majority domination.[15] In his "Facing the Challenge of a New Age" address, delivered in Montgomery, Alabama, in late 1956, King announced to the world that they "were starting a movement that would rise to international proportions." According to King, this was "a movement whose lofty echoes would ring in the ears of people of every nation; a movement that would stagger and astound the imagination of the oppressor, while leaving a glittering star of hope etched in the midnight skies of the oppressed." King further announced that "freedom must ring from every mountainside," a phrase he would later adopt for his "I Have a Dream" speech in Washington, D.C., in 1963.[16]

Through his broad, universal approach, King established a link between the African American struggles not just with the African bloodline but with a global kinship based on freedom for the oppressed and downtrodden. He not only encouraged Black immigration to assist in the continent's developmental aspirations but also maintained a very close relationship with African nationalist leaders of the 1950 and 1960s, including anti-apartheid leaders in South Africa.[17] On his way to Oslo to receive his Nobel Peace Prize in December 1964, King stopped over in London, where he addressed incidents of racism in

South Africa and Britain: "In our struggle for freedom and justice in the United States, which has also been so long and arduous, we feel a powerful sense of identification with those in the far more deadly struggle for freedom in South Africa. We know how Africans there, and their friends of other races, strove for half a century to win their freedom by non-violent methods."[18]

In the speech, King honored Chief Luthuli, Nelson Mandela, Robert Sobukwe, and others for their leadership, and King talked about how the apartheid leaders had responded to their nonviolent approach with increasing violence and repression, "culminating in the shootings of Sharpeville."[19] King further noted: "Clearly, there is much in Mississippi and Alabama to remind South Africans of their own country, yet even in Mississippi we can organize to register Negro voters, we can speak to the press, we can in short organize the people in non-violent action. But in South Africa even the mildest form of non-violent resistance meets with years of imprisonment, and leaders over many years have been restricted and silenced and imprisoned."[20]

King was not merely an exponent of Pan-Africanism and decolonization in Africa and elsewhere but personally participated in the swearing-in ceremonies of those African postcolonial leaders with whom he had special relationships: Kwame Nkrumah of Ghana on March 6, 1957, and Nnamdi Azikiwe of Nigeria on November 16, 1960.[21] Over a private lunch with Nkrumah during Ghana's independence celebration in 1957, the newly installed president of Ghana told King that he "would never be able to accept the American ideology of freedom until America settles its own internal racial strife."[22] Kevin Gaines emphasized that Nkrumah's air of confidence bolstered King's hope that "somehow the universe itself is on the side of freedom and justice. King was confident of the ability of Nkrumah and Ghanaian leadership to meet the challenge ahead."[23]

THE HISTORICAL CONTEXT

As a mass protest movement against racial segregation and discrimination that came to national prominence during the mid-1950s, it is important to highlight in brief the sociopolitical milieu in which the civil rights movement in the United States emerged and how King became its most distinguished leader and symbol. For generations, Euro-Americans led by slavocrats employed a White-based constitutional doctrine to justify a deeply entrenched culture of enslavement and exploitation of Africans. In 1865, Congress enacted a short-lived experiment in racial democracy in the Reconstruction era, which ended in 1877. From this point onward, Blacks lived under a formal, constitutionalized system of White racial authority that denied them voting rights and full citizenship rights. These conditions persisted and started to improve piecemeal from the turn of the twentieth century until the 1960s, when the struggle for civil rights and racial equality was in a full swing, and ended after President Lyndon Johnson signed the Civil Rights Act of 1964.

In 1838, the southern states promulgated a series of laws of racial segregation that targeted Blacks. (South Africa passed similar laws after the National Party came to power in 1948, such as the apartheid segregationist acts of the 1950s and 1960s.) By 1900, those laws, known across the nation as Jim Crow laws, became virulent. Feeble attempts to expunge the laws with the 1875 Civil Rights Act came to no effect. Instead, the Jim Crow laws expanded and persisted to a dangerous proportion after the Supreme Court ruled on October 15, 1883, that the 1875 act, which had prohibited racial discrimination in trains, hotels, and other public places, was unconstitutional.[24] From this point, segregation persevered because Congress wanted absolute control over corporations and people in the private spheres of the southern states. Lawmakers, who were predominantly Whites, rejected any suggestions for changes to the Jim Crow laws until the Civil Rights Act of 1964 effectively repealed them.[25] The new act invoked the commerce clause, outlawing discrimination in public accommodations. In 1965, Congress passed the Voting Rights Act, which secured the rights of Black people to vote in elections.[26]

Under the Jim Crow laws, many states and cities imposed harsh legal punishments. For example, Blacks and those Whites who attempted to consort with or marry with other races faced severe legal sanctions. The most stringent enforcement of the laws was in the South, where authorities made it a crime for Blacks to ride in public transportation reserved for Whites or to use public parks, schools, cemeteries, restaurants, hospitals, and many other public spaces and facilities reserved for Whites. In Whites-only hospitals, for example, White nurses could only attend to White patients. Different areas were designated to Whites and Blacks in trains, buses, restaurants, schools, hospitals, parks, cemeteries, and other spaces. White-owned newspapers segregated "Black news" from "White news"—that is, when they found it imperative to mention Blacks in the pages of their newspapers.[27]

Bruce M. Tyler has noted that early in the 1940s, Blacks and other people of color, such as Mexican Americans, had confronted the "American Dilemma" with proracial pride movements in response to the supremacist and segregationist ideologies and mass incarceration of minorities, particularly Blacks and Japanese Americans during World War II.[28] In an era when oppressed groups around the world perceived capitalism as exploitative and communism as a liberating force, the leaders of the Black civil rights movement of the 1950s and 1960s were identified as aiding and abetting international communism, whether real or imagined. The U.S. government branded prominent Black leaders of the movement across the country, including King, Malcolm X, and the Honorable Elijah Muhammad, as radicals and enemies of the state who preached doctrines of anarchy, civil disobedience, and militant agitation aimed at destabilizing the United States of America.

In the 1960s and 1970s, a great majority of Blacks remained trapped in poverty, hopelessness, and crime. Since poverty often engenders petty crimes, a record number of Black and Hispanic men ended up in prison. The question arises as to why men of minority groups remained marginalized in the socioeconomic system. The answer to this enduring historical question is simple but difficult to accept. Social expectations are part of the problem. Historically, the "American Dream" most often implied that anyone (specifically White men who dominated society before the Black civil rights and feminist movements gained traction) could rise to the highest levels of wealth and power, and every man had not only a duty but also an obligation to do so. The American Dream, while subject to diverse interpretations, remains open to objections. Philosophers like Horace Kallen have challenged the concept.[29] However, as defined by Saul Padover, the American Dream connotes "a dedication to individual freedom, justice under law, equality of educational and economic opportunity, and finally, constant material improvement and well-being."[30]

Regrettably, for American minorities in general and Blacks in particular, pursuing the Dream often proved difficult if not impossible because of their marginalization and social locations. The civil rights struggle, then, was a fight to overcome segregationist laws and the socioeconomic and political practices that limited the social mobility of disadvantaged groups who were often locked out of the American Dream. This state of society was the topic of Malcolm X's speech in 1964, when he asserted that he saw the America of his time "through the eyes of the victim. . . . I do not see any American dream; I see an American nightmare."[31] Yet, implicit in President Franklin D. Roosevelt's New Deal, Harry Truman's Fair Deal, and Lyndon B. Johnson's Great Society's War on Poverty was that the American Dream was open to all Americans through government assistance.[32] This was the rationale behind federal government legislation such as social welfare programs for the needy and affirmative action programs to ameliorate the conditions of the minorities.[33]

Some observers of the social welfare state and affirmative action programs have charged that these forms of diversity policies were flawed. The critics variously contend that the "culture of poverty" gripped the poor and rendered them socially immobile; that continued discrimination handicapped others; and that the so-called collapse of family values and the demise of traditional two-parent families resulted in individuals with flawed characters and work habits that made them unable or unwilling to work. Yet, others argue that government programs did not go far enough or needed adjustments to remedy these problems. Some other commentators have further argued that the postindustrial society left vast sectors of the labor force unable to adjust to the new skills required for employment.[34]

The adverse social conditions of Africans in the colonies after the Second World War parallel those of African Americans in the United States. The war, which left Britain, France, Portugal, and other imperial powers in desperate economic situations, forced them to ignore the urgent needs of the colonies as the Europeans tried to rebuild their war-ravaged economies. For instance, Robert Gordon's study of the impact of the Second World War in colonial Namibia reveals that the war opened the eyes of the Namibians recruited to fight in the South African theater to the many practices of exploitation and subjugation in the colonies.[35] Besides the fact that the war provided African ex-soldiers with a rich stock of experience and arguments to counter hegemonic claims predicated on the doctrine of racial superiority, Africanists are divided on the impact of African veterans on the emergence of postwar African nationalist movements. David Killingray, for example, argues that the African veterans played a no more significant role than other social groups in the independence movement. Anthony Smith asserts that the war also "marked a turning point in the Namibian people's struggle for freedom. Thousands of auxiliaries returned battle-hardened and victorious from the frontline, their eyes opened to a new dimension of coexistence and freedom."[36]

In Algeria soon after the war, deadly military responses to civil protests led Ahmed Ben Bella to found the militant nationalist party Organisation Spéciale (OS) in 1947. The OS led Algeria to freedom from French colonial rule in 1962. It became the National Liberation Army in 1958. On November 18, 1949, in eastern Nigeria, a civil protest against the colonial authorities by Enugu coalworkers over poor conditions of service (later blamed on Nnamdi Azikiwe) resulted in twenty-one deaths and fifty other casualties in one of the bloodiest suppressions of a labor union movement in Nigerian history.[37] In the British Kenya colony, the Mau Mau uprising emerged in 1952 and persisted until 1964 as a reaction to post–World War II oppressive and unfair political and economic policies by the British in East Africa. These and hundreds of similar instances across the African continent represented ways in which the colonized and oppressed masses chose to announce to the colonizer that they wanted to live in a free, equal, and democratic society.

In the United States, dire socioeconomic problems, most often associated with inner cities where the majority of poor Blacks lived, produced similarly violent agitations and brutal responses. In suburbs where Whites lived, violence was absent because most of the available opportunities for high-paying jobs were located in those areas. Apart from the fact that employment opportunities were unavailable in Black communities, public transportation to the White suburbs was problematic for the poor minorities. In practices reminiscent of the Boer-led segregationist socioeconomic and residential order in apartheid South Africa, some Whites who either despised Blacks or were afraid of crimes inspired by poverty relocated their homes farther away from the minority communities. Blacks in Los Angeles, Birmingham, Montgomery, Chicago, Louisville, and many other large U.S. cities suffered from these problems more than most other racial or ethnic groups in the entire United States of America. The practices of racism and violence went along with drug peddling and abuse and became more intractable everywhere across the United States. The old patterns of racial animosity changed to a new pattern with the emergence of a large Black population and a Black middle class in the major cities. The changing social problems brought about conservative political and strict police responses to the new counterculture as exhibited by Blacks of varying social and economic statuses. The persistence of racial isolation and discrimination and expanding ethnic consciousness were a result of a long history of political and police practices of containment and repression.

It was in the aforementioned socioeconomic and political milieu that African Americans in the South and other places embarked on a determined and bitter struggle for equality and freedom from the 1950s to end racial segregation; denial of opportunities for growth, citizenship rights, and the right to education; police brutality; and many other racist policies. Martin Luther King emerged in the mid-1950s as a community organizer, ordained minister, and civil rights activist in this historical milieu (Fig. 9.1).

Essentially, the civil rights movement of the late 1950s and 1960s was a struggle for equality, a call by African Americans to the U.S. society for due recognition as people who existed in body and mind and had the same God-given abilities as Whites, and the space to exercise their inalienable rights as humans and citizens of America. In December 1955, when the brave and courageous Black woman and NAACP official Rosa Parks declined to yield her seat on a segregated public bus in Montgomery, Alabama, and the police arrested her, the modern civil rights movement kicked off dramatically. This incident announced King's arrival to the civil rights protest theater. Although he planned to pursue a career in the academy, in 1954 King accepted an opportunity to serve as pastor of Dexter Avenue Baptist Church in Montgomery. Therefore,

Figure 9.1. Martin Luther King, Jr. *U.S. National Archives.*

King was in a strategic location when the bus crisis broke out. In reaction, Montgomery's Black leaders—among them his longtime friend Ralph Abernathy, Jo Ann Robinson, and E. D. Nixon—quickly tapped King as president of the Montgomery Improvement Association, the new organization they founded to resist segregation in Alabama.

In his role as the primary spokesperson for the Montgomery bus boycott, which lasted over twelve months, King deployed the leadership abilities he had gained from his religious background and academic training to forge an effective protest plan that involved the enlistment of Black churches and diplomatic petitions for White support. King would later recall in his memoir *Stride Toward Freedom* that "Mrs. Parks was ideal for the role assigned to her by history." According to King, "her character was impeccable and her dedication deep-rooted"; she was "one of the most respected people in the Negro community."[38]

King succinctly summed up this cardinal precept of the struggle in 1963: "We have waited more than 340 years to exercise our constitutional and God-given rights." King pointed out that African and Asian countries were quickly advancing toward political independence, but the United States was moving at a very slow pace that failed to ameliorate the racial climate and lives of Blacks.[39]

The urgent note struck by King validates the connection between decolonization and the civil rights movement. The successes gained by African nationalists in the late 1950s and 1960s hastened the impetus and imperative of the civil rights movement in America. This bond underpinned the decision of many young civil rights activists in the United States to take charge of the destiny of the movement by replacing the White liberals who were holding back the pace of the desired social reforms. Addressing thousands of Ghanaians at Accra's Polo Grounds on March 6, 1957, Socialist and labor leader A. Philip Randolph told the audience that Black Americans, "your brothers and sisters in color," were "fired [up]" by Africa's independence crusade.[40]

King recognized this bond when he contended, with the hindsight of the Black people's experience across time and space, that "freedom is never voluntarily given by the oppressor; it must be demanded by the oppressed." He condemned the timetable of White liberals "who have not suffered unduly from the disease of segregation," arguing that their familiar word "Wait!" has almost always meant "never." He stressed, "It has been a tranquilizing Thalidomide, relieving the emotional stress for a moment, only to give birth to an ill-formed infant of frustration. We must come to see with the distinguished jurist of yesterday that justice too long delayed is justice denied."[41]

Organized labor came under the control of White bureaucrats—many of whom seemed to have no honest sympathy for the conditions of the minority. The American Socialists were in too fragile a state to turn the situation around. Thus, Black Nationalism became the only viable course of action for leaders like Malcolm X and Stokely Carmichael (later Kwame Ture and one-time husband of Mariam Makeba). These and other African American figures traveled to Africa to confer with leaders of the emergent independent nations and anticolonial movements. Black advocates in the Student Nonviolent Coordinating Committee availed themselves of the violent rhetoric provided by Frantz Fanon in Algeria as a guide to action. By the mid-1960s, Black Nationalism had swept through the United States under the militant slogan of "Black Power."[42]

In a discussion on a radio show in New York on December 27, 1964, Malcolm X, one of the chief advocates of Black Power, who had just spent six months traveling across Africa, observed that Africans were waking up to the double standards inherent in the UN's deliberations in matters that affected people of African descent: "Neither was the case of Black people in this country ever linked with what was happening to people on the African continent. And if there's any drastic departure from past procedures that have been reflected already in the present UN session, it's the tendency on the part of African representatives one after another all to link what's happening in the Congo with what's happening in Mississippi."[43] In other words, there was an active dialogue and exchange of ideas between civil rights leaders in the United States and African anticolonial agitators. A further examination of United States-Africa exchanges and the manners in which public opinion leaders of the new postcolonial African society inserted themselves in the American civil rights struggle is crucial.

THE AFRICAN PRESS AND THE CIVIL RIGHTS MOVEMENT

Scholars who study the evolution of the Anglo-West African press have noted that its determination and outspokenness under colonial rule were unparalleled.[44] Often owned by the educated elite and nationalist leaders, it was in the 1950s that the conjoining movements for civil rights in America and sovereign rights across the world began to feed on one another. The civil rights movement gained significant support in 1954 following the *Brown v. Board of Education of Topeka, Kansas* Supreme Court decision ending segregation in public schools. This development did not escape the attention of the *West African Pilot* owned by Dr. Nnamdi Azikiwe, who was educated at Howard University and Lincoln University in the 1920s and 1930s.[45] Applauding the ruling in an article titled "Igirigiri, Searchlights: USA & Segregation," he declared that "action speaks louder than words. That is why I believe the U.S. Supreme Court ruling against segregation of white and Negro pupils in State schools to be far more effective than all the propaganda against the iron curtain."[46] It is noteworthy that the newspaper made an educated linkage of the event in America to the Cold War struggle to underscore the imperative of freedom and democracy for the oppressed.

Around the world, nations and peoples under imperial oppression saw hope in the 1954 defeat of the French army in Vietnam and the forced end of the Anglo-French invasion of Egypt in 1956 by the United States. Each movement took heart from the other. Then in the 1960s, the power of America's diplomatic influence and the demands of occupied peoples around the world exploded into popular, broad-spectrum social movements. Though Algeria was embroiled in a bloody war for independence against the French, the first year of the 1960s was arguably "the African year." When King inserted himself in the civil rights movement in Montgomery in 1956, no country in Black Africa had gained freedom from colonial rule. In 1960 alone, some seventeen African nations achieved their independence, all of them peacefully.[47]

After securing political freedom from Britain in 1957 without resorting to an armed struggle, Ghana emerged as a symbol of Africa's quest for freedom from colonialism. Both the United States and the Soviet Union sent groups to promote their interests in the new nation. For the United States, this influence took the form of the Peace Corps, the brainchild of then Sen. John F. Kennedy, who as presidential candidate in 1960 proposed "a peace corps of talented men and women" in a speech at the Cow Palace in San Francisco on November 2. The program offered for the peace and progress of developing countries was designed to use soft power both to better the world and to defeat global communism. The Communists tried to install their own groups as well but were less successful.

In Central Africa, the Congo presented the United States with two treacherous policy options. It had been evident for years that domestic politics could influence foreign policy. One only has to look at the Truman administration's intense antagonism toward China to see that in action. However, with the decolonization of Africa and American involvement to beat the Soviets to the new nations, foreign policy began to affect domestic politics in unexpected ways. Visiting the United Nations in July 1960, Patrice Emery Lumumba, the first prime minister of newly independent Congo, witnessed in person the nature of race riots in America. In many ways, decolonization of Africa forced many African Americans to reassess their own status in the home of democracy. Suddenly, the ugly bigotry and racism of the many White Americans were exposed for the entire world to see. This problem threatened more than just the ability of the United States to defeat the Soviets in Africa (as African nations were mortified to see how the most democratic society on earth treated its black citizens). Even more dangerously, it affected the domestic politics of the United States. If the president and other leaders did not begin reforms for African Americans' civil rights, the angry Black populace seemed ready to make these changes themselves through any means necessary.

With the intent to pry the conscience of the federal government to implement the promise of the *Brown v. Board of Education* decision of May 17, 1954, Black civil rights leaders announced a march in front of the Lincoln Memorial in Washington, D.C. In the last speech of the day, King tasked President Dwight D. Eisenhower and Congress to uphold and enforce the Supreme Court's landmark decision ending segregation in public schools. Additionally, King called on the government to grant voting rights to African Americans: "Give us the ballot and we will quietly and nonviolently, without rancor or bitterness, implement the Supreme Court's decision of May 17, 1954."[48] In the speech, King accused the two political parties of "betraying the cause of justice": "This dearth of positive leadership from the federal government is not confined to one particular political party. Both political parties have betrayed the cause of justice. The Democrats have betrayed it by capitulating to the prejudices and undemocratic practices of the southern Dixiecrats. The Republicans have betrayed it by capitulating to the blatant hypocrisy of right-wing, reactionary northerners."[49]

During the historic March on Washington on August 28, 1963, King and the other organizers of the event drew the attention of the world to the founding ideas of the United States and the deprived status of African Americans. During the speech now considered the speech of the century, King declared that "in a sense, we have come to our nation's capital to cash a check." He reminded the audience that "when the architects of our republic wrote the magnificent words of the Constitution and the Declaration of Independence, they were signing a promissory note to which every American was to fall heir. This note was a promise that all men, yes, black men as well as white men, would be guaranteed the unalienable rights of life, liberty and the pursuit of happiness."[50] By locating the civil rights struggle within the discourses of the founding fathers' anticolonial war against Great Britain, the Black civil rights leaders sought to remind all Americans and international observers of the inherent paradox of the oppression of Blacks in the midst of freedom.

In Africa, particularly in Anglo-speaking African nations, the press followed prudently and oftentimes in depth the struggles of the African Americans they referred to as "their brothers and sisters," a reference to racial and cultural affinity. The empathies demonstrated by the Anglophone West African press were strong, as were the criticisms and anger channeled to the U.S political leaders and those they identified as White racists. The newspapers celebrated "whatever they perceived or chose to interpret as a victory for African Americans."[51] The menacing presence of the Soviet Union in Africa, while the United States was grappling with race issues, put the Americans in a precarious position in coveting African leaders' support.

Thus, the Cold War ideological struggle provided the enabling international climate under which the free and independent press in English-speaking Africa inserted their voices in the United States' internal political trends. The goal of the African media was to support and advance the quest of the African Americans for freedom and equality. The African public understood that the African diaspora had shared a similar experience of Western slavery and imperial exploitation with Africans. The African press routinely addressed what it perceived as "America's hypocrisy and double standards on race issues," and either celebrated every sign of progress made by African Americans in the struggle or condemned every twist and reversal.[52]

The African American struggle for equal access in the field of education was one of the most emotional and compelling issues the African press monitored with serious interest. In 1954, for instance, following the *Brown v. Board of Education* ruling, the *West African Pilot* declared this development was "of particular significance and special interest to Africa and people of African descent throughout the world. It entails that the American concept and practice of democracy within its own territory should acknowledge the necessity of equal opportunity for all citizens no matter the racial origins."[53]

In 1957, when Arkansas governor Orval Faubus, a segregationist, defied federal laws by preventing nine African American students from enrolling in Little Rock High School, the African press followed the episode with keen attention. In an article entitled "Race Crisis in Little Rock," the *Nigerian Daily Times* called the attention of Nigerians to the event.[54] The newspaper followed up with a September 25, 1957, report that President Eisenhower had issued a warning that he would "use the full power of the United States, including whatever force may be necessary, to prevent the obstruction of the law in the Little Rock schools' racial dispute."[55] However, what the African newspaper did not understand at this time was that President Eisenhower was dragging his feet on social reforms. This slow pace is despite Jackie Robinson's (the first African American athlete in major league baseball) appeal to the president to come up with a clear and "unequivocal statement backed up by action."[56] Rather than heed this call, the president reiterated a gradualist resolution of the crisis and was more concerned about the embarrassment the Little Rock episode caused his government. "It would be difficult to exaggerate the harm that is being done to the prestige and influence" of the United States, President Eisenhower lamented in a nationally televised address, adding that the enemies of the country "are gloating over this incident and using it everywhere to misrepresent our nation."[57] In response to Robinson, Eisenhower wrote, "Steadily we are moving closer to the goal of fair and equal treatment of citizens without regard to race or color."[58]

Following Eisenhower's appeal, a fleeting period of peace returned to Little Rock, and the school crisis ended, albeit temporarily, without recourse to federal troops. Again, the *Daily Times* in Lagos updated the Nigerian newspaper-reading public with the latest development, adding the voices of students at the center of the crisis: "Five of the Negro students who attended the school said everyone in it was friendly. The White students also said they held no ill will

against their Negro schoolmates."[59] Then in October, the newspaper reported
again that normalcy had returned to the school in an article captioned "All
Quiet in Little Rock."[60] Two days later, hell broke loose at the school following
a calculated attack on Black students by their majority White fellow students.
The *Daily Times* did not waste much time in updating its audience about the
new development under the headline "Negro Students Attacked by Whites at
Little Rock." The writer quoted one of the attackers as saying that the aim of the
assault was to make the Black students feel "so miserable."[61]

During his short tenure as president, John F. Kennedy, who succeeded Eisenhower on January 20, 1961, had to respond to the African press's unrelenting
criticism of persistent racism against African Americans in the United States,
as well as the problem of disenfranchisement of Africans under European colonial domination. After running a successful campaign on a liberal agenda,
however, the Democratic president stated that winning the Cold War rather
than pursuing a lasting resolution of the civil rights struggle would be the primary focus of his administration. This view came despite his acknowledgment
that segregationist politics in the American South were a severe liability in the
United States' drive to emerge victorious in the Cold War ideological struggles.
Moreover, "even the most right-wing African groups and regimes made their
solidarity with African Americans known."[62] The new African leaders wanted
the United States to show that they would be treated with respect and not with
the racist disrespect meted out to the African American population.

The Africans perceived these racist policies as hypocritical in light of the
United States' coveting of the emergent African nations as allies in the Cold
War struggle. In a series of editorials and news reports and publications, the
Africans urged the U.S. government to restore social order in America. For instance, when President Kennedy announced in 1961 that it was the top priority of his government to land a crew of men on the moon and return them
home safely before the end of the decade, the *Ashanti Pioneer*, considered by
the American diplomats in Accra as "the most Western-oriented" and "responsible newspaper in Ghana," carried an article titled "Can White Americans
Answer?" in which the editor criticized the proclivity to racial discrimination
in the United States.[63] The *Ghanaian Times*, a government-owned newspaper
published in Accra, lashed out that rather than focusing on space travel, the
Negro condition demanded a more urgent consideration.[64] Four days later, the
Ethiopian Herald called on the U.S. government to put its "own house in order
before condemning others," adding that "any segregation against the Negro is
simultaneously segregation against Africans."[65]

In September 1962, when James Meredith, an African American World War II
Air Force veteran, enrolled at the University of Mississippi, Gov. Ross Barnett

sided with the segregationists, triggering a crisis in which federal troops were dispatched to Mississippi to protect Meredith and enforce federal laws. Following the incident, the *Nigerian Morning Post* sent a message of goodwill to President Kennedy for his handling of the incident.[66] The ensuing melee led to the loss of two lives and more than 300 injuries. The *West African Pilot* also celebrated the victory of Meredith, reporting that his decision was to use the resources at his command to liberate his people through his philanthropic organization known as the Meredith Fund Campaign for Afro-American Education. The nationalist paper linked Meredith's and other, related stories to the admission of Harvey Gantt into Clemson College in Columbia, South Carolina.[67]

On March 1, 1963, the Nigerian *Daily Express* called on President Kennedy's government to hasten civil rights reforms. The newspaper cited Kennedy's remarks that racial discrimination in the United States diminished America's "world leadership by contradicting at home the message we preach abroad."[68] In a similar tone, an editorial "Breaking the Color Line," in the *Ghanaian Times* of April 15, 1963, pronounced that "the man who screams friendship to the black man outside his borders only to discriminate against him in his home . . . is not causing a happy picture in anybody's mind."[69]

Indeed, segregation and the deplorable condition of African Americans were severe sources of embarrassment for U.S. democracy and the quest for global leadership. On April 12, 1963, the police in Birmingham, Alabama, arrested King for violating a law that prohibited a public demonstration. On May 9, 1963, the *Ghanaian Times* ran a commentary in which it branded Birmingham a "Race Riot City." The report included a picture of Gloria Floyd, a young African American girl, reportedly killed and dragged through the streets of Jackson, Mississippi. The paper posed the rhetorical question, "Is this America the beautiful?"[70] Echoing a speech by King, the *Ghanaian Times* editorial noted that "Birmingham is now the focal point of the freedom struggle . . . if we can crack segregation here, it will not be long before we crack it all over the south."

About a month later, on May 10, 1963, a cover story in the *Ghanaian Times* headlined "Luther Is Jailed for 6 Months" reported that the authorities in Alabama jailed King and his colleague Ralph Abernathy on May 9 for six months for organizing a public protest without a permit.[71] The paper also emphasized the prediction of Ralph Bunche, an official of the United Nations and the first African American to win the Nobel Peace Prize in 1950, that the struggle for racial equality in the United States would be resolved within the decade.

When the Birmingham Board of Education voted on May 20, 1963, to expel all 1,081 students who participated in the "Children's Crusade," a rally organized to protest Birmingham city's commissioner for public safety, Eugene "Bull" Connor, and his brutal police actions, the *Ghanaian Times* provided the reading audience in Ghana a full account of the events.[72] The paper also diligently covered any piece of action or legislation passed, which appeared as progress in the quest for racial equality. Among these was the news that some restaurants in Durham, North Carolina, had begun serving African American clientele even though many others continue to refuse to serve them. It also reported that in a civil rights case before the Supreme Court of the United States, the Court overturned the conviction of some African Americans by a local court for organizing a sit-in demonstration. Likewise, an editorial entitled "The Color Bar Problem in America" in the *Cameroonian Times* complained that the Americans "cannot pretend to assist African countries in the 'process of development' while torturing their kith and kin."[73] Similar but more comprehensive coverage of the Supreme Court ruling was in the Nigerian *Daily Express*. In an article headlined "U.S. Court Rules Against Racism: Conviction of Negroes by States Set Aside," the *Daily Express* reported that "the United States Supreme Court has declared unconstitutional state laws requiring racial segregation in public facilities."[74]

On June 10, 1963, the *Ghanaian Times* carried a very critical story linking Tehran, Birmingham, and South Africa as axes of evil. In powerful terms, the article decried racial policies in the United States, drawing a comparison between the United States and the apartheid policy of South Africa with the restrictive rules of the shah of Iran. The writer condemned what he perceived as unfulfilled "election promises about the Negro civil liberties." The article also accused President Kennedy of being fearful of introducing a transformative civil rights bill in Congress that would change African Americans' condition for good.[75] In a June 13, 1963, report, the Nigerian *Daily Express* insinuated that President Kennedy was acting more because of pressure than out of any personal commitment to civil right reforms in the United States, but also included the report that the president was optimistic that "U.S. Negroes shall Win Racial War." A couple of days later, the *Daily Express* carried a story titled "Kennedy Pledges New Race Law as Negro Leader Slain."[76] The *West African Pilot* added its voice to the growing international condemnation of the race problem in the United States by reporting the call by the Geneva-based International Commission of Jurists that the U.S. government change the attitude of White Americans, especially those "in the south."[77]

While the African newspapers spoke the minds of their government and people, the emergent African leaders continued to voice their feelings at every occasion that presented the opportunity. Early in 1959, Nnamdi Azikiwe was invited to address the NAACP on the organization's jubilee. When the Nigerian nationalist took the stage, he addressed a broad spectrum of subjects related to the civil rights struggle—including the 1954 Supreme Court decision, the spirit of the Blacks as exemplified by NAACP constitution, and the decolonization movement in Africa. Without hesitation, Azikiwe stated that "in Africa, the NAACP spirit of active resistance to the forces, which are inconsistent with democratic principles, has fired our imagination. We have relentlessly fought any attempt to foist upon us the horrible stigma of racial inferiority. We have successfully challenged cant and hypocrisy among those who pay lip service to democracy. And we have severed forever the chains of autocracy in many African countries where millions of Africans were held in political bondage."[78]

This speech would serve as one of the earliest and most direct comments made by an African nationalist leader about the civil rights movement on American soil. Many other similar remarks would follow as the decolonization train in African gained traction. On March 22, 1959, Congolese nationalist Patrice Lumumba expressed the African nationalist leaders' identification of the aspirations of colonized and enslaved peoples as one. In a speech at an international seminar held at the University of Ibadan, Lumumba declared that "the aims pursued by nationalist movements in any African territory are also the same. The common goal is the liberation of Africa from the colonialist yoke. . . . We hold out a fraternal hand to the West. Let it today give proof of the principle of equality and friendship between races that its sons have always taught us as we sat at our desks in school, a principle written in capital letters in the Universal Declaration of the Rights of Man. Africans must be just as free as other citizens of the human family to enjoy the fundamental liberties set forth in this declaration and the rights proclaimed in the United Nations Charter. The period of racial monopolies is now at an end."[79]

Then on May 24, 1963, for example, a correspondent of the *Ghanaian Times* reported from Addis Ababa, Ethiopia, that Prime Minister Milton Obote of Uganda had attacked the United States for the Alabama race riots. In a message to the president of the United States, Obote declared that "nothing is more paradoxical than that these events should take place in the United States and at a time when that country is anxious to project its image before the world screen as the architect of democracy and champion of freedom."[80]

Following Obote's comment was that from President Julius Nyerere of Tanzania. Nyerere attacked the United States for persistently experiencing the embarrassment that racial bigotry brings because of ignorance and intolerance. He pointed out the negative impression the race question had created about the country in the international arena. Echoing Du Bois's comment on the United States' claim to be the leader of democracy in the world while it could not rule Alabama, Nyerere also took America to task by saying, "America which claims to be a champion and guardian of democracy and an upholder of human dignity should have set a better example to the world."[81]

From May 3 to 8, 1963, the world cringed with horror at images of police brutality against schoolchildren as racial hatred boiled over again in Birmingham. In a slight reminiscence of the Sharpeville massacre of 1960 and the Soweto uprising of 1976 in South Africa, Bull Connor ordered the use of fire hoses, clubs, and rabid dogs against the demonstrating young people. After a series of meetings between Birmingham businesses and John M. Gore, the U.S. assistant attorney general for civil rights, Birmingham officials agreed to desegregate public facilities, and local businesses decided to hire more Blacks. However, the African press did not overlook the damage already done. In an article by Teshome Adera entitled "Justice Done," the *Ethiopian Herald* highlighted the increasing erosion of America's "enormous influence and prestige around the world" due to segregation.[82] Similarly, the *Cameroonian Times*, in an article headlined "The Colour Bar Problems in America" on May 21, 1963, argued that if what happened in Birmingham had occurred in the Soviet Union, American politicians would have "spoken out their lungs."[83] In other words, the United States would have spearheaded a global outcry against the Soviets.

It is noteworthy that the March on Washington on August 28, 1963, was part of the plan by African American leaders to support the civil rights bill proposed by President Kennedy and to lobby for its passage. The rally was attended by an estimated 250,000 people and received extensive coverage in Nigeria and Ghana. A day before the historic event, the *West African Pilot* published a report titled "4000 U.S. Troops Alerted as Negroes Plan to 'Invade' Washington."[84] The publication coincided with the announcement of Du Bois's death in Ghana at age ninety-five. Du Bois died two years after he had renounced his U.S. citizenship in 1961 due to frustrations with poor race relations in his country and moved to Ghana, where he took up Ghanaian citizenship on the invitation of Nkrumah. If King's "I Have a Dream" speech remains today as a powerful epitaph to the civil rights struggle, Du Bois's final words to Nkrumah on his deathbed on August 27, 1963, stand as a reminder of the essence of Pan-Africanism. He reminded Blacks around the world that their shared history and destiny made it compulsory to continue working with a common purpose for the greater good of their race. "I want to thank you," said Du Bois, "for all you have done to make the ending of my life bountiful and beautiful. . . . Good-bye! And bless you."[85]

As evidence reveals, the collective actions and thoughts of Africans and African Americans were instrumental in the success of the civil rights movement and the successful defeat of European colonial rule in Africa. In their vigorous and committed coverage of the struggle, the African press understood the need to project the deeds and misdeeds of U.S. politicians with regard to race relations and human rights as they related to African Americans' condition. The Africans were further conscious of the fact that racial discrimination in America diminished respect for the United States in the international arena and thus endangered its quest for global leadership in the world order.

More important, the African educated elite and opinion leaders were quite aware that the outcome of the struggle would have severe implications for Africa and its people on both the domestic and international fronts. While the postcolonial state in Africa used its independent press to cover myriad other issues converging on the global stage, the press devoted particular interest to the U.S. civil rights struggle and covered every event with consistency and analytical insight. It was to the credit of the Africans that the press leveraged the favorable global political climate offered by the Cold War ideological struggle to push forward various African agendas, including the quest for freedom on both sides of the Atlantic. The emergent African postcolonial leaders and nationalists provide the leadership and funds with which this struggle was prosecuted to a successful end. In his heartfelt tribute to the Africans in 1965, Malcolm X thanked the African leaders for organizing to help achieve freedom for Black people everywhere. Then he added that the only groups he saw not doing much during his trip to Africa in the 1960s were the "American Negros and the Afro-Americans" who were "just socializing and partying."[86]

10

THE COLD WAR: U.S. AFRICAN FOREIGN POLICY RESET

While scholars and practitioners of East-West diplomacy often present the Cold War as an ideological duel between the capitalist West and the communist East, or what Michael Wesley described as "democratic alliance versus authoritarian bloc," the focus here is on how the post–World War II rivalries between the two superpowers played out in Africa, along with the far-reaching consequences for the continent.[1] One may recall that on August 14, 1941, the United States under President Franklin D. Roosevelt and Great Britain under Prime Minister Winston Churchill had released a joint statement known as the Atlantic Charter setting forth the postwar goals of both countries. Among other things, the charter contained an avowal by the Allied powers not to seek territorial gains and to respect the right of people to self-determination, disarmament, and freer exchange of trade. Ultimately, the charter inspired nationalist agitations throughout the colonized world, including Africa, and the United States strategically nurtured and advanced the ideology of self-determination as a slogan for the anticommunist campaign on the international arena. The point is that the Atlantic Charter created the expectation of national self-determination that influenced African nationalism and decolonization in the 1950s. The Cold War intensified in the 1950s and 1960s, coinciding with the period of decolonization when America's interest in Africa rose to unprecedented heights. However, this sudden shift in attention had nothing to do with America's intent to engage with the emergent African postcolonial state in a reciprocal and respectful exchange of values and cultural, political, security, and economic ideas.

Instead, the driving motive was America's strategic interests articulated in terms of a zero-sum game, or what political leaders and policymakers in Washington perceived as necessary to curb the growing presence of the Soviet Union on the African continent. For the United States, the Soviet Union's conduct of foreign policy was a serious threat to America's rising global influence. But for America to be able to contain the spread of communism in the developing world, especially in Africa, it first needed to address its domestic problems of race relations, along with the international politics of colonialism in Africa. To capture properly the context in which the United States began to navigate these problems by getting more involved with Africa in the post–World War II era, it is crucial to revisit, albeit in brief, the African and African American response to Nazism and the Allied war effort.

NAZISM IMPERILS RACISM IN THE UNITED STATES

Britain's declaration of war on Germany on September 3, 1939, implied that its African colonies, along with those in Asia and the Pacific, were also at war with the Axis powers. Ashley Jackson has noted that the contributions of the African colonies in the numerous wars directed by the metropole are yet to be sufficiently noted by historians, even as those of India, Australia, New Zealand, Canada, and South Africa have received due coverage as an integral part of the global theaters of both World War I and World War II.[2]

There is no intent here to make up for the lacunas in the historiography, and it is quite impossible to give a detailed account of Africa's role in the two world wars. Rather, the following is a short background to the politics of the Cold War as it relates to Africa and United States-Africa relations in three related domains: Africa's strategic geography; Africa's material, financial, and manpower contributions to the Allied war effort; and the pitfalls of racist ideology inspired by Nazism.

By virtue of its geography in an age of European empires, Africa occupied a strategic position in the Allied war effort. Alexander Moorhead and others have provided glimpses of the North Africa campaign (the so-called Desert War) that raged from 1940 to 1943. The ultimate prize for the armies fighting in Africa north of the Sahara was for strategic control of the Mediterranean Sea, the adjoining Suez Canal, the Red Sea, and other sea routes connecting England's North and East African imperial holdings with British India. As Moorhead noted, the fact that the Desert War was the only theater in which Allied forces directly confronted combined German and Italian forces attests to the seriousness with which both sides in the war considered the African front strategic.[3]

The principal goal for the deployment of Germany's Afrika Korps, led by Gen. Erwin Rommel, was to deter the British Air Force from striking the Ploiesti oil fields in Romania, one of Germany's primary sources of oil. This intervention became urgent after Italy launched a failed offensive into British-occupied Egypt. As the German-led offensive scored initial successes, the possibility of a German-Italian conquest of the Middle East and a link-up with the German forces in the Caucasus region of the Soviet Union became a possibility. There was also an important campaign launched by Germany in Somalia and Ethiopia (parts of East Africa) in 1940–41, which bolstered its North African incursions. In the decisive Tunisian campaign, the Allied troops, with the help of Africans, seized as many as 275,000 Axis soldiers. Control of Italy's Libyan colony and parts of Egypt changed hands until the British Eighth Army, commanded by Lt. Gen. Bernard Montgomery, joined by Indian and African soldiers and supported by U.S. forces, flushed the Axis army out of North Africa and back into Europe, thus allowing the Allied forces to gain control of North Africa.[4]

The most important part of Africa's involvement in World War II was in the material and financial support people of the continent offered to the Allies.[5] Chima J. Korieh's study of Nigeria shows that like other British colonial dominions, Nigeria was obligated to contribute to the British Win-the-War-Funds campaign, with no compensation after the war. Everywhere in the continent, the elite and opinion leaders mobilized both human and material resources needed to execute the war.[6] For example, just a couple of weeks after Great Britain declared war against Germany, the faculty, staff, and pupils of the Qua Iboe Mission Institute in Uyo, Nigeria, wrote a letter to the king of England criticizing Germans and declaring that "our ardent wish is that the Germans be brought to their knees in the shortest possible time," in order to quickly restore global peace.[7] In similar terms, the local leaders of Ututu, Nigeria, wrote the British monarchy vowing loyalty and support to the empire and pledging "to render any assistance" in the fight "for world peace."[8] In more specific terms, the chiefs of Idomi, Nigeria, declared their willingness to assist Britain by "giving full attention to kernel production."[9] Africans sustained this level of assistance to the point that the people of Ondo Province contributed funds to assist the children of London rendered homeless by German bombing raids on civilian targets. Additionally, contributions from other parts of the country brought enough funds for the purchase of Spitfire fighter aircraft for the Royal Air Force.[10]

The African press, including the nationalist newspapers, played their part in promoting anti-German sentiments among the Africans. For example, the *Gold Coast Times* of March 13, 1939, depicted Great Britain as the "great protector of small nations" standing up to evil Germany and Nazi oppression.[11] The *West African Pilot*, owned by Nnamdi Azikiwe, offered the Allies unwavering support for the war. In an editorial of September 4, 1939, the editor noted that the youths of Britain and France were "shedding their blood in order that the ideals of liberty, democracy and peace might strive in the world."[12] In another editorial, in February 1942, the paper declared that it was "the duty of every citizen of this country, as it is of every liberty-loving soul in every part of the world, to bear the greatest sacrifice ungrudgingly and contribute his maximum in every way possible, little or great to bring the success of the Allied forces nearer."[13] The *Nigerian Daily Times* added that the war was a struggle "against habits of the jungle" and "a stand for fair and free negotiation."[14]

The third crucial factor that would affect United States-Africa relations after World War II was the peril of racism. The war exposed the problems of racism in the United States and the colonial territories in Africa. For African Americans, some of whom served as volunteers, there was an explicit similarity between Nazism and White supremacy. For instance, at the end of 1938, when the Nazis started separating Jews on German railways, the *New York Amsterdam News* quickly observed that Nazis were borrowing "a leaf from United States Jim Crow practices against the Negro."[15] The paper went on to explain how the German "Elite Guards" planned to "Jim Crow Jews on German railways," calling the policy "a guaranteed democratic example" in direct reference to the same system under U.S. democracy.[16] In reaction, the famous Black newspaper the *Chicago Defender* added that "the practice of Jim-Crowism has already been adopted by the Nazis." Therefore, World War II, like World War I before it, presented African Americans with an opportunity for a "double victory," as the influential *Pittsburgh Courier* announced: the simultaneous defeat of America's racist policies at home and German racial debauchery overseas.[17] In his message to a crowd of union workers in Detroit in July 1943, Vice President Henry Wallace warned that "we cannot fight to crush Nazi brutality abroad and condone race riots at home. Those who fan the fires of racial clashes for the purpose of making political capital here at home are taking the first step toward Nazism."[18] In response to the vice president's speech, John R. Williams, correspondent of the *Pittsburgh Courier*, noted that Wallace's comments stood as a solid endorsement of the "Double V" campaign launched by African American activists and leading journalists in January 1942 to promote civil rights and the genuinely democratic society that was obstructed by poor White-Black race relations in the United States.[19]

In Africa, a similar debate was in play against slavery and colonial subjugation. Omitting account of the practices of slavery and Jim Crow in America, the Allied forces had purposefully disseminated the propaganda that Hitler and Germans were the problems of the world and that the Axis powers intended to exterminate all the colored races. Allied propaganda emphasized that the war was waged for freedom and against racial bigotry.[20] In response, the Africans mobilized in support of the Allied forces in West, South, East, and North Africa. As the Africans deployed the dialectics of "freedom" and all that it implies, the imagery and semantic of slavery infiltrated colonial war propaganda. Bonny Ibhawoh has noted that the "propaganda literature stressed that the consequence of German victory in the war would be the enslavement, or more appropriately, the re-enslavement of Africans. Images of half-naked Africans bound in chains and flogged by menacing looking German soldiers were evocative of not so distant memories of slavery and the slave trade."[21]

In essence, Africans, like African Americans, were already negotiating their freedoms and building up hopes as World War II was running its course. In Morocco, the U.S. president, desirous of the support of Sidi Mohammed Ben Youssef (Sultan Mohammed V), verbally committed to decolonization after the war. This promise recalled the "self-determination" for colonized peoples of the world promised earlier by President Woodrow Wilson, who was succeeded by Warren G. Harding in 1921 after World War I.[22] In fact, on the eve of World War II, Mohammed V was already looking forward to the postwar era in the hope that French colonial rule in Morocco would end for good. Throughout the duration of the war, Mohammed V, once exalted as an "anti-Nazi Sultan," worked with France to ensure Allied victory.[23] Over a historic dinner in a suburb of Casablanca on January 22, 1943, the sultan secured the pledge of President Roosevelt, to France's displeasure, that his kingdom would be granted independence if the sultan would support the Allies in recruiting Moroccan troops for action on the European front. Referring to these developments in the wake of his deposition in 1955, a news report commented that "during the war, particularly from 1940 to 1943, he [Mohammed V] received much flattery from the Germans and later from other Powers. He came to regard himself as a personality and was persuaded by his entourage that all kinds of promises had been made him."[24] Not only did the sultan comply with Roosevelt's request, but Moroccan veterans served with distinction in the war.[25]

Thus, the post–World War II era was a difficult time for both colonial powers and defenders of Jim Crow in America, as civil rights activists in the United States and nationalists in Africa brought profound pressure on the Allied powers to follow through on their promises of "freedom" and "self-determination." U.S. and European politicians and policymakers found themselves in an unenviable moral dilemma. The choice involved either complying with the promise of freedom for the colonized peoples or maintaining imperial control, mostly for economic considerations. The justifications for racism in America and colonial control by Britain, France, Belgium, and Portugal had died in the fight against German Nazism. In Morocco, a move by French officials to renege on decolonization by undercutting the sultan's authority turned Mohammed V into a friend of radical nationalists there. The rebellious stances taken by the African rulers after 1945 and their consequent punishment by imprisonment, deportation, or exile—all attest to the incompatibility of the new nationalist Zeitgeist with either colonial control or practices of racism and domination.

World War II established the basis on which postwar United States-Africa relations makes sense. Following the death of President Roosevelt on April 12, 1945, President Harry S. Truman, who succeeded him and directed the end of the war, came out boldly to condemn racism. Truman was moved by the evil that Blacks who fought in the war had encountered segregation and mob actions at home. Truman unambiguously expressed his disgust: "No citizen of this great country ought to be discriminated against because of his race, religion, or national origin. That is the essence of the American ideal and the American Constitution." Truman emphasized the point by stating that his "stomach turned over when I learned that Negro soldiers, just back from overseas, were being dumped out of army trucks in Mississippi and beaten. Whatever my inclinations as a native of Missouri might have been, as President I know this is bad. I shall fight to end evils like this."[26]

The continuation of racism and segregation affected Truman so deeply that in late 1946 he established, by Executive Order 9808, the President's Committee on Civil Rights, charged with implementing the U.S. Bill of Rights to the letter.[27] "I want our Bill of Rights implemented in fact. We have been trying to do this for 150 years. We're making progress, but we're not making progress fast enough."[28]

The committee's report, made public in 1947, provided a detailed record of forms of racial discrimination in areas such as housing, voting rights, education, and public accommodations.[29] By this time, the Cold War was expanding like wildfire, fueled in part by the slow pace of changes in U.S. race relations despite President Truman's leadership to end discrimination. Also, the problem of decolonization in Africa and Asia was a severe and explosive flashpoint of conflict. Incidentally, President Truman also articulated the fundamental rules of engagement with which to confront the threat of communism around the world. The Truman Doctrine, enunciated on March 12, 1947, made available both the needed cash and logistics to combat communism.[30] These ground rules shaped U.S. foreign policy from this period to the fall of the Soviet Union in 1991.

Meanwhile, sensing that the pace of change in the U.S. was too slow, Du Bois and the NAACP were not ready to relent. In October 1947, the African American leaders found supporters in Communist China and the Soviet Union, who helped them tender a petition of the NAACP to the United Nations.[31] U.S. attorney general Tom C. Clark, a native of Jim Crow Texas, would later admit that the fact that it was the Soviet Union that brought the NAACP petition to the U.N. caused him to feel "humiliated."[32]

EISENHOWER COMES TO POWER

In his inaugural address on January 20, 1953, President Dwight D. Eisenhower (1953–1961), who succeeded President Harry S. Truman (1945–1953), spent a great deal of time highlighting the Soviet threat along with the principles of engagement that would guide his foreign policy in the new world order. "Abhorring war as a chosen way to balk the purposes of those who threaten us," Eisenhower said, "we hold it to be the first task of statesmanship to develop the strength that will deter the forces of aggression and promote the conditions of peace. For, as it must be the supreme purpose of all free men, so it must be the dedication of their leaders, to save humanity from preying upon itself."[33] How Eisenhower and the succeeding presidents of the United States would respond to the Soviet Union's presence on the African battlefront during the Cold War deeply affected the continent in many ways that are still ongoing.

To show these effects in the framework of United States-Africa relations, case studies of interest include the roles of the superpowers in supporting nonrepresentative minority governments, dictatorships, and military regimes in Africa, and in sponsoring coups d'état, assassinations, economic imperialism, and sabotage. Other frontiers of engagement include foreign aid, censorship, civil wars, and regional wars within and between African nation-states. African commentaries on and interpretations of capitalism and communism, such as Julius Nyerere's "African Socialism," Léopold Sédar Senghor's rejoinders, Siad Barre's reactions and responses, and Nnamdi Azikiwe's exploits, are discussed in light of U.S. policies toward Africa as the Western powers hunted down Marxist-Leninist "radicals" on the continent.

BACKGROUND: FLANKING AFRICA FROM
THE POSITION OF STRENGTH

Reflecting on United States-Africa relations in the context of the Cold War in 2007, Letitia Lawson reiterated the clear view that American foreign policy toward sub-Saharan Africa was governed by self-interest. Like other emergent and developing nations in Asia, Latin America, and the Middle East, African nations were just a "pawn in the great global game."[34] The key word from Lawson's conclusion is "game," but what transpired in Africa over the period was more than a regular game. In conventional games, there is an expectation of fair play and a referee enforces the rules. Games have spectators or fans who acknowledge winners and losers. The Cold Warriors on both sides of the struggle (the Soviet Union and America) held the delusion that every person not on their side was out to get them. Thus, in their delusional grandeur, the superpowers and their allies left no room open for the possibility of an alternative voice or a counterideological choice.

With hardliners like Premier Joseph Stalin (1941–1953) and Nikita Khrushchev (1953–1964) directing the Soviet Union's global expansionism, President Truman voiced his alarm at the pace with which the Soviet Union was extending its global influence. His response came in the form of the Truman Doctrine, which was a policy of containment formulated by the United States to keep the Soviet Union within its existing territories and spheres of influence.[35] The economic side of the doctrine was the Marshall Plan of 1948, an initial grant of $400 million (ultimately $12 billion) in financial assistance provided by the United States to aid the failing economies of Greece and Turkey, and later the rest of Western Europe.[36] In alignment with this doctrine, President Eisenhower warned in 1953 "that common sense and common decency alike dictate the futility of appeasement, we shall never try to placate an aggressor by the false and wicked bargain of trading honor for security. Americans, indeed, all free men, remember that in the final choice a soldier's pack is not so heavy a burden as a prisoner's chains."[37]

While the U.S. postwar economic gift was critical for rebuilding Europe's war-ravaged economies, the truth of the matter is that the Cold War was nothing but a bigoted ideological bazaar peddled by the emergent superpowers of the postwar world order. Armed with nuclear weapons, propaganda apparatuses such as films, radios, and televisions, espionage, assassinations, bullying, blackmail, and other instruments of coercion and intimidation, the Americans and the Soviets went about recruiting clients and supporters around the world with little or no consideration for the values of freedom, happiness, and peace they often claimed to protect. Manning Marable corroborated this view in 1984 when he noted that the "paranoid-mode of anti-communist America made it impossible for any other reform movement to exist."[38] Marable was speaking specifically about the prolonged and disturbing civil rights movement, a resolution of which some mischief-makers attempted to prolong, if not stop in total, under the false assumption that Communists drove it.

It is important to recall that before 1950, the United States had a diplomatic presence in only five African countries: Egypt (since 1849), Liberia (1864),

Morocco (1906), Ethiopia (1910), and South Africa (1930). At that time, most African countries were still colonies and, therefore, would not have qualified for diplomatic representation. However, the United States founded the colony of Liberia in 1816 and opened a consular office in Monrovia in 1864. This is irrefutable proof that America had little or no interest in African affairs until the rise of the Cold War. It is curious also that while Sierra Leone came into existence in 1787 as a symbol of freedom from the Atlantic slave trade, there was no U.S. diplomatic post there until April 27, 1961. Again, when Fascist Italy under Benito Mussolini (1883–1945) attacked Abyssinia (Ethiopia) with mustard gas, aerial assaults, and tanks on October 3, 1935, in violation of Article 15 of the Covenant of the League of Nations, both the United States (a nonmember) and the fifty-two nation-members of the world body refused to take concrete steps in defense of the African nation. This double-face was in spite of Italy's position as a founding member of the League of Nations and its verbal promises to adhere to the tenets of the league. This indifference led to the historic speech by Emperor Haile Selassie of Ethiopia at the Geneva summit in June 1936. "What [has] become of the promises made to me as long ago as October 1935? I noted with grief, but without surprise that three Powers considered their undertakings under the Covenant as absolutely of no value. Their connections with Italy impelled them to refuse to take any measures whatsoever to stop Italian aggression. On the contrary, it was a profound disappointment to me to learn the attitude of a certain Government, which, whilst ever protesting its scrupulous attachment to the Covenant, has tirelessly used all its efforts to prevent its observance."[39]

The preceding quote leads us to conclude that within the background from which contemporary American foreign policy relations with Africa emerged, Africa was a sidekick unless needed to achieve the specific interests of the superpowers. Thomas Noer highlights the United States' misconceptions of the continent and its people prior to the end of colonial rule: "Gaining their image of Africa from Tarzan movies, missionary slide shows in church basements, and Ernest Hemingway short stories, Americans saw the continent as a land of jungle and animals, not of nations in the international system. The rapid rise of independence movements in Africa and the growth of the American civil rights struggle following the Second World War finally combined to make the 'dark continent' an area of United States diplomatic activity."[40]

Then, in the 1950s and 1960s, the number of American embassies snowballed across the continent as Africans extricated themselves from the clutches of colonialism. The aim of this sudden hand of friendship extended to Africa from the 1950s by successive Republican and Democratic leaders was to support U.S.

Cold War clients in Africa and to destroy, at any cost, the legitimacy of those who were inclined toward the Soviet bloc. As the transition from colonial rule to self-rule was gaining traction, Richard Nixon, Eisenhower's vice president, acknowledged in late 1960 that "in the struggle with the Russians, Africa is the most critical area in the world."[41] Soon after Nixon's speech, President-Elect John F. Kennedy described Africa as the target of "a gigantic communist offensive."[42] These interpretations reveal that the American leaders understood that instability and chaos in Africa would not augur well for U.S. foreign policy goals on the continent, but rather would play into the hands of the Soviets. Through its actions and inactions, the United States helped create the unstable political situation it wanted to prevent in postcolonial Africa.

THE POSTCOLONIAL STATE AND CHAOS IN
UNITED STATES-AFRICA RELATIONS

Writing in in 1989, Thomas J. Noer, an authority on Kennedy's African foreign policy, suggested that the Congo crisis of the early 1960s was the most challenging diplomatic debacle for the president. Noer reinforced this idea with a quote from Roger Hilsman, director of the State Department's Bureau of Intelligence and Research under Kennedy, who in 1960 described the Congo crisis as the most "baffling and frustrating test" for the new administration.[43] Coming from a spy chief, there is no reason to challenge Hilsman's authoritative view. However, we cannot fully understand what transpired in the Congo without starting from Ghana, whose independence in 1957 predated Congo's in 1960.

Under Nkrumah's leadership, Ghana was the capital of nationalist agitation in Africa. Thus, it presents the most outstanding case study of U.S. attempts to influence the foreign relations of the newly developing African nations in the late 1950s and 1960s. In a message to Ghanaians on March 6, 1957, President Eisenhower, speaking through Vice President Nixon, who was in Accra to convey the goodwill of the administration and the people of America, congratulated Ghana on "joining the family of independent nations." He saluted Ghana's "statesman-like cooperative effort" with the United Kingdom, in an apparent reference to the absence of violence and bloodshed in the process of independence, and then added, "I am sure that this same spirit will characterize Ghana's relationship with the free world, including the great and voluntary association of nations, the British Commonwealth." Ironically, the United States also reiterated its belief in people who cherish their independence and right to exercise their free will: "I speak for a people that cherish independence, which we deeply believe is the right of all people who are able to discharge its

responsibilities. It is with special pleasure, therefore, that we witness the establishment of your new nation and the assumption of its sovereign place in the
free world." Nixon concluded by saying that he was proud that many of Ghana's
eminent leaders were educated in the United States and that "many of our most
accomplished citizens had their ancestry in your country. . . . I am confident
that our two countries will stand as one in safeguarding this greatest of all bonds
between us."[44]

What transpired throughout Africa in the following ten years, including in
Ghana and the Republic of the Congo, did not corroborate America's appreciation of other countries' "independence" and the belief in their "freewill" touted
by Eisenhower through Nixon in Accra in 1957. Likewise, neither Eisenhower's
successors, including Kennedy (1961–1963), nor others would respect those
words. Throughout the Cold War era, American presidents viewed Africa as a
region of symbolic significance and a battleground for the Cold War. In early
1953, Eisenhower had avowed, "Honoring the identity and the special heritage
of each nation in the world, we shall never use our strength to try to impress
upon another people our own cherished political and economic institutions."[45]
With Ghana as the first nation in sub-Saharan Africa to gain its independence,
the United States was desperate to win President Kwame Nkrumah's friendship
as a step to obtaining a firm foothold on the continent. This desire explains why
Eisenhower invited Nkrumah to Washington in the first year of his administration (Fig. 10.1).[46]

In a meeting with Eisenhower during his visit in 1958, Nkrumah with char-
acteristic candor told his host that his feeling while in the country was a general lack of understanding among the rank and file of the government about
Africa's needs and problems. He said that he had heard this particularly from
President Bourguiba of Tunisia.[47] President Eisenhower took Nkrumah's message literally, without realizing that while relating Bourguiba's message, the
Ghanaian president was also expressing his views about United States-Ghana/
Africa relations—especially about the economic needs of the Africans.[48] Uppermost on Nkrumah's mind was the Volta River Electricity Project, which he had
hoped the United States would help finance by way of foreign direct investment
rather than a grant. Nkrumah envisioned the Volta hydroelectric project as the
cornerstone of his massive industrialization program in Ghana.[49]

Perhaps more critical during Nkrumah's visit were those things not discussed:
specifically, the troubled racial relationship between White Americans and
African Americans, which troubled Nkrumah more than anything else. Kevin
Gaines informs us that in a discussion in March 1957, Nkrumah told Martin
Luther King, Jr. that he would not accept the American notion of freedom

Figure 10.1. President Dwight D. Eisenhower and President Kwame
Nkrumah. *Everett Collection Historical/Alamy Stock Photo.*

and democracy unless America first resolved its domestic racial conflict. This
confidential discussion inspired King to express his belief in Nkrumah's ability
as a leader "to meet the challenge ahead."[50] In other words, the line of conflict
between Nkrumah and the United States was marked on the sands of history
before the postcolonial state emerged and got itself entangled with American
Cold War interests.

    Despite his American education, Nkrumah gradually became a prominent
Communist ideologue who envisaged harnessing the principles of socialism
to reconstruct a postcolonial model nation in Ghana. The paradox of this re-
solve is evident in Nkrumah's initial vision of the liberty he wanted to bring to
Africa. Nkrumah would later write in *Ghana: The Autobiography of Kwame
Nkrumah* that on his way home from the United States after his studies in 1945,
he had accepted the American Statue of Liberty as a symbol of inspiration:
"You have opened my eyes to the true meaning of liberty. I shall never rest until
I have carried your message to Africa."[51] In essence, the Statue of Liberty was
for Nkrumah an inspiration in the struggle to free his country and Africa from

colonial domination. The context in which this original inspiration was lost to a Communist ideal is a flashpoint in the U.S.-African relations discourse.

To proceed, it is essential to add that America's sensitivity to its European allies and former colonial overlords in Africa shaped a good part of its African foreign policy. In his address before the Fifteenth General Assembly of the United Nations in New York on September 22, 1960, President Eisenhower enthusiastically welcomed the newly independent African nations to the "commonwealth of nations." To the world, Eisenhower talked about the challenges that lay ahead as the new nations emerged from decades of colonial rule. "We can strive to master these problems," he stated, "for narrow national advantage or we can begin at once to undertake a period of constructive action which will subordinate selfish interest to the general well-being of the international community." Of particular interest was his comment on outside interference in the internal affairs of the African countries. "Outside interference with these newly emerging nations, all eager to undertake the tasks of modernization, has created a serious challenge to the authority of the United Nations."[52] As is evident in what transpired in the Republic of the Congo, Ghana, and elsewhere in Africa over this period, the various European colonial powers were privy to the United States' actions and inactions.

With a political image that towered over the African continent as the Statue of Liberty towers over New York, Nkrumah's grand plan was to construct a United States of Africa with an African high command. Not only did this ambitious goal conflict with America's interests, Nkrumah aimed to achieve it under the banner of communism. In this context, Ghana became the foremost Cold War battleground in the East-West struggle, despite steps taken by Nkrumah to lead Ghana in a nonaligned framework. Increasingly, a significant gulf emerged between the United States and Ghana as succeeding American governments came to interpret most of Nkrumah's later policies and actions to strengthen the new nation to mean that Ghana had entirely moved to the Soviet bloc. This perception and the tension it generated both at home and overseas "became more intense and fraught with grave complications. In the end, America's clandestine activities in Ghana with British support demonized Nkrumah and culminated in a coup d'état that eventually toppled Nkrumah's administration on February 24, 1966, while Nkrumah was in Vietnam on a peacemaking mission."[53]

In his study of the U.S. Central Intelligence Agency's activities in Ghana, John Pradoes reminded us that the U.S. government encouraged the public to believe that it was making the West African country "safe for democracy."[54] Ironically, the opposite and most significant consequence of military intervention in a nascent democracy in Black Africa was apparent. The move created a long history of unstable military dictatorships that lasted until the 1990s, when Col. Jerry J. Rawlings (1981–2000), a hotheaded military officer, commenced a program of extrajudicial executions that targeted the former heads of state of Ghana.[55] Rawlings's actions inspired others of a similar nature in Burkina Faso, where Col. Thomas Sankara seized power in a radical move taken from Rawlings's political handbook.[56] Today, most Ghanaians and Africans continue to point accusing fingers at the United States for the end of Nkrumah's visions for Ghana and the lofty dream of a united Africa.

In a revealing work titled *How America Toppled Nkrumah*, Koojo Lewis claimed that through the covert operations of the CIA the Americans executed the coup d'état that ended Nkrumah's government. Lewis exposes the motive for and method of the CIA operation and the close personal role of President Johnson. As would be replicated in other countries in Africa, the CIA's clandestine oppressions involved identifying and using aggrieved individuals and groups within the rank and file of Ghana's army to destabilize the country.[57] David Rooney, in his study *Kwame Nkrumah: Vision and Tragedy*, suggested that idealistic mistakes imperiled Nkrumah's hopes and dreams for Ghana and Africa.[58] What Rooney did not point out is that Nkrumah, as an elected leader, had the mandate of the people to choose which economic model was best for Ghana.

Now it is time to return to the events in the Republic of the Congo, which contributed in no small measure to the painful relations between Ghana and the United States. In the Congo, a fellow traveler on the Communist road, Patrice Lumumba, whose death at the hands of the army led by then Col. Mobutu Sese Seko was followed by the assassination of President Kennedy in the United States, substantially impacted the calculus of United States-Africa relations. Nkrumah had developed personal relationships with both men, and the assassinations increased his resentment of the United States.[59] Lumumba and Nkrumah shared visions for Africa, and their Pan-Africanist determination to resist neocolonial overtures did not go down well with either the Americans or the Russians.[60]

One of the major fallacies of Cold War historiography is that African leaders abandoned their postcolonial nationalist agenda for the superpowers' interests. The truth, however, is that throughout the period, the African leaders remained committed to the ideals for which they fought for independence, and the Cold War, to them, was a means to an end. On December 11, 1958, Lumumba, as president of the Congolese National Movement, addressing the Assembly of African Peoples, an international Pan-African conference sponsored by Nkrumah, articulated that collective nationalist vision: "We wish to see a modern democratic state established in our country, which will grant its citizens freedom, justice, social peace, tolerance, well-being, and equality, with no discrimination whatsoever. In our actions aimed at winning the independence of the Congo, we have repeatedly proclaimed that we are against no one, but rather are simply against domination, injustices, and abuses, and merely want to free ourselves of the shackles of colonialism and all its consequences."[61] President Kenneth Kaunda of Zambia reemphasized the nationalist policy when he declared that his country, like many other African countries, would remain non-aligned in the Cold War: "Zambia stands like the other non-aligned nations, for the abolition of colonialism and neo-colonialism in all forms; and for the right to accept help from East or West without committing our people to accept their political beliefs. Or will purchase economic development at the cost of a new type of colonialism. . . . Therefore we ask that countries which offer us their aid should not exploit our need in order to infringe our sovereignty, for this is something which we shall guard jealously."[62]

It was therefore not surprising that after the murder of Lumumba, Nkrumah lost all respect for the U.S. government and intensified his attack on the manner in which the American government conducted its foreign policies. The crime Lumumba had committed against the United States was to profess communism so loudly, without fear or favor. Tim Weiner, who made a study of the covert operations of the CIA in Africa, concluded that the U.S. government masterminded the brutal assassination of the first prime minister of the Republic of the Congo.[63] However, the truth of the matter, as documented by Ludo de Witte and others, is that Belgium prioritized the killing, and in fact, directed it.[64]

After his election in a free and fair election, Joseph Kasavubu, the first president of the Republic of the Congo (1960–1965), which gained its independence on June 30, 1960, had appointed Lumumba the country's premier. Nevertheless, the Congo fell into chaos five days later. While the forces that led to the crisis are many, the primary issue was that Belgium, the former colonial power, was not comfortable with the nationalist rhetoric of Lumumba, who they feared would nationalize their billions of investments in Congo's mineral-rich region of Katanga. As a result, Belgium advised Moise Tshombe, its stooge in Katanga, to secede his province from the central government under Kasavubu and Lumumba. After Tshombe declared the secession of Katanga on July 11, 1960, President Kasavubu instructed Lumumba to stop the secession and restore order.[65] Two days later, the United Nations authorized a peace mission operation in the Congo. The calculation of Eisenhower was to accomplish a peaceful resolution of the crisis before the Soviets seized the opportunity to incorporate Congo into its sphere of influence.

However, Lumumba had appealed to the United States for military protection and assistance as the Congo transitioned from Belgium's brutal and exploitative colonial rule to self-government in 1960. Similar to the case with Ghana in 1957 and many other African states over the period, the appeal for help received no positive response—obviously because Belgium was opposed to Lumumba's designs for his country. Rather, the CIA in the Congo concluded that Lumumba was a Communist and marked him for elimination by poisoning.[66] In the ensuing crisis, Belgian troops invaded Leopoldville (later Kinshasa) in an attempt to retake control of the Congolese capital. At this point, Lumumba accepted Soviet planes, trucks, and "technicians" to bolster his barely functioning government.

The week the Belgian soldiers arrived, CIA Director Allen Dulles (1893–1969) sent Larry Devlin, the station chief in Brussels, to take charge of the CIA post in the capital of the Congo and assess Lumumba as a target for covert action. On August 18, after six weeks in the country, Devlin cabled CIA headquarters: "Congo experiencing classic communist effort takeover . . . whether or not Lumumba is actual commie or playing the commie game . . . there may be little time left in which to take action to avoid another Cuba."[67]

Confidential Senate testimony on "Project Wizard," delivered in 1975 by the U.S. National Security Council's recorder, Robert Johnson, reveals that at that meeting, President Eisenhower plainly instructed Dulles to have Lumumba assassinated. Eight days later, Dulles cabled the president: "In high quarters here it is the clear-cut conclusion that if LLL [Lumumba] continues to hold high office, the inevitable result will at best be chaos and at worst pave the way to a communist takeover of the Congo . . . we conclude that his removal must be an urgent and prime objective and that under existing conditions this would be a high priority of our covert action. Hence, we wish to give you wider authority along lines Leop 0772 and Leop 0785."[68]

It is difficult to detail the consequences of America's role in the destabilization of the Republic of the Congo in a work of this nature. In the meantime, following the death of Lumumba on January 17, 1961, a period of political turmoil followed as the U.N. tried to restore peace and stability in the country. The U.N. peace mission effort accomplished little because of America's determination to retain Col. Mobutu Sese Seko as a client in the Cold War struggle. In 1965, Mobutu, who would become one of Africa's most brutal dictators, launched a second coup that effectively ended Kasavubu's government. Throughout his tenure, from 1965 to 1997, Mobutu presided over a corrupt and cruel regime that brought about a catastrophic decline in national security, state service, and looting of the state treasury. Since the 1960s, civil war has been persistent, and foreign actors, mainly from Belgium and the United States, continue to fuel the conflicts and plunder the country's enormous mineral and agricultural wealth. The American government gave this systemic exploitation an official seal on February 12, 1990, following the "Reciprocal Encouragement and Protection of Investment" treaty between Washington and the Government of the People's Republic of the Congo.[69]

Angola was another flashpoint in the struggle between the United States and the Soviet Union for supremacy in Africa. At the height of the Vietnam War in 1975, the United States launched a covert mission to stop another Communist bid in Angola. While the effort fell short of preventing a Marxist government from ascending to power in the former Portuguese colony, it prolonged a chaotic civil war that resulted after the nationalists toppled the Portuguese colonial rule. The civil war involved the United States, the Soviet Union, and China in a grand proxy war that directly involved 50,000 Cuban soldiers on the side of the Communists, and apartheid South Africa and Congo-Zaire on the side of the United States and the rebel factions.

The making of the Angolan Cold War battleground goes back to around 1956, when in cities such as Luanda, Kinshasa, Algiers, Lisbon, Paris, and London, different progressive sectors of students, intellectuals, and European liberals promoted an anticolonial struggle through different left-wing and nationalist groups. These rather diverse groups of organizations with different nationalistic ideas mobilized around the purpose of overthrowing Portuguese colonial rule in Angola. After a rebellion in the main political prison in Luanda that caused general turmoil in 1961, those groups converged around a radical nationalist political structure: the Movimento Popular de Libertação de Angola (Popular Movement for the Liberation of Angola, or MPLA). Its militants carried out clandestine operations in urban areas and villages, enduring the repression mounted by the PIDE (Polícia Internacional e de Defesa do Estado, or International and State Defense Police). While the colonial government forced many of the insurgent leaders into exile in Europe or other African countries, the insurgents kept their eyes on the target: Angola's emancipation from the Portuguese colonial stranglehold.[70]

The Angolan MPLA nationalists projected a struggle based on a particular conception of the past, a historical representation expressed as discourses and practices, in which Angola's history became a foundation for the rise of a new postcolonial society.[71] In the Alvor Agreement of January 1975, all the warring parties agreed to put together a coalition government, and the independence of Angola was set for November of that year. However, fighting resumed in July, and when the Portuguese colonial regime caved in August 1975, the Marxist MPLA, who eventually emerged victorious, were already in control of Luanda, the capital city. However, the United States refused to recognize them but instead continued to sponsor the rebels from neighboring Congo-Zaire, the name of the Democratic Republic of the Congo in 1971. The United States gradually transferred its support to Jonas Savimbi, whom President Ronald Reagan welcomed to the White House in 1986 as a freedom fighter, to the outrage of the African heads of state who opposed his ambitious military and personal designs in Angola.[72] For nearly three decades, the United States supplied arms and materials to the rebels in the face of angry opposition by the Organisation of African Unity. As explained elsewhere, Savimbi was one of several career troublemakers, or "entrepreneurial warriors," who would rather go to any lengths in prosecuting and accomplishing their missions than accept any peace deals short of granting them total control of the ultimate "prize."[73] The careers of Liberia's Charles Taylor, Angola's Savimbi, and Sierra Leone's Foday Sankoh show how successful "war entrepreneurs think globally but act locally, using violence to exploit marketable natural resources without necessarily controlling the state."[74]

The eventual death of Savimbi on February 22, 2002, created an opportunity for scholars and policymakers to learn more about America's longest-lasting rebel ally in Angola. "A trove of recently declassified American documents seem to overturn conventional explanations of the war's origins."[75] These show that contrary to what the United States government had claimed, the Americans intervened in Angola weeks before the arrival of any Cubans. Additionally, it is now known that contrary to its denials, America collaborated with apartheid South Africa during the war in Angola.

Historian Piero Gleijeses, who has perused these classified documents, notes that "when the United States decided to launch the covert intervention, in June and July, not only were there no Cubans in Angola, but the U.S. government and the CIA were not even thinking about any Cuban presence in Angola." Rather, the Cuban intervention came as a response to the U.S. presence. Gleijeses further states that in a 1975 report delivered to the U.S. Senate toward the end of the year, "what you find is really nothing less than the rewriting of history."[76]

In his review of Gleijeses's book, Howard French "strongly challenges common perceptions of Cuban behavior in Africa. In the 1960s and 1970s, when Havana and Washington repeatedly clashed in central and southern Africa,

Cuban troops in the continent were typically seen as foot soldiers for Soviet imperialism." French stresses that Cuba intervened in Angola without seeking Soviet permission. The Soviets limited their activities "to providing 10 charter flights to transport Cubans to Angola in January 1976. The next year, Havana and Moscow supported opposite sides in an attempted coup in Angola, in which the Marxist government, Cuba's ally, prevailed."[77]

In Zimbabwe (formerly Southern Rhodesia, then known simply as Rhodesia after 1965), which regained its independence in 1980 after a prolonged and bloody guerrilla war against an abusive White minority rule, the path to Black freedom was complicated by the actions and inactions of the United States government and its small group of White supremacist citizens. On November 11, 1965, the minority government of Prime Minister Ian Smith chose to split from Great Britain, declaring Southern Rhodesia an independent nation. Smith's unilateral action threw the country's African majority population, estimated at 4.3 million, deeper into the vortex of racial subjugation under a European population of 224,000. Gerald Horne notes that in a country whose racial structure mirrored the apartheid system of neighboring South Africa, the route chosen by the minority government escalated a raging guerrilla war.[78]

In the United States, President Johnson timidly viewed the unfolding events in Rhodesia. His prime concern was that such a racial conflict in Africa had the potential to exacerbate America's already troubled racial discord. Unexpectedly, U.S. government officials expressed concerns over Rhodesia's actions, particularly with regard to human rights violations. The United States announced sanctions against the South Rhodesian government that it never intended to enforce. Instead, an attitude of tolerance explains the U.S. response to the conflict. Scores of White American fighters volunteered on the side of the White minority government, with no concerted effort by the U.S. government to stop them.

The actions and inactions of the U.S. government, as well as some of its citizens in the Southern Rhodesia conflict, mirrored the nature of Black-White relations in the United States and Africa. There was a virulent pro-Rhodesia lobby in the U.S. government during the late 1960s and 1970s, with an office located at 2852 McGill Terrace, NW in Washington. On March 29, 1977, during President Jimmy Carter's administration, John Goshko of the *Washington Post* reported that "the office has been run since its inception by Kenneth H. Towsey, who previously had been the Smith government's 'counselor for Rhodesian affairs' within the British embassy. Towsey is assisted by another Rhodesian national, H. J. C. Hooper, who deals primarily in information matters."[79]

A lover of Africa, President Carter, who was in office from 1977 to 1981, firmly supported majority Black rule in Rhodesia. He submitted a resolution to the

United Nations and successfully lobbied the members to support the closure of offices maintained by Southern Rhodesia in other countries. Smith's minority government fell in 1980, and African nationalists led by Robert Mugabe proclaimed the independent state of Zimbabwe.

Admittedly, the United States inserted itself into African affairs in a complicated context. Until the 1960s, the Americans saw the African continent as within the Europeans' sphere of influence by virtue of their imperial claims. In a memorandum of discussion at the 375th meeting of the National Security Council held on August 7, 1958, President Eisenhower asked his adviser on the Commission on Foreign Economic Policy, Clarence B. Randall (chairman of the board of the Inland Steel Company), how the United States was coordinating "our policies toward these colonial areas with the mother countries." In response, Randall explained that "this was a delicate problem." According to Randall, assisting the colonies was often less offensive to the European imperial powers "if offered in the framework of a multilateral organization, so that it appeared as a mutual effort." On this note, Eisenhower remarked that it was often difficult to cultivate good relations with colonies. The president went on to cite an occasion where "there was a great concern in Paris every time the United States spoke a friendly word to a French colony." The report of the discussion concluded that "in Africa South of the Sahara we must be careful not to get ourselves hated by both the colonies and the mother countries."[80]

Indeed, America's efforts not to infuriate its European allies did more harm to Africa than good. One of the most unfortunate incidents that took place in Africa between 1961 and 1967 was the series of seventeen nuclear-bomb tests carried out by the French government in the Algerian end of the Sahara Desert during the administration of President Charles de Gaulle.[81] To be fair, the United States did not openly support the French actions but condoned them in a desperate attempt to retain its European allies in the Cold War struggle. Discussions between President de Gaulle and U.S. secretary of state John Foster Dulles on July 5, 1958, concerning the use of nuclear weapons ended in disagreement because de Gaulle was intent on making France a nuclear power.[82]

The French nuclear-testing power show brought African masses and nationalists of all ideological persuasions into a unified front against what they perceived as open disdain for the continent and endangerment of the lives of its people. In August 1958, when the plans for a French test in the Sahara were first made official, Ghana's minister of transport and communications, Krobo Edusei, led a mass demonstration to the French Embassy in Accra. The French officials refused to give the peaceable demonstrators an audience and used embassy security staff to disperse the crowd. President Nkrumah immediately constituted a Ghana Council for Nuclear Disarmament (GCND) "to educate the people in the dangers of all such tests to the health and prosperity of the African peoples."[83] Through the awareness created by the GCND, every independent African state and every freedom movement in Africa, from Morocco and Tunisia in the North to the freedom movements in South Africa, condemned the French action with one voice.

Yet, the French were deliberate and bold in their resolve to acquire nuclear capability as a deterrent in a dangerously polarized period of international relations. On February 13, 1960, France conducted its first atomic test, code-named *Gerboise Bleue* (Blue Desert Rat). The first test was followed by four more held at the Reggane Oasis in the Sahara Desert of Algeria.[84] With an explosive capacity of seventy kilotons, the first test recorded four times more destructive capacity than the atom bomb the U.S. Army Air Force had detonated over Hiroshima, Japan, in 1945. Ignoring African demands to halt its plans for a follow-up test, the French government soon announced a further series of tests — this time underground.[85] As investigations later revealed, the French authorities were already making plans for underground nuclear testing in 1959, anticipating that "scenarios relative to international agreements on nuclear testing" could make it "impossible to carry out an aerial nuclear explosion. For this reason, the Minister of Armed Forces ordered a study of the conditions for an underground explosion."[86] France went on to conduct thirteen more nuclear tests because a U.N. ban on nuclear tests in 1963 did not include a prohibition on underground tests.

Enraged by these extra tests, African governments went to the United Nations to challenge the right of the French government to carry out these tests on African soil when it fully understood the consequences of its actions: "We say to the French Government today, 'If you don't want to test them in Paris don't come to Africa to test them!'"[87] In December 1960 and November 1961, the U.N. General Assembly adopted resolutions calling on member states to refrain from any nuclear tests in Africa.[88] Later, the United Nations also condemned further tests as proposed by France, by an overwhelming majority. The Ghanaian government also formed an international coalition under the leadership of Rev. Michael Scott, with representatives from Nigeria, Basutoland, the United States, Britain, and France, to protest France's actions. The team adopted a nonviolent approach to entering the testing site at Reggane, Algeria, "to challenge the right of France to endanger the life and health of innocent people, and to desecrate the soil of mother Africa."[89]

Considering that these dangerous tests came in the midst of the Algerian struggle for independence, it was predictable that African nationalists immediately linked the French actions to the political situation in Algeria. In his speech of September 1, 1960, Joseph Tawia Adamafio, the information and broadcasting minister under Nkrumah, charged that: "The political reasons for opposing these tests are no less powerful than the humanitarian; indeed, the two cannot be separated. Does it not mean the continuation of the Algerian war which has already cost over a million lives and condemned many millions to homelessness, hunger, and utter ruin—the reports of further tests, if true, shed a sinister new light on France's continued obstinacy to grant to the Algerian people the right of self-determination which harsh political facts have forced her to accept in her other colonial territories in Africa."[90] In response, the president of Mali, M. Modibo Keita, warned France that it could not support its repressive policies in Algeria and might shortly recognize the Algerian Provisional Government.

In defense of its actions, France claimed that "its nuclear operations were carried out as safely as possible." However, the confidential military report first acquired by the authoritative newspaper *Le Parisien* in 2010 indicated that soldiers who served in Algeria had been used as "guinea pigs" to study the effects of radiation on human health: "According to the report, a 1961 nuclear test involved military personnel advancing on foot and in trucks to within a few hundred meters of the epicenter of a nuclear blast less than an hour after detonation."[91] Also, a survey conducted in 2008 by Dr. Jean Louis Valatx of AVEN, an association representing veterans of the French nuclear test, revealed that "35 percent of the polled veterans had one or more types of cancer and one in five had become infertile."[92]

One of the participants in the *Gerboise Bleue* test, Michel Verger, disclosed that he "was wearing shorts. We were made to lie face down on the ground, eyes closed and arms folded, and not watch the flash, but immediately afterward we had to get up with an apparatus around our necks and measure and photograph the impact."[93] An Algerian scientist, Kathum El-Abodi, who has conducted a study on the nuclear testing in Algeria, noted that the test "resulted in environmental degradation, such as the movement of sand dunes in areas already affected by wind erosion. Radiation furthermore led to a decline in livestock and biodiversity, including the disappearance of several migratory and endemic reptiles and birds."[94] In addition to its own soldiers, the French government willfully exposed an estimated 30,000 Algerian civilians to radiation.[95]

It seems appropriate to conclude that United States' post–World War II African foreign policy evolved in the context of the Cold War. Two critical forces determined the nature of this policy: America's strategic interest in preventing the Soviet Union from gaining control of postcolonial African states, and America's desire not to offend its European allies—the former colonial powers Britain, France, Portugal, and Belgium. American leaders considered Africa as the Europeans' realm of influence and power. What the Americans did and did not do remains a critical factor in shaping the fate of Africa—whether we are looking at the class roots of Anwar Sadat's regime in Egypt or the international response to the Nigeria-Biafra civil war (1967–1970).[96] Other issues in which the United States' response or lack of it figured prominently involved the tensions between the "Monrovia" and "Casablanca" groups of African states (a critical Cold War political divide) that centered on African outrage at French nuclear tests in the Sahara. Across the continent, the impact of the Cold War in Nigeria, Senegal, Somalia, Morocco, Ghana, and elsewhere spurred a legion of intellectual and diplomatic discourses among African intellectuals and postcolonial political elite and leaders of opinion.

While some African leaders such as Dr. Nnamdi Azikiwe fought hard to stop short of endorsing communism as the right approach to Africa's development in the immediate postcolonial order, others like Julius Nyerere promoted Ujamaa, a form of African socialism, as a path to development in Tanzania and elsewhere. In the "Arusha Declaration" of February 5, 1967, President Nyerere outlined the principles of Ujamaa, rooted in the concept of self-reliance, that were to guide the economy of the newly independent nation. To each of these discourses, the Americans reacted with either force and emotion or hatred. Admittedly, several factors brought about the failure of Ujamaa—among them poor planning, government oppression of rural Tanzanians, drought, and the collapse of commodity prices. However, in reacting against Ujamaa, the United States and its European allies denied Tanzania any development aid or bilateral cooperation until the end of the Cold War in 1989. This policy persisted even though Tanzania demonstrated exemplary leadership in Africa and its promotion of the global nonaligned movement aimed to offset the dangers of the Cold War rivalry between East and West. The legacies of the Cold War are many; they range from arrested development, light armaments, landmines, migrations, lingering attachments to ideological thinking among leaders, and revolutionary adventurers to African university professors who continue to propagate Marxist ideologies in the minds of their students.

11

AFRICAN-BORN IMMIGRANTS IN THE UNITED STATES

Although a handful of Africans studied in the United States beginning in 1906, when the first native South African lawyer and African nationalist Pixley Ka Isaka Seme (1881–1951) graduated from Columbia University, the labor needs for building the African postcolonial state from the late 1920s to the 1960s urgently necessitated growth in university-level training for Africans. As a result, the mid-1960s saw an increased desire for American higher education among the new generation of Africans. Often the Africans who received American schooling returned to apply the knowledge and benefits of their sojourns in the United States to the socioeconomic and political developmental needs of their respective home countries. However, not all of these students and their families returned to Africa after graduation. For the small number of individuals who decided to remain in America, the chief reasons for their decision were the inability to complete their education, the increasing incidence of conflict on the continent, and/or the attractions of an American lifestyle.

As the civil crises that plagued the postcolonial state increased in the late 1970s, reaching a climax in the 1980s—prompting Basil Davidson to call this era "the decade of the AK-47"[1]—Africa witnessed what some observers today refer to as a massive "brain drain," the emigration of highly qualified professionals or intelligent people to countries where they would gain more profitable and steady employment.[2] Whether the Africans who emigrated were engineers, doctors, dentists, teachers, nurses, or writers, two things are clear: first, the immigrants took along with them some members of their families as well as elements of their inherited cultures. Second, their presence in the United States as visible minorities refreshed the long history of United States-Africa relations and enriched the exchange of cultural ideas across the Atlantic. Following the

229

Immigration Act of 1990, when the U.S. Congress passed the Diversity Visa Lottery program, more Africans and their families gained the opportunity to resettle in America as legal residents.[3] In 2015, the Pew Research Center estimated that there were 2.1 million African-born immigrants living in the United States (4.8 percent of the U.S. population).[4] These migrants constituted themselves into thousands of African communities across the United States that have instituted ethnic unions/associations, cultural events, and "national days" across America. Additionally, churches founded by African-born clergy (otherwise called African Instituted Churches, or AICs) have sprouted in the United States as one of the most powerful conveyors of African identity and socialization. Through different events and counseling support, these agencies provide their members with African foods, plays, music, religious practices, moonlight songs, films, and so on. Thus, African culture is imported and transmitted to a new generation of African Americans with African parents.

In the past two decades, scholars have shown a significant interest in the exponential rise in African migration to Europe and North America that began in the late 1990s. Before this time, the majority of African migrants were categorized as "economic migrants" and usually ended up in various European countries—particularly the metropoles of former colonial powers such as Britain, France, Belgium, Portugal, Germany, the Netherlands, and Spain. However, recent studies of African emigration indicate that the latest trends have produced one of the fastest growths in the African-born population in America. The records show that this rising pattern occurred mostly in the past two decades.[5] For instance, in 1970, eighty Africans landed in the United States. In 1980, the number rose to 200. Then it stood at 364 in 1990, 881 in 2000, and 2,060 in 2015.[6]

The bulk of the literature on cross-country, cross-regional migrations is more preoccupied with the causes of the population movements than with their cultural effects on the host societies.[7] Specifically, current research on the Africa-to-the-United States population flow generally focuses on the stream of skilled labor and refugees from Africa to the United States.[8] A more nuanced and informative study by Kevin Thomas in 2011 provides insights into three main areas: first, an estimate of the relative size of the overall trend in African emigration to the United States between 1992 and 2007, considering employment-related or family-reunification migration; second, the extent to which country-level socioeconomic and demographic factors determined the emigration trends; and third, whether emerging trends in African emigration to the United States vary across linguistic and developmental contexts.[9]

Some lacunas remain in the studies—among them are the cultural consequences of the African-born immigrants on their American host communities.

People move with their inherited culture and often try to reenact, although with limited success, their native habits and ideas in their host societies. Thus, our primary goal is to provide some perspective on how African-born immigrants of the past two decades have enriched the American cultural nexus as Africans in America strove to make the United States their new home and realize the American Dream. First, however, it is vital to outline the historical context in which recent African population movements to the United States have occurred.

HISTORICAL CONTEXT

The history of the trans-Atlantic slave trade, which uprooted millions of Africans to the New World, has been covered in detail in the preceding chapters. With the effective end to the human trade in the nineteenth century, a paltry 463 Africans arrived in the United States on average per year between 1861 and 1961.[10] Although there may have been other studies whose conclusions are not available, Walter Williams's seminal study of the ethnic relations of African students in the United States from 1870 to 1900 highlights that sixty-seven Africans attended seventeen American schools between 1870 and 1900. Williams reveals that the geographical origins of these students in Africa were diverse: thirty-two were from Liberia, seventeen from South Africa, eleven from Sierra Leone, four from the Gold Coast (modern Ghana), and one each from Ethiopia, Gabon, and Nyasaland. American missionaries sponsored nearly all of these students, and the goal was to train the Africans in the United States for missionary work in Africa. The American missionary bodies believed that converted and educated Africans would be more effective missionaries among their own people than outsiders would be. Above all, the belief was that indigenous Africans would remain healthy in a tropical climate infested with morbid disease vectors like mosquitoes and would have no language or cultural barriers with their congregations.[11]

The records of the U.S. Census Bureau further show that just 350 Africans arrived in the United States between 1891 and 1900.[12] Among them were twenty African students at Lincoln University in Pennsylvania, founded in 1854 by the Northern Presbyterians. Sixteen of these students were from Liberia. Other African immigrants included five students at Fisk University in Tennessee, a school sponsored by the American Missionary Association, an agency that had aided freed slaves in the South after the Civil War. One of the five students was of Mendi ethnic extraction in Sierra Leone.[13] The 2015 Pew Research Center study corroborates the fact that very little African migration across the Atlantic occurred in the century prior to the end of colonial rule in 1960. The research shows that in 1960, 84 percent of immigrants living in the United States were individuals born in Europe or Canada, about 6 percent were from Mexico, 3.8 percent from South and East Asia, and 3.5 percent from the rest of Latin America. Immigrants from other areas, including Africa, South and East Asia, and the Middle East, comprised 2.7 percent of the total.[14]

In contrast, the turn of the twenty-first century saw a significant change. The data from the U.S. Census Bureau estimates that about 60,000 African-born individuals arrived in the United States annually from 2000 to 2005.[15] In other words, the majority of the African-born population in the United States today came in the past two decades. In their separate studies, A. Gordon and Mary Kent concluded that the pre-1965 U.S. immigration laws that drastically curtailed African immigration to the United States for most of the twentieth century were responsible for the low or near absence of African-born movement to the United States before the late 1990s.[16] Indeed, the restrictions were so stringent that by the mid-1960s, African-born immigrants accounted for just 1 percent of all immigrants allowed into the country.[17]

Nonetheless, the unfavorable immigration laws enacted by the U.S. government were not solely responsible for the low immigration flow of Africans to the United States. A couple of other historical factors played decisive roles in this trend. First, the end of the trans-Atlantic slave trade in the Americas created a new situation in the late nineteenth century in which the priority of those involved in the Atlantic exchanges, particularly the U.S. government, was to repatriate as many Africans as possible to Africa. Most of these returnees resettled in Liberia, Sierra Leone, and other coastal enclaves in West Africa. Second, European colonial intrusion in Africa, which came on the heels of the thrust of Christian missionary evangelism in the late nineteenth century, effectively restricted the emigration of the Africans. In fact, from the late eighteenth century to the 1960s, Africa was the favored destination of global migrations as outside adventurers, colonial officials, Western missionaries, fortune hunters, and European settlers descended on the continent in search of its abundant natural and human resources.

The low or near absence of African-born emigration to the United States continued in the immediate postcolonial period despite the 1965 U.S. immigration reforms, which overturned the previous quota system that discriminated against individuals from certain countries. By the 1980s, however, African emigration to the United States began to pick up for the first time since the late nineteenth century. In their 2006 study, Kwadwor Konadu-Agyemang and Baffour Takyi discovered that the number of Africans arriving in the United States in the decade from 1982 to 1992 represented a whopping 500 percent increase on the total number of Africans who moved to the United States in the century between

1861 and 1961.[18] The primary reason for this remarkable rise was in connection with the labor needs of the Africans as European colonial dominions unraveled without creating opportunities in universities for the colonized people to train the critically needed African labor. In other words, most of the African migrants going to the United States in this period sought college education and skills needed to fill sectors of the postcolonial economy. Yet, in relation to immigrant groups from other parts of the world, the African-born population of the United States remained very small.[19]

A feature that separates Africans from other immigrant groups in the United States is their sharp growth rate, which spiked after 2000. The underpinning of this growth goes back to the mid-1980s, when the economies of many African states began to falter. The neoliberal reforms inspired by the International Monetary Fund (IMF) and World Bank in Africa, as in Asia and Latin America, brought into purview the continent's debt crises following the worldwide economic recessions in the early 1980s and the consequent collapse of world commodity prices. To support their weakening economies and increase production capacities, many African countries sought sanctuary in external loans from the IMF, World Bank, International Finance Corporation (IFI), European Investment Bank, and the Paris Club (Club de Paris in French) comprising officials from major creditor nations who decide on solutions for delinquent debtor countries. They also sought help from individual Western nations. In response, these governments and creditor institutions imposed strict conditions requiring conformity to neoliberalism for their loans and credits. The set of economic policies designed to enforce sanity in the troubled economies and to accelerate development in sub-Saharan Africa was labeled structural adjustment programs (SAPs). Between 1980 and 1993, thirty-six sub-Saharan African debtor nations implemented SAPs under other names, such as "economic survival programs" and "economic recovery plans."[20]

In general, the policies recommended by the Western credit institutions failed to help the African economies, and often the blame lay with the IMF. The plans offered by the IMF completely sidestepped the developmental needs of Africa and questions about what forms of integration were most suitable for the people. Making matters worse, African leaders engaged in gross mismanagement and corruption. Here resides the socioeconomic milieu in which, from the 1980s onwards, highly skilled African workers started to look for opportunities outside the continent.

The economic basis of African mass emigration from the late twentieth century accords with neoclassical migration theory, which conceptualizes migration as a product of wage differentials between origin and destination countries.[21]

Exponents of the neoclassical theory, initially formulated to explain population movements within a country, posit that migration on the international level is a product of the desire of the migrants from low-wage or labor-surplus countries to move to high-wage or labor-scarce countries. This tendency means that the apparent economic failures of the 1980s and 1990s created an income differential between the United States and Africa, which led to the appeal of the neoclassical paradigm's role in contemporary African migration research. In this regard, Jill Wilson and Shelly Habecker concluded that economic failures compelled African professionals to look for better opportunities outside the continent.[22]

A study by Amy Hagopian and others published in 2004 revealed that a majority of the roughly 5,334 African doctors then in the United States had come from the poorest African countries, with 86 percent coming from Nigeria, Ghana, and South Africa.[23] This revelation corroborates an earlier study by Carrington and Detragiache published in the IMF's quarterly periodical *Finance and Development* in 1999, which showed that 74 percent of all African immigrants in the United States are college graduates.[24] The Pew Research Center has drawn a similar conclusion that African-born immigrants in the United States are more educated than both the native-born U.S. population and migrants from other countries, and are more likely to gain profitable employment in the United States and the United Kingdom.[25]

The neoclassical paradigm is inclined toward Immanuel Wallerstein's World Systems theory, which claims that Western economic exploitation in the periphery gives rise to resource drain and, by implication, the "brain-drain." Carefully interpreted, the flow of human and material resources from more impoverished regions of the world to more prosperous areas is a product of both the permeation of capitalist economic relationships into developing countries and cultural and ideological linkages between the mother countries and the ex-colonial territories.[26] Monica Boyd emphatically contends that these colonial networks facilitate most international migrations drifting from the less-developed countries to the industrially advanced Western nations.[27]

To conclude, it is apparent from the preceding discussion that individuals and families emigrate from their original homelands to distant places primarily because of their economic necessities. Some scholars, among them A. R. Zolberg, have argued that the state's control of migration processes provides another perspective that explains recent African population movements to the United States.[28] The idea is that nations like the United States, Canada, Australia, and Britain can impose certain limits on the number of immigrant admissions and determine the characteristics of immigrants allowed to live within their borders. While this is true, it is fundamental to add that individuals, under normal conditions, would not leave their home countries regardless of favorable or unfavorable immigration laws. This caveat provides the basis for understanding the Diversity Visa (DV) Lottery program, through which more Africans have gained entry to the United States in the past twenty years than in the decades before the program's inception.[29] Barbara Dietz has noted that under the DV Lottery program, family-reunification policies tend to create more migrant networks and further strengthen familial ties between immigrants and their relatives in their origin countries.[30] Other auxiliary factors, such as improved means of communication and the increasing globalization of cultures, have helped to promote this pattern of immigration. Among other things, there are, however, limited studies on the role of kinship networks and African-born social institutions in easing the challenges that confront new African immigrants, and on their effects on identity formation and cultural productions to the United States.

In sum, the extant research on the recent movement of the African-born population to the United States is preoccupied with the factors behind this phenomenon. Scholars and policymakers have given little or no attention to the effects of the presence of the new migrant communities on the development of new habits and cultural practices in the United States. It is, therefore, important to examine how well the new African immigrants have successfully fused into U.S. society while lending aspects of their inherited culture to the host society. The sources for the discussion that follows include minutes of activities of ethnic unions such as the Nigerian, Igbo, Yoruba, Ghanaian, Sierra Leonean, and Liberian associations in various American cities, including Houston, Dallas, Austin, Baltimore, the District of Columbia, New York, and Louisville. Visual displays and textual accounts from popular magazines and newspaper sources from the United States and Africa provide an even more compelling story of the ongoing American consumption of African cultural inventions. Additionally, we have drawn on the *Constitution of Association of Congolese Community* in Los Angeles; the *Constitution of Mandingo Descendants Association* in Washington, D.C.; and *African Times USA*, which lists more than 100 African ethnic associations, clubs, and/or unions operating in the United States.

AGENCIES OF CULTURAL EXPRESSION AND TRANSMISSION

Comparable to other foreign-born groups in alien societies, African-born migrants in the United States try to keep their home traditions alive in several ways. These include visits back to their countries of origin; purchasing and distributing African films, particularly Nollywood movies; involvement in sporting activities; education; exchange of gifts; and foodways. All of these activities help maintain social relations. Religious worship, which builds trust in social relations, and memberships in village/ethnic/national associations also keep traditions alive. Among these and other agencies that connect friendship, marriage, and other forms of social and cultural expressions, the church and ethnic associations are the most popular and effective. In fact, among the African migrants, it is within these two agencies that their family, identity, habits, and social networks cohere. It is, however, important to state that not all African-born immigrants have belonged to these associations and churches.

Similar to hundreds of African ethnic associations in the United States, the Quardu-Gboni Mandingo Association in the United States, a kinship forum that represents U.S. African-born residents from Lofa County in Liberia, opens the preamble to its constitution with the statement: "Mindful of our obligation to uphold the virtues of our forefathers . . . as well as our own recent past history and our obligation to present and future generations; have resolved to organize ourselves for the purposes of promoting unity, peaceful co-existence, tolerance, equality, our traditional values and progress among ourselves and our compatriots and the world at large."[31]

Similarly, the constitution of the Houston-based Ghana Association purports to: "(1) foster a spirit of friendship, mutual understanding, and respect among the people of Ghana and the United States. (2) Act as a vehicle for the channeling of charitable contributions and donations from the public and business community to hospitals, and educational institutions in Ghana. (3) Act as the representative body and mouthpiece of people with interest in Ghana affairs, and living in the Houston Metropolitan area."[32] What immediately catches one's attention in these associations' documents is the interface among the members' inherited African culture, their historical connection with their native land, and their declared intent to use African symbols and value systems to promote unity and progress on both sides of the Atlantic. In this context, the ethnic associations have become a socialization agency with a Pan-African ideology.

Among other things, the Quardu-Gboni Mandingo Association uses its various committees to execute its numerous activities and developmental projects. However, top on its agenda is the promotion of Quardu-Gboni consciousness in America through organizing monthly and annual social events. Like the Sierra Leonean Youth Association in Philadelphia and the Achi Association USA, the Quardu-Gboni Association routinely provides medical and sanitary relief assistance to relatives in Liberia, including the purchase and shipment of medical supplies, drugs, equipment, and so on. The association also supports the educational needs of the Quardu-Gboni District of Lofa County in Liberia by awarding scholarships to qualified students at institutions of higher education at home.

The Ways, Means, and Financial Committee of the Quardu-Gboni Association is charged with raising funds for developmental projects such as "construction of schools, clinics/hospitals, feeder roads, etc."[33] Annually, the association, whose main chapters are located in New York and New Jersey, organizes Valentine's Day parties for members, families, and friends. During the occasion, all celebrants dress in African attire and offer their American guests and friends African dishes such as *dumboy* (or fufu), along with palm butter, palava sauce, meat, stew, jollof rice, and country chop. African music and dance provide entertainment for the guests. Such annual events afford opportunities for the members to raise money for the association's various projects. The two-day 2012 Valentine's Day "Black and Red" parties of the Quardu-Gboni held at the Sikira Night Club in Philadelphia and the Village Social Club in Newark, New Jersey, sold admission tickets for $20 per person.[34]

The Congolese community predominantly resettled in Los Angeles and New York because of the endless civil war in the Republic of the Congo, which has claimed nearly 5.4 million lives.[35] The Congolese Community of Southern California's program "An Evening of Healing and Hope," on April 30, 2005, was organized in partnership with KPFK Radio, Women for Women International, CARE International, and the City of Los Angeles Department of Cultural Affairs. As announced on the webpage of UCLA's African Studies Center, the program featured a live concert with "La Rumba, an Africana Oye Band, featuring Shimita, Dodo, Deesse, Nene, Chantal, Jado, Parigo, and dancers."[36] The event, organized by Jules Boyele and Ben Mandela, sold tickets for $10 and $15 in advance and at the gate, respectively. The festivities also featured a fashion show and a fundraising dinner to benefit the female victims of the Congolese civil war. Other aims of the occasion were to promote education among Africans and to increase awareness of the dangers of HIV/AIDS in the Democratic Republic of Congo.

Yet, some of the glitziest and most progressive African ethnic associations in the United States are found among the Nigerian (Igbo, Yoruba, Ibibio, etc.) ethnic communities. The reason for this goes beyond the large size of the Nigerian-born migrant population in the United States. The strength and efficiency with which the Nigerian ethnic associations operate and maintain historical linkages to their village communities in Nigeria go back to the African colonial period, when these associations sprouted up in the colonial cities and served as harbingers of development in their villages. The Nigerian ethnic associations in the United States sometimes include separate women's organizations such as the Umuada Ndi Igbo in the diaspora, which is based in Houston. Peter Ekeh has argued persuasively that under colonialism the notion of kinship was expanded considerably into the construction of ethnic groups.[37] Indeed, the Nigerian colonial cities saw a profusion of an expanded and complex practice of kinship belongingness. This culture was not limited to the Igbo or the Yoruba alone. In their attempts to create modern people and communities, other ethnic groups in colonial Nigeria, like the Calabar, Ibibio, Urhobo, Edo, and Efik, also established progressive unions; other such groups are found in both the eastern and midwestern regions of the United States. Most of these associations and their subnationalities not only rallied to help members who had come from the countryside to urban centers in search of new opportunities for social mobility, but also sponsored the overseas education of their indigenous sons.

Historian Austin Ahanaotu asserts that the leading Igbo lineage organizations in colonial Nigeria were founded in about 1920.[38] However, this might not be entirely true because Christopher Fyfe's study of James B. Africanus Horton (1835–1889), the Igbo-born Sierra Leonean medical doctor and intellectual, reveals that Horton was a member of the Igbo union in Freetown, Sierra Leone, where he lived and died.[39] This fact means that the Igbo union was already in existence at least four to five decades before its Nigerian colonial antecedents, as noted by Ahanaotu. In the colonial cities, the smallest Igbo "lineage" was the village group, and this expanded kinship network, or "brotherhood," provided the basis for organizing group action.[40] The lineage organizations later flowered into formal patriotic and improvement unions. They eventually became a defining part of Igbo life and culture in the third and fourth decades of the colonial era.[41]

For the Igbo, like their Nigerian neighbors, these colonial organizations represented Igbo forms of mobilization and communal expression. While memberships in the Igbo lineage/improvement unions were hypothetically voluntary, the truth is that individuals who declined to identify with the kinship were perceived as social and ethnic outcasts. For the Afikpo Association, for example, "membership shall only be terminated by death, permanent insanity or expulsion."[42] The ethnic organizations also pressured their members to make financial contributions to community projects. The Igbos carried over this invented tradition from the colonial era to the postcolonial order, and from there to the various African diasporas in the Americas and elsewhere today.

Like the other numerous ethnic and national unions of African origin, contemporary Nigerian ethnic associations in the United States perform identical functions, which include socialization among members and promotion of community and ethnic consciousness. The Association of Nigerians in the Capitol District (ANCD) of the State of New York in New Albany, established in 1999, fulfills similar identity and socialization functions. The constitution of the ANCD professed its purpose as follows: "(1) To dedicate ourselves to the unity, progress, and strength of our Association and the community, and to promote the general welfare of members. (2) To keep the community clearly and reliably informed about Nigeria and its people. (3) To organize and implement social, cultural, and educational activities that meet the needs and interests of members. (4) To work in collaboration with public and private agencies, business, industry, and community organizations to share information, exchange ideas on issues of interest to members and the community."[43] Within this constitutional framework, the members prioritize the following goals: enhancing cultural awareness of Nigerians through active participation in the community; assisting new immigrants to acclimate in the Capitol District; promoting volunteerism among members; instilling positive values, civic responsibility, and skills for good citizenship in adult and youth community members; and strengthening the educational/career aspirations of young people through mentoring.[44]

The ANCD usually holds annual cultural and social celebrations in September and in October, when Nigeria celebrates its independence anniversary. According to the association, the overall "strategic purpose is to foster a sense of community among diverse ethnic and racial groups and build lasting relationships through cultural performances and historical presentations for area schools and community-based organizations."[45] The ANCD's annual events, which continuously draw good attendance, consist of invited speakers who deliver keynote addresses on diverse topics of interest to members and the community at large. The "event also features Nigerian cultural shows, including fashions and cultural dances. In most cases, the association displays Nigerian cuisine and dance at the occasions."[46]

Often, the various Nigerian ethnic unions in the United States organize free family summer picnics for young people and their American friends. In Louisville, Kentucky, for example, the Community of Nigerians in Kentuckiana (CONK) holds picnics every July for members and their families, and their American friends are strongly encouraged to join the association. The association also uses the annual U.S. Independence Day celebration to raise money for various community projects. At the end of the school year, the Nigerian-born populations in Louisville and southern Indiana organize social events around graduation ceremonies and other occasions. Similarly, times of marriage and bereavement bring together members who support the families affected in both financial and emotional ways. During each of these events, Nigerian foodways, fashion, dancing, and shows, such as masquerade plays and folk music, are presented for the entertainment of the audience.

We can go on to highlight similar functions and activities of other African-born ethnic unions or associations, but it will amount to repetition, for they all perform the same role in the lives of members and their children, most of whom were born in the United States and are identified as African Americans. This group of African Americans is unique in the sense that they straddle two worlds: the Africana and the United States. Their values and habits follow these two paths.

It is no surprise, then, that the strong commitment of the African diaspora to their kith and kin in Africa, especially in the form of remittances, has become an enormous source of economic development in the mother continent.[47] World Bank data shows that in 2017, the African diaspora remitted $37.8 billion to Africa. This amount increased to $39.2 billion in 2018, and was projected to rise to $39.6 billion in 2019.[48] Of these totals, remittances from Nigerians accounted for $22.3 billion, and payments from Liberians living overseas accounted for a whopping 25 percent of the home country's GDP. Remittances from the African diaspora, which are projected to be about 140 million globally, help "to reduce poverty and grow the economy."[49] In fact, many agree that this kind of soft money is far "better than foreign aid funds."[50]

The other institutions that have helped to mold the lives of this group of African Americans are the African churches brought to the United States by the parents of the new generation of African Americans. In his classic study of religion as a cultural system, Clifford Geertz explains that religion serves as a guide to action for the group that professes the belief system. It is "a system of symbols, which acts to establish powerful, pervasive and long-lasting moods and motivations in men by formulating conceptions of a general order of existence and clothing these conceptions with such an aura of factuality that the moods and motivations seem uniquely realistic."[51] Geertz's anthropological definition of religion is vital to this discussion because it highlights how those who subscribe to a particular mode of cosmology may see every other thing in life through that religious prism. Religion has the potency to create a group within a group. It comes with a certain kind of emotion, which influences the social order. As Max Weber noted, a collective religious identity forges bonds of the sort that opposing belief systems cannot appropriate.[52]

The preceding offers a background to a deeper appreciation of the new-generation Christian churches (those that are not affiliated with the colonial churches from Western Europe) established by Africans as one of the most powerful vehicles through which the African-born community in the United

States has enhanced its identity, character, and strength and transmitted African cultural troupes in the host society. Although not all African-born immigrants living in the United States are members of these new-generation churches, their membership includes diverse migrant countries such as Nigeria, Ghana, Liberia, Sierra Leone, Ethiopia, South Sudan, Kenya, Uganda, and the Democratic Republic of the Congo.[53]

Found in diverse sizes in almost every nook and cranny of the country today, most African immigrant churches in the United States are located in major metropolitan areas with large African-born populations. Among them are Baltimore and Lanham, Maryland; New York City and throughout New York; Houston and Dallas, Texas; Everett, Washington; Atlanta, Georgia; Los Angeles, California; Minneapolis-St. Paul, Minnesota; Louisville, Kentucky; and Chicago, Illinois.[54] Among these Christian churches, the most prominent are the Redeemed Christian Church of God, the African Christian Fellowship, the Church of God Mission International Inc., Christ Chosen Church of God, Christ Embassy, the Synagogue Church of All Nations, Mountain of Fire and Miracles, Living Faith Church Worldwide, Deeper Christian Life Ministry, Christ Apostolic Church (or Assemblies of God), and numerous others. There are at least 150 African immigrant congregations in New York City alone. The *Washington Post* has noted that "the greater Washington area is home to an estimated 250,000 Ethiopians, many of whom worship in 35 different Ethiopian churches."[55]

We will use the Redeemed Christian Church of God (RCCG), a Pentecostal ministry established in Nigeria in 1952 by Rev. Josiah Akindayomi, to illustrate the dominant influence of the African-born churches on the African communities in the United States. In his study "African Immigrants and Their Churches," Adebayo Oyebade writes that African countries have established these "indigenous" Christian churches to serve the needs of their respective communities. As the study reveals, "more people in the African-born community are drawn to these churches than to any other social and cultural institutions they have established."[56] Worshippers include regular members, as well as occasional visitors in search of answers or solutions to a myriad of problems that sometimes transcend the ordinary fulfillment of the individuals' spiritual needs.

As the example of RCCG demonstrates, the African-born churches are conduits of social and cultural identity across national and regional boundaries. The constant national and international travels of religious leaders and church members facilitate the flow of information and communication between the homeland and host countries. Afe Adogame has characterized this exchange of religious ideas and material culture as "spiritual remittance."[57] Itinerant church leaders and ordinary members connect extensive transnational networks in a solid reciprocal exchange between the mother church and the global branches.

In short, the African immigrant church has served as a multipurpose institution not just for the African immigrants but also for the predominantly American Christian population. The influential U.S. magazine *The Atlantic* reported in 2017 that studies conducted in the past two decades reveal that "Americans—long known for their piety—were fleeing organized religion in increasing numbers. The vast majority still believed in God. But the share that rejected any religious affiliation was growing fast, rising from 6 percent in 1992 to 22 percent in 2014. Among Millennials, the figure was 35 percent."[58] In a related commentary in 2013, Wesley Granberg-Michaelson of the *Washington Post* noted: "Much has been written about the way that growing numbers of 'millennials' are walking away from the church. Yet while millennials are walking out the front door of U.S. congregations, immigrant Christian communities are appearing right around the corner, and sometimes knocking at the back door. And they may hold the key to vitality for American Christianity."[59]

These reports underline the relevance of the African Instituted Churches brought by African-born immigrants in modern America.

In the United States, the aspirations of the RCCG embody what Ibigbolade Aderibigbe has described as "an apocalyptic movement."[60] Oyebade has argued that the goal of the Redeemed Church is to "plant churches like Starbucks," the popular American coffeehouse that has proliferated across the nation. Indeed, this observation is literally correct.[61] The extensive studies of the RCCG show that it is one of the fastest-growing new-generation churches in the world. Its core mission is to plant a member in "every family of all the nations" of the world, and to establish parishes "within five minutes' walking distance" of every inhabitant "in every city and town of developing countries." In the developed parts of the world, the church plans to establish branches "within five minutes' driving distance" of every city and town dweller.[62] The RCCG has pursued this extraordinary goal through fervent evangelism and extensive church planting. As of 2018, the church has established about 5,000 branches worldwide, including more than 2,000 in Nigeria. The overseas branches cover 150 countries in Africa, Europe, Asia, the Middle East, and the Americas.[63]

The growth and expansion of hundreds of African Christian churches in the United States, serving millions of African-born immigrants and their friends and families, is a reliable indication of the growing presence of the Africans in contemporary America. As they face the everyday challenges new immigrants face in every region of the world, these churches, like the immigrants' ethnic associations, have served as a bridge in the transitions from the homeland to American society. The older members of the African-born churches often play a significant role in helping Africans integrate into the American social fabric by providing temporary shelter, food, and employment opportunities. Thus, the African-born immigrants have successfully created their own social, cultural, and religious institutions to meet their needs. Of the many civic institutions established by African immigrants, the church appears to be the most vibrant because of its high level of patronage among the community.

In her study of African-born migrant youth and assimilation in the United States, Shelly Habecker concludes that "immigrant youth, particularly those living in smaller U.S. cities, regularly cross, reinforce, and blur social boundaries among a range of social groups in a process better described as hybrid assimilation, which often causes feelings of identity confusion as well as opportunities for daily navigating, contesting, and adding new meaning to an African American identity."[64] Indeed, as the study discovered, children of African-born immigrants either born in America or raised as children in the United States have mixed feelings about balancing the American culture in which they were raised against the African culture inherited from their parents.

In a provocative piece in the *Globalist* on November 16, 2013, Joseph Conteh, a Sierra Leonean immigrant to the United States, describes what he has perceived as "a huge chasm between African-Americans and African immigrants in the United States." According to Conteh, the problem "has widened over the years," causing "deep animosity between many African-Americans and their African immigrant cousins."[65] On the one hand, this discord has prevented African American investors from taking advantage of the current economic boom in Africa. On the other, many African immigrants find it difficult to access the available opportunities for economic advancement in the United States.

The animosity between African-born immigrants and African Americans draws attention to underlying misconceptions that are sometimes fueled by misunderstandings of African and African American history, primarily related to the Atlantic slave trade. Additionally, the U.S. media promotes the view that Africans are backward, and many African Americans have accepted this view unquestioningly. As a result, African Americans often make jokes about Africans, who retaliate with the erroneous notion that African Americans are lazy and violent. What is evident from Conteh's study is that Africans on both sides of the Atlantic have passed through a similar experience of slavery, economic exploitation, and racial discrimination.

The opportunities available today for mutual dialogue and exchange between Africans and African Americans must not be sacrificed on the altar of inter- and intra-Black bigotry. In Chicago, for instance, where Black-on-Black violence has reached epidemic proportions, African American and African-born collaboration in civic engagement has the potential to curb uncivil behaviors among the Black community. Instead, as the *Chicago Tribune* reported in 2013, the African immigrant population, one of the city's fastest-growing immigrant groups, now "seeks a Chicago community on par with Chinatown, the Hispanic enclave at 26th Street."[66] Segregation of this nature has the potential to cause ethnic groups to retreat into their inner selves. Unity, rather than separation, has always been the spirit of Pan-Africanism, which has saved the Black race from the challenges of slavery, colonialism, and other forms of oppression.

Intermarriage among new immigrants from Africa and African Americans offers a substantial opportunity to repair the damage that slavery and racism have caused to the Black family. Also, when the Nigerian community in the United States recently announced its plans to create a community bank to serve the needs of Nigerians both in the United States and in Nigeria, one quickly sees an area for collaboration between African American investors and Nigerian and other African-born businesspeople.[67]

The high educational drive and achievements identified with the African-born immigrants and their families could serve as a source of motivation for African American youth. Even more, opportunities exist for African Americans and African-born immigrants to further promote Black music with new ideas from Africa. This opportunity inspired Makinde Adeagbo, the Nigerian-born genius and founder of People of Color in Tech (POCIT), who has worked with Facebook, Dropbox, Pinterest, and other successful high-tech firms. In founding his not-for-profit company, Adeagbo cited the need to help mentor people of color in the American high-tech professional field as the primary motivation behind his business. "I thought to myself, why is it just me doing this? I know other people who could be doing this, and they want to, but they just don't have any setup or system in which to do it. They also need help from people more senior than them. Again, there's no easy way to find that. That was the start of it, was figuring out what community I would want to be a part of and how do we build that?"[68]

In the field of sports, the sky remains the limit for Africans and African Americans. There are no successful programs in college basketball and track and field today that do not have at least one African American athlete of African parentage. For example, the University of Notre Dame's 2018 Women's Basketball victory could not have been possible without Arike Ogunbowale's clutch shots in the final seconds of the 2018 semifinals and championship matches against the University of Connecticut and Mississippi State University, respectively.

Upcoming stars from high school sports are Chinma Njoku of Century High School, Pocatello, Idaho, and Sudanese-born Bul Ajang of Patrick High School in Elizabeth, New Jersey. Udoka Azubuike of the elite University of Kansas basketball team has dominated its center position for three years. These young Africans are following the records set by their African and African American idols in the National Basketball Association such as Michael Jordan, Hakeem Olajuwon, Dikembe Mutombo, Kobe Bryant, LeBron James, Dwayne Wade, Serge Ibaka, and other superstars. Above all, the emphasis on the church as a compelling force in character molding and civic training is ultimately available through the Black churches and African Instituted Churches to win American youth back to Christianity.

12

U.S. PRESSURES: HUMAN RIGHTS AND DEMOCRATIZATION MOVEMENTS IN AFRICA, 1989–2016

U.S. foreign policy on human rights and democratization in the developing world since the 1990s has brought about more positive results for democratically elected governments in Africa than it did during the Cold War. In other words, the end of the Cold War marked by the collapse of the Berlin Wall in 1989 helped create opportunities for a more purposeful dialogue between the United States and the postcolonial African states. Even with several disturbing and bold attempts by sitting leaders to reverse democracy in the past two decades, Africa has witnessed fewer incidents of successful military coups d'état. Instead, there has been a rise in democratic transitions across the continent. Numerous explanations exist for the decline in new dictatorial regimes. Some dictators have been cautious in the manner in which they handle demands for electoral reforms in their respective countries. Besides, Western donor nations and institutions have pressed for democratic transitions as a prerequisite for loans and the extension of credit. Strident agitation on the part of opposition parties and human rights advocacy groups has led to the decline of dictator-led governments in Africa, making them both a problematic and a risky venture.

Foremost among the risks that stand in the way of dictators and would-be dictators today is the dread of U.S. military intervention, especially after the military invasion of Iraq and the ouster of Saddam Hussein in 2003. The brutal murder of Libya's strongman, Col. Muammar Gaddafi, in October 2011 with the aid of U.S. forces reinforces these fears. The crisis that claimed Gaddafi emanated from the Arab Spring that occurred in North Africa and the Middle East in 2011. The mass demonstrations for democratic reforms that deposed Zine El Abidine Ben Ali of Tunisia and Hosni Mubarak of Egypt and ignited wars in Syria and Yemen also threatened monarchies in Morocco, Saudi Arabia, and Bahrain. The television and Internet transmitted gory images of angry and bloodthirsty insurgents. French and American warplanes and armed forces struck terror in the hearts of African dictators and their cronies. Through this form of intense but understated selective military pressure, along with threats of economic sanctions, the United States and its allies have helped stop some dictators from stifling democratic opposition and influenced the course of democratic transitions in Africa in the past two decades.

However, selective pressures from the United States have not always worked to sway the ambition of African strongmen. On July 11, 2009, during his first visit to Africa as president of the United States, Barack Obama declared in Accra, Ghana, that "Africa does not need strongmen, it needs strong institutions" and that the United States would challenge "leaders whose actions threaten the credibility of democratic processes. . . . Our message [to antidemocratic actors] who would derail the democratic process is clear and unequivocal: the United States will not stand idly by when actors threaten legitimately elected governments or manipulate the fairness and integrity of democratic processes."[1]

Obama's clear but idealistic statements appear to have made a limited impression on African strongmen as time passed. This indifference was because there was a comparable decrease in the aggressive manner with which President George W. Bush had pursued the United States' advocacy of human rights and democracy in the developing world. Basking in the widespread euphoria that greeted his election, Obama began his foreign policy agenda by backpedaling from President Bush's big-stick foreign policy tactics. Above all, the destabilizing consequences that the fall of Saddam engendered in the entire Middle East contributed to Obama's cautious approach in the early years of his administration. Taking advantage of this restraint on the part of President Obama, African dictators attempted to impose their selfish interests on the continent's political order. Those leaders resorted to a cat-and-mouse game with the United States. In Zimbabwe and Uganda respectively, for example, Robert Mugabe and Yoweri Museveni entrenched themselves in power. In Cameroon, Gabon, and Togo, personal rulers persisted.

African rulers became more vigilant again in the period following Gaddafi's death (Fig. 12.1). The lessons to be drawn from the demise of Libya's longest-ruling dictator seemed lost on them. Between 2014 and 2015, dictatorial tendencies and human rights abuses flared up again, threatening the political gains made in the previous years. In Burkina Faso, for instance, we saw a popular uprising in response to longstanding leader Blaise Compaore, who was in power for more than twenty-seven years. Burkinabés of all ages and affiliations strongly rejected his desire to change the constitution so that he could run for another

Figure 12.1. Col. Muammar Gaddafi of Libya.
ZUMA Press, Inc./Alamy Stock Photo.

term in office. Through the combined actions of civil-society watchdogs, the opposition, and the masses, a preemptive coup executed by officers loyal to Compaore was aborted. At the end, the country completed what was considered a fair and peaceful "election with a clear winner accepted by the other candidates."[2]

In his address to the fifty-four-member African Union in Addis Ababa, the Ethiopian capital, President Obama frowned at the emerging undemocratic tendencies, warning that Africa's democratic growth is endangered "when leaders refuse to step aside when their terms end." According to the president, "No one should be president for life. I have to be honest with you: I just don't understand this." Obama further chided African governments against going after the opposition groups. In Ethiopia, where the government claimed that some journalists and opponents had been incarcerated for crimes, President Obama emphasized that the country could not "unleash the full potential of its people."[3]

Despite Obama's excellent advice, the year 2017 evinced democratic backsliding, although some sit-tight leaders suffered embarrassing setbacks. Early in 2015, President Pierre Nkurunziza moved to change the constitution of Burundi laws in order to perpetuate his hold on power. After encountering difficulties, he pressured Burundi's high court to revise the law to allow him to stand for two further seven-year terms. The plan, which was later approved in a dubious May 17, 2018, referendum, enabled Nkurunziza to stay in power until 2034.[4] This move came in clear violation of the 2000 Arusha Peace Agreement, which has guided Burundi's political order since the end of its bloody civil war.[5] President Nkurunziza's unconstitutional power grab caused a severe split within the country's fragile interethnic relations and brought significant violence and bloodshed. In a failed attempt to restore the political order, a section of the army led by Maj. Gen. Godefroid Niyambare, a dismissed former intelligence officer, announced on May 13, 2015, that "President Pierre Nkurunziza is removed from office, the government is dissolved."[6] In response, President Obama signed an executive order on November 23 that sanctioned individuals within Nkurunziza's regime who had contributed to the turmoil.[7] President Nkurunziza succeeded in turning himself into what the *Economist* of May 19, 2015, described as "Supreme Eternal Guide," with no plan for retirement in sight.[8]

While the Burundi imbroglio was going on, the heads of state of Rwanda, the Republic of the Congo (Congo-Brazzaville), and the Democratic Republic of the Congo (Kinshasa) were watching these trends carefully and calculating how to manipulate the constitutions of their countries in order to extend separate terms of office, regardless of the probable consequences of this plan. In August 2017, with a 98.95 percent majority of the popular vote, President Paul Kagame of Rwanda ended up securing a third-term, seven-year extension that will keep him in power to 2024.[9] Kagame's "landslide" victory at the polls replicated that by his counterpart in the Republic of the Congo, President Denis Sassou Nguesso, who in March 2016 extended his thirty-two-year-old rule with a third-term election victory, claiming over 60 percent of the vote.[10]

In the adjoining the Democratic Republic of the Congo (DRC), President Joseph Kabila reneged on an agreement he signed with the opposition on December 31, 2016, to organize a peaceful election and handover of power. After a seventeen-year rule, the agreement spelled out clear terms for Kabila's exit after his second presidential term ended on December 19, 2016. The agreement stipulated that, if needed, the president could take a one-year extension "on condition that he would neither seek a third term nor attempt to amend the constitution to remain in power beyond December 2017."[11] As of August 2018, Kabila had continued to leave everyone in suspense as he contemplated whether to remain in power or not. In what is the first peaceful transition of power in the country since its independence, Kabila eventually stepped down on January 24, 2019 and handed over power to Etienne Tshisekedi. The new president was Kabila's former prime minister.[12] Overall, both the 2015 and 2017 Mo Ibrahim Democracy Index Reports highlight the problem of "more wide-spread declines in [political] participation and human rights" abuses in Africa. The reports concluded that more than a third of African countries are backsliding on democratic governance.[13]

In its end-of-the-year 2017 executive summary of United States-Africa partnerships, the Institute for Defense Analysis (IDA) acknowledged that not all is promising on the democratic front. The report noted that while African opposition parties have made positive gains in countries such as Burkina Faso, Ghana, Malawi, Nigeria, South Africa, Gambia, and Zambia, authoritarianism has resurfaced in key states such as Ethiopia, Rwanda, and Uganda. The report observes that several factors are behind the troubling trends, including poor leadership, corruption, unfair elections, dictatorial tendencies, abuses of civil-society groups, and media censorship. Other serious issues include persistent inequalities in income and opportunity. In countries like Ghana, Kenya, Mozambique, Nigeria, South Africa, and Uganda, gaps between rich and the poor are widening. High levels of economic growth have not always translated into substantial poverty reduction. Unfortunately, they often have increased the economic rewards of political control.[14] Many African political watchers are concerned that Africa may be returning to the old order of military coups and dictatorships after the hiatus of the previous two decades. Military and one-party dictatorships remain a serious threat to democracy and institution building in Africa. As African dictators continue to test the waters to assess the possible reaction of the international community, how the United States responds is critical to the future of democracy on the continent. How Saddam and Gaddafi exited from power remains a powerful deterrent against efforts to reverse democracy and a return to full-blown authoritarianism. Reminding sit-tight leaders of the fate of Saddam and Gaddafi is a powerful lesson that could preserve and strengthen Africa's nascent democracies.

THE SADDAM-GADDAFI DOCTRINE

The images of the brutal execution of Saddam Hussein that were broadcast around the world in 2006, coupled with pictures of Muammar Gaddafi's murder in 2011 and the ensuing deaths of the dictators' favorite sons, left a terrifying impression in the minds of African dictators. InterAksyon.com, an online news portal, captured this gloom among African leaders in the title of its October 22, 2011, article "Disquiet Grows over How Gaddafi Met His End."[15] A day after this account was published, Josh Kron, a *New York Times* correspondent reporting from Nairobi, Kenya, published an article entitled "Many in Sub-Saharan Africa Mourn Qaddafi's Death." Citing the reaction of people in Zimbabwe, where Gaddafi had helped President Robert Mugabe overthrow a White-minority regime that ended in 1980, government spokesperson George Charamba commented that Colonel Gaddafi would not be forgotten: "The government cannot accept drawing blood as a model for changing political systems on the continent. More so, when that blood is drawn at the instigation of foreign countries."[16]

During his rule, Gaddafi was an enigma to the West and a divisive personality to the Africans. While he diversified Libya's oil-rich economy by investing in other countries such as Kenya, Senegal, Mali, and Burkina Faso, Gaddafi also sponsored civil crises in Liberia, Uganda, and Chad, and he often treated other African countries, such as Nigeria, and Western nations with contempt.

Nigerians reacted to the explosions that hit the Ikeja Military Cantonment in Lagos, Nigeria, on January 27 and 28, 2002. The blasts killed about 1,000 people inside the military complex. The report of this "unprecedented occurrence" in Lagos's *Punch Newspaper* on January 28, 2002 stopped short of linking the incident with a military attack that Nigerians widely speculated was an outgrowth of Gen. Sani Abacha's regime (1993–1998). That speculation and fear remained strong among Nigerians several years after the demise of Abacha. *Punch* described in detail the fear and confusion that seized many Nigerians who were not sure what was going on: "People, understandably, started running helter-skelter. And whilst scampering for safety, they heard several other explosions, of the same intensity, and in the imagination of many, it was as if another war had started. The vibration shattered windows, roofs and brought down buildings several kilometers away."[17] Ikeja resident and teacher Mrs. Francisca U. Uzodinma, whose home was located half a mile from the cantonment, recalled that she had never seen anything like the explosions before: "I saw the sky lit up with fire and thunder. I thought that airplanes were throwing bombs all over Lagos, I told my children that we are in serious trouble; Americans are here to bomb us as they did to Saddam Hussein."[18] It is remarkable that Mrs. Uzodinma had these thoughts in 2002, a year before President George W. Bush ordered the invasion of Iraq.

Such speculations among Nigerians were common and well founded. Early in 1997, during the heyday of General Abacha's government, the *New York Times* reported about the worsening relationship between the United States and Nigeria's leaders. At the center of the diplomatic tension was "a series of unexplained bomb attacks that senior Nigerian officials have said were backed by Western nations."[19] According to the report, attacks targeting mostly military personnel and property mainly occurred in Lagos. Lagos was a commercial capital with a population of over 18 million. One of the strikes destroyed a military-owned bus just outside an army barracks, killing two and injuring twenty-seven soldiers. The Nigerian army perceived itself as the sole target of the insurgent bombings and the government "blamed the country's largest opposition group, the National Democratic Coalition, or NADECO, many of whose members live in the United States."[20]

It was from the NADECO experience that this foreboding about a potential U.S. strike came about. Mrs. Uzodinma's statement referenced the March 2001 U.S. and British aerial assault on Baghdad. The bombing was to enforce U.N. Security Council Resolution 687, which authorized the "destruction, removal, or rendering harmless" of all Iraqi biological, chemical, and nuclear weaponry, the machinery and facilities used to develop them, and ballistic missiles with a range greater than 150 kilometers (about ninety-three miles). The weapons inspection resolution that came after the 1991 Gulf War invoked Chapter VII of the U.N. Charter, which allows for military action.[21]

With General Abacha in power, Nigerians had expected America's anger and military fury. This foreboding is because Abacha's ascendance involved the previous military government of General Ibrahim Badamasi Babangida, nullifying a free and fair democratic election won by Chief M. K. O. Abiola in June 1993. A few months later General Babangida stepped aside in favor of a transition government. General Abacha wrestled control from the interim government, commencing a reign of terror that left all Nigerians thinking in the morning, "What will Abacha do today?" and at night, "What will Abacha do tomorrow?"[22]

Throughout his reign, Abacha's devil-may-care attitude toward power and human rights elicited parallels to Saddam Hussein's Iraq, and the common apprehension in the country was that similar U.S. measures could happen anytime in Nigeria. When Abacha suddenly died on June 9, 1998, his death paved the way for a transition to civilian rule, which brought Gen. Olusegun Obasanjo to power in May 1999. Since then, Nigeria has maintained a democratic government and, for the first time, passed "the second election test," which is a handover of power from one elected government to another. This transition has happened despite many serious challenges, including the Boko Haram insurgency, the resurgence of Biafra secessionist agitation, and continuing looting of the public treasury.

We, therefore, attribute the democratic consolidations taking place in sub-Saharan Africa since 2000 to what we refer here to as the Hussein and Gaddafi effect. The construction of this violent therapy goes back to 1990–1991, when Iraqi caused an international outcry by invading Kuwait. This fear caught up with the rest of the continent after the death of Gaddafi. Both Hussein (1979–2003) and Gaddafi (1969–2011) had been in power for decades, during which time they resorted to extrajudicial executions that emasculated the will of the opposition and disrupted civil society. During those long years, Hussein and Gaddafi promoted their power and their family privilege in what one might describe as "fictional royalties," with no cultural and historical legitimacy. At the same time, these dictators projected international personas and seeming invincibility that other dictators around the world admired. Democracy and human rights activists around the world criticized these dictators. Their ultimate ends explain why the twenty-first century has seen perhaps the best period of democratic government and fewer successful military coups in Africa.

Writing in 2007, African historian Paul Tiyambe Zeleza observed that struggles for and the practice of human rights have grown in Africa and elsewhere despite the challenging economic conditions. Zeleza analyzed the complex problems and "contradictory tapestry and trajectory of human rights" in light of the changing contexts of "democratization, globalization, regionalization, and militarization" that have together shaped African political economies since the 1990s.[23] Overall, the recent trends witnessed in Africa implicate the struggles of the postcolonial African state to overcome what some scholars have identified as the pitfalls of Third World politics.[24] This syndrome, which is not unique to Africa, remains a challenge as the postcolonial states struggle to reconfigure the societies that have emerged since the end of European colonial rule.

THE PITFALLS OF THIRD WORLD POLITICS

The spate of conflicts that have continued to characterize African politics and society since the end of colonial rule reflected a definition of Third Worldism in the political usage of the term. According to Nigel Harris, scholars employ the term *Third World* in reference to states without the attributes of democracy, capitalism, market liberalization, and protection of human rights.[25] The argument goes that the political situation in a given society explains its socioeconomic progress. Therefore, bad politics in Africa hampers its growth. Corruption is a common feature of Third Worldism and remains a severe obstacle to institutional stability in the continent. One crucial factor was the change in the aid policies of Western donors, who introduced new political conditions that required an end to single-party rule and the fostering of "good governance." In other words, Western leaders presented democracy to the African leaders as an answer to development. In early 1990 in the West African subregion, the Benin Republic declared its commitment to democratic reforms. Many francophone countries witnessed similar events as local opposition arose in polities where state repression had previously confronted them.

In Arusha, Tanzania, in February 1990, signatories endorsed the "African Charter for Popular Participation in Development and Transformation," by which the participants representing 500 NGOs and governments hoped to encourage development and change through popular participation in government.[26] As the transitions to democracy encountered problems, the question resurfaced as to whether multiparty democracy was best for Africa or not. Michael Bratton and Robert Mattes contend that multipartyism would aid African development. They base their argument on the "successes" achieved in Ghana, Zambia, and South Africa in the 1990s.[27] However, Joel Barkan and others call for cautious optimism, asserting that there are several reasons why the current political opening may encounter a reversal.[28]

François Bayart, Stephen Ellis, and Béatrice Hibou have made a study of the role of the state, groups, and individuals on the impact of criminal activities on African nations. These studies, among other things, expose the patterns of illegal activities initiated by multinational companies, government employees, and foreign institutions and organizations at both the local and transnational levels. Also covered are the international crimes of money laundering, drug trafficking, currency counterfeiting, credit card fraud, conversion of cash of dubious origin into legal goods, and theft of foreign food aid, among other issues that militate against Africa's development.[29] Nonetheless, a critical observer should add that political corruption is not unique to Africa. Instead, as the Paul Manafort case from Robert Mueller's Russia-collusion probe shows, political corruption and graft are a common problem in both developed and developing nations. In 2018, Manafort, a U.S. political lobbyist and political consultant who worked for candidate Donald Trump's presidential campaign, was convicted on multiple financial charges including eight charges of tax and bank fraud. He also pleaded guilty to two charges of conspiracy to defraud the United States.

In some instances, collaborations between the developing world and Western leaders result in corruption. The recent arrest of former French president Nicolas Sarkozy for tax evasion, money laundering, and, more serious, allegations that he received €50 million from Libyan dictator Gaddafi further shows that Third Worldism and political corruption have no geographical boundaries.[30] Thus, we see that the difference between the consequences of public graft in Africa and the Western world is that the public treasury is more significant in the developed world than in the developing world, where corruption and looting of public funds often lead to human rights abuses that victimize individuals and groups and thus provoke intra- and interethnic conflicts and wars. On this note, therefore, it is crucial for American policymakers to observe that civil wars and human rights abuses in Africa, as markers of Third Worldism, need to be revisited.

REIMAGINING CIVIL WARS IN AFRICA

Although violent and nonviolent conflicts were not alien to the continent, in the colonial period, a sharp rise in armed conflict marked African political culture. Resistance to colonial rule radicalized the indigenous peoples. Irrespective of the nature of the resistance movement, it is apparent that most Africans communicated their displeasure at the colonial presence through acts of violence. This manner of expression has persisted in postcolonial Africa. Some of the factors that trigger these conflicts, such as economic and political domination, are not dissimilar to those that ignited civil conflicts in the colonial period. The extant literature on civil wars in Africa tends to emphasize the proximate rather than the remote causes of these wars. Scholars such as Paul Collier and Anke Hoeffler emphasize what they call the "greed versus grievance" debate. The debate revolves around the idea that greed more than grievance may have ignited some of the wars in Africa, particularly those in Sierra Leone, Liberia, and the Democratic Republic of the Congo.[31] Paul Richards challenges the views expressed by Collier and Hoeffler, noting that ethnographic factors— more than economic factors—triggered some of the civil conflicts in Africa. He argues that war is sociological and, therefore, a social project, among other social projects.[32]

While economic and ethnographic factors are inherent in most conflicts in Africa, they cannot account for the proliferation of conflicts on the continent. Many of the civil wars in Africa are mainly a consequence of what Brandon Valeriano has described as the hubris of "power-politics": the brazen act of desperation often exhibited by African political actors bent on attaining power through violent means with support from external agents. This desperation for power manifests as an act of insurgency.[33] Therefore, power politics is particularly inherent in the insurgent wars in Sierra Leone, Liberia, Ivory Coast, Sudan, and the DRC. In short, while greed, grievance, and ethnographic factors play essential roles in the outbreak of civil wars in Africa, these factors are mainly surpassed by the quest for territorial and political aggrandizement by both local and foreign agents.

A quick look at the incidences of authoritarian leadership and sit-tight governments reveals that they are more rampant in the francophone African countries than in the others. From Cameroon, where Paul Biya has been in power since 1982, to Senegal, where the two ex-presidents retired to Paris, many Africans have a very negative impression of France's heritage and policies in Africa. As Matia, a Ugandan student in Orebro, Sweden, noted in 2008, "It would appear all trouble and suffering in Africa is mostly in Francophone Africa."[34] Indeed, all the African countries where French is spoken—Cameroon, Mali, Togo, Equatorial Guinea, Rwanda, Congo, Chad, the DRC, the Central African Republic, Senegal, Ivory Coast, Burkina Faso—are ridden with endless conflicts exacerbated by French economic and neocolonialist policies. While France is not doing anything to bring these conflicts to an end, the terror perpetrated by dictators like Biya in Cameroon is complicated by the economic repercussions of a French mandate that its former colonies deposit a certain percentage of their GDP in the Bank of France as a trust. In 2014, about $20 billion of African money was in the trust of the "French government and earning just 0.75 percent interest."[35] This neocolonialist practice deserves scrutiny as it leads to unending political and economic crises in those African nations by limiting the amount of funds available for development programs.

Whatever the principal cause of civil conflicts, the African people are the losers. Stephen Ryan has aptly summarized the influences of social conflicts on development initiatives; he argues that protracted social conflict institutionalizes underdevelopment through the destruction of infrastructures and the diversion of wealth to excessive security expenditure.[36] E. E. Azar adds that "a vicious circle of underdevelopment and conflict deprives not only the victimized communities but also the dominant groups, of the economic resources for satisfying their needs."[37] These brutal wars have often destroyed the social fabric of African society, thus raising questions as to the validity of human rights in the indigenous culture.

CULTURE AND HUMAN RIGHTS

Incidences of socioeconomic and political decay have further brought into debate the imperative of freedom as a prerequisite for human development and societal progress.[38] As the indictments of African leaders for human and group rights violations increase, the leaders put forth arguments to justify their actions. At the center of the debate is the issue of whether Western notions of human rights should serve as a yardstick to judge human rights violations in Africa. Jack Donnelly and Rhoda Howard contend that precolonial African society had no notion of human rights. They emphasize the universality of fundamental human rights in scope and application and reject the idea that these rights are vested in the community instead of the individual. At best, the authors contend that these indigenous societies had notions of human dignity but not rights.[39] Donnelly and Howard's perspective not only represents some of the mainstream scholarship opposed to the idea of ethical relativism in human rights, but also reflects the familiar arrogation of liberal values to Western culture. Donnelly argues that there are alternative arcs or notions of human rights within the liberal discourses, but these are difficult to articulate because they do not focus on the individual. As a result, they are "atomistic and alienated from society and the state."[40]

Timothy Fernyhough and others who oppose Donnelly and Howard contend that precolonial Africa had clear concepts of human rights and that African peoples enjoyed specific rights.[41] Indeed, a critical reexamination of indigenous African human rights reveals that its beliefs about capital punishment differed from those imposed by British colonial governments beginning in the twentieth century. To make this more intelligible, it is imperative to briefly highlight the underlying concepts of the state, authority, and power, and the spiritual and cultural symbolism of the death penalty. Among most indigenous societies, such as the Igbo, Kikuyu, Akan, and Pigmy, the idea of human rights and the death penalty was a judicial and political concept based on the idea of the individual's relationship to the culture in general, as well as the cultural articulation of "proper" behavior. Such offenses as armed robbery, murder, and treasonable felony are subject to the death penalty in some of the United States but were rarely considered punishable by death in the indigenous penal code. Rather, certain individuals who committed manslaughter in the local culture were honored and rewarded with titles. Such cases were adjudicated through negotiations between the relatives and community of the victim and the culprit. In this sense, the African socio-cultural and political derivative of capital punishment predates the recent abolition of the death penalty by the European Union. The debate over human rights resonates with the ongoing reconfiguration of the African postcolonial state and the enormous challenges presented by cultural reforms. The reforms that Africans expect of American foreign policy concerning the continent will have a better chance of succeeding only if all the nuances involved in the political and economic convolutions of Africa are properly articulated and addressed accordingly. One proposed path toward this end is to create a way for Africa to partake of the economic spoils of globalization through support for the various regional economic commonwealths in Africa.

REGIONALISM AND GLOBALIZATION

In the mid-1990s, the entire idea of the African postcolonial state was revisited amid doubts as to whether the current notions of politics and the state (and related political strategies) were outdated. Some argued that, under some conditions, local, regional, or Pan-African "units of accountability" might better serve the move to democratization. The new discourses corresponded to global intellectual developments in the 1990s. The state itself was conceived as part of a complex process that acquired different roles at different times. Starting from this period also, the social organization "beyond the state" came into focus. The Franco-African François Bayart was one of the leading exponents of the general shift in interest from "'high politics' to 'low politics' as well as the introduction of the idea of civil society in the academic debate about Africa."[42]

As an academic discourse, civil society first attracted the political imagination of many Eastern European opposition intellectuals as the power of the former Soviet Union began to wane. From the late 1980s, the concept caught the attention of many intellectuals in other parts of the globe. The concept of civil society has been part of the mainstream of European political thought and had several different meanings. In the influential Hegelian-Marxist tradition, for instance, civil society equaled a vibrant social life under capitalism. In the revival of the concept in the 1990s, however, civil society embodied an attempt to define a new political vocabulary that transcended the divide between liberal and socialist traditions. Unlike the Marxist paradigm, class is not considered the conditioning factor of civil society. Social movements are viewed primarily as forms of self-organization or as intermediaries between state and society, rather than as actors in a socioeconomic power struggle. The idea of a civil society expresses "a program that seeks to represent the values and interests of social autonomy in the face of both the modern state and the capitalist economy, without falling into new traditionalism."[43]

With respect to Africa's development, the road ahead lies in adaptation to neoliberalism as an ideology based on the firm conviction in the promotion of common good. This shift would involve following the principles of a free market and open competition, limited state intervention and welfare, individualistic self-interest, rational utility maximization, and comparative advantage in free trade. Unfortunately, President Donald Trump's focus on bilateral trade rather than free trade may not serve the best interests of Africans at this point. Globalization poses an unpredictable question for African countries given the continent's disadvantaged position in the global economic order. Despite efforts to create regional economic blocs, externally funded developmental projects, and incentives for foreign capital investment, economic development on the continent and its integration into the global economy have been very slow.

It is, therefore, important for Africans to reinforce the various economic blocs already in existence on the continent. Among these are the Economic Community of West African States, East African Economic Commission, South African

Economic Commission, Economic Community of Central Africa, Community of Sahel-Saharan States, Common Market for East and Southern Africa, and Arab Maghreb Union. The 2015 consolidated report of Africa's regional economic communities sponsored by the African Union's Capacity Development Division reaffirms the continent's goals to develop large-scale capacity development interventions and to involve the main stakeholders and actors in supporting capacity efforts. Other aspirations include promoting the impact and value of historic efforts and the lessons learned from these efforts, removing the barriers and challenges embodied in developing coherence for capacity development, and identifying and resolving capacity development gaps for specific areas and sectors of the economy, including identifying possible areas of future intervention.[44]

In sum, we have highlighted the dynamics in which U.S. policies for human rights and democratization have brought pressures on authoritarian African leaders to permit reforms to the political systems in Africa. While African despots have attempted to make a comeback, many have suffered serious embarrassment, and sometimes misfortunes. We do not encourage any form of military attack from the United States and its allies similar what happened to Gaddafi of Libya in 2011. Instead, the opportunity has never been more favorable for the United States and other Western nations to collaborate with Africans to bring about a mutual political and economic order in the continent. In essence, Africa may have witnessed some relapses in capacity building and democratic transitions in the past decade, but it has also created agencies through which more positive and permanent results will come.

The collaborative approach fits in well with an observation made by Johnnie Carson, U.S. assistant secretary of state for African affairs, in 2012 that the United States' overarching policy goal for Africa "is to nurture the development of stable and democratic partners who are committed to the rule of law, human rights, transparent governance, and the welfare of their citizens." The term *nurture* is central to this realization because "the long-term strategy of supporting, strengthening and sustaining democratic institutions is already paying off." Therefore, it is incumbent on the United States to prioritize supporting democracy programs that "reinforce good governance and the rule of law, and promote participation of women and civil society."[45]

13

━━◆━●━◆━━

AFRICA AND THE NEW GLOBAL AGE: CHINA'S GIANT STRIDES

> Africa has chosen China; we do not have any regrets about this.
> —*President Roch Kabore*[1]

In February 2018, the Center for Strategic and International Studies reported that in the past ten years the United States had given almost $90 billion in foreign aid to Africa while China, over the same period, had emerged as the largest exporter of goods to the continent. The report, therefore, called for a need to create "a new U.S. and Africa partnership."[2] This call is overdue. Although some may disagree with him, President Roch Kabore of Burkina Faso sounded adamant when he stated on August 29, 2018, that Africa's new partnership with China in the twenty-first century is the right way to ensure the continent's future. In the new global age, Africans are eagerly looking for opportunities to transcend centuries of international exchanges that have perpetuated poverty, undermined developmental infrastructure, and arrested development in the continent. President Kabore's position toward China resonates with W. E. B. Du Bois's 1959 Peiping speech, in which he called on the emergent postcolonial African leaders to seek redemption from Communist China. "Come to China, Africa, and look around. You know America and France and Britain to your sorrow. Now know the Soviet Union and its allied nations, but particularly know China. China is the flesh of your flesh and blood of your blood. China is colored, and knows to what the colored skin in this modern world subjects its owner."[3]

The recent Afro-Sino détente has its roots in the 1970s. While many African states faced an economic decline in the 1970s and 1980s, others saw boom

260

periods resulting from the discovery and exploitation of enormous petroleum reserves and/or mineral deposits. These, along with cash crops such as cocoa, rubber, and groundnuts, defined Africa's involvement with the world capitalist system established by the Western world. Rather than bringing wealth and development, however, the so-called "resource curse" (or the paradox of plenty) often led to extensive corruption, conflict over the distribution of wealth, and ecological destruction. The resource curse involves the critical socioeconomic and political issues confronting oil-, gas-, and mineral-rich countries that inhibit them from benefiting "fully from their natural resource wealth, and [make it impossible] for governments in these countries to respond effectively to public welfare needs."[4]

All the oil-producing countries in Africa are members of the Organization of the Petroleum Exporting Countries (OPEC)—a cartel established in Baghdad, Iraq, in 1960 to advocate for the welfare of its members. In the two decades following decolonization in 1960, OPEC came in conflict with most of the industrialized nations of the world. The 1973 and 1979 energy crises emanating from the Arab oil embargo on Western countries briefly enriched the oil-producing nations of the world, along with Nigeria, Algeria, Gabon, and Libya. It also made the offshore oil in the Cabinda enclave of Angola and the Rossing uranium mine in Namibia more lucrative to these two countries' economies. However, the commodities market bust, and the ensuing recession, dogged African economies throughout the 1980s and 1990s. Among the economic trends of the twenty-first century is a resurgence of the commodities boom, the largest sustained one since World War I.

In many ways, the early twenty-first-century boom reflects earlier booms (and busts), but it has also been accompanied by infrastructure development. From the standpoint of this study, these trends were driven less by U.S. policies than by other global dynamics, especially the rise of China and its latest involvement in Africa. Thus, the successes and shortcomings of centuries-old United States-Africa relations can be gauged by the achievements of China in Africa today. The impetus for the Africans to embrace China can be viewed in regard to U.S. actions (and inactions) toward the postcolonial states over the years. Inconsistency and apathy have characterized this historical relationship. This discussion highlights unequal exchanges, especially with regard to Africa's state of underdevelopment, the proper distribution of oil and mineral revenues, and commentaries on and protests against corruption and the consequences of ecological damage resulting from petroleum and mineral "booms and busts."[5] The point is that the responses of the United States and the former colonial powers to African issues—whether concerning trade, investment, interventions

in times of political crisis, or provision of developmental aid—have been remarkably different from China's twenty-first-century approach. China brings a
different vision and mission that are tilting the scale of the continent's future in
its direction.

BACKGROUND TO AFRICA'S RECENT GRAVITATION TO CHINA

To understand Africa's recent gravitation to China, one has to go back to the
1970s and 1980s, when the oil and commodities markets tumbled, and many African economies ended up in serious difficulties. Concerned by the global economic trend and the dangerous consequences it presented to peace and security
in the region, African heads of state and governments began in earnest to plan
for a better future for their people irrespective of language barriers and ideological differences imposed by colonialism. One of the strategies the Africans found
expedient was economic regionalism. These included the formation of the Economic Community of West African States (ECOWAS) in 1975, the Economic
Community of Central African States (ECCAS) in 1983, the Intergovernmental
Authority on Development (IGAD) in 1986, the Arab Maghreb Union (UMA)
in 1989, the Common Market for Eastern and Southern Africa (COMESA) in
1994, the Community of Sahel-Sahara States (CEN-SAD) in 1998, and the East
African Community (EAC) in 2000. There is no space here to examine each of
these economic blocs in detail. For our purposes, we will use ECOWAS, the
foremost of these regional economic initiatives, as a case study.

In the Lagos Treaty, signed on November 5, 1976, in Lomé, Togo, the sixteen-
member organization laid out five protocols, which finally became operational
in March 1977.[6] Among other things, ECOWAS aimed to harness the abundant
natural resources of its member nations to promote human and infrastructural
development in the region. These include significant sources of energy, such as
oil, coal, and hydroelectric power, and substantial deposits of gold, diamonds,
copper, bauxite, phosphate, silica, uranium, iron ore, tin, chromium, and man-
ganese. The organization planned to promote free movement of people in the
region, to promote free trade by removing customs barriers by May 1981, and to
work out a single monetary zone. It further inaugurated an ECOWAS endow-
ment to help fund joint projects and provide loans for other regional infrastructural needs, such as the proposed 2,060 miles (3,315 km) of coastal highway
linking Lagos, Nigeria, to Nouakchott, Mauritania.[7]

Seven years after its launch, ECOWAS remained a healthy and positive idea
in Africa. Nevertheless, it had failed to attain its full potential because of many

problems that were identified in a report titled "World Economic Challenges."[8] The 1980s oil glut, and the energy crisis that preceded it, slowed down the economies of industrialized nations such as the United States, Canada, the Western Europe countries, Japan, Australia, and New Zealand. The crisis was a direct result of the Arab states' response to the crisis in the Middle East. First, in 1973, the Yom Kippur War between Israel and the Arab states disrupted the global oil supply, which caused the price of oil to skyrocket. When sanity was about to be restored, the 1979 Iranian Revolution that brought the Ayatollah Khamenei–led theocracy to power further depleted the global oil supply and caused prices to rise steeply from $15 to $35 per barrel. Thus, reduced demand for goods and increased production combined to unleash an "oil glut" and the economic slowdown that also affected all commodity market economies.[9]

The most immediate and critical challenge that confronted the OPEC members over the period was the Nixon administration's unilateral decision to pull out of the Bretton Woods agreement and abandon the gold-exchange standard in 1971–1973.[10] Nixon took this step to counter the consequences of OPEC's oil politics. The move led to the U.S. dollar becoming the standard linked to the price of gold. As a result, the U.S. dollar became the unit for measuring all other national currencies. The sudden change was tumultuous for world currencies, and it led to a depreciation of the U.S. dollar. OPEC members suffered a sharp decline in real revenue because producers priced oil in dollars.[11]

In Africa, the energy crisis produced results that mirrored the Igbo legend of the trickster Ekwensu, a deity of bargains and vengeance who is reputed to snatch the life of a person right at the moment the offending individual's life is at its peak. First, during the 1970s interruption in oil production, producers such as Nigeria, Libya, Algeria, Angola, and Gabon reaped substantial windfalls in revenues from oil exports. The bust that soon followed affected not only the oil-based economies in Africa, but the majority of the African economies anchored by agricultural commodities such as cocoa, maize, groundnuts, sorghum, and millet. The bust also impacted mineral-rich countries such as Botswana, the Democratic Republic of the Congo, Mauritius, and Sierra Leone.

In Mauritania, for instance, the iron ore industry, representing about 80 percent of the country's foreign currency earnings, declined drastically. The recession in Japan, a major importer of Mauritanian iron ore, caused a drop in exports from 686,000 tons in 1981 to 400,000 tons in 1982. The Western European nations (France, Belgium, Italy, Britain, Spain, and Germany) that bought the bulk of Mauritania's iron ore made similar import cuts. The panic and pain brought about by the economic downturn caused the government to award significant concessions to foreign countries, giving them greater control over

Mauritania's mineral wealth. For example, the United States–based Oxoco International received an offshore permit to mine 12,427 square miles (20,000 km), the largest concession ever granted by the government to a foreign company to survey and drill oil.[12] European oil companies from France, Italy, and Britain secured similar deals. The deals were not based on a mutual partnership but represented opportunism on the part of former colonial powers, gained when the West African nation was most vulnerable and its economic and political distress left it with few choices.

In Liberia under President Samuel Doe (1980–1990), Western governments and creditor nations denied the government's bid to secure a $500 million "Save-Our-Soul" loan. As a result, Liberia was forced to put strict economic measures in place, including a wage bill that consolidated an existing $13 million debt to $8.5 million. As Liberia's rubber-based economy continued to struggle, the government approached the Paris Club and commercial banks for debt relief totaling about $45 million. The agreement deferred payments on principal loans that were already two years overdue. In 1982, the delinquent payments totaled $27 million. At this time, the U.S. government tried to support Liberia's economy by giving it a $115 million loan, and Liberia borrowed $180 million from the International Monetary Fund (IMF).[13] Unfortunately, these measures were too little and came too late to resolve the enormous economic and political crisis facing Liberia.

President Reagan made a wrong policy decision to support President Doe despite his human rights abuses and the aggressive crackdown against his opposition.[14] In 1986, when the former military ruler became a civilian president, Thomas Quiwonkpa, Doe's former commanding army officer, launched an armed insurgency to dislodge him from power. Soon afterward, another militant faction, led by Charles Taylor, joined the civil war. In 1990, a rebel group splintered from Taylor's camp. Led by Prince Y. Johnson, the rebels captured and killed President Doe at ECOWAS headquarters. Liberia then fell into the hands of the Americo-Liberian Charles Taylor. Taylor would prove to be the most brutal dictator the country had ever seen.

The most significant problem faced by the African countries was environmental degradation and famine caused by drought. The insufficiency or near absence of rain in the Sahel region in the early 1980s caused severe and widespread economic hardship. From Mali, Cape Verde, the Gambia, Senegal, Mauritania, Guinea, Upper Volta, Chad, and the Republic of Niger to Northern Nigeria, the problem became perennial.[15] In the Gambia, for instance, Vice President Bakary Barbo announced in February 1984 that "the majority of the rural population of 500,000 are now exposed to serious risk of famine."[16]

Details of the impact of the drought on the production of cereal crops in these West African countries were presented at a summit of the Inter-State Committee for the Combat of Drought in the Sahel, held in January 1984.[17] The report noted that the drought had brought about a deficit of 1.5 million tons in cereal production, double the deficit in 1973. As a result, Senegal needed 300,000 tons and Mali 280,000 tons of cereal to make up for the shortages.[18] Across the African continent, half the population faced starvation. The drought in Ethiopia, Eritrea, and Somalia reached epic proportions. A report from Washington, D.C., warned that Africa was in "a state of emergency" and that the world had "an international disaster on [its] hands."[19]

In 1984, the Agency for International Development announced a $500 million special initiative aid for Africa, spread over five years.[20] The agency further submitted a supplemental aid package to the U.S. Congress for $90 million to help offset Africa's food needs.[21] In the end, the goodwill shown by the United States came up short, perhaps due in part to the fact that Congress ignored the voices of the African people it attempted to help. There was neither a concerted effort to forge a mutual partnership with the Africans nor a policy to help the continent achieve self-reliance in food production. Instead, cheap rice imports from the United States and other countries decimated rice production in Togo and Nigeria. African countries also had limited access to modern farming equipment and lacked important market information.[22] In the end, these countries became dumping grounds for foreign rice, and the local markets collapsed.

Looking inward for a solution to the worsening economic slowdown across the continent, African heads of state, government officials, and ECOWAS convened again in Lomé, Togo, in November 1984 to discuss strategies for economic recovery and security for the subregion. At the end of the two-day summit, the leaders resolved to:

(1) Adopt a common strategy for economic development based on a joint plan of action for the sub-region, to make the best possible use of the resources available to the Community.
(2) Promote the rehabilitation of the productive sectors of our national economies.
(3) Adopt and implement appropriate adjustment policies to combat the worsening balance of payment situation.
(4) Adopt, as soon as possible, measures to encourage the creation of an ECOWAS Monetary Zone, to promote stable monetary and financial conditions for sustained growth of the regional economy.

(5) Take the necessary measures to ensure the achievement of food self-sufficiency, the rationalization of manufacturing industries, and the improvements of their productive capacity. In the field of agriculture, the leaders resolved to use every effort to implement the decision relating to the establishment, on a zonal basis, of committees for agricultural development.

(6) Continue to pursue the current community policies on infrastructure development in transport and communications, aimed at the promotion of social and economic intercourse among the people of the sub-region.

(7) Initiate immediate action to combat desertification through the implementation of Community reforestation programs.

(8) Adopt collective measures to minimize the effects of unemployment within the Community.

(9) Take concerted action in the application of the findings of research institutions in the field of developmental problems in the sub-region and provide these institutions with all the facilities necessary for the successful performance of their functions.[23]

During the Tenth Ordinary Session of the ECOWAS summit held in Abuja, Nigeria, on July 7–9, 1987, African leaders drew attention to the unfavorable international economic environment "which continues to thwart the development aspirations of the Member States of the Community."[24] They spoke about the need to come up with the discernible changes, within the subregion and elsewhere in Africa, as the most reasonable approach to the myriad economic problems facing African economies. In place of the previous ad hoc measures designed to correct short-term disequilibria, ECOWAS decided on "well-structured" programs that would guide Africa's economic future.[25] The summit reiterated "the ECOWAS objective of economic integration and reliance on the resources of the sub-region for achieving balanced and sustainable growth and development. It was emphasized that only the adoption of appropriate reform policies could lay the foundation for the economic and social transformation necessary for the elimination of ignorance, poverty, and backwardness from the West African society."[26]

Within the search-for-survival frame of reference emerged the inclination of African leaders to look toward China for economic partnership. For the Africans, China appeared to offer them something that neither the United States nor the European colonial legacy had provided: the opportunity to work together as partners, not in a master–servant or superior–inferior relationship, but as equal partners in a win-win exchange.

While the genesis of United States-Africa and Europe-Africa relations run back several centuries, the Sino-African collaboration began to take shape in the 1960s. It took a new form in the late 1980s, following a thaw in the Cold War.[27] Without doubt, economic interests lay at the center of this collaboration. Africa's abundant "natural resources . . . are critical to [China's] continued economic growth."[28] Nonetheless, there is more to this change than some critics are willing to admit today. Historically, China has often supported Africa's course in the United Nations, from various liberation movements against colonial domination in Zambia, Zimbabwe, Algeria, Cape Verde, and Namibia to protests against Portuguese atrocities in Maputo, Mozambique, and apartheid in South Africa.[29] Influential African leaders such as Kwame Nkrumah of Ghana and President Julius Nyerere of Tanzania admired China. In particular, Nyerere modeled his ideology of Ujamaa on China's brand of communism, which represents a bottom-up approach rather than the top-down system to which Nkrumah was more inclined.[30]

Thus, some scholars now realize that the "global hunt for energy," as described by David Zweig and Jianhai Bi, does not fully explain the rapport between China and its African allies.[31] Some observers now acknowledge that the "allure of the Chinese model," predicated on mutual partnership and respect for the indigenous elite, connects with the "greater historical context" where "Cold War rationales have evolved towards convergence of economic interests."[32] On this basis, Liu Hongwu and Mulugeta Gebrehiwot Berhe conclude that the new Sino-African relationship represents "a significant break from the yoke of foreign interference in their economic policy,"[33] a Sino-Africa relationship that Wei Zhang perceives as enjoying "popular support" in Africa and China.[34]

Viewed from a geopolitical standpoint, the emergence of China as a new force in Africa has brought about a situation where the influence of the former colonial powers and the United States is now under challenge as never before.[35] In other words, the African countries perceive China's presence as a counterhegemonic force in a geopolitical sphere in which the Western powers held sway for several centuries. China's ability to clinch bilateral relations with several African countries provides a refreshing approach in a new world of globalism. In the pursuit of its own economic interests, China has constructed a post–Cold War vision in which it has projected itself into the new century.[36]

Theoretically, the nature of contemporary Sino-African relations has led to the adoption of concepts such as the "rediscovery of Africa."[37] China commemorated this rediscovery in 2000 with the founding of the Forum on China–Africa Cooperation (FOCAC).[38] Through this forum, which convenes alternately in China and Africa, China manages its relationship with the continent to increase aid to Africa significantly.[39] Anja Manuel has noted that while

China was the largest recipient of Asian Development Bank and World Bank loans in the 1980s and 1990s, "in recent times, China alone loaned more to developing countries than did the World Bank."[40]

In November 2006, China hosted the third FOCAC, which brought forty-one heads of state and an additional forty-eight African delegations to Beijing, the Chinese capital. FOCAC provides a platform for Chinese and African political and business leaders to allow "collective consultation and dialogue and a cooperation mechanism between the developing countries, which falls into the category of [the global] North-South cooperation."[41] Great pomp and ceremony characterized the 2006 event. In his closing remarks, Chinese president Hu Jintao praised the "new strategic partnership" with Africa and called for reform of the United Nations to give Africa a permanent seat on the Security Council. More remarkable was China's promise to increase its bilateral trade with Africa from $40 billion per annum to $100 billion over the next three years. The Chinese further pledged to set up three to five special economic zones and institute a $5 billion development fund to further Chinese investments in Africa. China also committed to build 100 new rural schools and train 16,000 professionals to introduce the Chinese language and culture into Africa.[42]

The Chinese initiative has since blossomed, reaching $163 billion in 2011 alone. In February 2007 President Hu Jintao, who came to power in 2003, made his third visit to Africa. The twelve-day trip included stops in eight African countries. President Jintao focused on trade, aid, and investment. He canceled debt during stops in Mozambique, Cameroon, Zambia, Liberia, and Sudan, and pledged soft loans and grants to Namibia (USD $139 million), Sudan (USD $117 million), Cameroon (USD $100 million), and Seychelles (USD $35 million). He also inaugurated a major mining partnership in Zambia's copper belt and pledged a new "strategic partnership" with South Africa: "The visit illustrated China's way of using high-level personal contact to reach out to virtually every country on the continent with which it has diplomatic relations."[43]

For the United States and the former colonial powers of Western Europe, nothing could be more indicative than this concept of rediscovery, in which the Chinese address a convergence of themes surrounding geopolitics, foreign interference, economic aid, development and underdevelopment, and emancipation issues that have lingered in the wake of decolonization. The salient features of the Sino-African relationship include weaving together economic solutions with the aspirations of citizens on both continents. This newfound focus arrived when Africa's economies were experiencing their most severe deterioration, engendered in part by foreign exploitation, civil conflict, mismanagement, and corruption. This development is contrary to the world capitalist system paradigm as articulated by Immanuel Wallerstein, in which the developed countries of the West aim to drain resources from the African periphery to the core economies.[44] The failed "structural adjustment policies" imposed on the African economies by the IMF and the World Bank did not help the African economies. Africans came to see these Western-owned international credit houses as neocolonialist apparatuses.[45] The lesson Africans learned from this experience inspired them to assert new priority goals in the age of globalization. A brief look at China's economic policies in a few African countries, such as Nigeria, Zimbabwe, and Kenya, offers perspective on the idea of Africa's rediscovery.

China's GDP has grown astronomically, from $2.7 trillion in 2006 to $12.8 trillion in 2017. China has achieved some of its ambitious economic goals through considerable investments in Africa. Writing in 2007, Jeremy Youde noted that Zimbabwean president Robert Mugabe was a close ally of a succession of Chinese leaders. Those who supported Zimbabwe's foreign policy toward China point to the fact that the country demonstrated "resourcefulness" in the face of Western economic sanctions and condemnations arising from President Mugabe's land redistribution policy of the late 1990s.[46] Youde points out that Zimbabwe's "Look East" foreign policy strategy alarmed many Western countries, particularly Britain and the United States. At the center of President Mugabe's Asian foreign policy was a pragmatic attempt to secure an alternative source of foreign aid and "to redirect the public imagination toward a different identity at the domestic and international levels: The government seeks to draw on its image as a freedom fighter and liberator to shore up its domestic legitimacy, while simultaneously reasserting its role as an important international actor."[47] However, China did not interject itself into Zimbabwean politics with no precedent. As in many other countries, China helped Zimbabwe in its fight against colonialism. It helped train and arm Zimbabwean guerrilla fighters. The fighters include current Zimbabwean president Emmerson Mnangagwa. China also provided ideological encouragement during the anticolonial struggle.[48]

In 2013, Charity Manyeruke, Shakespeare Hamauswa, and Aaram Gwiza analyzed Chinese influence on Zimbabwe in the wake of Western sanctions that blacklisted Zimbabwe's President Mugabe in the international community.[49] China helped Zimbabwe resist economic sanctions. When President Mugabe stepped down in November 2017, after thirty-one years in power, China played a subtle but crucial role in the transition.[50] China's Sinohydro financed the 300-megawatt expansion of the Kariba South project, estimated to be worth hundreds of millions of dollars. Chinese companies were also major players in Zimbabwe's diamond fields, until the government decided to terminate all licenses and establish a state monopoly in 2016.[51]

Thus, inherent in Sino-African relations is idealism founded on the tenets of cooperation and noninterference in the local politics of its African partners. This approach remains a compelling and defining hallmark of the Chinese foreign policy thrust in Africa. While this view is relevant to understanding China's relations with Africa, it paints a picture of a conflict-free and competition-free foreign policy strategy. Scholars such as Phineas Bbaala have a dissenting view and question whether the Sino-African relationship is indeed a "win-win or win-lose" relationship.[52] Kenneth Thompson concludes that idealism implicates an approach grounded in humanitarian concerns to avoid competition and conflict, as well as a bifurcated structure that has the potential to generate conflict.[53] Indeed, China's African mission is not a humanitarian project. So far, it has not turned into another colonial project either.

During his state visit to Beijing on April 3, 2018, President Mnangagwa thanked Chinese president Xi Jinping for political support, and Mnangagwa vowed to reinforce ties between the two countries. In his welcoming comments at the Great Hall of the People, President Jinping reassured President Mnangagwa that he was "an old friend of China": "I appreciate your efforts to develop relations in all areas."[54] He praised the Zimbabwean leader's efforts to "improve people's lives. As Zimbabwe's good friend and partner, we are very happy about this."[55] Ahead of an election scheduled for August 2018, President Mnangagwa was under pressure to recruit new foreign investors and address a currency shortage in the country, along with mass unemployment and dramatic price increases. The Zimbabwean delegation, bedecked with scarves in the colors of Zimbabwe's flag, recalled the military training China provided during the Zimbabwean anticolonial struggles in the 1960s, when China helped train and supply guerrilla fighters from the military wing of Zimbabwe's African National Union in the fight for independence in the Southern African country. Then seventy-five-year-old President Mnangagwa had fought against the White minority regime of Ian Smith in Southern Rhodesia. He applauded President Jinping's re-election as president and praised his political theory, referred to as "Xi Jinping Thought": "I will take this mantra to Zimbabwe and hope to develop some socialism in Zimbabwe with Zimbabwean characteristics."[56]

On April 7, 2018, the Harare daily *The Herald* reported that President Mnangagwa had signed a memorandum of understanding to unlock $1.2 billion worth of investments in the country's tourism and hospitality industry through a Chinese company.[57] The deal came after Zimbabwe's president visited China with an eight-member delegation to strengthen the partnership, which reflected the growing respect among some African countries for China as a powerful partner. Especially during Mugabe's tenure as president, China and Zimbabwe shared a common disdain for the West. Throughout his fight with the West, President Mugabe leveraged China's policy of noninterference. China showed support for Zimbabwe in various ways, including denouncing Britain's plan under Prime Minister Tony Blair to attack Zimbabwe in 2009 because the plan violated Zimbabwe's sovereignty. China instead increased its business dealings with the country—much to the chagrin of the West.[58]

In other places in Africa, China continues to leverage its massive economic investments to project its friendship and goodwill in the face of intrepid American and European engagement with the continent. In a report on Chinese activities in Nigeria, Mark A. McDowell of the U.S. Army noted that although the United States initially viewed Chinese–Nigerian relations with suspicion, it has since turned out that this relationship has prospered without any reason for the United States to consider it a threat to either the Nigerians or the Western powers. Although the Chinese-Nigerian partnership is predicated on "strategic partnership in economic terms," as enunciated in the memorandum of understanding between the two countries, both security and cultural elements are finding "resonance in the relationship."[59]

While McDowell's study was meant to assess the safety of America's military interests, it reveals that the China-Nigeria partnership is more economic than military. In McDowell noted that in 2012, for example, the Nigerian Navy's $62.7 million budget contained an agreement with China Shipbuilding and Offshore International Limited to build 50 percent of its patrol vessels at an estimated cost of $21 million. The 2012 Nigerian Navy procurement budget provides $42 million for two 1,800-ton offshore patrol vessels. Additionally, the Nigerian Air Force purchased twelve Chinese-made Chengdu F-7NI fighter aircraft and three F-7NI trainer aircraft.[60] Despite the attempt by McDowell to present this bilateral security cooperation in mostly economic terms, we see a strategic geopolitical maneuver aimed to secure the Nigerian import and export markets by China.

As in Sudan and Angola, China has strategic interests in Nigeria's massive oil industry, and its pursuit of oil exploration wells and drilling licenses in Nigeria has been ongoing since 2006. A memo dated August 2012 from the office of the president of Nigeria reveals that China's state-controlled China National Offshore Oil Corporation (CNOOC) is strategically targeting control of 16.6 percent of Nigeria's oil reserves. In 2012, it acquired a $2.7 billion offshore oilfield in Nigeria.[61] When China finally reaches its targeted goal of 16.6 percent, CNOOC will come in conflict with Western-owned oil companies such as Chevron, Shell-BP,

Texaco, Agip, Total, and Elf that currently have contracts in Nigeria.[62] In 2011, the Brookings Institution reported that China's strategy for securing and diversifying its energy supply made its involvement in Africa inevitable.[63]

Other sectors of the African and Chinese economies reinforce each other. Conceptually, Olugboyega Oyeranti and others have observed that infrastructure and capital deficiencies are the banes of development in Nigeria, while China owns one of the world's largest and most competitive construction industries in the world. Additionally, China's capacity to fund large projects is something Nigeria needs to push its economy on the road to progress.[64] Indeed, construction and infrastructure development are China's prime commercial inroads into Africa.[65] The most significant aspect of Nigeria-China cooperation is in the railway sector. China's largest overseas construction project is the $8.3 billion Nigerian Railway Modernization Project. The Abuja–Kaduna Railway was built by China and opened for operation in July 2016. Exactly two years later, the Abuja Rail Mass Transit project was commissioned in July 2018. Additionally, the government is about to celebrate the completion of the Lagos–Ibadan railway line in 2019. Among other things, the Chinese are modernizing the Nnamdi Azikiwe International Airport in Abuja and managing and funding the Lekki Deep Water Port project. Meanwhile, an essential step in Nigeria-China relations is the Naira-RMB currency swap. The purpose of this economic initiative is to sidestep the necessity of conducting trade between the two nations in U.S. dollars.[66]

Early in 2007, Nigeria turned to China to build NigComSat-1, Africa's first geosynchronous satellite. It subsequently ordered three additional satellites from China. As a report published in *Vanguard* on August 30, 2017, noted, Nigerians have realized that space technology is in the future of Nigeria's economy.[67] Additionally, China is collaborating with Nigeria to construct a 3,050-megawatt hydroelectric power project in Mambilla and gas-fired power stations in Geregu, Papalanto, and Omotosho.[68] In September 2018, during the Sino-African Summit, Nigeria and China signed the new $328 million National Information and Communication Technology Infrastructure Backbone Phase II. China's Export-Import (EXIM) Bank will fund the project, a joint venture of China's Huawei Technologies and Nigeria's Backbone Limited. The project is part of the Nigeria National Economic Recovery and Growth Plan.[69]

KENYA AND THE OBOR

In September 2013, President Xi Jinping of China announced a major initiative to resurrect the original Silk Road in a twenty-first-century trading network named "One Belt, One Road" (OBOR). The Silk Road, the ancient transcontinental trading circuit, linked China all the way from Far Asia (encompassing East Asia and Southeast Asia) through East Africa to Rome (Fig. 13.1). Via this 4,000-mile highway, China exchanged its silk, porcelain, sugar, tea, fragrances, and spices for imports like carpets, curtains, various woolen goods, rugs, spaghetti, and blankets from Central Asia and the eastern Mediterranean. With OBOR, China plans to connect trading relations with no less than forty countries with territories stretching from Asia through Africa and the Middle East to Europe. In 2015, the Chinese government released an action plan known as the Belt and Road Initiative (Fig. 13.2).

What makes the proposed New Silk Road unique and promising is that this gigantic infrastructural project promises something for all the partners involved in the network, or at least so it seems on paper. The cost of putting the infrastructure in place is estimated at USD $8 trillion. China's annual trade with countries along the Belt could reach USD $2.5 trillion.[70] Also factored into the calculation for this megaproject is time. The delivery time for goods exported from China to Rotterdam, the Netherlands, by sea is currently sixty days. The new initiative will cut down the time to fourteen days by land. Although China sells OBOR as a trade policy and not foreign policy, it will certainly enhance China's geopolitical power in countries along the route.

Meanwhile, the Chinese government's initiative is already in the advanced implementation phases. For example, the new Mombasa-Nairobi Standard Gauge Railway in Kenya opened in May 2017. The railway strategically links Nairobi, the inland capital, to the port city of Mombasa. The project's budget was estimated at USD $3.2 billion, with 90 percent of the costs financed by a loan from the EXIM Bank of China.[71] At the ceremony marking the opening of the railway, the local newspaper recalled that "more than 100 years ago, the British opened the 'Lunatic Express,' a 600-mile railway running through Uganda and Kenya, to cement its territorial claims over rival European powers in East Africa. Today, Kenya has replaced that decrepit rail line with a new one, this time built by a new foreign power in the region."[72]

Under colonial rule, the British built the East African railroads that connected Kenya with Uganda and Tanganyika (Tanzania) to facilitate the movement of raw materials from the African hinterlands for export to Europe. After the end of colonialism, these railway lines were not updated to meet contemporary needs. Instead, Britain and the Soviets turned down a plea from Tanzania and Zambia to complete the East African railroad as an economic necessity.[73] "Then, China was also an underdeveloped country, but out of frustration, Nyerere during his February 1965 visit to China raised the issue and surprisingly, China committed itself. In a follow-up visit by Kaunda in June 1967, China agreed to the construction. Then, Chinese leader, Chairman Mao Tse-Tung said, given the

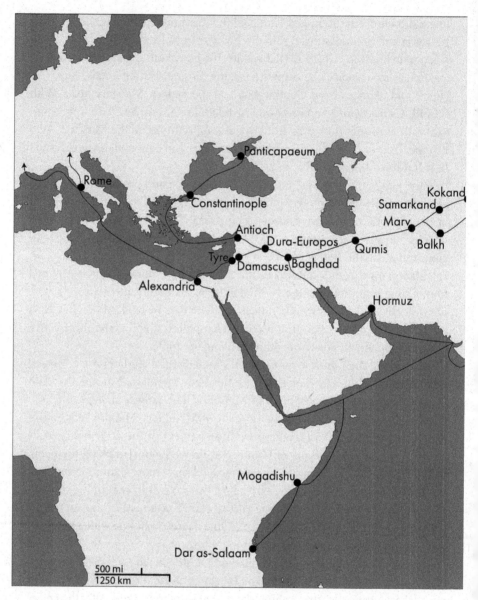

Figure 13.1. The ancient Silk Road. *Toyin Falola and Nathan McCormack.*

need for total African liberation and African development, China would build the railway even when it means his country suspending some of its development projects."[74]

The 1,155-mile (1,860-km) railway linking Dar es Salaam, Tanzania, to Kapri Mposhi, Zambia, was funded with an interest-free loan of USD $500 million

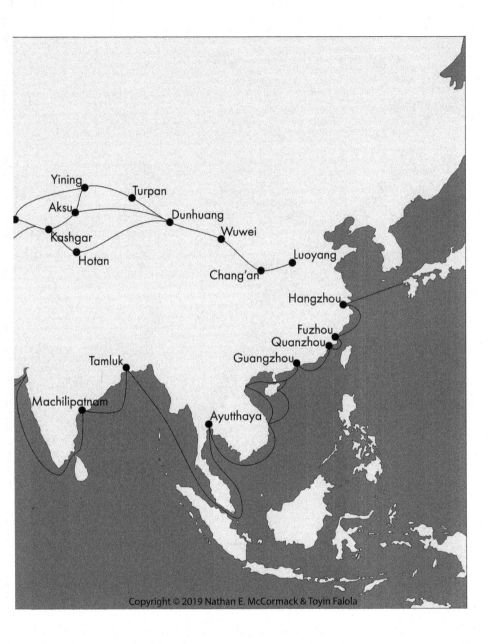

from China; construction began in 1968. Today, TAZARA, as the railway line is called, is part of the grander OBOR project that also connects the entire East African corridor, including Kenya and Uganda (Fig. 13.3). The massive accomplishment represented by the completion of the Kenya railway was celebrated in a skit at a Chinese New Year gala in February 2018 attended by the

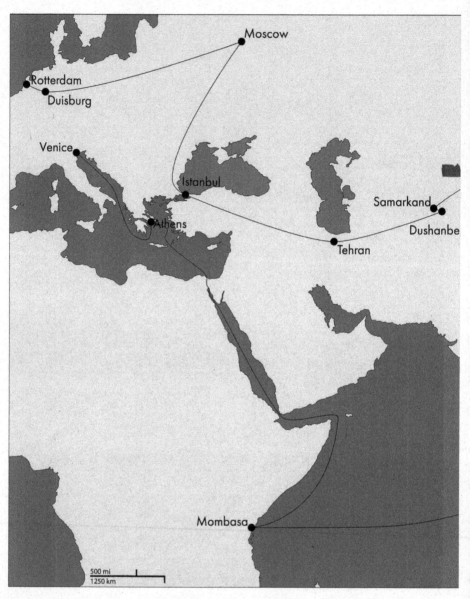

Figure 13.2. OBOR, China's proposed New Silk Road.
Toyin Falola and Nathan McCormack.

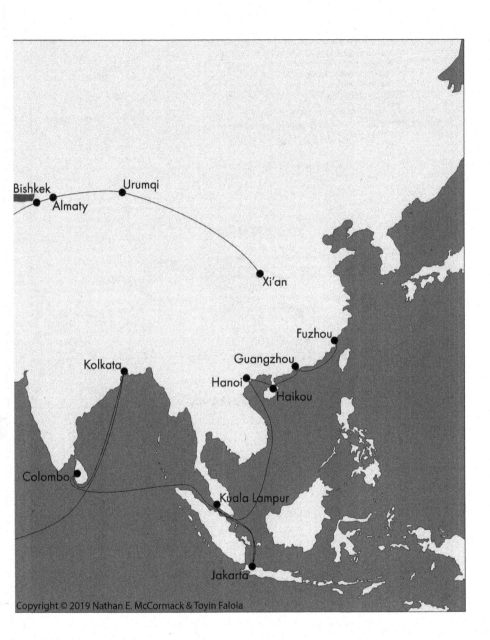

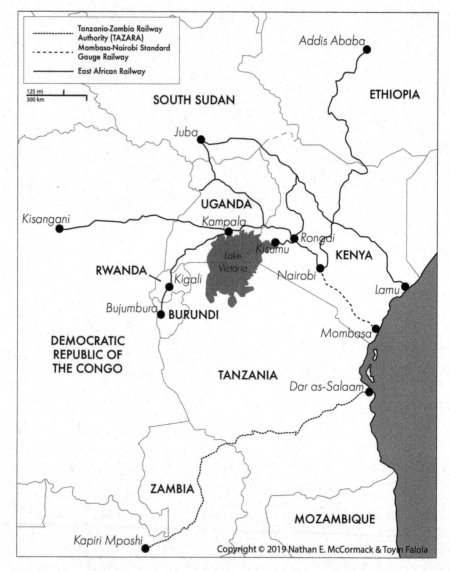

Figure 13.3. Tanzania–Zambia Railroad (TAZARA), built
by China. *Toyin Falola and Nathan McCormack.*

country's leaders and televised to an estimated 800 million viewers around
the world.

It is essential to realize that there are about 100,000 sub-Saharan African students pursuing different degree programs at Chinese universities in 2019. This
number represents a 13 percent increase from 2014. Over the same period, all

other international students enrolled in Chinese universities grew by just 2 percent. In perspective, there were 39,479 sub-Saharan African students comprising 4 percent of all international students studying in the United States in the 2017–2018 academic year. Many Chinese universities have now instituted programs dedicated to the study of Africa. Cultural interchange, especially in the field of education, has been growing, and some of these students helped put together the skit with an African theme that highlighted the fruits of OBOR for a Chinese audience in February 2018.[75] In the end, the skit drew much criticism because of its racial bias. Chinese society has a history of discriminating against African students. Besides, the skit episode also brought up the concern of China being the next colonial power to exploit the natural resources of Africa.[76]

The path to the New Silk Road may be bumpy, but China has mapped out strategies to continue to connect economic partnerships with South Asia, Central Asia, Africa, and Europe. Anja Manuel of the *Atlantic* writes that the project is "staggering" in scope and "is quietly reshaping the world."[77] The Chinese have demonstrated their willingness to learn from their bold moves in the various regions of Africa and to make amends for their mistakes. The key to China's record of successes in Africa and elsewhere has been the use of what Wei Liang identifies as "soft power," defined as the deployment of economic investments with potential benefits for all parties involved.[78] This tradition goes back to the period of decolonization in the 1950s and 1960s, when China used its veto power in the U.N. Security Council to support Africa's anticolonial movements. In the space of ten years (2000–2010), China invested about USD $90.5 billion in the energy and power sector. This investment sent a strong message that China is not the same as either the European imperialists or the American slaveowners, who milked Africa dry and more or less abandoned its people's future. Now, let us contrast China's aggressive economic designs with the 2018 U.S. trade policy agenda submitted to Congress by President Donald Trump.

UNITED STATES TRADE POLICY, 2018

The trajectories inherent in the most recent Chinese and U.S. trade policies present further insights into missed opportunities for the United States to forge closer relations with Africa and perhaps reshape its engagement with the continent in a more positive light. Both what China is currently doing in Africa and its future intentions on the continent provide ideas as to what the United States can learn from the past.

Unlike the Chinese OBOR, the highpoints of President Trump's policy initiative, announced on March 2, 2018, are: "supporting the U.S. national security, strengthening the U.S. economy, negotiating better trade deals, aggressive enforcement of U.S. trade laws, and reforming the multilateral trading system."[79] Focusing on three of these proclamations—America first, bilateral negotiations, and aggressive enforcement of U.S. trade laws—will highlight the point.

The America First paradigm, which is the overall theme of President Donald Trump's 2018 trade and foreign policy goals, did not start with his administration. In the interwar years, "America First" was the slogan deployed by a group led by Charles Lindbergh that wanted the United States to stay out of the looming Second World War.[80] A similar argument was advanced by President Barack Obama's administration to avoid any significant new military confrontations, especially after the U.S. misadventure in Iraq. In each of these instances, the United States ended up doing the opposite after realizing that in the new global age, engagement rather than isolationism is the first principle of survival.

The second aspect of the 2018 U.S. trade policy is the emphasis on bilateral trade negotiation instead of multilateral talks. This focus is consistent with candidate Trump's promises during the campaign for the 2016 presidential election and his acceptance speech during the GOP convention: "I pledge to never sign any trade agreement that hurts our workers or that diminishes our freedom and independence."[81] In what the *Washington Post* of July 21, 2016, called "the dark speech," Trump further stated that he would focus on exclusive deals with individual countries. "No longer will we enter into this massive transaction with many countries that are thousands of pages long—and which no one from our country even reads or understands."[82]

Anyone can criticize President Trump's trade policy of "America First," but no one can fault it just for the sake of fault finding. Every nation-state projects its national interests first in the classical idiom of realism or realpolitik.[83] What is crucial, however, is that President Trump's trade policies need to be complemented by other systems and strategies in order to be effective. First, as King Yik has noted, "the American president projects the United States as his number one focus, but there is no mention of who is number two."[84] In other words, all other countries come second, but in what order? More important, the mentality behind President Trump's "trade wars" is that the United States will always emerge victorious in trade negotiations and that its trading partners, the enemies, will always be the losers. However, the reality of twenty-first-century international trade relations is that there is no single winner and loser: everyone has some benefits and some losses to count in an interdependent world. This is where Africa's priority in the new global age comes into play. For a continent that has been at the losing end since the fifteenth century, the expectation today is to close this wide historical disparity. The world is a marketplace where players win some and lose some. President Trump's bilateral trade policy presents a "we-against-the-world" vision of conflict. The danger for the United States resides in a tendency to focus solely on bilateral negotiations, while losing sight of the grander trading networks that are springing up outside of this two-way trade fight—namely, the ambitious and elaborate belt China is constructing from the Far East through Africa and the Middle East to Europe.

The United States has identified China as an unfair player in global trade, charging that the Asian giant is not playing according to the rules. In a January 2018 announcement, President Trump publicized America's imposition of a punitive tariff on washing machines and solar panels from China. "For imports of large residential washers, the President approved applying a safeguard tariff-rate quota for three years with the following terms."[85] So far, China has chosen to engage the United States in this battle with cautious retaliatory policies. All indications so far are that it is going to be a long, drawn-out battle. Down the line, the United States will probably win the trade war, and supporters of this policy both in the Congress and in business will celebrate the victory. However, while the trade war lasts, China's OBOR initiative will continue to produce significant growth in the volume of trade with Europe (which is growing already), Central Asia, South Asia, and Africa. Then the United States will belatedly realize that it has won an insignificant battle but lost the peace. In essence, President Trump's emphasis on winning in bilateral negotiations poses a significant risk of ignoring what is happening outside the proposed bilateral frameworks.

In the sixteenth century, Ming China traveled the path the United States is currently following today by closing its markets and shutting down its successful voyages of discovery under the legendary Zheng He. The introspective policy led to the demise of China's competitive advantage in both trade and international relations. One of the consequences was the rise and eventual domination of Europe. A more egregious mistake describes Africa's narrow conduct of international trade relations with Europe and the Americas throughout the 400 years that the trans-Atlantic slave trade lasted. The African traders were not only preoccupied with goods like mirrors, glasses, guns, umbrellas, cheap clothes, and other finished products, but also failed to invest their profits in a manner that would have protected the continent from unending exploitative commercial exchanges.

If President Trump's trade policy, as illustrated by the punitive import tax on washing machines, succeeds, it will help companies like Whirlpool regain the American market. In 1983, President Ronald Reagan imposed an import tax policy that helped a U.S. company emerge stronger when he raised the import tax on motorcycles from Japan from 4.4 percent to 49.4 percent. The beneficiary, Harley-Davidson motorcycles, overcame the fierce competition it faced from Japanese makers Yamaha, Kawasaki, and Honda. The high import tax was scheduled to go down every year, and after five years, a decision would be made to either rescind or extend it. After four years—that is, a year before the potential sunset of the protective tariff—Harley-Davidson told the U.S. government to remove the tariff and announced that they were ready to compete with the Japanese corporations. In 2017, the Cato Institute published a comprehensive review of all instances of U.S. protective tariffs from 1947 to the present, which showed that Harley-Davidson's success story was an exception. Other U.S. tariff-protected firms continued to decline. In other words, the benefit of helping these firms is not justified by the costs.

In 1986, the United States accused Japan of dumping memory chips on the U.S. market and thereby hurting U.S. makers. As a result, the government imposed a punitive tariff on Japanese memory chips. Within a decade, all but one U.S. memory chip manufacturer had closed its doors. This closure happened even though the U.S. government considered the semiconductor industry an essential strategic industry for the future and repeatedly urged U.S. makers not to close their plants. However, Intel chip makers declined the government's support. In other words, the United States has many great companies that can make the right business decisions without the government's help. While the import tax on Japanese motorcycles certainly helped Harley-Davidson, the company also did a lot to help itself. It retooled its production system by introducing the innovative 1340 cc V2 Evolution engine. The company further developed the Softail hidden rear suspension system and switched from rigid-mounted to rubber-mounted engines. Additionally, Harley-Davidson introduced inventory management systems to optimize the supply chain for authorized dealers of its products.[86]

Concerning Africa, it is imperative to call out an unfair trading partner. Punitive tariffs are a useful tool to get a dishonest partner to change. By gravitating toward China, Africa is calling on both the United States and the former European colonial powers to address historical discriminatory trading policies that have drained resources from Africa and left its people in perpetual penury. Thus, instead of too much emphasis on wielding the weapon, U.S. bilateral trade negotiations must give due consideration to Africa's place in the new global order. President Trump remains the most suitable U.S. leader to address the main question. He has shown courage in questioning orthodoxy and righting the wrongs of centuries past.

Speaking in Addis Ababa, Ethiopia, on March 9, 2018, during a tour of Kenya, Djibouti, and other African states, former U.S. Secretary of State Rex Tillerson sounded an alarm that the Chinese money flooding Africa risked bringing dependency, exploitation, and intrusion on the nations' basic sovereignty. According to Tillerson, while Chinese investment is "badly needed," African countries should "carefully consider the terms."[87] In response to Tillerson's comments, a blogger who self-identified as Chris responded with the observation that "China means infrastructure, investment, progress, peace. On the contrary, the only thing that the US can offer to Africa is second hand, refurbished, obsolete military equipment."[88] Another who identified as Timur wrote: "Africa did not know much about China until the 1960s. The relationship built ever since, through thick and thin. I suppose in 60 years; you get to know a people or a country. No need for the West to see sour grapes or to give advice."[89] These sentiments are real, and Africans are not afraid to express them.

The views of ordinary Africans corroborate those of their leaders. In his comment at the 2018 FOCUC summit, President Roch Kabore of Burkina Faso described China's Belt and Road Initiative as a "sound initiative" focused on developing the critically needed infrastructure and improving commercial exchanges among nations. "I think it is an initiative that should be supported . . . if we want to develop international trade."[90] Commenting on the growing tariff barriers and unilateralism pursued by President Trump, President Kabore noted that the China–Africa summit "shows the interest of multilateralism."[91] According to President Kabore, "This is what we have always defended together because protectionism in our current times raises problems as it is a real threat to international and world peace. Therefore, the holding of this summit is a real success as we tell supporters of protectionist policies that we have opted for multilateralism. We expect to reinforce cooperation with China in all areas."[92]

Owei Lakemfa provides an apt summary, which mirrors the crisis inherent in United States-Africa relations on the one hand, and the essence of a true partnership exemplified by the Sino-African ties on the other, when he contrasts America's recent squabbles with countries such as Turkey and Iran: "It [America] insists that other countries [should either] join its economic sanctions, or be punished. China also teaches Africa that human circumstances and the world order can be changed not by threats, but in practice." Lakemfa writes that the coalition involved in building the BRICS (an acronym for the combined economies of Brazil, Russia, India, China, and South Africa) and the Belt and Road (that is, the New Silk Road project) is laying the foundation "for a New Economic World Order. Unlike our colonial and neocolonial experience, the Chinese have taught us that a candle does not lose its brightness by lighting other candles; rather, it makes the world brighter."[93] In this light, President Kabore emphasizes that the China-Africa partnership is founded on the principles of mutual benefit, equal opportunity, and the need to develop international trade. "We don't have any regrets about this existing China-Africa cooperation, which is developing day by day in favor of our respective peoples."[94]

14

THE OBAMA PRESIDENCY AND AFRICA: OPPORTUNITIES AND DISAPPOINTMENTS

Congratulations, Our Son, Our Hope.
— *Kenyan banner for Barack Obama's inauguration*[1]

The rise of Barack Hussein Obama II, the forty-fourth president of the United States (2009–2017) and son of a Kenyan father and a White American mother, conceivably epitomizes one of the most important outcomes of the long history of United States-Africa exchanges. The end of Obama's second term in office on January 20, 2017, afforded an opportunity to analyze the expectations and disappointments his presidency presented for Africa. The myriad hopes Africans held for Obama as the president of the most powerful nation in the world is reminiscent of the promises of independence from colonial exploitation. During the period of decolonization in the late 1950s and 1960s, the African nationalists and immediate postcolonial leaders had, by either commission or omission, suggested to the masses that with self-government, at least as Dr. Kwame Nkrumah assured his Ghanaian countrymen, Africa would transform itself into the proverbial paradise on earth.[2]

For a continent that has continued to suffer from entrenched neocolonialist exploitation and racial abuse, the election of Obama was symbolic of the second coming of independence. Expectations of his administration ranged from the absurd to reasonable optimism. In Kenya, for instance, a popular rumor spread that the entire Kogilo clan (Obama's extended family clan) would receive free visas to the United States. Similarly, in 1980, after Robert Mugabe and the Zimbabwe African National Union (ZANU) forced the White minority regime of Ian Smith out of power, Zimbabweans had talked about "moving proudly into the ranks of the first class [with] signs and symbols of modernity such as cars, suits, and fine cloths [*sic*]."[3] The Kenyans, like most Africans, believed that by immigrating to the United States, similar symbols of modernity and affluence would flow their way.

Inside and outside the continent, the general optimism remained that with a son of the soil in charge of the high American power, Africans would reap respect and fortune through Obama's presidency.[4] Nelson Mandela, the anti-apartheid icon and former president of South Africa, summed up the mind of the average and well-informed sub-Saharan African in a congratulatory message to Obama in 2008: "Your victory has demonstrated that no person anywhere in the world should not dare to dream of wanting to change the world for a better place. We note and applaud your commitment to supporting the cause of peace and security around the world. We trust that you will also make it the mission of your presidency to combat the scourge of poverty and disease everywhere."[5]

African historian Paul Tiyambe Zeleza echoed the feeling expressed by most Africans in a deeper historical context. Zeleza noted that Obama's presidency "marked a watershed in the cruel history of Euro-African relations . . . characterized by the savagery of racism and the dehumanization of peoples of African descent." Zeleza continued, "The symbolism of this historic moment was palpable, although its full substance remains to unfold. It is part of the remaking of the Pan-African world that began with the abolitionist movement, followed by the struggles for independence in Africa and the Caribbean, the civil rights movements in America, and crowned by the demise of apartheid in South Africa."[6]

Perceptively, the points of connection that Obama represented for Africa and the United States stretched beyond the potential the first African American president presented to remake the United States-Africa relationship symbolized by trans-Atlantic crossings and multiracialism. This view that Obama was a symbol of Black man's progress in America is substantial, particularly in the minds of many diaspora Africans who played a remarkable role in Obama's 2008 and 2012 electoral successes. For them, the Obama presidency brought a new moment of hope despite the centuries of inequality inherent in United States-Africa exchanges. This unique role in Obama's victory in 2008 profoundly influenced Africa's expectations of him as president. During the campaign, the Democratic Party mobilized the African American and African diaspora bases to support the party's candidate.

In the past five decades, the records of the U.S. Census Bureau show that about two million Africans have taken residence in the United States, compared with the 305,326 people forcibly brought to the present-day United States from

1619 to the late 1800s during the trans-Atlantic slave trade.[7] The recent African immigrants in the United States constitute an essential sector in the quest for stronger United States-Africa relations. The African-born population is the most educated immigrant group in the United States, and therefore a significant part of the economy. Data released on September 30, 2016, reveals that nine out of ten African-born residents of the United States had a high school diploma or higher degree. Government records further show that African-born residents average higher median wages than every subgroup born outside the country.[8] Annual remittances to the continent from Africans in the United States total about $6 billion. Out of this estimate, Nigerians alone remit more than $3 billion per year.

The votes of the African diaspora have never carried such weight in the history of U.S. presidential elections. The Democrats recognized that Obama's biracial ancestry would play a critical role in his presidential bid. The Africans responded actively by coming together to support Obama. Groups like the "African Diaspora for Obama," "Eritreans for Obama," "Ethiopians for Obama," and the "African Immigrant Movement for Obama" sprouted in major cities across the United States. In Virginia, the Democrats lobbied for the votes of 10,000 Ethiopian Americans to help win the votes of state delegates to the presidential conventions in the 2008 elections. The party also carried the swing state of Ohio by mobilizing Nigerian Americans living in Akron, Cleveland, and other places. In Minneapolis, the Somali American community turned out in mass to help the Democrats win the state. In other parts of the nation, African migrants joined forces with African Americans. The Democrats made it clear that "all those of African descent have the potential to be a key game changer in this election."[9] It is in this context of partnerships between the Democratic Party and Africans that the cadence of hopes and impediments in the Obama presidency resides. The Africans actually invested in the elections and therefore expected some returns from the Obama presidency.

Thus, when Ruth Prince, Alemayehu Madiega, and others speak about "the scramble for Obama," they specifically refer to a common political culture involving a network of patrons and clients in a political system that encouraged the hope that Obama would bring benefits to "his people" in the western part of Kenya in particular and Africa in general.[10] In 2006, when Obama was elected to the Illinois State Senate, Frederick Otieno, a Kisumu resident of Kenya, told his compatriots, "We will get support from America, as Africans, as Kenyans, and particularly as Luo." His other Luo fellow citizens were even more optimistic that Obama would turn western Kenya into an "Illinois Kenya Chapter" or Luo settler colony in Illinois.[11]

To someone outside Africa, these expectations may sound unreasonable, but they were widespread in Africa, where client–patron dynamics rule the political and socioeconomic spheres and, by extension, interpersonal and international relations. In the established anthropological meaning, clientelism broadly defines a controlled exchange of relationship between actors in an ordered system with very complex social linkages.[12] Nicolas van de Walle has noted that these dynamics are high in rural, low-income societies, because opportunities for social mobility are few due to poorly developed financial markets, particularly "insurance and credit markets." As a result, client–patron exchanges represent a mechanism to reduce risk, gain mobility, and "smooth consumption over time."[13] "The fact remains," writes the British journalist and author Michela Wrong, "that Africa's rural poor expect to be rescued by the ones who got away. And the higher the individual rises, the greater the anticipation."[14]

However, it is evident that sociopolitical practices of clientelism denote more than the anthropological interpretation. It is an interlocking network defining ways the state and its citizens interact. This system is not peculiar to Africa, despite the assumptions of the mainstream discourses.[15] Ultimately, all social relationships are political, and clientelism is more pervasive in all societies than previously conceived in the extant literature. Within the system, clients pledge loyalty to the patron, who is usually a person or a politician with a lot of socioeconomic and political power. The implicit understanding in the patron–client exchange is that with the electoral victory, the spoils of office will trickle through the patron to his or her subordinates in a redistributive chain linking the patron to the ordinary person at the bottom of the social order.[16]

The relationship among the masses, the indigenous culture of communalism and patronage, and the postcolonial African state is complicated. Much of the modernization literature tended to view the postcolonial state as the remnant of colonial rule and to assume that its culture would inevitably vanish with urbanization, higher education, and the development of a middle class.[17] Nevertheless, time has shown that such paradigmatic postulations are replete with poor judgment of the African system. The argument then is that while Africans, including those in the diaspora, held some legitimate hopes for Obama's presidency, many of these expectations were quite idealistic and based on the notion that Obama shared cultural connections with the African continent. This misconception betrays a shallow grasp of Obama's family background and his multiple identities, which transcend his African identity. Understanding these identities in a global context is key to a proper review of Obama's foreign policy priorities for Africa. Obama's successes and failures reflect the reality and challenges of American power; Democratic and Republican Party dynamics; and the resilience of the politics of race in America. Other factors that affected the intent of and expectations for Obama's presidency are the problem of global terrorism and transnationalism in the cyber age, economic crisis, and corruption of leadership.

BACKGROUND AND IDENTITY

A deeper insight into Obama's presidency and his African foreign policy agenda must start with the immediate period before his presidential run: from his brief tenure as a U.S. senator to the electrifying euphoria of his victory. African American political scientist Ricky Jones describes the euphoria as "Obamamania."[18] During his campaigns, Obama often claimed that he understood Africa's needs better than his political peers in Washington, and he provided some clues about his priorities for Africa, mainly through his legislative participation in policies related to the continent. His campaign promises on the road to the White House at least alluded to these claims at several points. Carefully examined, at the level of rhetoric, Obama sourced his notions of the African continent from his shallow experiences of Africa. While he held a belief in the fundamental ties between the well-being of Africans and American politics, he did not, as was later revealed, possess a particularly profound knowledge of the continent and its people. Obama also appeared to understand the United States-Africa relationship "outside of the narrow realism of war on which virtually all of his presidential predecessors have relied in their dealings with African nations in the past."[19] Before we proceed, a quick look at Obama's family background is crucial to gaining a deeper insight into his political career and relationship with Africa (Fig. 14.1).

Born in Honolulu, Hawaii, on August 4, 1961, to Barack Obama (Sr.) and Stanley Ann Dunham, young Barack's early life journey followed several trajectories that would shape his identity, values, and political journey. While Obama obviously inherited his father's brilliant mind, which saw him navigate successfully through his Harvard education, his mother also played a predominant role in his upbringing.[20] The couple divorced in 1964, but Dunham raised Obama as a single mother almost from his birth. In 1965, Dunham married Lolo Soetoro, an Indonesian.[21]

Dunham was a global citizen, cosmopolitan in thought to a degree far ahead of her time. Her multicultural, inclusive, and adaptive worldviews shaped Obama's outlook on the world. These were the essential values that raised Obama's political stock and which he espoused throughout his time in the

Figure 14.1. President Barack Obama. *Official White House photo by Pete Souza.*

White House. In his autobiography *Dreams from My Father*, Obama tells a complex story of race and personal inheritance. What particularly catches the reader's interest is his calculated emphasis on his mother's White race and his father's Black race.[22] It is hard to overlook Obama's attempt to cast his father as the other while depicting Dunham as the shy, innocent girl who fell head over heels for the African. In some other places in the same book, she comes across as a naïve idealist who chose to sojourn in Indonesia, while possibly underestimating its sociocultural energy and the possible implications for her welfare and happiness.

At his 2004 Democratic National Convention keynote speech in Boston, Obama traced his Kenyan origins to his paternal grandfather, who served as "a cook, a domestic servant" to British settlers: "You see my Grandfather was a cook to the British in Kenya. Grew up in a small village and all his life, that's what he was—a cook and a houseboy. They called him a houseboy. They wouldn't call him by his last name." Likewise, Obama also extended the picture of his mother as a metonym for her parents' hardworking midwestern ethos. Obama's maternal grandfather, he writes, "worked on oil rigs and farms through most of the depression . . . my grandmother raised her baby and went to work on a bomber assembly line."[23] Within the disparate realities of the African and U.S. cultural milieus, Obama inserted himself as a symbol of the American dream, a unique vision embodied by his identity rooted in both sides of the Atlantic.

It is hard to draw reliable deductions based on what *Dreams from My Father* says and what it does not say because it is primarily Obama's way of introducing himself to the American public, who knew little to nothing about him before he made his presidential ambitions public. The Igbo-born American slave and abolitionist Olaudah Equiano reminds us that autobiography is a self-interested genre: "I believe it is difficult for those who publish their own memoirs to escape the imputation of vanity; nor is this the only disadvantage under which they labour: it is also their misfortune, that what is uncommon is rarely, if ever, believed, and what is obvious we are apt to turn from with disgust, and to charge the writer with impertinence."[24] With this hindsight, one questions the motives behind Obama's repeated characterization of his mother during the presidential campaign as a poor single mother with no health coverage who relied on government food stamps for survival. It is hard to deny that this narrative was intended to win personal electoral connections with average voters. If Dunham conformed to the different portrayals of her in the book, she was also, at least in the eyes of Obama's political foes, an enigmatic Marxist and atheist who once left her son in the care of his grandparents. The critics also, without any credible evidence, peddled the lie that Obama was born in Kenya instead of Hawaii.

Whichever story one chooses of Obama's childhood, it is pertinent not to obscure an extraordinary story of a man whose mother was courageous to marry a Black man at a time when parents frowned on interracial unions, and Jim Crow laws lingered in nearly twenty-four states. We may never know whether Jim Crow played a part in Dunham's decision, at the age of twenty-four, to move with her son to Jakarta, Indonesia, a predominantly Muslim country in the throes of a bloody anti-Communist purge. In Indonesia, Janny Scott of the *New York Times Magazine* explains, Dunham presented a strange picture with two biracial children, Barack and his half-sister Maya. Dunham believed that Barack was destined to be great, and her inspiration set him on the road to greatness. Dying at fifty-two, she did not live to see what her son would accomplish.

Obama directly linked the imprudence of his absentee father with the failure of his parents' relationship. "At the time of his death, my father remained a myth to me, both more and less than a man. He had left Hawaii back in 1963 when I was only two years old so that as a child I knew him only through the stories that my mother and grandparents told."[25] This disclosure has implications for Africa in terms of Obama's policy. It reveals Obama's distant familiarity with the people and their culture despite his often-touted close relationship with his paternal grandfather and numerous cousins back in Kenya. It is evident that Obama was closer to his maternal grandparents, who helped raise him when his mother was not available. In a revised preface to the 2004 edition of *Dreams from My Father* (first published in 1995), Obama admitted that if he had known that illness would claim his mother's life in November 1995, his memoir would have been different. Explicitly, he concluded that it would have been "less a meditation on the absent parent, more a celebration of the one who was the single constant in my life."[26]

The four years Obama and his mother sojourned in Indonesia were his formative years. His mother inculcated in him some of her values, such as politeness and respect for others, and structured his understanding of the world. She also taught him how to deal with racial slurs. Elizabeth Bryant, who was a resident of Yogyakarta at the same period Obama and his family were there, recalls that a group of Indonesian children taunted young Barack because of his color while throwing rocks in his direction. Nine-year-old Barack remained unfazed, dancing around the stones coming in his direction as if he was in a dodge-ball game with "with unseen players." This revelation reminds us of Obama's repeated encounter with racial epithets throughout his presidency. The most publicized episode was his experience with the ill-tempered president of the Philippines, Rodrigo Duterte, who reportedly called him "son of a whore." The Philippine president was responding to a reporter's question about how he planned to explain to the U.S. president the ongoing drug war in his country involving extrajudicial killings when the two leaders meet in Laos for the 2016 Association of Southeast Asian Nations summit. Duterte, who had at other times called Americans "monkeys" and "fools" over minor disagreements, chose the opportunity to question the purity of President Obama's mother: "You must be respectful," he said to the U.S. president through the press. "Do not just throw away questions and statements. Son of a whore, I will curse you in that forum. We will be wallowing in the mud like pigs if you do that to me."[27] Speaking later at the G20 summit in China in 2016, Obama explained that "clearly he [Duterte] is a colorful guy" and that when he had heard about Duterte's "colorful" choice of words he advised his aides to see if meetings with Duterte would still be "productive."[28] Here, Obama's training in Indonesia had adequately prepared him to handle even the worst provocations. Dunham sometimes used humor to defuse racist behavior toward her children.

Dunham's colleague, Richard Hook, who knew her well in the late 1980s and early 1990s in Jakarta, said she revealed to him that as a mother, she consciously strived to impart in her son a sense of civic leadership. She wanted Obama to have a sense of obligation to give something back. Obama's encounter with racism in Indonesia is not different from the resilient history of Black racism in America, and the values of respect and fearlessness are critical survival tools everywhere racism exists. Speaking later about Obama, Elizabeth Bryant, a long-time acquaintance of Dunham, noted, "This is one reason he's so *halus* [polite, refined, or courteous]," adding that Obama was also "patient, calm, and a good listener. If you're not a good listener in Indonesia, you'd better leave."[29]

This brief account of Barack Obama's early years would not be complete without mention of his encounter with Islam. Our assertion is that young Barack, like most minors, identified with the religion of his parents and guardians. Barack embraced the Islamic religion because of his stepfather's Muslim faith, although Dunham was uncommitted to the faith. Barack may not have understood the implications of his journey with Islam, and the impact the religion may have had on his psyche is anyone's guess. In an interview with Jeffrey Goldberg of the *Atlantic* in March 2016, the president "described how he has watched Indonesia gradually move from a relaxed, syncretistic Islam to a more fundamentalist, unforgiving interpretation; large numbers of Indonesian women, he observed, have now adopted the hijab, the Muslim head covering."[30] This story resonates with Obama's comment in 1995 regarding how the Islamic culture in Indonesia strained his mother's second marriage. In his book, Obama described his mother's unwillingness to comply with such cultural expectations in Indonesia as accompanying his stepfather on social occasions: "He would ask her how it would look for him to go alone, and remind her that these were her own people." Dunham would yell at the top of her lungs, "They are not my people." Obama continued,

> What tension I noticed had mainly to do with the gradual shift in my mother's attitude toward me. It had always encouraged my rapid acculturation in Indonesia: It had made me relatively self-sufficient, undemanding on a tight budget, and extremely well mannered when compared to other American children. She had taught me to disdain the blend of ignorance and arrogance that too often characterized Americans abroad. But she now had learned, just as Lolo had learned, the chasm that separated the life chances of an American from those of an Indonesian. She knew which side of the divide she wanted her child to be on. I was an American, she decided, and my true life lay elsewhere.[31]

In the United States, Obama understood that it would be more difficult for a cow to pass through the eye of a needle than for a self-identified Muslim to get into the White House. Throughout his 2008 campaign, Obama's religious identity became a subject of agitation and controversy. In 1992 at Trinity Church in Chicago, Obama, then a community leader in disadvantaged Chicago neighborhoods, embraced the African American community his mother had envisioned for him as an American. His encounter with Rev. Jeremiah Wright, a maverick and fearless pastor with an Afrocentric theology, was episodic. The practice of Christianity at Holy Trinity infused both Obama's life and his political ambition. This drive was evident when he made his presidential announcement with the familiar phrase associated with Black churches in the United States: "Giving all praise and honor to God." The impact of Reverend Wright's style was so deep that Obama entitled his second book *The Audacity of Hope*, after one of Wright's sermons.[32]

In the preceding, Obama comes across as a man wired with his mother's adventurous, imaginative, if not conflicted persona. Like his mother, he is a global figure with a mind broader than that of the average liberal ideologue. "If you want to grow into a human being," Obama remembers his mother saying, "you're going to need some values."[33] When appropriate, Dunham disciplined her kids: "We were not permitted to be rude, we were not permitted to be mean, we were not permitted to be arrogant," Maya disclosed. "We had to have a certain humility and broad-mindedness. We had to study. . . . If we said something unkind about someone, she [our mother] would try to talk about their point of view."[34]

Perhaps the best evidence of Dunham's influence on Barack Obama is in her strong belief in what the future held for her son. Invested in Obama's rare talent, Dunham would brag about his intelligence, bravery, and achievements. Benji Bennington, an acquaintance of Dunham's from Hawaii, disclosed that sometimes Dunham would say, "Well, my son is so bright, he can do anything he ever wants in the world, even be president of the United States—the first black president."[35]

OF EXPECTATIONS: DREAMS AND DEEDS

Belgian anthropologist Karin van Bemmel, who had a firsthand encounter with the homeland Kenyans in the months immediately after Obama took the oath of office in 2009, observed that the euphoria was so intense that *benga* musician Kevin Omondi Migot, also known as "Dola Kabarry," and his Orchestra Super Haki Haki Band produced an album entitled *Change the World*, which has a familiar message: "We Want Change, Obama." The title of the album is in line with candidate Obama's presidential campaign slogan, "Change you can believe in." The Kenyan artist challenged Obama to live up to his words:

"Change the world, son of Kenya. Change the world, son of Luo."[36] In a poetic retort mirroring the hunting tradition of the Kogelo of Kenya, a village elder added, "Our son has shot a large animal and is now going to bring it home."[37]

Brian Larkin has expressed intense apprehension about the role of both local and international media in building up false hopes for Obama that had no foundation on more profound and authentic experiences with the then-obscure young politician from Illinois.[38] During his historic visit to Ghana in 2009, Obama's first trip to Africa as president, Ghanaian businesspeople and government officials went into a frenzy, believing that the tour would bring Africa many investment opportunities.[39] The same media added that Obama chose Accra ahead of all other African capitals for his first formal visit "because [Ghana] represents the hope for a new Africa."[40] Indeed, Arjun Appadurai, who has made a study of disjuncture and differences of cultural globalization, is right to observe that the lines between the realistic and fictional landscapes people see in media are blurred, likely to result in the construction of worlds that are chimerical, aesthetic, and even fantastic imaginaries.[41]

In an insightful essay on Obama's African foreign policy, Sehlare Makgetlaneng, head of the Governance and Security Program at the African Institute of South Africa, a think-tank in Pretoria, delivered a neorealistic perspective on what shaped United States-Africa relations in the Obama years. Makgetlaneng explains that the Democratic Party failed to construct a foreign policy tailored explicitly to Africa's needs. The United States under Obama followed the previous Republican administration's neoconservative Africa policy orchestrated by President George W. Bush. Articulating these thoughts barely two months after Obama assumed office in 2008, Makgetlaneng predicted that Obama's African plan would not deviate from the same old imperialist approach "in satisfying the needs, demands and exigencies" of the United States and its European allies.[42] Obama's eight years of African foreign strategies vindicated Makgetlaneng's prognosis. U.S. foreign policy interests continued to stand in the way of even the most modest of Africa's expectations. Obama's African and African American connections to Africa were not enough to meet the African people's unrealistic hopes. The Africans expected Obama to influence the United States to guide the continent toward a more meaningful, productive, and mutually beneficial partnership in a manner never seen with the previous presidents. As it turned out, President Obama failed to articulate a political, economic, and ideological position sympathetic to the African view.

Nonetheless, one may argue that the widespread practice of corruption and leadership failures by postcolonial African states were a severe hindrance to building a better United States-Africa relationship under President Obama.

The postcolonial African state has done little to promote the economic well-being of the masses. Poor leadership continues to stall the lofty expectations of independence, and the lack of development and progress in Africa was something that Obama was not in a position to tackle. Obama visited Ghana in 2009 after a trip to Cairo, Egypt, where he launched his "A New Beginning" speech with the Arab world. In Cairo, Obama outlined the four themes upon which he believed the future of Africa would depend: "democracy, opportunity, health, and the peaceful resolution of conflict."[43] During the Ghana trip, part of the president's speech was symbolic of his snub of Nigeria, the most populous nation in Africa and the largest economy in Africa.[44]

Nigeria was then seen as one of the most corrupt nations in the world because its government had failed to address the basic needs of the masses despite its massive oil wealth. Reacting to Obama's snub, some Nigerians, such as Nobel laureate Wole Soyinka, who has been a staunch advocate of democracy and human rights, saw Obama's action as appropriate. "If Obama decides to grace Nigeria with his presence, I will stone him. The message he is sending by going to Ghana is so obvious, is so brilliant that he must not render it flawed by coming to Nigeria any time soon." Soyinka's colleague Wale Ade chided Nigeria's government for being angry over the matter. "The presidency guys should cover their faces in shame for attacking or reacting too negatively to Professor Soyinka for declaring the open truth. If Obama had chosen to come to Nigeria, I would personally have organized a Two Million Man March against him."[45]

Indeed, as Makgetlaneng and others assert, it is perhaps a gross mistake on the part of Africans to have expected Obama to resolve all the "problems internal to African countries—problems [African leaders] have actively created" and perpetuated by acts of war.[46] Through his actions and inactions, President Obama communicated to African leaders that his administration was only going to defend and expand the United States' strategic interests in Africa and elsewhere. The question remains: What are the vital interests that guide the foreign policy of the United States?

Since the Cold War, U.S. foreign policy has revolved around what some observers have identified as an expansive, conservative, militaristic, capitalistic, brutal, and ruthless projection of power around the world. This observation is central to this study and has been consistent since the early sixteenth century, when the British colonists started importing African slaves to facilitate the exploitation of America's abundant resources and influence around the world. In other words, the history of the United States' relations with the developing countries in general, and Africa in particular, has been defined by the quest to expand America's power, zone of control, and sphere of influence.

With a self-image of itself as a model for the rest of the world, the United States has continuously asked the world to accept its projection of American influence as enshrined in the notion of "manifest destiny." Consistent with this phrase, which the journalist John L. O'Sullivan coined in 1845, America's relations with the rest of the world have followed the philosophy that guided the United States' nineteenth-century territorial expansion. Exponents of manifest destiny claim that God intended the United States to exert its influence across the globe, spreading the ideals of capitalism and democracy, particularly in the Northern Hemisphere. Emerging stronger than ever from the Second World War, the United States began to extend this ideology far beyond the North American continent. This paradigm for international relations is a yardstick for measuring the United States' insatiable appetite for external expansion.

President Obama did not deviate from this guiding spirit of U.S. foreign policy. The purveyors of his strategies for Africa throughout Obama's two administrations were members of the established political order going back to Presidents Bill Clinton (1993–2001) and George W. Bush (2001–2009). On closer examination, it is more or less the same principle Obama had articulated during his presidential campaign when he called upon the United States to continue being "the leader of the free world, in battling immediate evils and promoting the ultimate good," and "to promote the spread of freedom" in the world.[47]

While most Africans had high expectations of Obama to change their lives and the continent for the better, not everyone took him literally. For instance, during his 2006 visit to Kenya as a U.S. senator, Wycliffe Muga, a local commentator in Kenya, asserted that the widespread enthusiasm came from the fact that the average Kenyan was tired of watching their elected leaders unabatingly practice corruption at unimaginable and often lawless levels. They placed their hopes in outsiders like Obama, who they thought would help them from abroad. "Call it the donor mentality," Muga said. "People are saying, 'We have a senator now; we have a man in power.' They forget he is a U.S. senator representing the state of Illinois."[48]

Therefore, hope was the message: the message and the substance Obama offered not only to Africa but also to the rest of the world. The world celebrated Obama's victory as a victory in the struggle against racism, particularly racism against people of African descent. This topic was one of the main targets of his campaign, and in his inaugural address Obama stated, "we have chosen hope over fear, unity of purpose over conflict and discord." He vowed that he would lead "a new way forward based on mutual interests and mutual respect."[49] Reacting to the address, Frida Ghitis, writing in the *Miami Herald*, cautioned that Obama might bring about less change than he promised. "So, America will work with allies, friends, former foes and as a friend of each nation and every man, woman, and child who seeks a future of peace and dignity." The implicit question was whether Obama could accomplish all of these things.[50] Without doubt, however, these avowals were far from being the reality as racial prejudices and attacks against Black people increased throughout Obama's presidency, particularly during his second term in office.

OBAMA'S AFRICA AGENDA

In 2008, Witney Schneidman, adviser on Africa to Barack Obama's presidential campaign, identified three foreign policy priorities for the continent: (1) Accelerate Africa's integration into the global economy. (2) Improve peace and security among African states. (3) Reinforce the efforts of those African governments, civil societies, and institutions that support the growth of democracy, poverty reduction, equal opportunity, and transparency in the continent.[51]

AFRICA'S ECONOMIC INTEGRATION

During the 2008 presidential campaign, Obama pledged to fight poverty in Africa by doubling U.S. annual foreign assistance from $25 billion in 2008 to $50 billion by the conclusion of his first term in 2013. Implicit in this initiative was to support the United Nations' Millennium Development Goals, which aimed to cut extreme poverty in half by 2015 by fully funding debt cancelation for heavily indebted poor countries, thus stimulating internal development in Africa. Additionally, the promise was that the U.S. government would invest at least $50 billion by 2013 in the global effort to eradicate HIV/AIDS, including its fair share of the Global Fund, a Geneva-based international partnership and financing organization that supports efforts to eradicate AIDS, tuberculosis, and malaria in the developing countries.[52] The overall idea was that Obama's administration would expand prosperity by establishing an Add Value to Agriculture Initiative (AVAI), creating a fund that would extend seed capital and technical assistance to small and medium enterprises, and reform the World Bank and International Monetary Fund.

Obama further promised to work with the international community to launch the Global Energy and Environment Initiative (GEEI) to ensure that African countries had access to low-carbon energy technology. Their participation in the new global carbon market would ensure stable economic growth even as global leaders continued to search for ways to curtail greenhouse gas emissions. Obama also planned to strengthen the African Growth and Opportunity Act

(AGOA), initiated by President Bill Clinton in 2000 and enhanced during the Bush administration, which amended and extended the AGOA with bipartisan support three times and created a Millennium Challenge Account along with the President's Emergency Plan for AIDS Relief (PEPFAR) program.[53] In the end, Obama failed both to ensure that African producers had access to the U.S. market and to encourage a higher number of American companies to invest on the continent. Obama further failed to make good on his promise to facilitate the availability of credit to African small and medium businesses by partnering with the Overseas Private Investment Corporation (OPIC). This idea was a viable route to enhance the capital base on which Africa's private entrepreneurs could create job opportunities for young people.[54]

Obama further conceived the Add Value to Agriculture Initiative as a tool to enhance Africa's position in the world economy and improve the standard of living for the average African. Through partnerships with colleges, businesses, and nongovernmental organizations, Obama hoped to propel scientific research and innovation in the continent. The grand idea was to help develop better irrigation systems, advanced and high-yielding seed plants, and fertilizers that are not dangerous to health and at the same time inexpensive. This plan, intended to resolve widespread hunger and the rising cost of food in most parts of the sub-Saharan region, did not materialize. On the other hand, PEPFAR placed 1.7 million people in Africa on antiretroviral drugs and has been an important initiative, similar to the Bush administration's program to eradicate malaria and address neglected tropical diseases. So far, shortage of essential materials and needs such as food, medicine, clean water, stable electricity, and adequate housing remains the most dangerous cause of morbidity in Africa.

The various programs planned by Obama were intended to bequeath to the continent a long-lasting legacy that was supposed to help resolve Africa's myriad problems. To advance these schemes that began before Obama's presidency, U.S. development support was increased from $2 billion in 2000 to $6 billion between 2004 and 2007.[55] However, the more significant part of new funding under the Obama administration was earmarked to reduce the debilitating burden of foreign debt that continued to hinder Africa's progress. Other targeted areas included humanitarian aid, limiting the spread of HIV/AIDS, and treating those patients already affected by the disease. In reality, the portion of funding available for development assistance to the neediest countries fell by about 50 percent during the Obama administration. At the same time, development assistance earmarked for polities ranked by the Democracy Index (an organ of the United Kingdom–based Economist Intelligence Unit) as having the most viable democracies on the continent plunged by two-thirds.

With $3.7 billion in aid committed to ten sub-Saharan African countries under the Millennium Challenge Account, the expectation was that this money would help offset the overall reduction in development aid to the continent.[56] However, building education capacity, enacting judicial reform, strengthening democracy and the rule of law, supporting parliaments, and building human resources and entrepreneurial skills remained areas of critical need. President Obama led a new push aimed at reducing what many perceived as lack of parity in education between the developed and developing countries of the world. The result was the institution of a Global Education Fund intended for primary school education in sub-Saharan Africa in particular and in the developing countries in general. In this context, the Millennium Development Goals became Obama's responsibility for America under his administration. Unfortunately, the effort did not produce any visible positive results.

PEACE AND SECURITY OF STATES

The hopeful rhetoric of change that distinguished Obama's political campaign did not adequately consider what needed to be changed and what did not. As a member of the Senate Foreign Relations Committee (2005–2008), Obama worked to increase America's responsiveness to the hard challenges facing Africa. For instance, he was at the forefront of the concerted effort to end the genocidal debacle in Darfur, Sudan, perpetrated by the Arab-allied Janjaweed on the Fur, Zaghawa, and Masalit communities of southern Sudan.[57] Obama also worked to help pass congressional legislation to promote stability in the Democratic Republic of the Congo, a nation wracked by a perpetual civil war that has claimed more than 5.3 million lives since 1960.[58] Other initiatives Obama supported as a member of the Foreign Relations Committee included bringing Charles Taylor, the former Liberian president and a war criminal, to justice at the Hague. He also led international campaigns to bring about a more democratic and safe government in Zimbabwe; to fight corruption in Kenya; to demand honesty about HIV/AIDS in South Africa; and to develop a coherent strategy for stabilizing Somalia. Obama traveled across the continent, promoting awareness for these critical issues. Also, he helped increase America's attention to the constant challenges of sustainable economic development, disease control, poverty reduction, education, and the strengthening of democratic institutions in the continent.

On the genocide in Darfur, Sudan, Senator Obama and Sen. Sam Brownback (R-KS) worked diligently to pass the Darfur Peace and Accountability Act in 2006. As a presidential candidate, Obama promised to take quick action to end the genocide by pressuring the Sudanese government to stop the massacres and support the deployment of a robust international peacekeeping force in the country. Additionally, Obama promised to hold the Sudanese government responsible for complying with its obligations under the Comprehensive Peace Accord that ended the three decades of war between northern and southern Sudan.[59]

INSTITUTIONAL CAPACITY BUILDING

During his visit to Kenya in 2006, Senator Obama decried poor leadership and corruption of power in Africa. He called upon South African leaders to demonstrate transparency on HIV/AIDS so that facts would guide America's engagement with the country to fight the scourge of the disease in sub-Saharan Africa. Obama also advised Ethiopia and Eritrea to end their interregional struggles. In the East African nation of Djibouti, where the Combined Joint Task Force-Horn of Africa base is located, Obama visited with American military commanders to discuss pressing issues connected with the threat of terrorism and how to combat the threat to the interests of the United States and its allies in the region. He pressed the government of Kenya, his father's homeland, to settle a postelection conflict that troubled the East African nation. To gain direct knowledge of the refugee situations in several parts of Africa, Obama made a trip to refugee camps in Chad, where he met with homeless women from Sudan who had been separated from their families because of the government's genocide against people from southern Sudan. Obama also took on Robert Mugabe of Zimbabwe, who had been in power since the country emerged from White minority rule in 1980. Obama decried Mugabe's refusal to vacate power after the 2003 election and his use of violence against the opposition.

Cognizant of the fiasco that was the U.S. humanitarian mission to Somalia in the early 1990s, Obama called for retooling the nation's attitude toward interventions in Africa. It was Obama's view that U.S. notions of and preoccupation with state building in other countries and execution of humanitarian assistance had not always produced the desired results. He argued that to make these engagements effectual in the era of terrorism, it was vital to develop fundamental ideas and strategies. To fully understand the background to Obama's comments, it is crucial to briefly highlight the disastrous U.S. military mission in Somalia in the early 1990s, which created the U.S. "Somalia syndrome" and influenced the U.S. role in minimizing the genocide in Rwanda in 1994.

Following the collapse of Siad Barre's regime in January 1991, conditions in Somalia took a frightening turn, with famine, looting, and continuing civil war among different political factions and militia groups built around clans and subclans. Across the country, the incessant warring and the absence of a central government compounded the problem of severe drought and famine, which made life very precarious.[60] The United Nations estimated that 300,000 people died during this time, another 2 million were displaced, and all regulatory and infrastructural developments were destroyed. The daily deaths were about 3,000 during this time. The plight of both aid workers and Somalis evoked a more active interest in Somalia's affairs by the international community, sparking fervent public and political pressure in the United States and Europe for stronger action by the U.N. Security Council.[61] International nongovernmental humanitarian organizations that arrived to assist the civilian population were unable to operate amid the crisis, thereby making it necessary for the United Nations to create a more robust intervention.[62]

Commentators have different views about the United Nations' humanitarian intervention in Somalia in light of the mission's initial goals and all that subsequently emerged in its expanded nation-building role. Some scholars have mercilessly attacked the role played by the United States in the mission.[63] Others, including some Somalis, acknowledge with appreciation the achievements of the U.N. peacekeepers, particularly the American soldiers who offered their lives for a cause from which they derived no direct benefits. Whatever view one might hold, one cannot diminish the urgent humanitarian circumstances in which the international community acted. Whether the intervention helped or complicated the crisis in Somalia is a different matter.

Disparaged for demonstrating an unwillingness to be involved, U.S. president George H. W. Bush (1989–1993) announced the U.S. mission to Somalia in December 1992. Under the broader framework of the U.N.'s United Task Force (UNITAF), the U.S. contingent was charged with executing Operation Restore Hope.[64] The joint UNITAF-U.S. forces began to deploy to Mogadishu on December 9, 1992, and were empowered under Chapter VII (Articles 39–51) of the U.N. Charter to use force (if required) to create a stable and secure environment for deliveries of humanitarian supplies. The mandate of the mission also involved the risky task of disarming those factions who were breaching the ceasefire agreement. In the end, the mission proved a disaster mainly because the U.S. military abandoned its initial mandate and instead pursued an agenda of nation building. On October 3, 1993, U.S. commanders decided to act on critical intelligence that presented them with an opportunity to capture top two officers serving under Mohammed Farah Aideed, the chief protagonist in the Somali civil war. Assembling nineteen aircraft, twelve fighting vehicles, and 160 soldiers, the Delta Force troops successfully captured their targets.

Unfortunately, the operation ran into an unforeseen situation when Somalis began rushing to the area as soon as the attack started. The crowd blocked the roads and armed men fired automatic weapons and RPGs at the U.S. forces, bringing down two Black Hawk (UH-60) helicopters and apprehending a pilot named Michael Durant. Enraged by propaganda that the Americans were in Somalia to destroy their Islamic religion, the mob began hacking apart the bodies of the dead soldiers and dragging them through the streets.[65] In the end, eighteen U.S. soldiers died in the ill-advised operation, and Somali casualties totaled about 500 dead and 1,000 injured.[66]

The episode of shooting down the two UH-60s, butchering the bodies of dead U.S. soldiers, and dragging them along the streets provoked a widespread outcry in the United States and Europe. As a result, U.S. lawmakers decided on October 5, 1993, to pull American forces out of Somalia. This outcome forced the United Nations to modify the mandate of the United Nations Operation in Somalia (UNOSOM II) to exclude the use of coercive measures. By 1995, all U.N. forces had left Somalia.[67] The behavior of the Somalis implanted a dangerous belief in individual Western minds that it is the people rather than their leaders who turn terrible countries into a mess. One U.S. official claimed that "Somalia was the experience that taught us that people in those places bear much of the responsibility for things being the way they are. The hatred and the killings continued because they want it to. Or because they don't want peace enough to stop it."[68] A year later, this unfortunate perception held by some U.S. lawmakers influenced American policy toward other areas of conflict in Africa. A good example was the Clinton administration's refusal to stop acts of genocide in Rwanda (1994) and Zaire (1997). Clinton's successor, President George W. Bush, was also reluctant to intervene in the Darfur crisis (2006).

The truth is that Africa's history is complex, and this requires a more in-depth understanding. A critical look beyond Barre's rule reveals some serious structural problems that made violence and separatism rife in the land. Some of these problems were endemic in society; some were created by colonial rule and compounded by neocolonial tendencies of the Western world, particularly in the context of the Cold War era. The trend for Western powers to meddle in the affairs of the postcolonial African state was a significant factor in the Somali quandary. In Somalia after 1960, this manifested either through arms supplies or the praxis of East–West ideological competition.

In the Congo, where civil war has proved resilient, there was a need to back the U.N. armed command, MONUC (later renamed MONUSCO—United Nations Organization Stabilization Mission). There was also the critical need of transforming the goals and strategies of the "tripartite plus" process, which brought together senior officials from the DRC, Rwanda, Burundi, and Uganda. The idea was to move the process from being a mere discussion forum to one in which all the partners involved would be committed to the process and hold one another accountable for the region's needs for security. In the oil-producing areas of Nigeria, particularly the Niger Delta, Obama made a campaign pledge to assist in bringing peace and security to the region. The approach would be to partner with the Nigerian government, the African Union, the European Union, and other stakeholders. In Zimbabwe, Obama held to the belief that it was time for President Mugabe to relinquish power and to empower civil society and other prodemocracy organizations and institutions. Above all, it was vital for Mugabe to respect the will of his people, as demonstrated in the March 29, 2008, election won by the Movement for Democratic Change (MDC).

Obama also considered the physical security of Africa as a foundation for its economic and human security. Thus, the United States Africa Command (USAFRICOM, also AFRICOM) was established in October 2007 to help build the continent's defense capability and security forces capacity in coopera-tion with other U.S. agencies and regional partners. One of Obama's agenda items under the auspices of USAFRICOM was to create a Shared Security Part-nership Program and lay the groundwork for an operational counterterrorism response force, especially as it related to collaborative action against al Qaeda and its associates in Africa, such as al Shabab and Boko Haram. The planned security partnership envisaged assisting with information sharing and training, crucial for cross-border security, destroying sources of funds for terrorists, and eliminating corrupt practices.

In response to the concerns about climate change around the world, Obama planned to launch a Global Energy and Environment Initiative (GEEI) to bring developing countries into the global effort to develop alternative sources of energy and mitigate the apparent threats of climate change. In the end, there was nothing to celebrate in regard to this initiative, and poor energy supplies remain one of the banes of economic development in sub-Saharan Africa.

By every measure, Obama's election to the White House was a milestone in the history of United States-Africa relations. In 2008, on his way to the presi-dency, Obama's African policy adviser Witney Schneidman told Africans on both sides of the Atlantic that "in voting for Barack Obama, you will be voting for genuine change and, when it comes to Africa, a deepening of those partner-ships that benefit Africa and benefit America."[69] In real terms, the Africans be-lieved him, although as the evidence now reveals, there were miscommunica-tions at different levels. From the African perspective, the United States and the rest of the Western world can help move African aspirations of development to the next level. From the Western standpoint, Africans alone can move forward and sustain their developmental expectations and human security.

Objectively, Obama did not have the legislative power to satisfy even the modest expectations the Africans held. He also lacked both the educated and cultural connections with the continent to understand the intricacies of the Africans' needs. Some of his core mission of neo-American globalism and sociocultural liberal preachments were at odds with African traditionalism and values. Obama arrogated comprehensive knowledge of every topic to himself, and this mindset led him to lecture people rather than accept alternative views. As disclosed by Steve Hilton, a former close adviser to the British prime minister, Obama "thought he was smarter than everyone." According to Hilton, "My old boss, former British prime minister David Cameron, thought Obama was one of the most narcissistic, self-absorbed people he'd ever dealt with." Speaking on Fox News following the fallout from the publication of Michael Wolff's *Fire and Fury*, Hilton added that "Obama never listened to anyone, always thought he was smarter than every expert in the room, and treated every meeting as an opportunity to lecture everyone else. This tendency led to real-world disasters, like Syria and the rise of Isis."[70] As a consequence, Obama's African policy failed to leverage the potentials of mutual engagement and dialogue with African leaders. Additionally, he was unable to tap resources from America's Western European allies and former colonial overlords who understand the continent's myriad problems. Also, for other G8 countries, such as Russia and Canada, as well as emerging economies like India, China, Brazil, and South Africa, the private sector and global philanthropy could have supported important African aid initiatives if Obama had led the way.

Several insurmountable issues plagued Obama's presidency, which coincided with the challenge that America and the entire democratic and capitalist Western world face today in the form of China's fast-growing influence in Africa. While there are genuine concerns for the continent, China's new African policy is attractive for Africa. This interest resides in the demonstrated readiness of China to assist various African governments with infrastructure development. The consequences of China's African foreign policy and economic partnerships are anybody's guess. Top among the dangers are the environmental degradations perpetrated by Chinese companies, mounting new debts accruing from foreign loans and development projects, and increasingly the decline in Africa's share in the global market. Sadly, Obama's America neither offered Africans a realistic alternative to China nor engaged the Chinese to establish the procedures for engagement with the continent and ensure that the United States and Africa are partnering to safeguard the historical relationship that both sides of the Atlantic have come to share.

More pitifully, Obama failed to deviate from the tradition of lecturing Africa established by previous U.S. presidents. The killing of Muammar Gaddafi was the worst foreign policy misadventure on the continent under President Obama. At those moments, Obama abandoned the wisdom that African governments are part of the effort and part of the dialogue to bring change both in Africa and America and on the global stage. Obama failed to end the days when external powers took advantage of Africa by deciding what was best for the continent. Obama's vision of leadership betrayed his aspiration by failing to uphold the fundamental problem his campaign acknowledged in 2008: "the security and well-being of each and every American is tied to the security and well-being of those who live beyond our borders, including in Africa." By that deadly mistake with Gaddafi, Obama failed himself and his pledge to lead: "We must lead not in the spirit of a patron, but in the spirit of a partner." Obama would later admit that his most significant foreign policy gaffe was the Libyan fiasco. However, he blamed the European "free riders" for the mess of Libya.[71]

The inclination to shift blame for his unrealized African policies onto the Europeans has some merit, but it also betrays Obama's shallow knowledge of Africa and its dynamics. Horace Campbell concluded, "When Obama was a presidential candidate for the first time, he was fond of saying that he understands Africa. He found out clearly in the debacle of Libya and Benghazi that whatever his understanding, it will only go so far unless he stands up to the foreign policy establishment" in Washington and the former colonial metropolis in Europe. As Campbell noted, "This he has refused to do and has surrounded himself with those elements of the intellectual and academic circuits that had supported apartheid."[72]

For centuries, the Europeans have perpetrated, as Patrick Bond rightly describes, a destructive extraction of resources from Africa.[73] Since 1960, this theft has gone hand in hand with capital flight because of the World Bank's domination of economic arrangements in Africa. The World Bank and the IMF know that Africa still owns the lion's share of global natural resources. To covertly continue their endless theft of Africa's resources, Western creditor nations and institutions "disguised the reality that Africa was a net creditor to the advanced capitalist countries (termed 'donors' in the neo-liberal parlance)."[74] As a result, America continues to ignore its moral responsibility to assist Africa to overcome centuries of exploitation by actors from outside the continent. At least, if Obama had led a campaign to recover some of the trillions of dollars corrupt African leaders stashed away in Western countries since 1960, the continent would have had enough funds to turn its development dreams around. But he did not.

Overall, Obama was wholly unprepared for the task he took on. Even some of his best supporters, such as MSNBC's Joe Scarborough, stated the obvious:

"There are so many great things personally about Barack Obama, even though so many of his policies drive me crazy." Scarborough, a former Republican congressman from Florida who turned Democrat after the 2016 election, adds that "Barack Obama wasn't ready, in my opinion, to be president. He was, as I said, a glorified state senator."[75] This observation implicates Obama's own admission in 2007 that "I recognize there is a certain presumptuousness—a certain audacity—to this announcement." Obama admitted his lack of experience during the address: "I know I haven't spent a lot of time learning the ways of Washington. But I've been there long enough to know that the ways of Washington must change."[76]

It is then apparent that Obama came to Washington and planned to change the order of things, but he never conquered. Lack of experience was the most significant real impediment in Obama's African foreign policy collapse. He lacked in-depth knowledge of the problem and underestimated what it would entail to effect a meaningful and lasting legacy for Africa. It was not his failure to grant visas to all Kenyans or to create a new "Illinois Kenya" settler colony in the United States. Indeed, such expectations of Obama held by Africans were unrealistic, naïve, and trivial. Nevertheless, his emergence as a global leader brought a few developmental changes in the Kenyan "Obama village" over the last few years. For example, a day after his presidential election victory in November 2007, Kogelo, Obama's paternal village in Kenya, was connected to the electrical power grid. Electrification was "perhaps the most vivid symbol of modernization and development"; as an image of universal connection with the classical motif of lighting the dark, it was "an irresistible piece of symbolism for the modernist state, . . . a compelling symbol of inclusion, a sign that Africans, too, were to be hooked up with the 'new world society.'"[77] To his credit also, President Obama supported a robust fight against al Shabab, the Somali-based terrorist group linked to al Qaeda. Additionally, the Young African Leaders Initiative (YALI), through which the president brought African youths for training in Washington, D.C., remains one of the most laudable programs instituted by Obama for Africa. Indeed, these were the kind of tangibles and symbols the Africans had expected from the Obama presidency in America. Unfortunately, it was not the way Obama understood the African expectation of his ascendancy.

CONCLUSION: REFLECTIONS

The overall intent of this book is to give the reader a volume covering six centuries of Africa's relationship with the Americas. For reasons already explained, the focus on the United States is to fully account for the exemplarity of this former British colony and how the strivings of African Americans from slavery to freedom and empowerment shaped the trans-Atlantic relationship. The concluding lessons for America and Africa are many, but only a brief report is necessary at this point.

This account of United States-Africa relations through the prism of Africa and the African American odyssey reveals that the trans-Atlantic union is akin to a forced marriage, which often goes hand in hand with gross abuse of dignity and autonomy. The European slave dealers from Britain, France, Portugal, the Netherlands, and Spain arranged and officiated at the historic marriage. The bride was the enslaved African and the abusive bridegroom was the plantation owner/slavocrat. As with people forced into marriage, the enslaved Africans became alienated from their kin in the ancestral homeland. It is usual to see victims of forced marriage trapped in a cycle of domestic abuse with serious long-term consequences, including self-harm and suicide. This reality explains why the White-Black relationship in the Americas flares up now and then like an autoimmune disease, with no evidence of final relief.

In other words, life is a constant struggle from cradle to death. As Frantz Fanon, the eminent psychologist and expert on race relations, notes, as soon as one life trial ends, another comes up; thus, the struggle continues. Without doubt, this process has been the order of events defining the experiences of all the individuals, groups, and nations involved in trans-Atlantic relations. Under oppression—whether racial or that of the colonial social order—the group or

307

people under siege "are called upon to fight against oppression; after national liberation, they are called upon to fight against poverty, illiteracy, and under-development. The struggle, they say, goes on. The people realize that life is an unending contest."[1] This course is an apt description of the Black experience in both America and Africa, and the struggle is ongoing in different shades today.

While relentless contest may define the nature of United States-Africa rela-tions, it is vital not to see this dynamic only from a negative viewpoint. A popu-lar understanding among the Igbo of Nigeria is the notion that the world is an enigma that comes in a dualist context. The Igbo, who from the seventeenth century dominated the export trade in slaves from the Bight of Biafra port to the Americas, have noted long in the past that when one thing or event stands, another stands beside it (*ife kwulu, ife ákwudebe yá*—that is, "Anything that is has a complement").[2] Interpreted in light of this book, one begins to appreciate the struggles between servants and masters, Whites and Blacks, colonized and colonizers, protagonists and antagonists, exploiters and exploited, and so on. In these dualist contexts, the United States-Africa relationship emerged and grew. It is evident that the course of history sometimes follows a planned path; sometimes, it proceeds in an ad hoc manner. In other words, specific patterns of oppression such as economic exploitation perpetrated by the privileged groups of slavocrats in the Atlantic world may appear as a preconceived decision, but sometimes these only assume a "planned" form after the fact.

Yet, it is human to draw the conclusion that economic considerations, fear, power, privilege, and racial identity often truncate fairness based on moral val-ues and rational principles. Whether in relation to the culture of slavery in America and Africa or to colonial practices on both sides of the Atlantic, the record indicates that economic reality, inequality, and immense differences in ways of life are often the major factors that shape the course of human history, including United States-Africa relations. This reality explains why no one has been able to offer precise answers to the question of why White people treat people of color so mean, posed by a five-year-old boy in 1963 as the civil rights movement became more volatile.[3] Matters related to race, ideology, and social conscience are manifestations of human follies and psychiatry; they defy com-mon understanding, and they are the cemetery of civilizations.

There is no gainsaying that rather than the Civil War, the racial abuses per-petrated under the Jim Crow laws constituted the worst single domestic threat to America's survival. One of the chief revelations of the present study is the problem of democracy in America before 1970. The civil rights movement of the 1950s and 1960s exposed the dubious nature of America's claim to liberal de-mocracy and the nation's moral rights to challenge totalitarian polities around the world. The reality is that the United States long held on to slavocracy—the most extreme form of illiberal democracy—using a corpus of racially induced laws to practice violent tyranny against minority groups. John Owen has noted that the purpose of liberalism is "life and property, and its means are liberty and toleration."[4] Liberalism implies sureties of the rights of the individual and groups, with freedom from arbitrary authority, the right to hold private property, rights to equal opportunities in education, employment, health care, and political participation and representation in the decision-making process of their country. American democracy was devoid of all of these characteristics of a liberal democracy until the end of the civil rights movement.[5]

The preceding leads to our coming to terms with how, indeed, the African American experience schooled American political leaders in the basic rudiments of a democratic order. As we now know, liberal democratic societies do not lynch individuals solely because of their skin color or gender; they follow due process of law and order and do not disenfranchise their citizens. As this study shows, these social ills internal to the United States were some of the most contentious issues that troubled the African American condition in America and poisoned United States-Africa relations for centuries. They made African nationalists and political leaders look down on America and drove them toward the Communist bloc.

Indeed, one of the lessons to be drawn from slavery through emancipation and Jim Crow, and from Pan-Africanism through the American civil rights struggle to anticolonial agitations in Africa, is that the dangers confronting people of African descent around the world may mutate or change their appearances, but never completely disappear. Therefore, a resilient spirit of Pan-Africanism is in order because the ideology of unity will continue to provide people of African descent, wherever they may be, a powerful front for self-preservation in a world where power is might and Blackness presents uncommon challenges to life and survival.

Finally, as China charts and pursues its new African foreign policy, the relevant and crucial question for U.S. leaders is to deeply consider the enduring bonds between Africa and the United States. For a nation now sweltering from a convoluted "America First" nationalist dogma, what are the potential implications of turning its back on Africa? Can America afford to ignore its long-time bride and unique relationship with Africa, and for how long? What are the likely consequences?

NOTES

INTRODUCTION

1. We duly recognize that before 1776, there was no country known as the United States of America except the individual states that existed as colonies of the British Empire. The German cartographer Martin Waldseemuller, who drew the map of the "New World" in 1507, called the southern part of the continent "America." See John W. Hessler and Chet A. Van Duzer, *Seeing the World Anew: The Radical Vision of Martin Waldseemuller's 1507 and 1516 World Maps* (Delray Beach, FL: Levenger Press in association with the Library of Congress, 2012).
2. John Rolfe to Sir Edwin Sandys, January 1619/20, in Susan Myra Kingsbury, ed., *The Records of the Virginia Company of London . . .*, 4 vols. (Washington, DC, 1906–1935), 3: 234.
3. David R. Ransome, ed., *Ferrar Papers, 1590–1790*, reel 1,159. See also William Thorndale, "The Virginia Census of 1619," *Magazine of Virginia Genealogy* 33 (1995): 155.
4. Martha McCartney, "Virginia's First Africans," *Encyclopedia Virginia*, Virginia Foundation for the Humanities, September 21, 2018. Web. Dec. 22, 2018.
5. Northampton County Court Records, Deeds, and Wills, etc., Book III, folio 83, and Book V, 54–60, of November 1, 1654, show that 17 persons identified as Negroes paid tithes and lived in households as free individuals.
6. Extract from a letter of Peter Fontaine, Westover, VA, March 30, 1757, printed in Ann Maury's *Memoirs of a Huguenot Family* (New York, 1853), 351, 352.
7. Barbara Palmer citing David Brion Davis, in "Historian Situates 'Back-to-Africa' Movement in Broad Context," *Stanford Report*, March 1, 2016.
8. *The Herald*, "The Pragmatics of African Politics," Harare, September 2, 2015.
9. Alexander Crummell, "The Attitude of the American Mind Toward the Negro Intellect," *Occasional Papers of the American Negro Academy*, No. 3 (Washington, DC, 1898); and W. E. B. Du Bois, *The Souls of Black Folk* (Chicago: A. C. McClurg and Co., 1903); David Levering Lewis, *W. E. B. Du Bois, 1919–1963: The Fight for Equality and the American Century* (New York: Holt Paperbacks, 2001).

10. President Jimmy Carter, remarks at the National Arts Theater, Lagos, Nigeria, April 1, 1978. See also "A New Framework for the U.S.-Africa Relations," *African Review of Business and Technology*, March 12, 2018, and Charles Onunaiju, "U.S., China, and Africa: Issues in Tillerson's Visit," *The Nation*, Lagos, March 13, 2018.

11. Curtis A. Keim, *Mistaking Africa: Curiosities and Inventions of the American Mind* (Boulder, CO: Westview Press, 1999); Joseph E. Holloway, ed., *Africanisms in American Culture* (Bloomington: Indiana University Press, 2005).

12. Peter Duignan and L. H. Gann, *The United States and Africa: A History* (Cambridge: Cambridge University Press, 1987). For this critique, see Peter J. Schraeder, *African Politics and Society: A Mosaic in Transformation* (Boston: Bedford, 2000); and Peter J. Schraeder, *United States Foreign Policy toward Africa: Incrementalism, Crisis and Change* (Cambridge: Cambridge University Press, 1994).

13. Macharia G. Munene, J. D. Olewe Nyunya, and Korwa G. Adar, eds., *The United States and Africa: From Independence to the End of the Cold War* (Nairobi: East African Educational Publishers, 1995).

14. Toyin Falola, *The African Diaspora: Slavery, Modernity, and Globalization* (Rochester, NY: University of Rochester Press, 2013), and Linda M. Haywood, ed., *Central Africans and Cultural Transformations in the American Diaspora* (Cambridge: Cambridge University Press, 2002).

15. Ibrahim Sundiata, *Brothers and Strangers: Black Zion, Black Slavery* (Durham, NC: Duke University Press, 2004); Alvin B. Tillery, Jr., *Between Homeland and Motherland: Africa, U.S. Foreign Policy, and Black Leadership in America* (Ithaca, NY: Cornell University Press, 2011); and James Meriwether, *Proudly We Can Be Africans: Black Americans and Africa, 1935–1961* (Chapel Hill: University of North Carolina Press, 2002).

16. Schraeder's *United States Foreign Policy toward Africa*; Elliot P. Skinner, *African Americans and U.S. Policy toward Africa, 1850–1924: In Defense of Black Nationality* (Washington, DC: Howard University Press, 1992); Raymond W. Copson, *The United States and Africa: Bush Policy and Beyond* (London: Zed Books, 2007); and David F. Gordon, David C. Miller, and Howard Wolpe, eds., *The United States and Africa: A Post–Cold War Perspective* (New York: W. W. Norton, 1998).

17. For a good read on this, see Kenneth W. Thompson, *Schools of Thought in International Relations: Interpreters, Issues, and Morality* (Louisiana: Louisiana State University Press, 1996), 8–20; and Mark D. Gismondi, *Ethics, Liberalism and Realism in International Relations* (New York: Routledge, 2008).

18. Jamal Greene, "Thirteenth Amendment Optimism," *Columbia Law Review* 112, no. 7 (2012): 1733–68.

19. Among the seminal works are Philip D. Curtin, *The African Slave Trade: A Census* (Madison: University of Wisconsin Press, 1969); J. D. Fage, "African Societies and the Atlantic Slave Trade," *Past and Present* 125 (1985): 97–115; J. D. Fage, "Slavery and Society in Western Africa, 1445–1700," *Journal of African History* 21 (1980): 289–310; and Joseph E. Inikori, "Measuring the Atlantic Slave Trade: An Assessment of Curtin and Anstey," *Journal of African History* 17 (1976): 197–223.

20. The contribution of African slaves to the emergence of the U.S. as an industrialized power is a subject of heated controversy. For recent discourses on this, see Edward E.

Baptist, *The Half Has Never Been Told: Slavery and the Making of American Capitalism* (New York: Basic Books, 2016); and Eric Williams, *Capitalism and Slavery* (Philadelphia: The Great Library Collection, 2015).

21. Albert J. Raboteau, *Slave Religion: The "Invisible Institution" in the Antebellum South* (New York: Oxford University Press, 1978), 92; and also Albert J. Raboteau, *African American Religion* (Oxford: Oxford University Press, 1999), 58.

22. An engaging work on this topic remains Mary Louise Clifford, *From Slavery to Freetown: Black Loyalists after the American Revolution* (Jefferson, NC: McFarland and Company, 2006). See also James W. St. G. Walker, *The Black Loyalists: The Search for Promised Land in Nova Scotia and Sierra Leone, 1783–1870* (Toronto: University of Toronto Press, 2017).

23. See Francis J. Bremer, "John Winthrop and the Shaping of New England History," *Massachusetts Historical Review* 18 (2016): 1–17; and Richard M. Gamble, *In Search of the City on a Hill: The Making and Unmaking of an American Myth* (New York: Continuum, 2012).

24. Delindus R. Brown, "Free Blacks' Rhetorical Impact on African Colonization: The Emergence of Rhetorical Exigence," *Journal of Black Studies* 9, no. 3 (1979): 251–65; and Eric Burin, "Rethinking Northern White Support for the African Colonization Movement: The Pennsylvania Colonization Society as an Agent of Emancipation," *The Pennsylvania Magazine of History and Biography* 127, no. 2 (2003): 197–229.

25. Adrian Hastings, *The Church in Africa, 1450–1950* (Oxford: Oxford University Press, 1996), and David Killingray, "The Black Atlantic Missionary Movement and Africa, 1780s–1920s," *Journal of Religion in Africa* 33, no. 1 (2003): 3–31.

26. The early studies on the missionary enterprise in Africa largely ignored the African American contribution. See, for instance, E. A. Ayandele, *The Missionary Impact on Modern Nigeria, 1842–1914: A Political and Social Analysis* (London: Longmans, 1967); Felix Ekechi, *Missionary Impact on Igboland, 1857–1914* (London: Frank Cass, 1972); and John Mbiti, *The People of God: The Church and the Bible* (Geneva: World Christian Student Federation, 1963).

27. Martin Luther King, Jr., speech at the laying of wreath at Garvey's shrine, Kingston, Jamaica, June 20, 1965. See also "Garvey's UNIA: A Vital and Historic Vision," *Jamaica Observer*, July 20, 2014; Barbara Palmer, "Historian Situates 'Back-to-Africa' Movements in Broad Context," *Stanford Report*, March 1, 2005; E. U. Essien-Udom, Introduction, *Philosophy and Opinions of Marcus Garvey Compiled by Amy Jacques Garvey* (London: Frank Cass, 1967), xxvi; Alistair Kee, *The Rise and Demise of Black Theology* (Aldershot: Ashgate, 2006), 32; and Mary G. Rolinson, *Grassroots Garveyism: The Universal Negro Improvement Association in the Rural South, 1920–1927* (Chapel Hill: University of North Carolina Press, 2007), 190.

28. See, for instance, Pixley Ka Isaka Seme, "The Regeneration of Africa," in Gwendolyn M. Carter and Thomas Karis, *From Protest to Challenge*, vol. 2: *A Documentary History of African Politics in South Africa, 1882–1964: Hope and Challenge, 1935–1952* (Stanford, CA: Hoover Institution Press, 1973), 69–71.

29. See Amos O. Odenyo, "An Assessment of the African Brain Drain, with Special Reference to the Kenyan Mid-Career Professional," *Issue: A Journal of Opinion* 9, no. 4

(1979): 45–48; and George J. Sefa Dei and Alireza Asgharzadeh, "What Is to Be Done? A Look at Some Causes and Consequences of the African Brain Drain," *African Issues* 30, no. 1 (2002): 31–6.

30. Emmanuel Yewah and Dimeji Togunde, eds., *Across the Atlantic: African Immigrants in the United States Diaspora* (Champaign, IL: Common Grounds, 2010); and Randy Capps, Kristen McCabe, and Michael Fix, "Diverse Streams: Black African Migration to the United States," *Migration Policy Institute*, April 2012.

31. Martin Luther King, Jr., "King's Mountaintop Speech," Mason Temple, Memphis, TN, April 3, 1968.

1. AFRICAN LABOR AND THE BRITISH AMERICAN COLONY, 1619–1865

1. It is challenging to periodize the trans-Atlantic slave trade. We see 1460 as the beginning of the trade because it was the year the Portuguese began to use enslaved Africans on the sugar plantation located on the West African island of Madeira. However, the Spanish rerouted the first batch of African slaves from Europe to the Americas in 1503; and the first direct shipment of West African captives to the Americas happened after the 1518 Edict by King Charles I of Spain authorizing the direct shipment of slaves from Africa to the Americas. The year 1867 marked the last documented slave landing in Cuba, but the Atlantic slave voyages report shows that last groups of slaves were smuggled into Brazil, Uruguay, and United States between 1851 and 1875. Brazil abolished slavery in 1888. See D. R. Murray, "Statistics of the Slave Trade to Cuba, 1790–1867," *Journal of Latin American Studies* 3, no. 2 (1971): 131–32. However, information on the website www.slavevoyages.org shows figures covering the period 1501–1875.

2. For a quick look at the slave imports from the Caribbean, see for instance Gregory E. O'Malley, "Beyond the Middle Passage: Slave Migration from the Caribbean to North America, 1619–1807," *William and Mary Quarterly* 66, no. 1 (2009): 141–42. According to the study, from 1670 to 1808, about 21,122 slaves were imported from the Caribbean to North Carolina alone and 12,060 to Virginia over the same period.

3. See for instance Philip D. Curtin, *The African Slave Trade: A Census* (Madison: University of Wisconsin Press, 1972); J. D. Fage, "Slavery and the Slave Trade in the Context of African History," *Journal of African History* 10 (1975): 393–404; J. D. Fage, "The Effect of the Slave Trade on African Population," in *The Population Factor in African Studies*, ed. R. P. Moss and R. J. A. R. Rathbone (London: University of London, 1975), 15–23; David Eltis and David Richardson, eds., "A New Assessment of the Transatlantic Slave Trade," in *Extending the Frontiers: Essays on the New Transatlantic Slave Trade Database* (New Haven, CT: Yale University Press, 2008), 46–47. For an engaging read on the effects of the trans-Atlantic slave commerce on the Bight of Biafra and its hinterlands, see Carolyn A. Brown and Paul E. Lovejoy, eds., *Repercussions of the Atlantic Slave Trade: The Interior of the Bight of Biafra and the African Diaspora* (Trenton, NJ: Africa World Press, 2011).

4. Despite the number of studies on slavery and the agitated debates on whether the economics of slavery was good for capitalist development or not, few have carefully considered either slavocracy, an oligarchic system comprising majority plantation/slaveholders, or the inherent ideology of this mode of economic production from the mindset of the operators.

5. To Thomas Jefferson from Abigail Adams with Enclosures, June 6, 1785; see enclosure dated May 8, 1785 (National Historical Publications and Records Commission [NHPRC] National Archives Project).

6. Theodore E. Watson, "Socialists and Socialism," *Watson's Jefferson Magazine* 3, no. 10 (October 1909): 742.

7. Hans J. Morgenthau, "The Six Principles of Political Realism," in *The Politics among Nations: The Struggle for Power and Peace*, 7th ed., ed. Kenneth W. Thompson and David Clinton (Boston: McGraw Hill, 2005), 4–5.

8. Ibid., 4–16; and Hans J. Morgenthau, *Politics among Nations: The Struggle for Power and Peace*, 5th ed. (New York: Alfred A. Knopf, 1978), 4–15.

9. Chauncey S. Boucher, "In re That Aggressive Slavocracy," *Mississippi Valley Historical Review* 8, nos. 1 and 2 (1921): 13–79.

10. Watson, "Socialists and Socialism," 742.

11. National Archives Kew (NAK), FO 84/1310, East African enslaved people released from a dhow by HMS *Daphne*, 1 November 1868. For secondary literature on this, see Moses D. E. Nwulia, *Britain and Slavery in East Africa* (Washington, DC: Three Continents Press, 1975), 125; Ray W. Beachery, *The Slave Trade of Eastern Africa*, vol. 1 (London: African Books Center Limited, 1976); and Robert W. Harms, Bernard K. Freemon, and David W. Blight, eds., *Indian Ocean Slavery in the Age of Abolition* (New Haven, CT: Yale University Press, 2013).

12. A. E. Afigbo, "The Aro Slaving Oligarchy," *Nigerian Magazine* 110–12 (1974): 66–73; A. E. Afigbo, "The Eclipse of the Aro Slaving Oligarchy of Southeastern Nigeria, 1901–1927," *Journal of the Historical Society of Nigeria* 6, no. 1 (1971): 15; Nigerian National Archive Enugu (NNAE), Arodiv 20/1/3, Report on the Long Juju of Arochukwu, 1909–1923.

13. Adaobi Tricia Nwaubani, "My Great-Grandfather, the Nigerian Slave-Trader," *New Yorker*, July 15, 2018. See also Ayomide O. Tayo, "Nigerian Writer Opens Up about Her Family's Dark Past," *The Pulse*, Lagos, July 16, 2018.

14. For thoughts on realism, see John J. Mearsheimer, *The Tragedy of Great Power Politics* (New York: W. W. Norton, 2001).

15. Adam Smith's 1776 lecture is entitled "Juris Prudence, Or Notes from the Lectures on Justice, Police, Revenue, and Arms Delivered in the University of Glasgow." See also Smith's *An Inquiry into Nature and Causes of Wealth of Nations in Three Volumes* (Edinburgh: Printed for Oliphant, Waugh & Innes, 1814), 132, 202, 338.

16. Joshua S. Goldstein and Jon C. Pevehouse, *International Relations*, 8th ed. (Boston: Pearson Education, 2008), 4–9.

17. By way of illustration, President Ronald Reagan betrayed this fact in the 1980s when he advocated for a ban on chemical and biological weapons while at the same time

funding the United States' stockpiles of these weapons. Len Ackland, editorial: "Checking What He Did," *Bulletin of the Atomic Scientist* 45, no. 1 (1989): 2; and William Arkin, "The Buildup That Wasn't," *Bulletin of the Atomic Scientist* 45, no. 1 (1989): 6–10, here 6.

18. Competition for unbridled profit has been one of the critical problems of neoliberalism and the good economy. See for instance David Whyte and Jorge Wiegratz, eds., *Neoliberalism and the Moral of Fraud* (New York: Routledge, 2016), 1–16, 123; and Norman P. Barry, *The Morality of Business Enterprise* (Aberdeen: Aberdeen University Press, 1991), 29.

19. There is hardly a consensus on what the term "relativism" stands for. However, a typical definition of the concept is to assert that that a phenomenon (e.g., values, epistemic, aesthetic, and ethical norms, experiences, judgments, and even the world) is somehow dependent on and covaries with some underlying, independent variable (e.g., paradigms, cultures, conceptual schemes, belief systems, and language). See M. Baghramian, "Relativism: A Brief History," in *Relativism: A Contemporary Anthology*, ed. M. Krausz (New York: Columbia University Press, 2010), 31–50; M. Krausz, *Relativism: Interpretation and Confrontation* (Notre Dame, IN: University of Notre Dame Press, 1989); and M. Kolbel, "Relativism," *Philosophy Compass* 10, no. 1 (2013): 38–51.

20. James Kellenberger, *Moral Relativism, Moral Diversity, and Human Relationships* (University Park: Pennsylvania State University Press, 2013), esp. 23, 120–27. See also James Kellenberger, *Relationship Morality* (University Park: Pennsylvania State University Press, 2010), 43–50.

21. Neil Levy, *Moral Relativism: A Short Introduction* (London: One World Publications, 2002), 138.

22. Thurstan Shaw, "Bronzes from Eastern Nigeria: Excavations at Igbo-Ukwu," *Journal of the African Historical Society of Nigeria* 2, no. 1 (1960): 162–65.

23. Adam Smith, *Lectures on Jurisprudence: Report Dated 1766*, ed. R. L. Meek, D. D. Raphael, and P. G. Stein, vol. 5 (Indianapolis, IN: Liberty Fund, 1981).

24. NAK, CO 137/222, David Woods Emancipation, 167/44 no. 8: 7 March 1818. For secondary accounts on this, see Douglas Charles Stange, *British Unitarians against American Slavery, 1833–65* (Madison, NJ: Fairleigh Dickinson University Press, 1984), 65; and Adrienne Shadd, *The Journey from Tollgate to Parkway: African Canadians in Hamilton* (Ontario, CA: Natural Heritage Books, a Member of the Dundurn Press, 2010), 58.

25. For an insight into the weight of power exercised by these two politicians in the life of people resident in the Borough of Liverpool, see for instance a collection of letters and political treaties in City of Liverpool, *The Poll for the Election, or Members of Parliament for the Borough of Liverpool; Taken Between Colonel Tarleton and Bamber Gascoyne* (Liverpool: Printed by T. Johnson, Castle-Street, 1790), 39.

26. Marika Sherwood, *After Abolition: Britain and the Slave Trade since 1807* (London: I. B. Tauris, 2007); "Slavery: Atlantic Trade and Arab Slavery," *New African Magazine*, October 1, 2012. The 1833 Emancipation Act applied to only four parts of the

British Empire: the Caribbean, Cape Town, Ceylon (Sri Lanka), and Canada. Other colonies, or British trading posts, that eventually became colonies, including West and East Africa and India, were omitted from the act. The freedmen, women, and children received no compensation.

27. Christian Arnsperger and Yanis Varoufakis, "What Is Neoclassical Economics? The Three Axioms Responsible for Its Theoretical Oeuvre, Practical Irrelevance and, Thus, Discursive Power," *Panoeconomicus* 1 (2006): 5–18.

28. Marvin Brown, "Free Enterprise and the Economics of Slavery," *Real-World Economics Review* 52, no. 7 (2010): 28–39. On p. 33, Brown admits that Smith was antislavery, but at the same time faults his treatise on the subject. He cannot have it both ways.

29. Thomas Wells, "Adam Smith's Real Views on Slavery: A Reply to Marvin Brown," *Real-World Economics Review* 53, no. 26 (2010): 156–60. Charles L. Griswold, *Adam Smith and the Virtues of Enlightenment* (Cambridge: Cambridge University Press, 1999), 198–201.

30. For engaging discussions on the origin of this American creed, see Julius W. Pratt, "The Origin of 'Manifest Destiny,'" *American Historical Review* 32, no. 4 (1927): 795–98; Jorie Graham, "Manifest Destiny," *Grand Street* 42 (1992): 65–78; and R. H. Sloddard, "Manifest Destiny," *The Aldine* 5, no. 2 (1872): 47.

31. There may have been other Africans in Virginia before this event. See John Rolfe to Sir Edwin Sandys, January 1619/20, in Susan Myra Kingsbury, ed., *The Records of the Virginia Company of London . . .*, 4 vols. (Washington, DC: Government Printing Office, 1906–1935), 3: 234; David R. Ransome, ed., *Ferrar Papers, 1590–1790*, reel 1, 159. See also William Thorndale, "The Virginia Census of 1619," *Magazine of Virginia Genealogy* 33 (1995): 155; and Martha McCartney, "Virginia's First Africans," *Encyclopedia Virginia*, Virginia Foundation for the Humanities, Sep. 21, 2018. Web. Dec. 22, 2018.

32. See David Olusoga, "The Roots of European Racism Lie in the Slave Trade, Colonialism—and Edward Long," *The Guardian*, London, Sept. 8, 2015; Benjamin P. Bowser, ed., Introduction to *Racism and Anti-Racism in World Perspective* (Thousand Oaks, CA: Sage, 1995), ix–xxii. See also Thomas Jefferson, *Notes on the State of Virginia* (London: John Stockdale, 1787), 6. Jefferson argues that "race might be the effect of subjugation."

33. Geoffrey Gertz, "What Will Trump's Embrace of Bilateralism Mean for America's Trade Partners?" *Future Developments*, Feb. 8, 2017.

34. See Brenda E. Stevenson, *What Is Slavery?* (New York: John Wiley & Sons, 2015); Daniel Barros, Dominquez da Silva, and David Eltis, "The Slave Trade to Pernambuco," in *Extending the Frontiers: Essays on the New Transatlantic Slave Trade Database*, ed. David Eltis and David Richardson (New Haven, CT: Yale University Press, 2008), 117.

35. All the sworn witnesses to this document affirm that Garrido was free (*horro*) when he arrived in Spain. Matthew Restall, "Black Conquistadors: Armed Africans in Early Spanish America," *The Americas* 57, no. 2 (2000): 171–205.

36. Ibid.

37. Juan Garrido's *probanza* (proof of merit) dated Sept. 27, 1538; and Archivo General de Indias, Servile (hereafter AGI), Mexico 204, folio 1. See also Ricardo E. Alegria, *Juan Garrido, el Conquestador Negro en las Antillas, Florida, Mexico y Californis, c. 1503–1540* (San Juan: Centro de Avanzados de Puerto Rico y El Caribe, 1990), 6, 127–38; Restall, "Black Conquistadors," 171; and Leslie K. Best, *The Afro-Latino: A Historical Journey* (Matteson, IL: Becslie Publishers, 2010), 6.

38. While the names of the Black conquistadors hardly survive in the historical record, nor do we know their actual number, it is undeniable that more Black auxiliaries were involved in the secondary conquests that radiated outward from Mexico City than participated in the first victory over the Aztec Empire. Ben Vinson III, "The Free-Colored Military Establishment in Colonial Mexico from the Conquest to Independence," *Callaloo* 27, no. 1 (2004): 150–71, here 153.

39. Robert O. Keohane and Joseph S. Nye, *Power and Interdependence: World Politics in Transition* (London: The Book Service, 1977). See also Robert O. Keohane and Joseph S. Nye, "Power and Interdependence Revisited," *International Organization* 41, no. 4 (Autumn 1987): 725–53.

40. Robert O. Keohane and Joseph S. Nye, "Globalization: What's New and What's Not? (And So What?)," *Foreign Policy* 118 (2000): 104–19.

41. Richard N. Cooper, *The Economics of Interdependence: Economic Policy in the Atlantic Community* (New York: McGraw-Hill for the Council on Foreign Relations, 1968).

42. Keohane and Nye, "Power and Interdependence Revisited," 727.

43. See http://www.slavevoyages.org/assessment/estimates (accessed on April 20, 2017). The full extent of the time covered is 1501–1866.

44. U.S. Bureau of the Census, Historical Statistics of the United States, 1970, collected in ICPSR study number 0003, "Historical Demographic, Economic and Social Data: The United States, 1790–1970."

45. For instance, Marcus Garvey reminds us that all people of African descent are Negroes. He sees no difference between the African-born and the African American. See Aija Poikane-Daunke, *African Diaspora: African German Literature in the Context of the African American Experience* (Berlin: Lit Verlag, 2006), 28.

46. Gwendolyn Midlo Hall, *Africans in Colonial Louisiana: The Development of Afro-Creole Culture in the Eighteenth Century* (Baton Rouge: Louisiana State University Press, 1992), 157, 187.

47. *Turner v. Johnson*, 7 Dana 435, 440 (Ky. 1838).

48. Ibid.

49. Judgment in the U.S. Supreme Court Case *Dred Scott v. John F. A. Sanford*, March 6, 1857; Case Files 1792–1995; Record Group 267; Records of the Supreme Court of the United States; National Archives. The transcript of *Dred Scott v. John F. A. Sanford*, April 1857, was by courtesy of the Library of Congress.

50. Fay A. Yarbrough, "Power, Perception, and Interracial Sex: Former Slaves Recall a Multiracial South," *Journal of Southern History* 71, no. 3 (2005): 559–88. Yarbrough, citing testimonies of ex-slaves, writes that "in the eyes of many ex-slaves, relationships between whites and blacks were usually matters of forced sex between the powerful and the powerless: Immoral white men have, by force, injected their blood into our

veins." On free black women, see Emily Clark, *The Strange History of the American Quadroon: Free Women of Color in the Revolutionary Atlantic World* (Chapel Hill: University of North Carolina Press, 2013); Amrita Chakrabarti Myers, *Forging Freedom: Black Women and the Pursuit of Liberty in Antebellum Charleston* (Chapel Hill: University of North Carolina Press, 2011); and Daniel L. Schafer, *Anna Madgigine Jai Kingsley: African Princess, Florida Slave, Plantation Slaveowner* (Gainesville: University Press of Florida, 2003).

51. "Official Register of Free Persons of Color in Richmond County, Georgia, 1819," reprinted in the Augusta (GA) *Chronicle*, March 13, 1819.

52. Extract from a letter of Peter Fontaine, Westover, Va., March 30, 1757, reprinted in Ann Maury's *Memoirs of a Huguenot Family* (New York, 1853), 351, 352.

53. Peter Fontaine, "Slaveholding Hard to Avoid," extract from a letter to Moses Fontaine, Virginia, March 30, 1757, reprinted in *A Documentary History of American Industrial Society: Plantation and Frontier*, ed. John Rogers Commons, Ulrich Bonnell Phillips, Eugene Allen Gilmore, Helen Laura Sumner, and John Bertram Andrews, vol. 2 (Cleveland, OH: Arthur H. Clark Company, 1920), 29–30.

54. Ronald Segal, *Islam's Black Slaves: The Other Black Diasporas* (London: Atlantic Books, 2003).

55. Fontaine, "Slaveholding Hard to Avoid."

56. Ibid.

57. Ibid.

58. Ibid.

59. Ibid.

60. David M. Kennedy and Thomas A. Bailey, *The American Spirit: United States History as Seen by Contemporaries*, 13th ed. (Boston: Cengage Learning, 2016), 45. Peter Fontaine, "Slaveholding Hard to Avoid"; Albert Bushnell Hart and Blanche Evan Hazard, *Colonial Children* (New York: The Macmillan Company, 1902), 158; Junius P. Rodriguez, *Slavery in the United States: A Social, Political, and Historical Encyclopedia*, vol. 1 (Santa Barbara, CA: ABC-CLIO, 2007), 551; Ulrich Bonnell Phillips, *Plantation and Frontier*, vol. 2: 1647–1862 (New York: Cosimo, Inc., 2008), 30.

61. Advertisement from the Charlestown *South Carolina City Gazette*, March 10, 1796.

62. *Boston Gazette and County Journal*, July 22, 1776.

63. Ibid.

64. Dorothy Schneider and Carl J. Schneider, *Slavery in America* (New York: Facts on File, 2007), 70.

65. Wilma A. Dunaway, *The African-American Family in Slavery and Emancipation* (Cambridge: Cambridge University Press, 2003), 49.

66. Michael Tadman, "The Interregional Slave Trade in the History and Myth-Making of the U.S. South," in Walter Johnson, ed., *The Chattel Principle: Internal Slave Trade in the Americas* (New Haven, CT: Yale University Press, 2004), 122.

67. Alvan Stewart, *Writings and Speeches of Alvan Stewart, on Slavery*, vol. 3 (New York: A. B. Burdick, 1860), 176.

68. Dorothy Schneider and Carl J. Schneider, *Slavery in America* (New York: Infobase Publishing, 2007), 66; Pierce Butler, *The Letters of Pierce Butler, 1790–1794: Nation*

Building and Enterprise in the New American Republic, ed. Terry W. Lipscomb (Columbia: University of South Carolina Press, 2007), 265; Michael Tadman, *Speculators and Slaves: Masters, Traders and Slaves in the Old South* (Madison: University of Wisconsin Press, 1989), 14; and Howard Dodson, *In Motion: The African-American Migration Experience* (Washington, DC: National Geographic Society, 2004), 46.

69. Ulrich Bonnell Phillips, *American Negro Slavery: A Survey of the Supply, Employment and Control of Negro Labor as Determined by the Plantation Regime* (New York: D. Appleton and Co., 1918); Robert Francis Withers Allston, *The South Carolina Rice Plantation as Revealed in the Papers of Robert F. W.* (Charleston: University of South Carolina Press), 2; Herbert Ravenel Sass and Daniel Elliot H. Smith, *A Carolina Rice Plantation in the Fifties: 30 Paintings in Water-Colour* (New York: William Morrow & Co., 1936); and Lewis Cecil Gray, *History of Agriculture in the Southern United States to 1860* (Washington, DC: Carnegie Institute of Washington, 1933).

70. See also Ulrich Bonnell Phillips, *Life and Labor in the Old South* (Boston: Little Brown & Co., 1929).

71. Duncan Clinch Heyward, *Seed from Madagascar* (Chapel Hill: University of North Carolina Press, 1937).

72. Judith Ann Carney, *Black Rice: The African Origins of Rice Cultivation in the Americas* (Cambridge, MA: Harvard University Press, 2001). See also Julia Floyd Smith, *Slavery and Rice in Low Georgia, 1750–1860* (Knoxville: University of Tennessee Press, 1985; reprint 1991), 4; Edda L. Fields-Black, *Deep Roots: Rice Farmers in West Africa and the African Diaspora* (Charleston, SC: Charleston Museum, 1970), 5.

73. Walter Rodney, *How Europe Underdeveloped Africa* (London: Bogle-L'Ouverture, 1972).

74. Daniel C. Littlefield, "The Varieties of Slave Labor," National Humanities Center, http://nationalhumanitiescenter.org/tserve/freedom/1609–1865/essays/slavelabor.htm (accessed on June 18, 2018).

75. Stewart, *Writings and Speeches of Alvan Stewart on Slavery*, 177. Alvan Stewart Papers, Special Collections, University of Miami Libraries, Miami, Florida.

76. Mss2 W5205 b.4, Sale, 1863, of African-American Slaves at "Lower Market House," Unknown No Longer Records, Virginia Historical Society.

77. Wilma A. Dunaway, *The First American Frontier: Transition to Capitalism in Southern Appalachia, 1700–1860* (Chapel Hill: University of North Carolina Press, 1996), 245–46.

78. U.S. Constitution, Article 1, Section 2, 1878. James Wilson and Roger Sherman proposed the three-fifths compromise at the Constitutional Convention of 1787. Source: Gilder Lehrman Institute.

79. Excerpted from Schomburg Center for Research in Black Culture, *Jubilee: The Emergence of African-American Culture*, https://news.nationalgeographic.com/news/2003/01/0131_030203_jubilee2_2.html (accessed on June 23, 2018).

80. George R. Woolfolk, "Planter Capitalism and Slavery: The Labor Thesis," *Journal of Negro History* 41, no. 2 (1956): 103–16.

81. Frederic Bancroft, *Slave Trading in the Old South* (Baltimore: J. H. Furst Company, 1931), 67, 343–48, 407.

82. Phillips, *American Negro Slavery*, 394–95, 401; and Phillips, *Life and Labor in the Old South*, 185.

83. Lewis Cecil Gray and Esther Katherine Thompson, *History of Agriculture in the Southern United States to 1860, with an Introduction by Henry Charles Taylor* (Washington, DC: Carnegie Institute of Washington, 1933), 1, 476. See also Thomas P. Govan, "Was Plantation Slavery Profitable?" *Journal of Southern History* 8, no. 4 (1942): 513–35, here 514; and Charles Crowe, "Slavery, Ideology, and 'Cliometrics,'" *Technology and Culture* 17, no. 2 (1976): 271–85. Crowe attacks Phillips's works as based on sentimentally conceived plantation life. For an engaging discussion, see John David Smith, "The Historiographic Rise, Fall, and Resurrection of Ulrich Bonnell Phillips," *Georgia Historical Quarterly* 65, no. 2 (1981): 138–53.

84. Henry Bolingbroke, *A Voyage to the Demerary, Containing a Statistical Account of the Settlements There* (London: R. Phillips, 1807), 84–86. See also Ulrich Bonnell Phillips, *Plantation and Frontier Documents, 1649–1863* (1909; reprint New York: Cosimo, Inc., 2008).

85. Cited in Ralph B. Flanders, *Plantation Slavery in Georgia* (Chapel Hill: University of North Carolina Press, 1933), 220–21; D. B. De Bow, *The Industrial Resources, etc., of the Southern and Western States*, vol. 1 (New Orleans: 1853), 161–64; D. Lee, "Cotton," in Report of the Commissioner of Patents for the Year, 1849, Part II, Agriculture (Washington, DC: Government Printing Office, 1850), 307–13.

86. De Bow, *The Industrial Resources*, 163–64.

87. Govan, "Was Plantation Slavery Profitable?" 535.

88. George R. Woolfolk, "Cotton Capitalism and Slave Labor," *Southwestern Social Science Quarterly* 37, no. 1 (1956): 43–52.

89. Ibid., 52.

90. Kenneth M. Stampp, "The Historian and Southern Negro Slavery," *American Historical Review* 57, no. 3 (1952): 622.

91. Walter Johnson, *River of Dark Dreams: Slavery and Empire in the Cotton Kingdom* (Cambridge, MA: Harvard University Press, 2013); and Edward E. Baptist, *The Half Has Never Been Told: Slavery and the Making of American Capitalism* (New York: Basic Books, 2016).

92. This estimate covers the period 1619–1865, and it is compounded at 6 percent interest through 1993. See Bakari Kitwana, "Did John Hope Franklin Want $100 Trillion for Blacks?" *HuffPost*, May 7, 2009, https://www.huffingtonpost.com/bakari-kitwana/id-john-hope-franklin-wan_b_183656.html (accessed on Feb. 13, 2017).

2. THE AFRICAN DIASPORA

1. *The Boston Evening Post*, Sept. 22, 1735.

2. Oliver Wendell Holmes, "An Address Delivered before the Massachusetts Medical Society at the Annual Meeting, May 30, 1860," in *Currents and Counter-Currents in*

Medical Science with Other Addresses and Essays (Cambridge, MA: Harvard University Press, 1861), 39.

3. Boston, City Registrar's Report for 1859, Boston City document no. 85, 1860 (Government Documents Section, Boston Public Library), 10.

4. Boston, City Registrar's Report for 1873, Boston City document no. 48, 1874 (Government Documents Section, Boston Public Library), 6.

5. Alvan Stewart, *Writings and Speeches of Alvan Stewart on Slavery*, ed. Luther Rawson Marsh (New York: A. B. Burdick, 1860), 177; ASM0429, Alvan Stewart Diaries, Special Collections, University of Miami Libraries, Miami, Florida.

6. Rhode Island Census Board, *Report upon the Census of Rhode Island, 1865* (Providence, 1867), xlvii.

7. See for instance Romeo B. Garrett, "African Survivals in American Culture," *Journal of Negro History* 51, no. 4 (1966): 239–45.

8. Ira Berlin, Steven E Miller, and Mark Favreau, eds., *Remembering Slavery: African-Americans Talk about Their Personal Experiences in Slavery and Freedom* (New York: The New Press, 1998).

9. Sidney W. Mintz and Richard Price, *An Anthropological Approach to the Afro-American Past: A Caribbean Perspective* (Philadelphia: Institute for the Study of Human Issues, 1976). The authors republished this work as *The Birth of African-American Culture: An Anthropological Perspective* (Boston: Beacon Press, 1992).

10. Vicente M. Diaz, "Creolization and Indigeneity," *American Ethnologist* 33, no. 4 (2006): 577.

11. Viranjini Munasinghe, "Theorizing World Culture through the New World: East Indians and Creolization," *American Ethnologist* 33, no. 4 (2006): 556.

12. Daniel Segal, "Nationalism in a Colonial State: A Study of Trinidad and Tobago" (Ph.D. diss., University of Chicago, 1989), 76.

13. See Charles Darwin, *On the Origin of Species by Means of Natural Selection, on the Preservation of Favored Races in the Struggle for Life* (New York: D. Appleton and Company, 1859).

14. George Champlin Mason, *Reminiscences of Newport* (Newport, RI: Published by Charles E. Hammett, Jr., 1884), 157.

15. William Mein to Pierce Butler, May 24, 1803, folder 27, box 6, Series II: Plantation Management, Miscellaneous Correspondence 1802–1803, Butler Family Papers (Historical Society of Pennsylvania, Philadelphia). See also Michael A. Gomez, *Exchanging Our Country Marks: The Transformation of African Identities in the Colonial and Antebellum South* (Chapel Hill: University of North Carolina Press, 1998), 17–18.

16. See Paula Marshall, *Praisesong for the Widow* (New York: Dutton, 1983), 38–39. See also Lorna McDaniel, "The Flying Africans: Extent and Strength of the Myth in the Americas," *Nieuwe West-Indische Gids / New West Indian Guide* 64, nos. 1 and 2 (1990): 28–40; and Silvia del Pilar Castro Borrego, *History, Memory, Recovery and Representation in Contemporary Fiction by African American Women Writers* (La Cañada, Spain: Universidad de Almeria, 1990), 83.

17. McDaniel, "The Flying Africans," 31. Also, see Victor Turner, *The Forest of Symbols: Aspects of Ndembu Ritual* (Ithaca, NY: Cornell University Press, 1967), 30.

18. *The Boston Evening Post*, Sept. 22, 1735.
19. Jack Tannali, Georgia Writers' Project interview, in Georgia Writers' Project, *Drums and Shadows: Survival Stories among the Georgia Coastal Negroes* (1940; Athens: University of Georgia Press, 1986), 108; and Floyd White, in *Drums and Shadows*, 185.
20. Andrew C. Pearse, liner note to *The Big Drum Dance of Carriacou*, Ethnic Folkways Library, Folkway Records P1011, 5.
21. Terri L. Snyder, "Suicide, Slavery, and Memory in North America," *Journal of American History* 97, no. 1 (2010): 39–62, here 40.
22. Harriet Ann Jacobs, *Incidents in the Life of a Slave Written by Herself* (Boston: Published by the author, 1861). Jacobs's biography reveals that she was born a slave in Edenton, NC, in 1813. Following the death of her mother, Delilah, and father, Elijah, Harriet' s maternal grandmother took custody of her and her younger brother John.
23. Georgia Kreiger, "Playing Dead: Harriet Jacobs's Survival Strategy in *Incidents in the Life of a Slave Girl*," *African American Review* 42, nos. 3 and 4 (2008): 608–09.
24. Jeffrey R. Young, "Ideology and Death on Savannah River Rice Plantation, 1833–1867: Paternalism amidst 'A Good Supply of Disease and Pain,'" *Journal of Southern History* 59, no. 4 (1993): 673–706.
25. Orazio P. Attanasio and Carl Emmerson, "Differential Mortality in the UK," *Journal of the European Economic Association* 1 (2003): 821–50; Orazio P. Attanasio and Hillary Williamson Hoynes, "Differential Mortality and Wealth Accumulation," *Journal of Human Resources* 35, no. 1 (2000): 1–29; and A. Bommier, T. Magnac, B. Rapoport, and M. Roger, "Droit à la retraite et mortalité différentielle" (Pension Entitlement and Differential Mortality), *Économie et prévision* 168 (2006): 1–16; A. Deaton and C. Paxson, "Mortality, Income, and Income Inequality over Time in Britain and the US," in D. Wise, ed., *Perspectives in the Economics of Aging* (Chicago, IL: University of Chicago Press, 2004), 247–86.
26. Michael Marmot, "Multi-level Approaches to Understanding Social Determinants," in *Social Epidemiology*, ed. L. Berkman and I. Kawachi (Oxford: Oxford University Press, 1999), 349–67; and R. Adams, M. Hurd, D. McFadden, A. Merrill, and T. Ribeiro, "Healthy, Wealthy, and Wise? Tests for Direct Causal Paths between Health and Socioeconomic Status," *Journal of Econometrics* 112 (2003): 3–56.
27. Adeline Delavande and Susann Rohwedder, "Differential Survival in Europe and the United States: Estimates Based on Subjective Probabilities of Survival," *Demography* 48, no. 4 (2011): 1377–1400, here 1377.
28. Ibid., 1398.
29. Clifton D. Bryant, *Handbook on Death and Dying* (Thousand Oaks, CA: Sage Publications, 2003), 189.
30. Robert W. Fogel and Stanley L. Engerman, "The Anatomy of Exploitation," in Robert Whaples and Dianne C. Betts, eds., *Historical Perspective on the American Economy* (Cambridge: Cambridge University Press, 1995), 153. See also Richard H. Steckel, "The African American Population of the United States, 1790–1920," in *A Population History of North America*, ed. Michael R. Haines and Richard H. Steckel (New York: Cambridge University Press, 2000), 433–81.

31. Steven Mintz, "The Origins and Nature of New World Slavery: What Was Life Like under Slavery?" *Digital History*, http://www.digitalhistory.uh.edu/disp_textbook.cfm?smtID=2&psid=3040 (accessed on March 10, 2018).

32. Ibid. See also Howard Bodenhorn, *The Color Factor: The Economics of African American Well-Being in the Nineteenth-Century South* (Oxford: Oxford University Press, 2015), 222–23; and the excellent study on a Jamaica sugar estate by Richard S. Dunn, "'Dreadful Idlers' in the Cane Fields: The Slave Labor Pattern on a Jamaica Sugar Estate, 1762–1831," *Journal of Interdisciplinary History* 17, no. 4 (1987): 795–822.

33. Richard H. Steckel, "A Dreadful Childhood: The Excess Mortality of American Slaves," *Social Science History* 10, no. 4 (1986): esp. 430.

34. Robert W. Fogel and Stanley L. Engerman, *Time on the Cross: The Economics of American Negro Slavery* (Boston: Little, Brown, 1974), 122.

35. John Campbell, "Work, Pregnancy, and Infant Mortality among Southern Slaves," *Journal of Interdisciplinary History* 14 (1984): 793–812.

36. Richard H. Steckel, "Slave Height Profiles from Coastwise Manifests," *Explorations in Economic History* 16 (1979): 363–80.

37. Kenneth F. Kiple and Virginia H. King, *Another Dimension to the Black Diaspora: Diet, Disease, and Racism* (Cambridge: Cambridge University Press, 1981).

38. Steven Mintz, Introduction to Steven Mintz, ed., *African American Voices: A Documentary Reader, 1619–1877* (Sussex, England: Wiley-Blackwell, 2009), 22.

39. Ibid.

40. Charles Manigault to Jesse T. Cooper, Naples, Jan. 10, 1848. See also James M. Clifton, ed., *Life and Labor on Argyle Island: Letters and Documents of a Savannah River Rice Plantation, 1833–1867* (Argyle Island, GA: Beehive Press, 1978), 62.

41. For an engaging discussion on this, see Peter H. Wood, *Black Majority: Negroes in Colonial South Carolina from 1670 through the Stono Rebellion* (New York: Alfred A. Knopf, 1974), 190.

42. Despite this loss in "capital" (the dead slaves were worth at least $44,000), Gowrie still managed to yield a 4 percent return on investment between 1848 and 1854. "Charles Manigault's Gowrie—A Starting Point," https://www.sciway.net/afam/slavery/gowrie .html (accessed on July 20, 2018).

43. William Dusinberre, *Them Dark Days: Slavery in the American Rice Swamps* (Athens: University of Georgia Press, 2000), 61.

44. Ibid., 5–6.

45. Jay D. Edwards, "Creolization Theory and the Odyssey of the Atlantic Linear Cottage," *Etnofoor* 23, no. 1 (2011): 50–83.

46. Josephine A. Beoku-Betta, "We Got Our Way of Cooking Things: Women, Food, and Preservation of Cultural Identity among the Gullah," *Gender and Society* 9, no. 5 (1995): 535–55, is an excellent account of cultural practices related to food and women's roles among the Gullah communities of the Sea Islands of Georgia and South Carolina. See also Herbert C. Covey and Herbert Eisenach, *What the Slaves Ate: Recollections of the African American Foods and Foodways from the Slave Narratives* (Santa Barbara, CA: Greenwood Press, 2009), 60–62.

47. Vilet Lester to Patsey Patterson, Aug. 29, 1857; from the Joseph Allred Papers, 1819–

1903: An Online Archives Collection, Special Collections Library, Duke University. In the letter, Vilet mentioned that she was sold several times before ending up with the household of James B. Lester. Vilet's account indicated that she had been away from the Pattersons' home for at least five years by the time she sent this letter. The record further reveals that Vilet had a child while owned by the Pattersons.

48. Marie Jenkins Schwartz, "Family Life in the Slave Quarters: Survival Strategies," *OAH Magazine of History* 15, no. 4 (2001): 36–41, reprinted as Annenberg Learner, "African Americans in the Early Republic," https://www.learner.org/courses/amerhistory/pdf/MOH/REF_MOHarticle.doc (accessed on Aug. 1, 2018).

49. John W. Blassingame, *The Slave Community: Plantation Life in the Antebellum South* (Oxford: Oxford University Press, 1979).

50. Schwartz, "Family Life in the Slave Quarters: Survival Strategies," 37.

51. Frederick Douglass, *My Bondage and My Freedom* (New York and Auburn: Miller, Orton and Co., 1957), 132.

52. Schwartz, "Family Life in the Slave Quarters: Survival Strategies," 38.

53. Ibid.

54. Douglass, *My Bondage and My Freedom*, 189.

55. U.S. Congress, The Fugitive Slave Law or Fugitive Slave Act, Sept. 18, 1850. The law was part of the Compromise of 1850 between southern slave-holding interests and northern Free-Soilers.

56. Wilbur H. Siebert, "The Underground Railroad," *New England Magazine* 27 (1902/1903): 565–78, here 567; and Henrietta Buckmaster, "The Underground Railroad," *North American Review* 246, no. 1 (1938): 142–49.

57. Wilbur Henry Siebert, *The Mysteries of Ohio's Underground Railroad* (1891; reprint Columbus: Long's College Books Company, 1951).

58. Fred B. Joyner, "Review of *The Mysteries of Ohio's Underground Railroads* by Wilbur Henry Siebert," *Mississippi Valley Historical Review* 39, no. 2 (1952): 336–37.

59. Lisa Pfueller, "Review of *The Underground Railroad in Montgomery County: A History and Driving Guide* by Anthony Cohen," *Washington History* 8, no. 2 (1996/1997): 89.

60. See Stanley Harrold, "Freeing the Weems Family: A New Look at the Underground Railroad," *Civil War History* 42, no. 4 (1996): 289–306.

61. Pfueller, "Review of *The Underground Railroad in Montgomery County*," 89. See also Howard Dodson, "America's Cultural Roots Traced to Enslaved African Ancestors," *National Geographic*, Feb. 5, 2003, https://news.nationalgeographic.com/news/2003/02/jubilee-america-culture-enslaved-africans/ (accessed on June 23, 2018).

62. Dodson, "America's Cultural Roots."

63. Albert J. Raboteau, *Slave Religion: The "Invincible Institution" in the Antebellum South* (Oxford: Oxford University Press, 1978), esp. 47–49.

64. Melville Herskovits, *Myth of the Negro Past* (Boston: Beacon Press, 1958), 6; Sterling Stuckey, *Slave Culture: Nationalist Theory and the Foundation of Black America* (Oxford: Oxford University Press, 1987), 3–10, 31, 78, 33; and Walter C. Rucker, *The River Flows On: Black Resistance, Culture, and Identity Formation in Early America* (Baton Rouge: Louisiana State University Press, 2007).

65. Jason Young, "African Religions in the Early South," *Journal of Southern Religion* 14 (2012), http://jsr.fsu.edu/issues/vol14/young.html (accessed on Nov. 19, 2017).

66. Sylviane A. Diouf, *Servants of Allah: African Muslims Enslaved in the Americas* (New York: New York University Press, 1998); Yvonne P. Chireau, *Black Magic: Religion and the African American Conjuring Tradition* (Berkeley: University of California Press, 2003); and Allan D. Austin, *African Muslims in Antebellum America: Transatlantic Stories and Spiritual Struggles* (New York: Routledge, 1997).

67. Jason Young, "African Religions in the Early South," *Journal of Southern Religion* 14 (2012), http://jsr.fsu.edu/issues/vol14/young.html (accessed on Nov. 19, 2017).

68. Jon Butler, *Awash in a Sea of Faith: Christianizing the American People* (Cambridge, MA: Harvard University Press, 1990), 153.

69. Robert W. Nicholls, *Old-Time Masquerading in the USVI* (St. Thomas, USVI: VI Humanities Council, 1998). One of the strengths of Nicholls's works is his due acknowledgment of the complications of ethnic identification in the African diaspora.

70. Ivor Miller, "Cuban Abákuá Chants: Examining New Linguistic and Historical Evidence for the African Diaspora," *African Studies Review* 48, no. 1 (2005): 23–58.

71. Dodson, "America's Cultural Roots Traced to Enslaved African Ancestors."

72. See Ted Widmer, "The Invention of a Memory: Congo Square and African Music in Nineteenth-Century New Orleans," *Revue française d'études américaines* 98, no. 2 (2003): 69–78.

73. Midge Burnett, eighty years old, interviewed on Aug. 7, 1937, at 1300 S. Bloodworth Street, Raleigh, NC, in *Slave Narratives: A Folk History of Slavery in the United States from Interviews with Former Slaves* (Washington, DC: Library of Congress, 1941), 156.

74. The term "musician" is used in the generic sense. As elaborated in Chapter 8, the spiritual and the blues, two indigenous African American musical forms, were invented by enslaved Africans during the slavery era. African American religious and secular songs trace their roots to the spiritual and the blues, respectively.

75. George Champlin Mason, *Reminiscences of Newport* (Newport, RI: Published by Charles E. Hammett, Jr., 1884), 154.

76. A quick read is J. Southern, "Newport Gardner (1746–1826)," *Black Perspective in Music* 4, no. 2 (1976): 202–07. Information on Captain Gardner came from court cases and deeds related to the Gardner family of Rhode Island. See Cato Gardner, 6 Oct. 1796, An Order of Removal, "Providence Town Papers," MSS 214 Vol. 26 #11261; Prince Thurston, 5 June 1793, An Order of Removal, "Providence Town Papers," MSS 214 Vol. 18 #7980, Rhode Island Historical Society (Providence), 373.

77. Mason, *Reminiscences of Newport*, 154–59. See also Eileen Southern, *Readings in Black American Music* (New York: W. W. Norton, 1971), 36–40; and Christy Clark-Pujara, *Drak Work: The Business of Slavery in Rhode Island* (New York: New York University Press, 2016), 115.

78. Mason, *Reminiscences of Newport*, 158.

3. FROM LAND OF FREEDOM TO CROWN COLONY OF SIERRA LEONE

1. Christopher Fyfe, *A History of Sierra Leone* (New York: Oxford University Press, 1962).

2. Tara Helfman, "The Court of Vice Admiralty at Sierra Leone and the Abolition of the West African Slave Trade," *Yale Law Journal* 115, no. 5 (2006): 1122–56. See also Fyfe, *A History of Sierra Leone*, 107, 109, 115–17. For an account of Robert Thorpe's work in Sierra Leone, see Robert Thorpe, *Letter to William Wilberforce* (London: F. C. and J. Rivington, 1815), v; and Samuel Samo, *The trials of the slave traders, Samuel Samo, Joseph Peters, and William Tuft: tried in April and June 1812, before the Hon. Robert Thorpe, L. L. D. Chief Justice of Sierra Leone, &c., &c., with two letters on the slave trade from a gentleman resident of Sierra Leone to an advocate for the abolition in London* (London: Sherwood, Neeley, and Jones, 1813), 20.

3. Joseph Tracey, *An Historical Examination of Western Africa as Formed by Paganism and Muhammedanism, Slavery, the Slave Trade and Piracy* (Boston: Press of T. R. Marvin, 1845).

4. V. E. J. Buckle, "The Language of the Sierra Leone 'Creo,'" *Sierra Leone Studies* 21 (1939): 20–24.

5. A fire outbreak obliterated the first settlement, Granville Town, in 1787. A Temne chief burned the settlement in retaliation for the destruction of one of his villages by a British naval group.

6. Zachary Macaulay, *Life and Letters of Zachary Macaulay by His Granddaughter Viscountess Knutsford* (London: Edward Arnold, 1900), 52.

7. K. L. Little, "The Significance of the West African Creole for Africanist and Afro-American Studies," *African Affairs* 49, no. 197 (1950): 312 note.

8. Ibid., 318.

9. For clarity, the Monrovia project that led to the formation of Liberia as an American colony is different from Freetown, Sierra Leone, which occupies a central position in the history of the abolition and the later formation of Liberia.

10. See http://www.slavevoyages.org/assessment/estimates.

11. Ottobah Quobna Cugoano, in *Thoughts and Sentiments on the Evil of Slavery and Other Writings*, ed. Vincent Carretta (New York: Penguin, 1999), 156.

12. Isaac Land, "On the Founding of Sierra Leone, 1787–1808," *BRANCH: Britain, Representation and Nineteenth-Century History*, http://www.branchcollective.org/?ps _articles=isaac-land-on-the-foundings-of-sierra-leone-1787-1808. Land reminds us that there was once a different plan to establish the colony in the Caribbean Bahamas, New Brunswick (Canada), and even Australia.

13. Washington to George William Fairfax, June 10, 1774, in *The Writings of George Washington*, vol. 3, ed. John C. Fitzpatrick (Washington, DC: Government Printing Office, 1938), 224.

14. See Mary Wigge, "List of George Washington's Slaves, 1799," *Washington Papers*, http://gwpapers.virginia.edu/documents/list-of-george-washingtons-slaves-1799/ for a quick breakdown of his acquisitions comprising those slaves he inherited from his father (11), those he inherited from his brother Lawrence (12), those he owned outright, and those he leased at Mount Vernon. See also Charles Lee to Washington, Sept. 13, 1786, esp. note 3, https://founders.archives.gov/documents/Washington/04-04-02-0237; and Washington to William Triplett, Sept. 25, 1786, http://founders.archives.gov/ documents/Washington/04-04-02-0247, both in *Founders Online*, National Archives.

15. It was for his acts of hypocrisy and doublespeak that Washington's biographer calls him "an imperfect God." Henry Wiencek, *An Imperfect God: George Washington, His Slaves, and the Creation of America* (New York: Farrar, Straus, and Giroux, 2013).

16. Peter A. Dorsey, "'Corroborate Our Own Claims': Public Positioning and the Slavery Metaphor in Revolutionary America," *American Quarterly* 55, no. 3 (2003): 353–86, here 353.

17. Thomas Jefferson, *Notes on the State of Virginia* (Philadelphia: Printed and Sold by Pritchard and Hall, 1781; reprint 1785), appendix.

18. John Chester Miller, *The Wolf by the Ears: Thomas Jefferson and Slavery* (New York: Free Press, 1977), 22.

19. Jefferson, *Notes on the State of Virginia*, 172.

20. Ibid., 173–74.

21. E. A. Ijagbemi, "The Freetown Colony and the Development of 'Legitimate' Commerce in the Adjoining Territories," *Journal of the Historical Society of Nigeria* 5, no. 2 (June 1970): 243–56.

22. For clarity, the group initially assigned the term "Black Poor" in England were the lascar seamen brought home on the ships of the East India Company. However, the African Americans arriving from North America were in a much more miserable condition and the committee had to assist them in more significant numbers.

23. Ijagbemi, "The Freetown Colony," 244.

24. T. C. McCaskie, "Cultural Encounters: Britain and Africa in the Nineteenth Century," in *The Oxford History of the British Empire*, vol. 3, ed. Andrew Porter and Alaine Low (Oxford: Oxford University Press, 1999), 665–89, here 667.

25. See, for instance, Fyfe, *A History of Sierra Leone*.

26. Zachary Macaulay, journal entries for July 13 and 14, 1793, in Knutsford, *Life and Letters of Zachary Macaulay*, 37.

27. Suzanne Miers and Igor Kopytoff, Introduction to *Slavery in Africa: Historical and Anthropological Perspectives*, ed. Miers and Kopytoff (Madison: University of Wisconsin Press, 1977), 3–40. For a similar argument, see Paul E. Lovejoy, *Transformations in Slavery: A History of Slavery in Africa* (Cambridge: Cambridge University Press, 1984); and Paul E. Lovejoy, ed., *The Ideology of Slavery in Africa* (Thousand Oaks, CA: Sage Publications, 1981).

28. A. G. Hopkins, *The Economic History of West Africa* (London: Longmans, 1973), 23, 77.

29. Claude Meillassoux, Introduction to Claude Meillassoux, *L'Esclavage en Afrique précoloniale* (Paris: Maspero, 1975), 12–13.

30. For instance, see Henry Louis Gates, Jr., "Ending the Slavery Blame-Game," *New York Times*, April 23, 2010, in which the Harvard University professor called on African kings and chiefs to apologize for the enslavement of Africans in the Americas. More illuminating is the counterview provided by Eric Foner, "Africa's Role in the U.S. Slave Trade," *New York Times*, April 23, 2010.

31. Frederick Cooper, "The Problem of Slavery in African Studies," *Journal of African History* 20 (1979): 105.

32. Anselma Guezo, "Abolition and West African Societies: The Inconclusive Debate," *Journal of the Historical Society of Nigeria* 21 (2012): 1–20, here 2.

33. The full history is detailed in an excellent essay on King Adandozan by Ana Lucia Araujo, "Dahomey, Portugal, and Bahia: King Adandozan and the Atlantic Slave Trade," *Slavery and Abolition* 3, no. 1 (2012): 1–19.

34. Joseph J. Bangura, *Sierra Leone: African Agency in the Making of a British Colony* (Cambridge: Cambridge University Press, 2017), 6.

35. For full list of the cheap items the Temne chiefs received from the Europeans as tokens in exchange for the land, see Treaty No. 1 of Aug. 22, 1788, in A. Montagu, *Ordinances of the Colony of Sierra Leone* (London: Her Majesty's Stationery Office, 1857–1868), reprinted in Christopher Fyfe, *Sierra Leone Inheritance* (London: Oxford University Press, 1964), 112–13. The details show that no money exchanged hands. Fyfe stresses that this treaty was eventually "repudiated and declared invalid" (112).

36. Roy Lewis, *Sierra Leone: A Modern Portrait* (London: Her Majesty's Stationery Office, 1954), 25; and Bangura, *Sierra Leone*, 6.

37. See Ta-Nehisi Coates, "Inverse Nationalism: My Response to Henry Louise Gates Jr.'s Argument against Reparation," *The Atlantic*, April 26, 2010.

38. The original hymn was written in 1772 and first published in *The Olney Hymns* (London: W. Oliver, 1779) as hymn number xli by John Newton and William Cowper. See Steve Turner, *Amazing Grace: The Story of America's Beloved Song* (New York: Harper and Collins, 2009).

39. "Who Was Captain Paul Cuffe?" New Bedford Whaling Museum, https://www.whaling museum.org/explore/paul-cuffe/who-was-captain-paul-cuffe/.

40. Ibid. For details of this history, see Anita C. Danker, "African American Heritage Trails: From Boston to Berkshires," in *African American Heritage in the Upper Housatonic Valley*, ed. David Levinson (Great Barrington, MA: Berkshire Publishing Group, 2006), 17–32.

41. See Charles P. Keith, *Chronicles of Pennsylvania, from the English Revolution to the Peace of Aix-la-Chapelle, 1688–1748*, 2 vols. (Philadelphia: Patterson and White Co., 1917), 1: 228; J. William Frost, "Unlikely Controversialists: Caleb Pusey and George Keith," *Quaker History* 64 (1975–1976): 16–36.

42. Copied here in modern-day English. Original text: "it allways appeard a most iniquitous scheme to me. fight ourselfs for what we are daily [ebbing] and plundering from those who have as good a right freedom as we have—you know my mind upon this subject." See transcription and original letter, Abigail Adams to John Adams, Sept. 22, 1774, "Abigail Adams's letter to her husband, 1774," *Africans in America*, https://www.pbs.org/wgbh/aia/part2/2h23.html.

43. Laurie Carter Noble, "Abigail Adams," in Unitarian Universalist History and Heritage Society, *Dictionary of Unitarian and Universalist Biography*, http://uudb.org/articles/abigailadams.html.

44. Crooks, *A History of the Colony of Sierra Leone*, 20.

45. Among these are Justin Roberts, *Slavery and the Enlightenment in the British Atlantic, 1750–1807* (Cambridge: Cambridge University Press, 2013); and Louis Sala-Molins,

Dark Side of the Light: Slavery and the French Enlightenment, translated and with an
introduction by John Conteh-Morgan (Minneapolis: University of Minnesota Press,
2006).

46. Ijagbemi, "The Freetown Colony," 243–56.

47. National Archives of Canada (NAC), C-115424, Black Loyalists in Nova Scotia, 1783–
84—The Sierra Leone Company (Carleton Papers), Halifax, NS. Comprising about
19,000 Whites, Blacks, Native Indians, recent migrants, and other ethnic minorities,
most of the loyalists were poor farmers, tradespeople, laborers, and their families. For
more reading, see Mary Beacock Fryer, *King's Men: The Soldier Founders of Ontario*
(Toronto: Dundurn Press, 1980); Harvey Amani Whitfield, "Slavery in English Nova
Scotia, 1750–1810," *Journal of the Royal Nova Scotia Historical Society* 2010: 23–40; and
Harvey Amani Whitefield, "Black Loyalists and Black Slaves in Maritime Canada,"
History Compass, October 2007: 1980–97.

48. James W. St. G. Walker, *The Black Loyalists: The Search for a Promised Land in Nova
Scotia and Sierra Leone, 1783–1870* (Toronto: University of Toronto Press, 1976).

49. Sixty of the émigrés died of fever while in transit, 1,131 landed in Freetown, and forty
died within a few weeks. Thus, 1,091 survived the first few months after their arrival.
Fyfe records that sixty-seven died of the fever, while another thirty-seven died in the
first few weeks after they arrived. See Fyfe, *A History of Sierra Leone*, 38.

50. Names of the leaders came from annotations found in the Nova Scotia Museum,
Remembering the Black Loyalists, Black Communities in Nova Scotia, Halifax, NS,
2001.

51. Fyfe, *A History of Sierra Leone*, 36–37; and Vitella A. D. Thompson, "The Transformation of Freetown Christianity, 1960–2000" (Ph.D. diss., School of African Studies,
University of London, 2015), 42.

52. For details of these treaties, see *A Complete Collection of the Treaties and Conven-
tions, and Reciprocal Regulations at Present Subsisting between Great Britain and
Foreign Powers: and of the laws, decrees, orders in council, &c, concerning the same.
. . . Compiled from Authentic Documents, by Edward Hertslet*, Foreign Office, vol. 14
(London: Butterworth, 1880), 927–64.

53. For these figures, see National Archives Kew, ADM 51 and ADM 53, Royal Navy Operational Records 1660–1914. These files account for the sighting, chases, and capture
of slavers across the Atlantic.

54. V. R. Dorjahn and Christopher Fyfe, "Landlord and Stranger: Change in Tenancy
Relations in Sierra Leone," *Journal of African History* 3, no. 3 (1962): 394–95.

55. See for instance David Chalmers, *Report by Her Majesty's Commissioner and correspondence on the subject of the insurrection in the Sierra Leone Protectorate, 1898* (Great
Britain: Darling & Son, 1899), cited in Fyfe, *Sierra Leone Inheritance*, 267–69.

56. Robert Clarke, "Sketches of the Colony of Sierra Leone and Its Inhabitants," *Transactions of the Ethnographical Society of Britain and Ireland* 2 (1863): 329.

57. The story of the sixty White women was an attempt by the British government to rid
the country of social undesirables such as prostitutes. For a very interesting read on the
variety of peoples that formed the first batch of settlers in Freetown, see the eyewitness
account of (Maj.) J. J. Crooks, *A History of the Colony of Sierra Leone, West Africa*

with *Maps and Appendices* (1893; reprint London: Browne and Nolan, Limited, 1903), 27–29.

58. This analogy makes sense in that both the Chibok girls and British White women had no voice in their cruel fate.

59. Crooks, *History of the Colony of Sierra Leone*, 28.

60. For all the names of these women and other passengers aboard the two ships, see National Archives Kew, "Transcript, The Passenger List of the Vernon and the Atlantic . . . ," http://www.nationalarchives.gov.uk/pathways/blackhistory/work_community/transcripts/atlantic_passengers.htm. See also Tim Butcher, *Chasing the Devil: A Journey through Sub-Saharan Africa in the Footsteps of Graham Greene* (New York: Atlas and Co., 2011).

61. Anna Maria Falconbridge, *Two Voyages to Sierra Leone during the Years 1791-2-3, in a Series of Letters* . . . (London: Printed by the author, 1794), 70.

62. Caroline Bressey, "Geographies of Belonging: White Women and Black History," in Lucy Bland and Katherine Rowold, eds., *Reconsidering Women's History: Twenty Years of the Women's History Network* (Abingdon, Oxon: Routledge, 2015), 21–38, here 30.

63. Crooks, *History of the Colony of Sierra Leone*, 29. For a touching description of what happened to the White women, see Anna Maria Falconbridge, *Narrative of Two Voyages to the River Sierra Leone during the Years 1791–1793 . . .*, ed. Christopher Fyfe (Liverpool: Liverpool University Press, 2000). Falconbridge concludes that the entire idea emanated from "minds unsullied with evil [and] meaning" (69).

64. *Substance of the report of the Court of Directors of the Sierra Leone Company to the General Court held at London on Wednesday the 19th of October, 1791* (London, 1792), 37. For a similar declaration, see also *The Times*, London, Dec. 3, 1792.

65. *The Times*, "Report from the Sierra Leone Colony," London, Oct. 14, 1793.

66. Isaac Land and Andrew M. Schocket, "New Approaches to the Founding of the Sierra Leone Colony, 1786–1808," *Journal of Colonialism and Colonial History* 9, no. 3 (2008): 1–19.

67. Private correspondence with Dr. A., June 16, 2009. I gained this insight from a White Portuguese professor born in Africa who claimed that he suffered severe discrimination in Lisbon, Portugal.

68. Dorjahn and Fyfe, "Landlord and Stranger," 394–95. Fyfe, *Sierra Leone Inheritance*, 267–69; and Chalmers, *Report by Her Majesty's Commissioner*.

69. Anna Maria Falconbridge and Ann Parker, in Deirdre Coleman, ed., *Maiden Voyages and Infant Colonies: Two Women's Travel Narratives of the 1790s* (Leicester: Leicester University Press, 1999), 10.

70. Lamin Sanneh, "Prelude to African Christian Independency: The Afro-American Factor in African Christianity," *Harvard Theological Review* 77, no. 1 (1984): 6.

71. *Substance of the Report Delivered by the Court of Directors of the Sierra Leone Company to the General Court of Proprietors, on Thursday the 27th March 1794* (London: Printed by James Phillips, 1794), 23. See also Zachary Macaulay, *Life and Letters of Zachary Macaulay by His Granddaughter, Viscountess Knutsford* (London: Edward Arnold, 1900), 137; and EAP284/3/1 and EAP284/3, John Clarkson's Letterbook and Journal (1791–1792).

72. *Substance of the Report Delivered by the Court of Directors of the Sierra Leone Company*, 24.

73. The first name of this "Beveshout" is not available in the handwritten "Book of Negroes," which contains only the last names of the Nova Scotia Blacks. It is preserved at the Nova Scotia Museum in Halifax.

74. See *Life and Letters of Zachary Macaulay*, entry for Sept. 17, 1793. For more on the American Negro, Thomas Peters, who appointed Beveshout precentor in the church, see W. E. B. Du Bois, *Black Folk Then and Now: An Essay in the History and Sociology of the Negro Race*, ed. Henry Louis Gates, Jr. (Oxford: Oxford University Press, 2007), 48.

75. Macaulay, *Life and Letters of Zachary Macaulay*, 157; Zachary Macaulay, MS journals, microfilms, Fourah Bay College Library, Freetown, Dec. 10 and 15, 1790. See also Fyfe, *History of Sierra Leone*, 74–83. For clarity, Macaulay first served as governor from March 1794 to May 6, 1795. His second term lasted from March 1796 to April 1799.

76. Zachary Macaulay, MS journals, Dec. 21, 1796. The Nova Scotians have never forgiven the Maroons for their role in putting down the 1800 uprising.

77. EAP284/3, John Clarkson's Letterbook and Journal (1791–1792), 150. See also William Whitaker Shreeve, *Sierra Leone: The Principal British Colony on the Western Coast of Africa* (London: Simmonds and Co., 1847), 5. Shreeve reiterated that there was a broken promise between the Nova Scotia Blacks and the colony's leaders in "refusing to allot to them the quantities of land for which they had previously stipulated," so that "distrust and discontent, neglect of agriculture, and inveterate habits of idleness, became general."

78. For studies on African resistance to slavery, see Anne Laurentin, "Nzakara Women (Central Africa)," in *Women in Tropical Africa*, trans. H. M. Wright, ed. Denise Paulme (London: Kegan Paul, 1963), 121–29, 137–45, 173–75; and Chisi Ndjurisiye Sichyajunga, "Slave (Central Africa 1890s)," in *Strategies of Slaves and Women: Life Stories from East/Central Africa*, ed. Marci Wright (New York: Lilian Barber Press, 1993), 81–90.

79. P. E. H. Hair, "Africanism: The Freetown Contribution," *Journal of African Studies* 5, no. 4 (1967): 526. See also Lewis H. Gann and Peter Duignan, *Africa and the World* (Lanham, MD: University Press of America), 476.

80. See the Church Missionary Society (CMS) Archives, O/1/87 and O/88/235: Section IV: African Relations, West Africa (Sierra Leone), 1803–1880.

81. Fyfe, *A History of Sierra Leone*, 119; Jeffrey A Fortin, "'Blackened beyond Our Native Hue': Removal, Identity and the Trelawney Maroons on the Margins of the Atlantic World, 1796–1800," *Citizenship Studies* 10, no. 1 (2006): 5–34, here 23.

82. Falconbridge, *Two Voyages to Sierra Leone*, 193. The Sierra Leone Company recorded similar accounts. See Sierra Leone Company, *Substance of the Report: Delivered, by the Court of Directors of the Sierra Leone Company to the General Court of proprietors, on Thursday the 29th March, 1798* . . . (London, James Philips, 1798).

83. See David C. Cole, "The Struggle for Respect: Paul Cuffee and His Nova Scotia Friends in Sierra Leone," *Symposium Proceedings Exploring Paul Cuffee: The Man*

and His Legacy (New Bedford, MA: New Bedford Whaling Museum, Oct. 3, 2009), 32–49. Cuffee's name is a corruption of the Kumasi (Ghana) word *kofi*; the *i* is pronounced "ee." Two different spellings of the name are encountered in the literature, "Cuffe" and "Cuffee." For consistency, the latter form is used throughout this book except in titles of certain publications.

84. Elwood Watson, "Cuffee, Paul, Sr. (1759–1817)," https://blackpast.org/aah/cuffe-paul -sr-1759-1817. Also see *Maryland Colonization Journal* 8, no. 8 (July 1856): 218.

85. Paul Cuffee, *Memoir of Captain Paul Cuffee: A Man of Colour . . .* (London: C. Peacock, 1812), 8–9. For details, see Town of Westport, Paul Cuffee's tax records for 1807, 1808, 1811, 1813, 1814, 1815, and 1817, Vital Records of Westport, MA, to the Year 1850.

86. *Edinburgh Review*, August 1811. See also Paul Cuffee, Personal and Family Papers (1759–1817). See specific file: John Cuffee notes relief from taxes and plantings, 1789, and also his draft of 14 petitions for relief from taxes dated Oct. 2, 1780. Microfiche courtesy of New Bedford Free Public Library, Westport, MA.

87. See *Chamber's Pocket Miscellany Volume XVII* (Edinburgh: William and Robert Chambers, 1853), 91.

88. Mark Hanna Watkins, "The West African Bush School," *American Journal of Sociology* 43 (1943): 666–74; and K. L. Little, "The Role of Secret Society in Cultural Specialization," *American Anthropologist* 51, no. 2 (1949): 199–212.

89. Suzanne Schwarz, *Zachary Macaulay and the Development of the Sierra Leone Company, 1793–94*, vol. 1 (Leipzig: Leipzig University Papers on Africa, 2000), 43, 61, 62–63; Walker, *The Black Loyalists*, 47, 171–77, 184, 198, 208; and Cassandra Pybus, *Epic Journeys of Freedom: Runaway Slaves of the American Revolution and Their Global Quest for Liberty* (Boston: Beacon Books, 2006), 213.

90. Macaulay, *Life and Letters of Zachary Macaulay*, 97.

91. Schwarz, *Zachary Macaulay*, 66; and Boston King, "Memoirs of Boston King, a Black Preacher," *Methodist Magazine* 21 (March 1798): 106–10.

92. Sierra Leone Company, *Substance of the Report Delivered by the Court of Directors Of the Sierra Leone Company to the General Court of Proprietors, on Thursday the 27th March, 1794* (London: James Phillips, 1794), 49, 66.

93. M. Y. Frenkel, "Edward Blyden and the Concept of African Personality," *African Affairs* 73 (1974): 284–85.

4. PRESIDENT JAMES MONROE AND THE COLONIZATION SOCIETY

1. James Monroe, House Journal, 16 Cong., 1 sess., Dec. 7, 1819, p. 18.

2. An Act of March 3, 1819, Ch. 101, 3 Stat. 532 CHAP. CI.—An Act in addition to the Acts prohibiting the slave trade (a). See also James Monroe, Special Message to the Senate and House of Representatives of the United States, Dec. 17, 1819. in James D. Richardson, *A Compilation of the Messages and Papers of the Presidents*, vol. 2 (Washington, DC: Bureau of National Literature, 1897).

3. The War of 1812 was over British violation of U.S. maritime rights. For more on the designs to flush out the free Blacks, see Matthew Carey, *Letters on the Colonization Society with a Review of its Probable Results* (Philadelphia: Young Printer, 1832), 5–7;

P. J. Straudenraus, *African Colonization Movement, 1816–65* (New York: Columbia University Press, 1961), vii.

4. Robert T. Brown, "Simon Greenleaf and the Liberian Constitution of 1847," *Liberian Studies Journal* 9, no. 2 (1980–1981): 51. Brown's conclusion echoes the scholarly work of Charles Henry Huberich, *The Political and Legislative History of Liberia* (New York: Central Book Company, 1947).

5. This ideology has been thoroughly explored by Christina Spicer in "The Perpetual Paradox: A Look into Liberian Colonization," *The Corvette* 3, no. 2 (2015–2016): 1–17. See also Svend E. Holsoe, "Matilda Newport: The Power of a Liberian-Invented Tradition," *Liberian Studies Journal* 32, no. 2 (2007): 28–41.

6. William Blyden, letter to the editor, *New Africa*, Monrovia, Nov. 7, 1899. William Blyden, who arrived in Liberia in 1850, was born in St. Thomas, Virgin Islands. For a similar idea held by the American Pilgrims, see Anonymous, *The Spirit of the Pilgrims for the Year 1830*, vol. 3 (Boston: Peirce and Parker, 1830), esp. 348, 524.

7. See Olive A. Taylor, "Blacks and the Constitution (II): Chief Justice John Marshall," *Washington Post*, July 4, 1987. Paul Finkelman, *Supreme Injustice: Slavery in the Highest Court* (Cambridge, MA: Harvard University Press, 2018), 170, provides insights on what drove Marshall's Supreme Court proslavery adjudications and biases against Blacks. Justice Marshall was himself a slave owner.

8. George W. Ellis, "Political Institutions in Liberia," *American Political Science Review* 5, no. 2 (1911): 213.

9. *Corfield v. Coryell*, 4 Wash. C.C. 371 (1823) 6 Fed. Case 546 (No. 3. 230); Bernard H. Siegan, *The Supreme Court's Constitution: An Inquiry into Judicial Review and Its Impact on Society* (New Brunswick, NJ: Transaction Publishers, 1987), 48; Joseph Njoh, *Liberia: The Path to War* (Ibadan, Nigeria: Spectrum Books, 2007), 32; Tommy L. Lott and John P. Pittman, eds., *A Companion to African American Philosophy* (Malden, MA: Blackwell Publishing, 1995), 431; and Charles Marrow Wilson, *Liberia: Black Africa in Microcosm* (New York: Harper and Row, 1971), 13.

10. Rev. Robert Finley to John O. Mumford, Feb. 15, 1815, reprinted in Isaac V. Brown, *Biography of the Reverend Robert Finley, of Basking Ridge, N.J.* (Philadelphia, 1857), 60, 61. See also African Repository, II, 2, 3, and Matthew Carey, *Letters on Colonization and its Probable Results addressed to C. F. Mercer* (Philadelphia, 1834), 7.

11. Rev. Robert Finley to John O. Mumford, Feb. 15, 1815 (italics added). For an extended account of the plans proposed before 1816 for removing the colored population, see H. N. Sherwood, "Early Negro Deportation Projects," *Mississippi Valley Historical Review* 2, no. 4 (1916): 485–508.

12. Rev. Robert Finley to John O. Mumford, Feb. 15, 1815. Microfiche, New Bedford Free Public Library, Westport, MA.

13. For more thoughts on the "Negro peril," see Booker Taliaferro Washington, *The Story of the Negro* (New York: Doubleday, 1909). Chap. 9 discusses the slave rebellions and the perils that confronted the Negro.

14. Thomas Jefferson, *Notes on the State of Virginia* (Philadelphia: Prichard and Hall, 1784), 154.

15. See also George Washington William, *The Story of the Negro* (New York: G. P. Putnam's Sons, 1882).

16. It took William Nesbit a fact-finding journey to Liberia in the 1850s to confirm his fears. William Nesbit, *Four Months in Liberia; or, African Colonization Exposed*, reprinted in Wilson Jeremiah Moses, ed., *Liberian Dreams: Back-to-Africa Narratives from the 1850s* (University Park: Pennsylvania State University Press, 1998), 79–125.

17. In fact, Gov. James Monroe saw the threat as "unquestionably the most serious and formidable" question facing society. See James Monroe to Thomas Jefferson, Sept. 15, 1800, in James Monroe, *The Writings of James Monroe*, ed. Stanislaus Murray Hamilton (New York: G. P. Putnam's Sons, 1900), 3: 208–09.

18. In March 2, 1807, United States Statute: "Importation Prohibited: An Act to prohibit the importation of Slaves into any port or place within the jurisdiction of the United States, from and after the first day of January, in the year of our Lord one thousand eight hundred and eight." Bills to amend §8, so as to make less ambiguous the permit given to the internal traffic, were introduced on Feb. 27 and Nov. 27, 1807. Statutes at Large, II, 426.

19. For a detailed record of this rebellion and the court trials, see Calendar of Virginia State Papers and Other Manuscripts Preserved in the Capital at Richmond, 11 vols. (Richmond, 1875–1893), 9: 134–74. This and related documents remain the most detailed record of the rebel trial. See also Henrico County Order Book No. 9, 1799–1801, pp. 372–401.

20. James Monroe to Thomas Jefferson, Richmond, VA, June 11, 1802; in James Monroe, *The Writings of James Monroe*, vol. 3: 1796–1802, *including a collection of his public and private and papers and correspondences now for the first time printed*, ed. Stanislaus Murray Hamilton (New York: G. P. Putnam's Sons, 1903), 353. Under a Virginia law passed on Dec. 17, 1792, Gabriel Prosser was subject to the death penalty. See *Statutes at Large of Virginia*, 3 vols. (Richmond, 1835–1836), vol. 1, ed. Samuel Shepard.

21. James Monroe to Thomas Jefferson, Richmond, VA, June 11, 1802; in Monroe, *The Writings of James Monroe*, 3: 352–53.

22. Thomas Jefferson to Rufus King, July 13, 1802, *Thomas Jefferson Papers*, Series 1, General Correspondence, 1651–1827.

23. Thomas Jefferson, *Notes on the State of Virginia* (Philadelphia: Prichard and Hall, 1784), Query XIV, 138–39.

24. Thomas Jefferson and Henry Augustine, *The Writings of Thomas Jefferson, Being His Autobiography, Correspondences, Reports, Opinions, Messages, Addresses, and Other Writings Official and Private* (New York: Derby and Jackson, 1859), 333. David Reeves Goodloe, *The Southern Platform, or Manual of Southern Sentiment on the Southern Slavery* (Boston: John P. Jewett and Co., 1858), 36.

25. Jefferson and Augustine, *The Writings of Thomas Jefferson, Being His Autobiography, Correspondences Reports, Opinions*, 333.

26. From Thomas Jefferson to Jared Sparks, Feb. 4, 1824. About two decades later these controversial statements were used in a legal deliberation in London. See George

Sweet, *Cases on a Wife's Separate Estate and Equity to a Settlement Out of Her Equitable Property* (London: S. Sweet and Co., 1840).

27. Christa Dierksherida, "Jefferson and the Amelioration of Slavery," *Early American Studies* 6, no. 1 (2008): 165–97.

28. James Monroe to Gen. John Mason, Aug. 31 1829, James Monroe Papers, New York Public Library, reel 4. See also Monroe to Jefferson, June 15, 1801, in Monroe, *The Writings of James Monroe*, 3: 294, n. 52.

29. By way of emphasis, slave owners like Monroe and Andrew Jackson were determined to do everything humanly possible to avoid the threat of free and emancipated Blacks inciting rebellion among enslaved people in the U.S. southern states.

30. Act of March 3, 1819, Ch. 101, 3 Stat. 532, 532–34. The deal and terms of payment surrounding the purchase are not apparent. There are still doubts as to whether money exchanged hands. What is more apparent is that the African chiefs received goods including bottles of alcoholic spirits.

31. Jane Ailes and Marie Tyler-McGraw, "Leaving Virginia for Liberia: Western Virginia Emigrants and Emancipators," *West Virginia History*, n.s. 6, no. 2 (2012): 2–3.

32. Solomon D. Parker (Hampshire County, VA) to R. R. Gurley (Washington, DC), Nov. 18, 1834, Digital Image, RACS, http://www.fold3.com/image/ #27423925 (accessed on May 23, 2018).

33. See the will of Robert Parker, Hampshire County, WV, Loose Wills, Will No. 491, signed Sept. 13, 1805, proved Dec. 16, 1816; in Hu Maxwell and H. L. Swisher, *Hampshire County, West Virginia, from Its Earliest Settlement to the Present* (1897; reprint Parsons, WV: McClain Publishing, 1972), 723–34.

34. Sherwood, "Early Negro Deportation Project," 498.

35. Eli Seifman, "The United Colonization Societies of New-York and Pennsylvania and the Establishment of the African Colony of Bassa Cove," *Pennsylvania History* 35, no. 1 (1968): 23–44; and anonymous, "View of Bassa Cove," *Colonization Herald* 3, no. 54 (June 17, 1837): 4. See also Beverly C. Tomek, *Colonization and Its Discontents: Emancipation, Emigration, and Antislavery in Antebellum Pennsylvania* (New York: New York University Press, 2011), 15. As Tomek concluded, this is a proof of the sincerity of the staunch opposition to slavery by some of the gradualists and supporters of colonization.

36. Statute 47 George III., 1 sess., Ch. 36: "An Act for the Abolition of the Slave Trade," March 25, 1807.

37. See minutes of the action between U.S. frigate *Constitution* and H.M. ships *Cyane* and *Levant*, Feb. 20, 1815; and Roland P. Falkner, "The United States and Liberia," *American Journal of International Law* 4, no. 3 (1910): 529–45, here 531.

38. National Archives Microfilm Publications, Correspondence of the [U.S.] Secretary of the Navy relating to African colonization, 1819–1844 (Washington, DC: National Archives and Records Office, 1955), 4. See also *African Repository and Colonial Journal* 1 (March 1825): 3–4; and Allan E. Yarema, *American Colonization Society: An Avenue to Freedom?* (Lanham, MD: University Press of America, 2006), 39–40.

39. Falkner, "The United States and Liberia," 532.

40. President Monroe's Message to Congress, Nov. 14, 1820, Senate Journal, 16 Cong. 2 sess., pp. 16–17.
41. Falkner, "The United States and Liberia," 532.
42. See Mr. Gurley to the President, Washington, DC, Feb. 2, 1844; enclosure 28th Congress, DOC, No. 162, House of Reps. 1st Session, Executive.
43. Thomas Buchanan was a cousin of the fifteenth president of the United States, who was in office from 1857 to 1861.
44. This description of the African natives appeared in William Blyden, letter to the editor, *New Africa*, Monrovia, Nov. 7, 1899. For details of Buchanan's activities in Liberia, see Cuthbert Christy, "Liberia in 1930," *Geographical Journal* 77, no. 6 (1931): 521, 535. Dr. Christy read his paper at the evening meeting of the American Colonization Society on March 31, 1931.
45. For a vivid interpretation of the symbolic representations of the Stars and Stripes on the Liberian flag, see Frederick Starr, *Liberia: Description, History and Problems* (Chicago, 1913), 37, 87. The British were unable to stop the American slave ships because they had yet to acquire the right to search them.
46. Ibid., 87.
47. Liberia Independence Constitution, XIII, sect v.
48. Beverly C. Tomek, *Colonization and Its Discontents: Emancipation, Emigration, and Antislavery in Antebellum Pennsylvania* (New York: New York University Press, 2010), 39–40.
49. Forten cited in ibid.
50. See Forten, letter to Cuffee, in *Captain Paul Cuffee's Logs and Letters, 1808–1817*, ed. Rosalind Cobb Wiggins (Washington, DC: Howard University Press, 1996).
51. See Richard S. Newman, *Freedom's Prophet: Bishop Richard Allen, the AME Church, and the Black Founding Fathers* (New York: New York University Press, 2008).
52. Edward Wright Haile, ed., *Jamestown Narratives: Eyewitness Accounts of the Virginia Colony: The First Decade: 1607–1617* (Chaplain, VA: Roundhouse, 1998).
53. For an engaging discussion, see Antonio McDaniel, *Swing Low, Sweet Chariot: The Mortality Cost of Colonizing Liberia in the Nineteenth Century* (Chicago: University of Chicago Press, 1994). See also James W. Lugenbeel, *Sketches of Liberia: Comprising a Brief Account of the Geography, Climate, Productions, and Diseases, of the Republic of Liberia* (Washington, DC: C. Alexander, printer, 1850).
54. Jehudi Ashmun, *History of the American Colony in Liberia from December 1821 to 1823* (Washington, DC, 1826), 24. For an insightful account of the prejudices and arrogant ideas the ACS and the settlers brought to the colony, see Jehudi Ashmun, "Traits of the African Character," *African Repository and Colonial Journal* 1, no. 1 (1825): 56–62. See also Ralph Randolph Gurley, *The Life of Jehudi Ashmun, Late Colonial Agent in Liberia* (New York, 1839), 319, 331.
55. Gurley, *The Life of Jehudi Ashmun*, 155.
56. John Rolf to (Sir) Edwin Sandys, "20 and odd Negroes: An Excerpt from a Letter dated 1619/1620," transcription from *The Thomas Jefferson Papers*, Ser. 8. Virginia Records Manuscripts, 1606–1737. Other sources on the early periods of the colony also

suggest that the African presence was critical to the colony's survival. See also Susan Myra Kingsbury, ed., *The Records of the Virginia Company of London, 1606–1626* (Washington, DC: Government Printing Office, 1905), and H. R. McIlwaine, *Minutes of the Council and General Court of Colonial Virginia, 1622–1632, 1670–1676, with notes and excerpts from the original Council and General Court records* (Richmond, VA, 1924).

57. See James Barnett Taylor, *Biography of Elder Lott Cary, Late Missionary to Africa, with an Appendix on the Subject of Colonization, by J. H. B. Latrobe* (Baltimore: Armstrong and Berry, 1837), 46–47; G. S. Stockwell, *The Republic of Liberia: Its Geography, Climate, Soil, and Productions with the History of its Early Settlements* (New York: A. S. Barnes and Co., 1868), 82; and Gurley, *Life of Jehudi Ashman*, 233–34.

58. See "Treaty of Gourah," *Digest Art* 39, "Laws of the Colony of Liberia, 1820–1838," cited in Henk Dop and Philip T. Robinson, eds., *Travel Sketches from Liberia: Johann Büttikofer's Nineteenth-Century Rainforest Explorations in West Africa* (Leiden: Brill, 2013), 842; Gurley, *Life of Jehudi Ashman*, 233; Charles Henry Huberich, *The Political and Legislative History of Liberia: A Documentary History of the Constitution, Laws and Treaties of Liberia from the Establishment of the Republic . . .* (New York: Central Book Co., 1947), 339–40. See also Büttikofer, *Travel Sketches from Liberia*, 419–20.

59. Some of the most detailed and compelling treatments of these clashes include Ibrahim Sundiata, *Brothers and Strangers: Black Zion, Black Slavery, 1914–1940* (Durham, NC: Duke University Press, 2003), esp. chaps. 1–3; and Elliot Skinner, *African Americans and U.S. Policy towards Africa, 1850–1924: In Defense of Black Nationality* (Washington, DC: Howard University Press, 1992). The authors treat the history of these conflicts candidly and explicitly.

60. Gurley, *Life of Jehudi Ashman*, 55–56.

61. Davis in *Stanford Report*, March 1, 2016.

62. Ibid.

63. Such charitable support was part of a larger pattern of women's benevolence in antebellum America. Many considered the missions and schools natural interests of middle-class Christian women.

64. Karen Fisher Younger, "Philadelphia's Ladies' Liberia School Association and the Rise and Decline of Northern Female Colonization Support," *Pennsylvania Magazine of History and Biography* 134, no. 3 (July 2010): 235–61.

65. "Declaration of Independence in Convention," in *Liberia Statutes, 1847–1857* (Monrovia, 1857), 18.

66. Brandon Mills, "'The United States of Africa': Liberian Independence and the Contested Meaning of a Black Republic," *Journal of the Early Republic* 34, no. 1 (2014): 82; Etsuko Taketani, "Postcolonial Liberia: Sarah Josepha Hale's Africa," *American Literary History* 14 (2002): 479–504; and Bronwen Everill, "British West Africa or 'The United States of Africa'? Imperial Pressures on the Transatlantic Anti-Slavery Movement, 1839–1842," *Journal of Transatlantic Studies* 9 (2011): 136–50.

67. Martin Luther King, Jr., cited in Hollie I. West, "Marcus Garvey, Hero," *Washington Post*, Aug. 18, 1980. See also Barbara Gloudon, "When Dr. King Praised Us," *Kings-*

ton, Jamaica, *Jamaica Observer*, Aug. 30, 2013; and Leonard E. Barret, *Soul-Force: African Heritage in Afro-American Religion* (Norwell, MA: Anchor Press, 1974), 151.

5. AMERICAN MISSIONARIES IN AFRICA, 1780–1920S

1. Themes relating to the American Revolution, the founding of the colony of Sierra Leone, and the American settlement of Liberia, among other historical developments of this era, have been covered in separate chapters. These topics ran parallel across time and are, therefore, challenging to periodize.
2. See William C. Kashatus III, "The Inner Light and Popular Enlightenment: Philadelphia Quakers and Charity Schooling, 1790–1820," *Pennsylvania Magazine of History and Biography* 118, nos. 1 and 2 (1994): 87–116.
3. See for instance Sandy Dwayne Martin, *Black Baptists and African Missions: The Origins of a Movement, 1880–1915* (Macon, GA: Mercer University Press, 1989); Sylvia M. Jacobs, ed., *Black Americans and the Missionary Movement in Africa* (Westport, CT: Greenwood Press, 1982), and L. G. Jordan, *Up the Missions* (Nashville: National Baptist Publishing Board, 1901).
4. David Killingray, "The Black Atlantic Missionary Movement and Africa, 1780s–1920s," *Journal of Religion in Africa* 33, no. 1 (2003): 1–31; and Adrian Hastings, *The Church in Africa: 1450–1950* (Oxford: Clarendon Press, 1994), 175.
5. For more on this topic, see Ivana Elbi, "Cross-Cultural Trade and Diplomacy: Portuguese Relations with West Africa, 1441–1521," *Journal of World History* 3, no. 2 (1992): 165–204; and J. O. Ijoma, "Portuguese Activities in West Africa Before 1600: The Consequences," *Transafrican Journal* 11 (1982): 136–46.
6. John K. Thornton, *Africa and Africans in the Making of the Atlantic World, 1400–1800*, 2nd ed. (Cambridge: Cambridge University Press, 1998), 268. See also John K. Thornton, "On the Trail of Voodoo: African Christianity in Africa and the Americas," *The Americas* 44, no. 3 (1988): 261–78; and John Thornton, *The Kongolese Saint Anthony: Dona Beatriz Kimpa Vita and the Antonian Movement, 1684–1706* (Cambridge: Cambridge University Press, 1998).
7. Ann Laura Stoler, "Tense and Tender Ties: The Politics of Comparison in North American History and (Post) Colonial Studies," in *Haunted by Empire: Geographies of Intimacy in North American History*, ed. Ann Laura Stoler (Durham: Duke University Press, 2006), 23.
8. Tertius de Wet, Jef L. Teugels, and Pieta van Deventer, "Historic Bell: Moravian Missions in South Africa's Western Cape," *Historia* 59, no. 2 (2014): 94–119. See also B. Krüger and P. W. Schaberg, *The Pear Tree Bears Fruit: The History of the Moravian Church in South Africa-West*, vol. 2: *1869–1960, with an Epilogue, 1960–1980* (Genadendal, South Africa: Moravian Book Depot, 1984). The Moravians were committed to Christian evangelism and devoted to "the conversion of the heathen" (p. 96).
9. Thomas Thompson, *An Account of Two Missionary Voyages* (London: Society for the Propagation of the Gospel in Foreign Parts, 1758), vii, xiii.

10. Thompson, *An Account of Two Missionary Voyages*, xiii. For details of Quaque's career, see Richard J. Mammana, Jr., Review: *The Life and Letters of Philip Quaque, the First African Anglican Missionary, International Bulletin of Missionary Research* 35, no. 2 (2011): 112-113; and Vincent Carretta and Ty M. Reese, eds., *The Life and Letters of Philip Quaque, the First African Anglican Missionary* (Athens: University of Georgia Press, 2010), 44–45.

11. Katherine Reid Gerbner, "Christian Slavery: Protestant Missions and Slave Conversion in the Atlantic World, 1660–1760" (Ph.D. diss., Harvard University, 2013), iii.

12. David Killingray, "The Black Atlantic Missionary Movement and Africa, 1780s–1920s," *Journal of Religion in Africa* 33, no. 1 (2003): 1–31; and Adrian Hastings, *The Church in Africa: 1450–1950* (Oxford: Clarendon Press, 1994), 175.

13. Andrew Porter, *Religion versus Empire? British Protestant Missionaries and Overseas Expansion, 1700–1914* (Manchester: Manchester University Press, 2004), 76. See also Norman Etherington and David Maxwell, "Missions and Empire," *Journal of Religion in Africa* 34, nos. 1 and 2 (2004): 194–99.

14. Lamin Sanneh, "'A Plantation of Religion' and the Enterprise Culture in Africa: History, Ex-Slaves and Religious Inevitability," *Journal of Religion and Society* 27, no. 1 (1997): 15–49, here 16.

15. W. Garden Blaikie, *The Personal Life of Davis Livingston, Chiefly from the Unpublished Journals and Correspondence in the Possession of the Family* (London: John Murray, 1880), 19.

16. Vincent Carretta, *Equiano: Biography of a Self-Made Man* (New York: Penguin Books, 2007); and Vincent Carretta, "Olaudah Equiano or Gustavus Vassa? New Light on an Eighteenth-Century Question of Identity," *Slavery and Abolition* 20, no. 3 (1999): 96–105, here 103–04. While Carretta concludes that Equiano's autobiography—which claims that he was born in Africa—was in part a lie, he raises the possibility that Equiano may have been born in South Carolina. For a refutation of this idea, see Paul Lovejoy, Review of *Equiano, the African: Biography of a Self-Made Man* by Vincent Carretta, *Journal of Southern History* 73, no. 1 (2007): 150–51.

17. David Kofi Amponsah, "Christian Slavery, Colonialism, and Violence: The Life and Writings of an African Ex-Slave, 1717–1747," *Journal of Africana Religion* 1, no. 4 (2013): 431–57.

18. Martin Marty, *Modern American Religion: The Noise of Conflict, 1919–1941*, vol. 2 (Chicago: University of Chicago Press, 1991), 111.

19. Annette Laing, "Heathens and Infidels? African Christianization and Anglicanism in the South Carolina Low Country, 1700–1750," *Religion and American Culture: A Journal of Interpretation* 12, no. 2 (2002): 197–228.

20. Francis Le Jau to the Secretary, Feb. 1 and 19, 1710, and Sept. 18, 1711; in Frank J. Klingberg, *The Carolina Chronicle of Dr. Francis Le Jau, 1706–1717*, edited with an introduction and notes by Frank J. Klingberg (Berkeley: University of California Press, 1956), 69, 77, 102.

21. Francis Le Jau to Society for the Propagation of the Gospel (SPG), Nov. 15, 1708, in Klingberg, *Carolina Chronicle of Dr. Francis Le Jau*, 48.

22. See William Cotes to Society for the Propagation of the Gospel, St. George's Parish, Dorchester, Jan. 4, 1749, SPG Letter Books, B/16/147. See also Laing, "Heathens and Infidels?" 215.

23. Laing, "Heathens and Infidels?" 204.

24. See Frank Lambert, "'Peddler in Divinity': George Whitefield and the Great Awakening, 1737–1745," *Journal of American History* 77, no. 3 (1990): 812–37; and Peter Y. Choi and Mark A. Noll, *George Whitefield: Evangelist for God and Empire* (Grand Rapids, MI: William B. Eerdmans Publishing Group, 2018).

25. See Alan Gallay, *The Formation of a Planter Elite: Jonathan Bryan and the Southern Colonial Frontier* (Athens: University Press of Georgia, 1989), 38–39.

26. Travis Glasson, *Mastering Christianity: Missionary Anglicanism and Slavery in the Atlantic World* (Oxford: Oxford University Press, 2012), 125–26.

27. Gallay, *The Formation of a Planter Elite*, 52; Glasson, *Mastering Christianity*, 126; and Little, *Origins of South Carolina Evangelism*, 159.

28. Gallay, *The Formation of a Planter Elite*, 53; Laing, "Heathens and Infidels?" 216; and Leigh Eric Schmidt, "The Grand Prophet: Hugh Bryan and the Evangelical Movement in Colonial South Carolina," *South Carolina Historical Magazine* 87, no. 4 (1989): 238–50.

29. Laing, "Heathens and Infidels?" 216.

30. See Gallay, *The Formation of a Planter Elite*, 393.

31. Leon Terrell, *The History of Calvary Baptist Church at Bayou Chicot* (Bayou Chicot, LA: L. Terrell, 1992).

32. Cassandra R. Veney, "The Ties that Bind: The Historic African Diaspora and Africa," *African Issues* 30, no. 1 (2002): 6.

33. Lawrence Sanders Rowland, *The History of South Carolina: 1514–1861* (Columbia: University of South Carolina Press, 1996), 134–35.

34. Walter H. Brooks, "The Evolution of the Negro Baptist Church," *Journal of Negro History* 7, no. 1 (1922): 11–22, here 17. See also Langston Hughes, *African American History: Four Centuries of Black Life* (New York: Scholastic, 1990), 81; and Noel Leo Erskine, *Plantation Church: How African American Religion Was Born in Caribbean Slavery* (Oxford: Oxford University Press, 2014), 88.

35. James A. Quirin, "'Her Sons and Daughters Are Ever on the Altar': Fisk University and Missionaries to Africa, 1866–1937," *Tennessee Historical Quarterly* 60, no. 1 (2001): 16–37.

36. Walter L. Williams, *Black Americans and the Evangelization of Africa: 1877–1900* (Madison: University of Wisconsin Press, 1982), 4, 10–29.

37. Gayraud Wilmore, *Black Religion, Black Radicalism* (Maryknoll, NY: Orbis Press, 1986), 102. See also Gwinya H. Muzorewa, *The Origin and Development of African Theology* (Eugene, OR: Wipf and Stock Publishers, 1987), 118; and Larry G. Murphy, "All Things to All People: The Functions of the Black Church in the Last Quarter of the Nineteenth Century," in Larry G. Murphy, ed., *Down by the Riverside: Readings in African American Religion* (New York: New York University Press, 2000), 319.

38. See J. B. Bury, *The Idea of Progress: An Inquiry into Its Origin and Growth* (1920; reprint Auckland, NZ: The Floating Press, 2009), 178. See also Lawrence S. Smith, *Disciples of Liberty: The African Methodist Episcopal Church in the Age of Imperialism, 1884–1916* (Knoxville: University of Tennessee Press, 2000); and Ikenna U. Okafor, *Towards an African Theology of Fraternal Solidarity: Ube Nwanne* (Eugene, OR: Pickwick Publications, 2014).

39. See C. L. Woolworth, *Historic Correspondences in Africa and America* (Boston, 1889), 1, 6, 13–14; Williams, *Black Americans and the Evangelization of Africa*, 6–7; and Quirin, "Her Sons and Daughters," 18.

40. Williams, *Black Americans and the Evangelization of Africa*.

41. R. Drew Smith, "Black Religious Nationalism and the Politics of Transcendence," *Journal of the American Academy of Religion* 66, no. 3 (1998): 534.

42. Washington S. Chaffin, Sermons, January 1845–June 1962, in W. S. Chaffin Papers, Duke University Libraries, Manuscript Department, Durham, NC, 87–88.

43. James H. Thornwell, *Thoughts Suited to the Present Crisis* (Columbia, SC: n.p., 1850), 29.

44. Williams's biography makes it clear that the parent church in New York mistreated him. See John H. Hewitt, "Peter Williams Jr.: New York's First African American Episcopal Priest," *New York History* 79, no. 2 (1998): 119.

45. See Carter G. Woodson, *The History of the Negro Church* (Washington, DC: The Associated Publishers, 1921), 83.

46. Kenneth C. Barnes, "'On the Shore beyond the Sea': Black Missionaries from Arkansas in Africa during the 1890s," *Arkansas Historical Quarterly* 61, no. 4 (2002): 329–56, here 330–31; Williams, *Black Americans and the Evangelization of Africa*, 7–9, 184–90.

47. See L. G. Jordan, *Up the Ladder in Foreign Missions* (Nashville: National Baptist Publishing Board, 1901; reprinted New York: Arno Press, 1980), 88–90; and Sandy Dwayne Martin, *Black Baptists and African Missions: The Origins of a Movement 1880–1915* (Macon, GA: Mercer University Press, 1989), 56–106. See also Williams, *Black Americans and the Evangelization of Africa*, 39–40; and Sandy Dwayne Martin, "Black Baptists, Foreign Missions, and African Colonization, 1814–1882," in *Black Americans and the Missionary Movement in Africa*, ed. Sylvia M. Jacobs (Westport, CT: Greenwood Press, 1982), 63–76.

48. It was the AMA under the championship of Erastus Milo Cravath, Edward P. Smith, and John Ogden that served the Freedmen's Bureau of Tennessee, which worked to establish a school for freed slaves in Nashville in 1866. This school was renamed Fisk University in 1867.

49. Quirin, "'Her Sons and Daughters,'" 12.

50. Ibid., 16–37.

51. See Alferdeen Harrison, ed., *Black Exodus: The Great American Migration from the American South* (Jackson: University Press of Mississippi, 1991).

52. Kenneth C. Barnes, "'On the Shore beyond the Sea': Black Missionaries from Arkansas in Africa during the 1890s," *Arkansas Historical Quarterly* 2002: 329–56.

53. Data about the African American emigrants to Liberia in three voyages sponsored by the International Migration Society from 1894 to 1896 came from Edwin S. Redkey,

Black Exodus: Black Nationalist and Back-to-Africa Movements, 1890–1910 (New Haven, CT: Yale University Press, 1969), 205–51.
54. Williams, *Black Americans and the Evangelization of Africa*, 160.
55. Sylvia M. Jacobs, ed., "The Impact of Black American Missionaries in Africa," *Black Americans and the Missionary Movement in Africa* (Westport, CT: Greenwood Press, 1982), 219–28, here 220.
56. Ibid.
57. Turner, cited in *The Christian Recorder*, Jan. 22, 1883. Turner goes on to declare that he does not believe that God ordained slavery, but he maintains that "it was a providential institution and that God intends to make it the primal factor in the civilization and Christianization of that dark continent." See Thomas Allan Scott, ed., *Documents that Formed the State* (Athens: University of Georgia Press, 1995), 168.
58. See E. A. Anyandele, *'Holy' Johnson: Pioneer of African Nationalism, 1836–1917* (Oxford: Frank Cass, 1970), 366. See also Pieter Boele van Hensbroek, *Political Discourses in African Thought, 1860–the Present* (Westport, CT: Praeger, 1999), 43.
59. Edward Wilmot Blyden, *Christianity, Islam and the Negro Race*, with an introduction by Christopher Fyfe (1887; reprint Edinburgh: Edinburgh University Press, 1967), 278; Edward Wilmot Blyden, *The Prospects of the African: An Address Delivered at the Celebration of the Independence of Liberia, held in the Grounds of David Chinery, Esq., Monday, July 27, 1874*, in Edward Wilmot Blyden, *Selected Works of Edward Wilmot Blyden* (Robertsport, Liberia: Tubman Center of African Culture, 1976), 7–9; Robert W. July, "Nineteenth Century Negritude: Edward W. Blyden," *Journal of African History* 5, no. 1 (1964): 73–86, here 80.
60. Edward Wilmot Blyden, *Liberia's Offering: Being Addresses, Sermons, Etc. by Rev. Edward W. Blyden* (New York: John A. Gray, 1862), 75.
61. See K. J. King, "The American Negro as Missionary to East Africa: A Critical Aspect of African Evangelism," *African Historical Studies* 3, no. 1 (1970): 5–22, here 19–22. See New York Public Library (NYPL), Archives and Manuscript Division, Phelps-Stokes Fund Records, ScMG162, Schomburg Center for Research in Black Culture.
62. AA/M/636/6, letter from Secretary General on behalf of Minister for the Colonies to Governor General, dated May 20, 1920; African Archives of the Ministry of Foreign Affairs (Ministère des Affaires Étrangères), Rue des Petits Carmes, Brussels, Belgium.
63. Ibid.
64. See George Waveland Carpenter, "African Education and the Christian Missions," *The Phi Delta Kappan* 41, no. 4 (1960): 191–95; and Sylvia M. Jacobs, "James Emman Kwegyir: An African Intellectual in the United States," *Journal of Negro History* 81, nos. 1 and 4 (1996): 47–61.
65. Phelps-Stokes Commission, *African Education Commission: Education in East Africa*, abridged with an introduction by L. J. Lewis (1924; reprint London: Oxford University Press, 1962).
66. Edward H. Berman, "American Influence on African Education: The Role of the Phelps-Stokes Fund's Education Commissions," *Comparative Education Review* 15, no. 2 (1971): 132–45.

67. Edwin William Smith, *The Christian Mission in Africa: A Study Based on the Proceedings of the International Conference at Le Zoute, Belgium, Sept. 14–21, 1926* (London: The International Missionary Council, 1926), 122–23.

68. David Killingray, "The Black Atlantic Movement and Africa, 1780s–1920s," *Journal of Religion in Africa* 33, no. 1 (2003): 3–31, here 22.

69. Modupe Labode, "'A Native Knows a Native': African American Missionaries' Writings about Angola, 1919–1940," *The North Star: Journal of African American Religious History* 4, no. 1 (2000): 1.

70. H. C. McDowell, Sept. 16, 1919, HCM/Aug./2/4/3, Slavery Library, Talladega College.

71. Ibid.

72. H. C. McDowell, "Galangue News," *The Amistad*, February 1935: 5.

73. J. Mutero Chirenje, *Ethiopianism and African Americans in Southern Africa, 1883–1916* (Baton Rouge: Louisiana State University Press, 1987).

74. See "Memorandum on the Ethiopian Movement and the Attitude Toward It by the Several S.A.-Govts," 1904; TNA, DO 119/522, no. D 42/1, 1–2.

75. See Nyasaland Protectorate, Report of the Education Department, May 1926–December 1927, CO 525/125/15. 20; Annual General Report for Sierra Leone for 1927, CO 267/626/18. 24–25; and Gold Coast Colony, Report on the Education Department for the Year 1935–1936, CO 96/733/23. 19. All TNA.

76. William David Schermerhorn, *The Christian Mission in the Modern World* (New York: Literary Licensing LLC, 1912), 247.

77. See, for instance, "The Rev. S. B. A. Campbell, M.A., B.D., Ph.D.: A Brilliant Career," *Sierra Leone Guardian*, Feb. 7, 1930: 11; and "Wise Words by the Black Bishop," *South African Outlook*, June 1, 1922: 127.

78. The British colonial government, formed in 1910, issued the Immigration Restriction Act of the Union of South Africa (no. 22, 1913) prohibiting the entry of colored persons. This policy was intended to exclude the AME missionaries. For the act, see Office of the International Missionary Council, *Treaties, Acts and Regulations Relating to Missionary Freedom* (London: IMC, 1923), 27. For AME staff immigration, see Charles Spencer Smith, *A History of the African Methodist Episcopal Church . . .* (Philadelphia: AME Church Book Concern, 1922), 331–36; and Lillie M. Johnson, "Missionary–Government Relations in British and Portuguese Colonies," in *Black Americans and the Missionary Movement in Africa*, ed. Sylvia M. Jacobs (Westport, CT: Greenwood Publishing, 1982), 203.

79. Chirenje, *Ethiopianism and Afro-Americans*.

80. William Cohen, "The Great Migration as a Lever of Social Change," in *Black Exodus: The Great Migration from the American South*, ed. Alferdeen Harrison (Jackson: University Press of Mississippi, 1991), 72–82.

81. W. E. B. Du Bois, *The Negro Church: Report of a Social Study Made under the Direction of Atlanta University; Together with the Proceedings of the Eighth Conference for the Study of the Negro Problems Held at Atlanta University, May 26, 1903* (Atlanta: The Atlanta University Press, 1903).

82. Felix K. Ekechi, *Missionary Enterprise and Rivalry in Igboland, 1857–1914* (London: Frank Cass, 1972), 22. See also H. A. C. Cairns, *Prelude to Imperialism* (London: Routledge and Kegan Paul, 1965), 10–11.

83. James Fernandez, "Fang Representations under Acculturation," in *Africa and the West*, ed. Philip Curtin (Madison: University of Wisconsin Press, 1972), 25–26.

6. THE BACK-TO-AFRICA MOVEMENT/BLACK ZIONISM, 1916–1940

1. Marcus Garvey, "The Principles of the Universal Negro Improvement Association," Speech delivered at Liberty Hall, New York City, Nov. 25, 1922. Printed in *The Philosophy and Opinions of Marcus Garvey or Africa for Africans*, vol. 2, ed. Amy Jacques-Garvey and Tony Martin (1922; reprint Dover, MA, 1986), 93–100.

2. Howard Dodson and Sylviane Anne Diouf, *In Motion: The African American Experience* (New York: National Geographic, 2005), 74. See also William Lloyd Garrison, *Thoughts on African American Colonization* (New York: Firework Press, 1832). Among other things, Garrison accused the ACS of enabling slavery and deceiving and misleading the nation.

3. James Forten, "Address at the Mother Bethel African American Episcopal Church, Philadelphia," Jan. 15, 1817.

4. Peter Williams, "Slavery and Colonization: A Discourse Delivered at St. Philip's Church, 4 July 1830." This episode was not the first time the reportedly reserved antislavery crusader had spoken out against the evil trade. See, for instance, Peter Williams, "An Oration on the Abolition of the Slave Trade, delivered in the African Church in the City of New York, 1 January 1808." The text of both speeches is in Carter G. Woodson, ed., *Negro Orators and Their Orations* (Washington, DC: The Associated Publishers, 1925), 32–41, 77–85. See also Dorothy Porter, *Early Negro Writing, 1760–1837* (Baltimore: Black Classic Press), 297; and Christian G. Samito, ed., *Changes in Law and Society during the Civil War and Reconstruction* (Carbondale: Southern Illinois University Press, 2009), 32.

5. This point was the central message of the UNIA's 1921 convention in New York City.

6. For a detailed look at all the various cultural productions emerging from the Harlem Renaissance, see Cary D. Wintz, ed., *The Harlem Renaissance, 1920–1940*, vol. 5: *Remembering the Harlem Renaissance* (New York: Garland Publishing, Inc., 1996).

7. Pan-Africanism as a movement has captured the fascination of scholars. A few examples of the literature include George A. Shepperson, "Ethiopianism and African Nationalism," *Phylon* 14 (1953): 9–18; "Notes on the Negro American Influences on the Emergence of African Nationalism," *Journal of African History* 1 (1960): 299–312; George Padmore, *Pan-Africanism or Communism? The Coming Struggle for Africa* (London: Doubleday Anchor, 1956); Colin Legum, *Pan-Africanism: A Short Political Guide* (New York: Frederick A. Praeger, 1962); J. Ayodele Langley, *Pan-Africanism and Nationalism in West Africa, 1900–1945* (Oxford: Oxford University Press, 1973); Imanuel Geiss, *The Pan-African Movement* (London: Africana Publishing, 1974); and

P. Olisanwuche Esedebe, *Pan-Africanism: The Idea and Movement, 1776–1991* (Washington, DC: Howard University Press, 1982).

8. Letters from Marcus Mosiah Garvey to Booker T. Washington, West Indies, Sept. 8, 1914, and Sept. 11, 1915, http://btwsociety.org/letters/index.php?file=1914-09-08-from-marcus-mosiah-garvey (accessed on Sept. 27, 2018).

9. Marcus Garvey, "If You Believe the Negro Has a Soul" (1921); and "Garvey Explains the Objectives of the Universal Negro Improvement Association (New York, 1921). Courtesy of the Marcus Garvey and the Universal Negro Improvement Association (UNIA) Papers Project at the University of California, Los Angeles, http://historymatters .gmu.edu/d/5124/ (accessed on Sept. 27, 2018).

10. "Marcus Garvey 'Provisional President of Africa' has his African Plan Rejected," photograph (New York: Keystone View Company, [1920?]), Library of Congress, Reproduction No. LC-USZ62–109627, http://www.loc.gov/pictures/item/94509041/ (accessed on Sept. 27, 2018).

11. David Levering Lewis, *W. E. B. Du Bois: The Fight for Equality and the American Century, 1919–1963* (New York: Henry Holt and Company, 2000), 52.

12. For an interesting exposition on the origins, disposition, character, manners, and survival instincts of the Jamaica Maroons, including their war with the British, see Bryan Edwards, *Maroon Societies: Rebel Slave Communities in the Americas*, ed. Richard Price (Baltimore: The Johns Hopkins University Press, 1973), 231. Leeward and Windward Maroon communities' combined population reached well over 1,000 by 1735; these communities had developed an independent economy and material culture.

13. W. E. B. Du Bois, *The Souls of Black Folk* (Chicago: A. C. McClurg and Co., 1903), vii, 3–4, 108.

14. Marcus Garvey, "The Negro's Greatest Enemy," in Garvey, *Philosophy and Opinions*, vol. 2, ed. Amy Jacques-Garvey (New York: Athenaeum, 1969), 124.

15. "Mulatto" refers to an offspring of a Black and White parent. In Jamaica, this light-skinned (colored) group discriminated against darker-skinned Jamaicans and believed they should succeed the British colonialists. At the time of emancipation, mulattos numbered about 35,000, which was about the population of Whites. The Black population at this time was 310,000.

16. Marcus Garvey, "An Expose on the Caste System among American Negroes," in Garvey, *Philosophy and Opinions*, 2: 58.

17. Garvey, "The Negro's Greatest Enemy," *Current History* 18, no. 6 (1923): 951–57.

18. Tiki Sundiata and Phaon Sundiata, "A Portrait of Marcus Garvey," *The Black Scholar* 2, no. 1 (1970): 6–19.

19. Garvey, "The Negro's Greatest Enemy," 951–52.

20. For details of this social issue in America, see Willard B. Gatewood, *Aristocrats of Color: The Black Elite, 1880–1920* (Bloomington: Indiana University Press, 1990); J. M. Goering, "Changing Perceptions and Evaluations of Physical Characteristics among Blacks: 1950–1970," *Phylon* 33, no. 3 (1972): 231–41; and M. Hunter, "The Persistent Problem of Colorism: Skin Tone, Status, and Inequality," *Sociology Compass* 1, no. 1 (2007): 237–54.

21. Garvey, "The Negro's Greatest Enemy."

22. Amy Jacques Garvey, *Garvey and Garveyism* (reprint Baltimore: Black Classic Press, 2014), 7–8.
23. Claudius Fergus, "From Prophecy to Policy: Marcus Garvey and the Evolution of Pan-African Citizens," *The Global South* 4, no. 2 (2010): 29–48.
24. Garvey, "The Negro's Greatest Enemy."
25. *The Marcus Garvey and the Universal Negro Improvement Association Papers*, ed. Robert A. Hill (Berkeley: University of California Press, 1987; reprint Columbia, SC: Model Editions Partnership, 2000); hereafter *Garvey Papers*. An electronic version of the papers is now available on the web at http://mep.blackmesatech.com/mep/.
26. Colin Grant, *Negro with a Hat: The Rise and Fall of Marcus Garvey and His Dream of Mother Africa* (Oxford: Oxford University Press, 2008), 39, 41.
27. Booker T. Washington, *Up from Slavery: An Autobiography* (Garden City, NY: Doubleday and Company, Inc., 1901).
28. Garvey, "The Negro's Greatest Enemy," 126.
29. Letter from Marcus Mosiah Garvey to Booker T. Washington, Sept. 8, 1914.
30. Eric Arnesen, "Polarizing Figure," *Chicago Tribune*, March 22, 2008.
31. Marcus Garvey, *Aims and Objectives of Movement for Solution of Negro Problem Outlined* (New York: Press of UNIA, 1924).
32. For the full text of this address, see Washington, *Up from Slavery*, chap. 14.
33. Booker T. Washington, "The Speech at the Opening of the Cotton States' Exposition, and the Incidents Connected Therewith," in *The Booker T. Washington Papers*, ed. Louis R. Harlan and Raymond W. Smock (Champaign: University of Illinois Press, 1972), 1: 76; hereafter *Washington Papers*. See also Christopher E. Forth, "Booker T. Washington and the 1905 Niagara Movement Conference," *Journal of Negro History* 72, nos. 3 and 4 (1987): 54.
34. Washington, *Up from Slavery*, 217.
35. See Allen W. Jones, "The Role of Tuskegee Institute in the Education of Black farmers," *Journal of Negro History* 16, no. 2 (1975): 252–67.
36. For a scathing critique of Washington, see Ta-Nehisi Coates, "The Tragedy and Betrayal of Booker T. Washington," *The Atlantic*, March 31, 2009.
37. Library of Congress, Washington, DC, "How Tuskegee Helps Farmers," Typescript 1910, Box 979, *Washington Papers*; and Theodore Saloutos, *Farmer Movement in the South, 1863–1933* (Lincoln: University of Nebraska Press, 1964), 31–43.
38. See South African Native Races Committee, *The Natives of South Africa* (London, 1901), 332. The Very Rev. W. Rubusana, who later became the president of the South African Native Convention of 1909 and a vice president of the African National Congress in 1912, had also argued for a South African university modeled "after the fashion of Tuskegee in America." See also D. D. T. Jabavu, *The Black Problem: Papers and Addresses on Various Native Problems* (Lovedale, South Africa: Institution Press, 1920), 27, 66. Educated at Yale, Jabavu had been invited to submit a report on Tuskegee to the South African government.
39. Alvin Bernard Tillery, Jr., *Between Homeland and Motherland: Africa, U.S. Foreign Policy, and Black Leadership in America* (Ithaca: Cornell University Press, 2011), 51.

40. W. E. B. Du Bois, "The Future of Africa," *Advocate of Peace* 81 (1919): 12–13; and "Letters from Du Bois," "Africa," "Reconstruction and Africa," and "Not Separatism," *Crisis* 17 (1919): 163–66.

41. UNIA, "Preamble," Constitution of the Universal Negro Improvement Association, in effect July 1918 (amended 1920, 1921, and 1922).

42. Marcus Garvey, "An Expose of the Caste System among American Negroes," in Garvey, *Philosophy and Opinions*, 2: 57. For information on Mr. Dill, see Du Bois to Mr. Spingarn, New York, Oct. 28, 1914, Box 13, Joel E. Spingarn Papers, Manuscripts and Archives, New York Public Library. See also Box 1, folder 10, Joel Spingarn Collection, Yale Collection of American Literature, Beinecke Rare Book and Manuscript Library, New Haven, CT.

43. National Archives and Records Administration (NARA), Washington, DC, M2158, Marcus Garvey, the Black Star Line (BSL), and the Black Cross Navigation and Trading Company (BCNTC)—being part of Records of the United States Shipping Board, Record Group (RG) 32; Records of the Bureau of Marine Inspection and Navigation, RG 41; and General Records of the Department of Justice, RG 60.

44. *Maryland Colonization Journal* 8, no. 8 (July 1856): 218–23.

45. NARA, Washington, DC, M2158, Marcus Garvey BSL and BCNTC.

46. Ibid.

47. See Julia E. Johnson, *The Negro Problem* (New York: H. W. Wilson Company, 1921), 367–68.

48. Marcus Garvey, "Address to the Second UNIA Convention, New York," 1921.

49. Ibid.

50. Booker T. Washington and W. E. B. Du Bois, *Negro in the South* (Philadelphia: George W. Jacobs & Company Publishers, 1907), 33–35. Also see John W. Robinson, "Cotton Growing in Africa," in Booker T. Washington, ed., *Tuskegee, Its People, Their Ideals and Achievements* (New York: D. Appleton and Company, 1905), 184–99. In 1859, Delany with his colleague Robert Campbell went to Africa as representatives of the National Emigration Convention. In December of that same year, a treaty was signed with the Yoruba indigenous chiefs of Egbaland in western Nigeria for the settlement of American-born Blacks in the region. It was then that Delany stressed that "our policy must be Africa for the African race and black men to rule them." See Hollis R. Lynch, Preface, in Garvey, *Philosophy and Opinions*, 5.

51. For clarity, Liberia's financial crisis goes back to the late nineteenth century, but it became intractable during World War I when, in deference to its long-standing relationship with the United States, Liberia declared war on Germany, its most important trading partner, and suffered a massive drop in exports as a result. See Jo Sullivan, "The Kru Coast Revolt of 1915–1916," *Liberian Studies Journal* 14 (1989): 51–71, here 59.

52. See Garvey, *Philosophy and Opinions*, 2: 371–78. References to the UNIA colonization plan appeared in the *Negro World*, May 31 and June 7, 14, and 21, 1924.

53. For a more profound treatment of the Firestone transaction, see for instance Raymond Leslie Buell, *The Native Problem in Africa*, vol. 2 (New York: Macmillan Company, 1928) and George William Brown, *The Economic History of Liberia* (Washington, DC: Associated Publishers, Inc., 1941).

54. See for instance Arthur Knoll, "Harvey Firestone's Liberian Investment (1922–1932)," *Liberian Studies Journal* 14 (1989): 13–33; Harvey S. Firestone and Samuel Crowther, *Men and Rubber: The Story of Business* (New York: Doubleday, Page & Company, 1926); and Alfred Lief, *The Firestone Story: A History of the Firestone Tire and Rubber Company* (New York: Whittlesey House, 1951).

55. James J. Dossen, Monrovia, to UNIA, New York: May 2, 1924, quoted in Garvey, Philosophy and Opinions, 378–79. See also Memorandum for William R. Castle, Jr., Esq. from De la Rue—office of the General Receiver, Monrovia, Jan. 24, 1924, "Subject: Report on W. E. Du Bois, Minister Extraordinary, etc. specially appointed for the inauguration of the President of Liberia," Jan. 7, 1924, RG 59, National Archives, 6: 882.00/739-882.00/743.

56. Du Bois first floated this accusation in a scathing article published in the NAACP periodical edited by Du Bois. Du Bois, "Marcus Garvey," *Crisis* 21 (January 1921): 114.

57. Robert Bagnall, "The Madness of Marcus Garvey," *Messenger*, March 1923: 638–48.

58. Dana Johnson, "Separation or Death: One Hundred Years of White Supremacist–Black Nationalist Alliances in America," *The Spark*, Fall 2007, https://www.whitman .edu/spark/rel355fa07_Johnson.html (accessed on Jan. 10, 2018).

59. Marcus Garvey "Speech by Marcus Garvey, Liberty Hall, July 9, 1922," *Garvey Papers*, 4: 707–15. Details of the meetings and what the parties agreed upon are still shrouded in secrecy. What we know comes from Garvey's Liberty Hall speech and a letter written by Walter F. White, assistant secretary of the NAACP, to his lawyer, Lewis R. Gravis, dated Aug. 28, 1924, Library of Congress, NAACP, footnote 2 to "Cable by Marcus Garvey to Chairman, Liberty Hall, Atlanta, 25 June 1922," *Garvey Papers*, 4: 679–80.

60. See Du Bois, "A Lunatic or Traitor," *Crisis* 28 (May 1924): 9.

61. Du Bois, "Back to Africa," *Century Magazine* 55 (February 1923): 545. For a discussion of this characterization, see Zora Neale Hurston, *Collected Plays*, ed. Jean Lee Cole and Charles Mitchell (New Brunswick, NJ: Rutgers University Press, 2008), 79.

62. Garvey, *Philosophy and Opinions*, 1: 310.

63. Ibid.

64. For Garvey's reaction to this article, see "W. E. Burghardt Du Bois as Hater of Dark People," in ibid., 310–20.

65. Thamba E. M'bayo, "W. E. B. Du Bois, Marcus Garvey and Pan Africanism in Liberia, 1919–1924," *Historian* 66, no. 1 (2004): 19–25, here 20.

66. *The Gold Coast Leader*, "Editorial Notes," Cape Coast, July 19, 1924.

67. *New York Times*, "Du Bois, 91, Lauds China," March 5, 1959. See also UMASS Reel/ Frame 83/1282, "China and Africa," *Peking Review*, March 3, 1959.

68. See J. E. Hoover to A. Caminetti, Aug. 13, 1919, File OG 185161, RG 65, NA; and Mark Ellis, "Federal Surveillance of Black Americans during the First World War," *Immigrants and Minorities* 12 (March 1993): 1–20.

69. Marcus Mosiah Garvey, "Statement of Arrest," January 1922, in Garvey, *Philosophy and Opinions*, 98-100.

70. *West African Pilot*, May 24, 1940. Note that this article appeared in print two weeks before Garvey's actual demise. This error stemmed from several premature rumors of his death.

71. Hollis R. Lynch, "Edward Wilmot Blyden," *Pan Negro Patriot, 1832–1911* (London: Oxford University Press, 1967), 251; J. A. Langley, "Garveyism and African Nationalism," *Race* 11, no. 2 (1969): 157.

72. "African Brotherhood and the Right Spirit of Approach," *Times of Nigeria*, March 1, 1920.

73. Rina L. Okonkwo, "The Garvey Movement in British West Africa," *Journal of African History* 21, no. 1 (1980): 105–77.

74. G. O. Olusanya, "Garvey and Nigeria," in *Garvey, Africa, Europe, the Americas*, ed. R. Lewis and M. Warner-Lewis (Trenton, NJ: Africa World Press, 1994), 123.

75. Amy J. Garvey, *Garvey and Garveyism* (London: Collier, 1963), 300–301.

76. Lynch, "The Garvey Movement in British West Africa," 105. See also Michele Mitchell, *Righteous Propaganda: African Americans and the Politics of Racial Destiny after Reconstruction* (Chapel Hill: The University of North Carolina Press, 2004), 225. For a detailed read on Adelaide Casely Hayford, see Barbara Bair, "Pan Africanism in Process: Adelaide Casely Hayford, Garveyism and the Cultural Roots of Nationalism" in *Imagining Home: Class, Culture, and Nationalism in the African Diaspora*, ed. Sidney J. Lemelle and Robin D. G. Kelley (London: Verso, 1994), 122–45.

77. For a good read on Garveyism in South Africa, see Robert Trent Vinson, "'Sea Kaffirs': 'American Negroes' and the Gospel of Garveyism in Early Twentieth-Century Cape Town," *Journal of African History* 47, no. 2 (2006): 281–303; Robert A. Hill and Gregory A. Pirio, "'Africa for the Africans': The Garvey Movement in South Africa, 1920–1940," in Shula Marks and Stanley Trapido, *The Politics of Race, Class and Nationalism in Twentieth Century South Africa* (London: Routledge, 1987), 209–53.

78. See Amanda D. Kemp and Robert Trent Vinson, "'Poking Holes in the Sky': Professor James Thaele, American Negroes, and Modernity in 1920s Segregationist South Africa," *African Studies Review* 43, no. 1, Special Issue on the Diaspora (2000): 141–59. Thaele secured his B.A. and B.Sc. degrees from Wilberforce University in Ohio.

79. For a detailed account of this episode, see Robert Edgar, "The Prophet Motive: Enoch Mgijima, the Israelites, and the Background to the Bullhoek Massacre," *International Journal of African Historical Studies* 15, no. 3 (1982): 401–22.

80. See Gary Baines, "'In the World but Not of It': 'Bishop' Limba and the Church of Christ in New Brighton, c. 1919–1949," *Kronos: South African Histories* 19 (1992): 102–34.

81. Established in 1919 after the Bolshevik revolution, the Comintern was an international organization charged with supporting and spreading the Communist ideology around the world.

82. Michael O. West, "The Seeds Are Sown: The Impact of Garveyism in Zimbabwe in the Interwar Years," *Journal of African Historical Studies* 35, nos. 2 and 3 (2002): 336–37.

83. In a period when language was a marker of nationalist identity, the message of the Zimbabwean diaspora association carried implications for the internal politics of Southern Rhodesia. The letters allegedly charged that the Manyika people were "forbidden from their own tongue and forced to use a tongue which we never knew." See

Zimbabwe Province, Society of Jesus, Harare Archives (ZP/SJ Harare), Box 195/3: O'Hea to Monsignor, Sept. 11, 1930.

84. *Southern Rhodesia, Debates of the Legislative Assembly*, vol. 10, cols. 1979–80.

85. Ibid.

86. Kwame Nkrumah, *Ghana: The Autobiography of Kwame Nkrumah* (London: Thomas Nelson, 1957), 45. For a detailed study of the role of Lincoln University in the education of African nationalists and immediate postcolonial leaders, see Leonard Bethel, "The Role of Lincoln University in the Education of Leadership" (Ph.D. diss., Rutgers University, 1975).

7. THE PAN-AFRICANIST IDEA

1. Colin Legum, *Pan-Africanism: A Short Political Guide*, rev. ed. (New York: Praeger, 1967), 14.

2. P. O. Esedebe, "Origins and Meaning of Pan-Africanism," *Présence africaine* 73 (1970): 109–27. See also American Society of African Culture, *Pan-Africanism Reconsidered* (Berkeley: University of California Press, 1962).

3. Marcus Moriah Garvey, "The Principles of the Universal Negro Improvement Association," speech delivered at Liberty Hall, New York City, November 25, 1922. Printed in *The Philosophy and Opinions of Marcus Garvey or Africa for Africans*, vol. 2, ed. Amy Jacques-Garvey and Tony Martin (1922; reprint Dover, MA, 1986), 93–100; Kwame Nkrumah, *Towards Colonial Freedom: Africa in the Struggle against World Imperialism* (1942; reprint London: Heinemann, 1962).

4. Marcus Moriah Garvey, "Aims and Objects of Movement for Solution of Negro Problem" (1924), National Humanities Center Resource Toolbox, http://nationalhumanitiescenter.org/pds/maai3/segregation/text1/marcusgarvey.pdf (accessed on Jan. 30, 2019). See also Marcus Garvey, "Appeal to the Soul of White America" (1923), in Amy J. Garvey, ed., *Garvey, and Garveyism* (Kingston, Jamaica: Majority Press, 1963).

5. For a definitive history of his career, see Miles Mark Fisher, "Lott Cary, The Colonizing Missionary," *Journal of Negro History* 7, no. 4 (October 1922): 380–418, here 389; John Henderson Russell, *The Free Negro in Virginia, 1619–1865* (Mineola, NY: Dover Publications, 1969), 145–56; H. R. Lynch, *Edward Wilmot Blyden: Pan-Negro Patriot, 1832–1912* (Oxford: Oxford University Press, 1967), 6, 8.

6. For an engaging work on this figure, see Kevin G. Lowther, *The African American Odyssey of John Kizzell: A South Carolina Slave Returns to Fight the Slave Trade in His African Homeland* (Columbia: University of South Carolina Press, 2012).

7. Garvey, *Philosophy and Opinions*, in *Philosophy and Opinions*, vol. 2, ed. Amy Jacques-Garvey (New York: Athenaeum, 1969), 2: 132.

8. L. G. E. Edmondson, Review of Amy Jacques Garvey, *The Philosophy and Opinions of Marcus Garvey, or Africa for the Africans*, *Review of Politics* 31, no. 1 (1969): 132–35, here 135.

9. Benedict Anderson, *Imagined Communities: Reflections on the Origin and Spread of Nationalism* (New York: Verso, 1983).

10. Nikki Pal Singh, *Black Is a Country: Race and the Unfinished Struggle for Democracy* (Cambridge, MA: Harvard University Press, 2004), 69.

11. George Washington Williams, "An Open Letter to His Serene Majesty Leopold II, King of the Belgians and Sovereign of the Independent State of Congo by Colonel, the Honorable Geo. W. Williams, of the United States of America" (1890), in Adelaide Cromwell Hill and Martin Kilson, eds., *Apropos of Africa: Sentiments of American Negro Leaders on Africa from the 1800s to the 1950s* (London: Frank Cass, 1969), 98–109.

12. Paul Gilroy, *The Black Atlantic: Modernity and Double-Consciousness* (Cambridge, MA: Harvard University Press, 1993), 218.

13. Ibid.

14. W. E. B. Du Bois, *The Seventh Son: The Thoughts and Writings of W. E. B. Du Bois*, vol. 2 (New York: Random House, 1971), esp. 187–209.

15. George Padmore, "A Guide to Pan-African Socialism," in *African Socialism*, ed. William H. Friedland and Carl G. Roseberg, Jr. (Stanford, CA: Stanford University Press, 1964), 223–37; and George Padmore, *Pan-Africanism or Communism?* (New York: Doubleday, 1971).

16. Don C. Ohadike, *Pan-African Culture of Resistance: A History of Resistance Movements and the Diaspora* (New York: Global Publication, Binghamton University, 2002); Don C. Ohadike, *Sacred Drums of Liberation: Religions and Music of Resistance in Africa and the Diaspora* (Trenton, NJ: Africa World Press, 2007), xxx.

17. Horace Campbell, "Pan-Africanism in the 21st Century," *African Journal of Political Science*, n.s. 1, no. 1 (1996): 84–98, here 85.

18. See Edward W. Blyden, "Africa and Africans" (1878), in Blyden, *Christianity, Islam and the Negro Race* (London: W. B. Whittington & Co, 1888); James Africanus B. Horton, *West African Countries and Peoples, British and Native: With the requirement necessary for establishing that self-government recommended by the committee . . . 1865; and a vindication of the African race* (New York: W. J. Johnson, 1868).

19. Horace Campbell, "Pan-Africanism in the Twentieth Century," in *Pan-Africanism: Politics, Economy, and Social Change in the Twenty-first Century*, ed. Tajudeen Abdul-Raheem (New York: New York University Press, 1996), 213.

20. Ibid., 21–22. See also Walter Carrington, "Nigeria and the Future of the Black World," excerpts of a speech delivered by Ambassador Carrington at the First Eminent Lecture Series of the University of Benin, Nigeria, Oct. 13, 2015. This speech was published as "Nigeria and the Future of the Black World," *The Herald*, Oct. 22, 2015.

21. See Martin Robinson Delany, "The Condition, Elevation, Emigration, and Destiny of the Colored People of the United States, Politically Considered, Philadelphia, 1852," in *Apropos of Africa: Sentiments of Negro American Leaders on Africa from the 1800s to the 1950s*, ed. Adelaide Cromwell Hill and Martin Kilson (New York: Routledge, 2014), 21–25. Du Bois was firmly against the agitation for separatism, which was a topic of his 1919 speech at the Pan-African Congress. See W. E. B. Du Bois, "Not 'Separatism': The Pan-African Congress" (1919), in W. E. B. Du Bois, *The Seventh Son: The Thoughts and Writings of W. E. B. Du Bois*, vol. 2, ed. J. Lester (New York: Random House, 1971), 189–90.

22. Gayraud Wilmore, *Black Religion, Black Radicalism* (Maryknoll, NY: Orbis Press, 1986), 102. See also Gwinya H. Muzorewa, *The Origin and Development of African Theology* (Eugene, OR: Wipf and Stock Publishers, 1987), 118; and Lawrence S. Smith, *Disciples of Liberty: The African Methodist Episcopal Church in the Age of Imperialism, 1884–1916* (Knoxville: University of Tennessee Press, 2000).

23. Henry Sylvester Williams cited in Abdul-Raheem, ed., Introduction to *Pan-Africanism*, 1–2, 26.

24. See Gustav Spiller, ed., *Papers on Inter-Racial Problems Communicated to the First Universal Races Congress* (London: P. S. King and Sons, The World's Peace Foundation, 1911), 477; and Ulysses Weatherly, Albion Woodbury Albion, and Ernest Watson Burgess, eds., "The First Universal Races Congress," *American Journal of Sociology* 17 (1912): 315–28.

25. See W. E. B. Du Bois, *An A.B.C. of Color* (Berlin: Seven Seas, 1963), 19; Hollis R. Lynch, *Edward Blyden* (London: Oxford University Press, 1967), 245; E. S. Redkey, "Bishop Turner's African Dream," *Journal of American History* 54, no. 2 (1967): 259; and Clarence G. Contee, "Du Bois, the NAACP, and the Pan-African Congress of 1919," *Journal of Negro History* 57, no. 1 (1972): 13–28, here 13–14.

26. See Casely Hayford, "Race Emancipation: Particular Considerations" and "Race Emancipation: The Crux of the Matter," both in *Ethiopia Unbound: Studies in Race Emancipation*, 2nd ed. (1911; reprint London: Frank Cass, 1969).

27. See Abiola Irele, *The African Experience in Literature and Ideology* (London: Heinemann, 1990), 67–68; and Léopold Senghor, "What Is Negritude?" (1961), in *Readings in African Political Thought*, ed. G. M. Mutiso and S. W. Rohio (London: Heinemann, 1975), 83–84.

28. See David Williams, "How Deep the Split in West Africa?" *Foreign Affairs* 40, no. 1 (1961): 118–27; Russell Howe, "The Monrovia Conference," *Africa Today* 8, no. 5 (1961): 4; and Jon Kraus, "Pan-Africanism in Perspective," *World Affairs* 125, no. 4 (1962): 225–31.

29. Garvey, "Aims and Objectives of Movement," 5.

30. John Henrik Clarke, "Marcus Garvey: The Harlem Renaissance Years," *Black Scholar* 5, no. 4 (1973–1974): 17–23, here 20.

31. P. Kevin Tunteng, "George Padmore's Impact on Africa: A Critical Appraisal," *Phylon* 35, no. 1 (1974): 36.

32. Jon Kraus, "Pan-Africanism in Perspective," *World Affairs* 125, no. 4 (1962): 225–31, here 226.

33. Jason C. Parker, "'Made-in-America Revolutions'? The 'Black University' and the American Role in the Decolonization of the Black Atlantic," *Journal of American History* 96, no. 3 (2009): 727–50, here 728.

34. Rita Kiki Edozie, "The Sixth Zone: The African Diaspora and the African Union's Global Era Pan-Africanism," *Journal of African American Studies* 16, no. 2 (2012): 262–99, here 268.

35. See Emanuel Geiss, "The Development of Pan-Africanism," *Journal of the Historical Society of Nigeria* 3 (1967); and Vincent B. Thompson, *The Evolution of Pan-Africanism* (London: Longmans, 1969).

36. See Courland Cox, "Sixth Pan-African Congress," *Black Scholar* 5, no. 7 (1974): 32–34; Sylvia Hill, "Sixth Pan-African Congress: Progress Report on Congress Organizing," ibid., 35–39.
37. Cox, "Sixth Pan-African Congress," 33.
38. For compelling studies highlighting the contributions of African women to the liberation struggles, see Susan Geiger, "Tanganyikan Nationalism as 'Women's Work': Life Histories, Collected Biography and Changing Historiography," *Journal of African History* 37 (1996): 465–78; and LaRay Denzer, "Constance A. Cummings-John of Sierra Leone: Her Early Political Career," *Tarikh* 7 (1981): 20–32.
39. See African Association of Political Science, "Rebuilding the Pan African Movement: A Report on the 7th Pan African Congress," *Journal of Political Science* 1, no. 1 (1996): 1–8, here 6.

8. CULTURAL EXCHANGES AND TRANS-ATLANTIC BONDS

1. This book is now a reference manual for scholars of diverse disciplines interested in African studies. See W. E. B. Du Bois, *The Souls of Black Folk* (Chicago: A. C. McClurg and Co., 1903).
2. Fernando Ortiz, *Hampa afro-cubana: Los negros brujos, apuntes para un estudio de etnología criminal* (Madrid: Sociedad Española de Librería, 1906).
3. Fernando Ortiz, *Los bailes y el teatro de los negros en el folklore de Cuba (The Dances and Theater of Blacks in Cuban Folklore)* (1951; reprint La Habana: Letras Cubanas, 1981), esp. 37–166.
4. For some synopsis of the works of Rodrígues and Beltrán, see Nina Rodrígues, *Medica da Bahia* 38, no. 2 (1906): 57–67; Gazeta Robert V. Kemper, "Gonzalo Aguirre Beltrán (1908-1996)," in David Carrasco, ed., *Oxford Encyclopedia of Mesoamerican Cultures: The Civilizations of Mexico and Central America*, vol. 1 (New York: Oxford University Press, 2001), 8–9.
5. Marta Moreno Vega, "Interlocking African Diaspora Cultures in the Work of Fernando Ortiz," *Journal of Black Studies* 31, no. 1 (2000): 39–50.
6. For a list of some of the Harlem Renaissance writers, see Sidney H. Bremer, "Home in Harlem, New York: Lessons from the Harlem Renaissance Writers," *PMLA* 105, no. 1 (1990): 47–56.
7. See Brian Harker, "Louis Armstrong and the Clarinet," *American Music* 21, no. 2 (2003): 137–58; and Leroy Ostransky, "Early Jazz," *Music Educator* 64, no. 6 (1978): 34–39.
8. Gene Anderson, "The Origin of Armstrong's Hot Fives and Hot Sevens," *College Music Symposium* 43 (2003): 13–24; and Lee B. Brown, "The Theory of Jazz Music 'It Don't Mean a Thing,'" *Journal of Aesthetics and Art Criticism* 49, no. 2 (1991): 115–27.
9. There is a consensus among musicologists that "Potato Head Blues," released on May 10, 1927, on the Okeh label, may be one of Armstrong's best songs.
10. Louis Armstrong, *Swing That Music* (London: Longmans, 1936); and Louis Armstrong, *Satchmo: My Life in New Orleans* (New York: Prentice-Hall, 1954). Armstrong's two autobiographies are reference manuals in jazz studies. A third autobiographical state-

ment appeared in *Life* magazine of April 15, 1966. Richard Meryman revised this interview and published it as Louis Armstrong, *Louis Armstrong—A Self-Portrait*, ed. Richard Meryman (New York: Eakins, 1971).

11. Melville Jean Herskovits, *The Myth of the Negro Past* (1941; reprint Boston: Beacon Press, 1958), 6. See also Jerry Gershenhorn, *Melville J. Herskovits and the Racial Politics of Knowledge* (Lincoln: University of Nebraska Press, 2004), chap. 4.

12. See, for instance, Kenneth M. Bilby, *The Caribbean as a Musical Region* (Austin: University of Texas Press, 1985), 201; and Andrew Pearse, "Aspects of Change in Caribbean Folk Music," *International Folk Music Journal* 7 (1955): 29–35, here 34.

13. Don C. Ohadike, *Sacred Drums of Liberation: Religion and Music of Resistance in Africa and the Diaspora* (Trenton, NJ: Africa World Press, 2007).

14. Fredrick Kaufman and John P. Guckin, *The African Roots of Jazz* (Sherman Oaks, CA: Alfred Publishing, 1979).

15. Eddie S. Meadows, review of Frederick Kaufman and John P. Guckin, *The African Roots of Jazz*, *Ethnomusicology* 26, no. 3 (1982): 468–69. Meanwhile, it might be argued that while New Orleans hosted some of the earliest jazz musicians, other cities also had contemporary jazz artists.

16. Paul Oliver, *Savannah Syncopators: African Retentions in the Blues* (New York: Vista, 1970), 57, 164. See also William S. Pollitzer, *The Gullah People and Their African Heritage* (Athens: University of Georgia Press, 2005).

17. Samuel Charters, *The Roots of the Blues: An African Search* (Salem, NH: Marion Boyars, Inc., 1981).

18. Stanley Elkins, *Slavery: A Problem in American Institutional and Intellectual Life* (1959; reprint Chicago: University of Chicago Press, 1976), 91, 101–02. For an engaging analysis of these ideas, see Jason Young, "African Religions in the Early South," *Journal of Southern Religion* 14 (2012): 1–18.

19. David Evans, "African Elements in Twentieth Century United States Folk Music," *Jazzforschung* 10 (1978): 85–111, here 87–89.

20. Raphael Chijioke Njoku, *African Cultural Values: Igbo Political Leadership in Colonial Nigeria* (New York: Routledge, 2006), chap. 2. See also Toyin Falola, *The Yoruba Gurus: Indigenous Production of Knowledge in Africa* (Trenton, NJ: African World Press, 1999), esp. chaps. 1 and 9.

21. Philip McGuire, "Black Music Critics and the Classical Blues Singers," *Black Perspective in Music* 14, no. 2 (1986): 103–25.

22. Frank Tirro, *Jazz: A History* (New York: Norton, 1977), 71. It is notable that White writers, including Tirro, authored the earliest jazz books. See, for instance, James Lincoln Collier, *The Making of Jazz: A Comprehensive History* (London: Hart-Davis MacGibbon, 1978).

23. Tirro, *Jazz: A History*, xvii, 280–92; Gunther Schuller, *Early Jazz: Its Roots and Musical Development* (Oxford: Oxford University Press, 1986), 6; and Eddie Condon and Thomas Sugrue, *We Called It Music: A Generation of Jazz*, rev. ed. (London: Corgi Books, 1962), 173.

24. Marjorie Richie, review of Frank Tirro, *Jazz: A History*, *American Music Teacher* 29, no. 2 (1979): 36–37.

25. For more exploration of the origins of jazz, see Barry Ulanov, *A History of Jazz in America* (New York: Viking Press, 1995), 24–26.

26. See Cynthia Lejeune Nobles, "Gumbo," in *New Orleans Cuisine: Fourteen Signature Dishes and Their Histories*, edited by Susan Tucker with a foreword by S. Frederick Starr (Jackson: University Press of Mississippi, 2009), 98–100, 107–08; Amanda Watson Schnetzer, "Cajun and Creole Food," in *The Oxford Encyclopedia of Food and Drink in America*, vol. 1, ed. Andrew F. Smith (Oxford: Oxford University Press, 2013), 242–43; and Howard Mitcham, *Creole Gumbo and All That Jazz: A New Orleans Seafood Cookbook* (Reading, MA: Addison-Wesley, 1978).

27. E. Taylor Atkins, *Blue Nippon: Authenticating Jazz in Japan* (Durham, NC: Duke University Press, 2001), 47; and Bill Crow, *From Birdland to Broadway: Scenes of a Jazz Life* (New York: Oxford University Press, 1992), 211.

28. John Collins, "Music Feedback: African America's Music in Africa," *Issue: A Journal of Opinion* 24, no. 2 (1996): 26.

29. Marabi music is a township style of music that is rooted in the indigenous South African culture. It became identified with the keyboard style linked to American ragtime and blues.

30. For engaging reads on Dixieland jazz in New Orleans, see Alan C. Turley, "The Ecological and Social Determinants of the Production of Dixieland Jazz in New Orleans," *International Review of the Aesthetics and Sociology of Music* 26, no. 1 (1995): 107–21; and Ronald L. Davis, "Early Jazz: Another Look—II," *Southwest Review* 58, no. 2 (1973): 144–54.

31. John Collins, *West African Pop Roots* (Philadelphia: Temple University Press, 1992), 53–57.

32. John Collins, "Bye Jazz, Hello World," lecture delivered at the World Blend, June 28, 2013. Charlie Crooijmans published a transcription of the lecture edited by John Collins, "Parallels in the Development of Jazz and Ghanaian Brass Band Music," *News and Noise*, Sept. 22, 2013.

33. Collins, *West African Pop Roots*, 17–31; Collins, "Music Feedback," 26–27.

34. Samuel A. Floyd, Jr., "Black Music in the Circum-Caribbean," *American Music* 17, no. 1 (1999): 1–2. Floyd reminds us about the process of creolization or hybridization that gave birth to cultural products in the Americas.

35. Collins, "Music Feedback," 26–27.

36. Guy Warren, *African Rhythms: The Exciting Sounds of Guy Warren and His Talking Drums*, DL 74243, Decca West African Recording (WA), 1962. See Monique Ameyo, "It's Highlife Time: On the History of Ghanaian Brass Music," *Black Love Project*, March 6, 2016.

37. "He Is Off to the Gold Coast," *Daily Graphic*, Accra, Ghana, May 25, 1956: 9. See also Collins, "Music Feedback," 27.

38. *E. T. Mensah and His Tempo Band* (Julie Okine, singer), Decca West African Recording (WA) 806, matrix number KWA 5383, 1957. See also Collins, "Bye Jazz, Hello World"; and Lloyd Gedye, "Reliving West African Highlife," *Mail and Guardian*, Johannesburg, South Africa, April 20, 2017.

39. E. T. Mensah, *Ghana Freedom: Africa, 50 Years of Music, 50 Years of Independence*, West Africa CD1, Track 1, LC 14868-3218462, 1957.

40. Collins, "Bye Jazz, Hello World." See also Tyler Fleming, "A Marriage of Convenience: Mariam Makeba's Relationship with Stokely Carmichael and Her Music Career in the United States," *Safundi: The Journal of South African and American Studies* 13, no. 3 (2016): 312–38.

41. For more on Victor Olaiya, see Bode Omojola, "Politics, Identity and Nostalgia in Nigerian Music: A Study of Victor Olaiya's Highlife," *Ethnomusicology* 53, no. 2 (2009): 249–79; and "Elders' Forum to Celebrate Olaiya," *Punch Newspaper*, Ibadan, March 24, 2017; and Daniel Anazia, "Highlife Veteran Victor Olaiya Exits the Stage on Health Grounds," *The Guardian*, Lagos, Feb. 18, 2017. Dr. Olaiya renamed his band "All Stars" when they played at the 1963 Jazz Festival in Czechoslovakia.

42. Alexander Stewart, "Make It Funky: Fela Kuti, James Brown and the Invention of Afrobeat," *American Studies* 52, no. 4 (2013): 116. See also Michael Veal, *Fela: The Life and Times of an African Musical Icon* (Philadelphia: Temple University Press, 2000).

43. For Fela's activist musical career, see Randall F. Grass, "Fela Anikulapo-Kuti: The Art of an Afrobeat Rebel," *Drama Review: TDR* 30, no. 1 (1986): 131–48; and Justin Labinjoh, "Fela Anikulapo-Kuti: Protest Music and Social Processes in Nigeria," *Journal of Black Studies* 13, no. 1 (1982): 119–34.

44. Alexander G. Weheliye, "A New Groove: Black Culture and Technological Development," *Diverse Issues in Higher Education* 22, no. 21 (2005): 39.

45. Iain Anderson, "Reworking Images of a Southern Past: The Commemoration of Slave Music after the Civil War," *Studies in Popular Culture* 19, no. 2 (1996): 167–83, here 168. See also Eugene Genovese, *Roll, Jordan, Roll: The World the Slaves Made* (New York: Pantheon, 1975).

46. See Dena Epstein, *Sinful Tunes and Spirituals* (Urbana: University of Illinois Press, 1977), 68–72.

47. James Johnson and J. Rosamond Johnson, *The Book of American Negro Spirituals* (New York: Viking, 1940), 23–24; Henry Edward Krehbiel, *Afro-American Folksongs: A Study in Racial and National Music* (New York: G. Schirmer, 1914), 102; and Anderson, "Reworking Images of a Southern Past."

48. Johnson and Johnson, *The Book of American Negro Spirituals*, 25–26; and Anderson, "Reworking Images of a Southern Past," 168–69.

49. The Black musicians were mostly attracted to the big cities like New York, Boston, Detroit, New Orleans, and Chicago, where producers repackaged and commercialized these songs as a force in popular entertainment.

50. See for instance John Miller Chernoff, *African Rhythm and African Sensibility* (Chicago: University of Chicago Press, 1979), 36, 167; and Paul Gilroy, "Sounds Authentic: Black Music, Ethnicity, and the Challenge of a Changing Same," *Black Music Research Journal* 10, no. 2 (1990): 128–31.

51. Ndiouga Benga, "Meanings and Challenges of Modern Urban Music in Senegal," in Toyin Falola and Steven J. Salm, eds., *Urbanization and African Cultures* (Durham, NC: Carolina Academic Press, 2005), 158.

52. Brian Cross, *It's Not about a Salary: Rap, Race, and Resistance in Los Angeles* (New York: Verso, 1993), 3.
53. Arnold Shaw, *Black Popular Music in America: From the Spirituals, Minstrels, and Ragtime to Soul, Disco, and Hip-Hop* (New York: Schirmer Books, 1966), 292.
54. John Collins, *West African Pop Roots*, 56–57.
55. The annual Brussels area summer music exposition is usually held in August.
56. Lerone Bennett, Jr., "Sex and Music: Has It Gone Too Far?" *Ebony* 57, no. 12 (2002): 146.
57. Steven Best and Douglas Kellner, "Rap, Black Rage, and Racial Differences," *Enculturation* 2, no. 3 (1999): 4. For a critique of this manner of identity expression, see also Daniel Traber, "The Identity Joke: Race, Rap, Performance in CB4," *American Studies* 52, no. 1 (2012): 123–42.
58. Best and Kellner, "Rap, Black Rage, and Racial Differences," 4–5.
59. Emily Gray, "The Father and the Son: The Rhetoric of Rebellion in Marvin Gaye's 'What Is Going On,'" *Enculturation* 2, no. 2 (1999): 1–12.

9. THE CIVIL RIGHTS MOVEMENT MEETS DECOLONIZATION

1. Martin Luther King, Jr., "Letter from Birmingham Jail" or "Letter from Birmingham City Jail and the Negro Is Your Brother"), April 16, 1963. In the letter, King informed the reader that this was a question from a five-year-old boy.
2. Frantz Fanon, *The Wretched of the Earth*, trans. Constance Farrington with a preface by Jean-Paul Sartre (New York: Grove Press, 1963), esp. 254–70.
3. Theodore Isaac Rubin, *Anti-Semitism: A Disease of the Mind: A Psychiatrist Explores the Psychodynamics of a Symbol Sickness* (1990; reprint Fort Lee, NJ: Barricade Books, 2011), esp. 19. For a compelling review of Rubin's book by a fellow psychiatric practitioner, Werner Israel Halpern, see *Shofar* 9, no. 1 (1990): 118–19.
4. Kwame Anthony Appiah, *In My Father's House: Africa in the Philosophy of Culture* (Oxford: Oxford University Press, 1993).
5. See Mauricio Mazon, *The Zoot-Suit Riots: The Psychology of Symbolic Annihilation* (Austin: University of Texas Press, 1989), 1. Mazon writes, "What the riots lack in hard incriminating evidence they make up for in a plethora of emotions, fantasies, and symbols."
6. See for instance David J. Goldberg, "Unmasking the Ku Klux Klan: The Northern Movement against the KKK, 1920–1925," *Journal of American Ethnic History* 15, no. 4 (1996): 32–48; Robert Goldberg, *Hooded Empire: The Ku Klux Klan in Colorado* (Urbana: University of Illinois Press, 1981); and Nancy MacLean, *Behind the Mask of Chivalry: The Making of the Second Ku Klux Klan* (New York: Oxford University Press, 1994). See also Dieter D. Hartman, "Anti-Semitism and the Appeal of Nazism," *Political Psychology* 5, no. 4 (1984): 635–42; and Susanne Y. Urban, "At Issue: The Jewish Community in Germany: Living with Recognition, Anti-Semitism, and Symbolic Roles," *Jewish Political Studies Review* 21, nos. 3 and 4 (2009): 31–55.
7. Black Power is simply a crusade in support of rights and political power for Black people in Africa and the African diaspora, especially prominent in the United States

in the 1960s and 1970s. See Richard Rights, *Black Power* (New York: Harper and Row, 1954). Stokely Carmichael, chairman of the Mississippi Student Nonviolent Coordinating Committee, rallied marchers by chanting, "We want Black Power." A. P. MacDonald, Jr., in "Black Power," *Journal of Negro Education* 44, no. 4 (1975): 547–54, defines "Black Power" as referring to the Black man's right to control himself and his destiny. It "is one of the most important social events of recent history, and is crucial to the upgrading of black men everywhere" (p. 547).

8. John Karefah, *African People in the Global Village: An Introduction to Pan African Studies* (Lanham, MD: University Press of America, 1998), 79.
9. King, "Letter from Birmingham Jail."
10. Malcolm X, "Ballot or Bullet," speech delivered in Cleveland, Ohio, April 3, 1964.
11. Steve Biko, "Black Consciousness and the Quest for a True Humanity (1973)," in Steve Biko, *I Write What I like: Selected Writings*, ed. Aelred Stubbs (Chicago: University of Chicago Press, 1978), 87–98.
12. Jeremy I. Levitt, "Beyond Borders: Martin Luther King, Jr., Africa, and Pan Africanism," *Temple International Law Journal* 31, no. 1 (2017): 1–23.
13. This tribute came forty days before King's death on April 4, 1968.
14. Martin Luther King, Jr., "Honoring Dr. Du Bois" address delivered at Carnegie Hall in New York City on the hundredth birthday of W. E. B. Du Bois, Feb. 23, 1968.
15. Levitt, "Beyond Borders—Martin Luther King, Jr., Africa, and Pan Africanism," 2–4.
16. Martin Luther King, Jr., "Facing the Challenge of a New Age," address delivered at the first annual Institute on Nonviolence and Social Change in Montgomery, AL, on Dec. 3, 1956.
17. See letter from Oliver Tambo to Rev. Martin Luther King, Nov. 18, 1957, in *The Papers of Martin Luther King, Jr.*, vol. 4: *Symbol of the Movement: January 1957—December 1958*, ed. Clayborne Carson, Tenisha Armstrong, Susan Carson, Adrienne Clay, Virginia Shadron, and Kieran Taylor (Chapel Hill: University of North Carolina Press, 2000), 325.
18. Martin Luther King, Jr., address delivered at St. Paul's Cathedral, London, Dec. 4, 1964.
19. Ibid.
20. Ibid.
21. Martin Luther King, Jr., letter to Kwame Nkrumah, April 17, 1959. In the letter, King thanked Nkrumah for the "hospitality extended to me and my wife" during the Ghana independence celebration in March 1957 and described the event as "a most rewarding experience." See also Nnamdi Azikiwe to Martin Luther King, Jr., Oct. 26, 1960. In the letter, the newly appointed governor-general of Nigeria invited King to his inauguration, slated for Nov. 16, 1960. See *The Papers of Martin Luther King, Jr.*, vol. 5: *Threshold of a New Decade: Jan. 1959—Dec. 1960*, ed. Clayborne Carson, Tenisha Armstrong, Susan Carson, Adrienne Clay, and Kieran Taylor (Los Angeles: University of California Press, 2005), 533–34.
22. Kevin K. Gaines, *African Americans in Ghana: Black Expatriates and the Civil Rights Era* (Chapel Hill: University of North Carolina Press, 2006), 82.
23. Ibid.

24. See U.S. Civil Rights Cases 109 U.S. 3, 1883.

25. See the Library of Congress online exhibition "The Civil Rights Act of 1964: A Long Struggle for Freedom," https://www.loc.gov/exhibits/civil-rights-act/ (accessed on Jan. 7, 2019). The 1964 Civil Rights Act outlawed discrimination based on race, color, religion, national origin, or sex by private employers with fifteen or more employees; federal, state, and local governments; and educational institutions, employment agencies, and labor unions.

26. U.S. Department of Justice, Voting Rights Act of 1965.

27. See Gwyneth Mellinger, *Chasing Newsroom Diversity: From Jim Crow to Affirmative Action* (Urbana and Chicago: University of Illinois Press, 2013), 10; David Randall Davis, ed., *The Press and Race: Mississippi Journalists Confront the Movement* (Jackson: University Press of Mississippi, 2001), 5; and Michael C. Dawson, *Black Vision: The Roots of Contemporary African-American Political Ideologies* (Chicago: University of Chicago Press, 2001), 71. For comparative insights, similar segregation of the media was in play under apartheid South Africa. See Christina Scott, *The Future of Newspapers in Natal: A Discussion Document* (KwaZulu-Natal: University of Natal, 1992), 10.

28. Bruce M. Tyler, "Race, Violence and 'Culture War' in Los Angeles, 1940s–1970," unpublished working paper, July 2010.

29. For a consolidated study of Kallen's works and career as an intellectual and advocate of pluralism, see Milton M. Konvitz, ed., *The Legacy of Horace M. Kallen* (Rutherford, NJ: Fairleigh Dickinson University Press, 1987).

30. Saul K. Padover, "The American Dream," *American Journal of Economics and Sociology* 15, no. 4 (1956): 404.

31. Malcolm X, "The Ballot or the Ballot," address delivered in Cleveland, Ohio, April 3, 1964.

32. See, for instance, Joseph A. Califano, Jr., "Seeing Is Believing: The Enduring Legacy of Lyndon Johnson," keynote address at the Centennial Celebration for President Lyndon, Baines Johnson Kaiser Family Foundation, Washington, DC, May 19, 2008.

33. In broad terms, affirmative action encompasses any measure that allocates resources such as admission to selective universities or professional schools, jobs, promotions, public contracts, business loans, or rights to buy, sell, or use land through a process that considers individual membership in underrepresented groups. Its purpose is to increase the proportion of individuals from those groups in the labor force, entrepreneurial class, or student population excluded because of state-sanctioned oppression in the past or societal discrimination in the present.

34. See for instance M. E. Porter, "Location, Clusters and Economic Development: Local Clusters in the Global Economy," *Economic Development Quarterly* 14, no. 1 (2000): 15–31; H. W. Richardson, *Economic Recovery in Britain, 1932–9* (London: Weidenfeld & Nicolson, 1967); N. Rosenberg, *Inside the Black Box: Technology and Economics* (Cambridge: Cambridge University Press, 1983); and W. W. Rostow, *The Stages of Economic Growth* (Cambridge: Cambridge University Press, 1960); R. Rowthorn and J. Wells, *Deindustrialization and Foreign Trade* (Cambridge: Cambridge University Press, 1987).

35. Robert J. Gordon, "The Impact of the Second World War on Namibia," *Journal of Southern African Studies* 19, no. 1 (1993): 147–65.
36. See Anthony D. Smith, *State and Nation in the Third World: The Western State and African Nationalism* (New York: Wheatsheaf Books, 1983,), 48. See also N. I. Gavrilov and I. G. Rybalkina, "Africa and World War II," *Africa in Soviet Studies* (1987): 118–25; and SWAPO, *To Be Born a Nation* (London: Zed Press, 1981), 166. For the counterpoint argument, David Killingray, *Fighting for Britain: African Soldiers in the Second World War* (London: James Curry, 2010).
37. *Report of the Commission of Inquiry into the Disorders in the Eastern Provinces of Nigeria*, November 1949 (Colonial No. 256) (London: HMSO, 1950), 35. See also S. O. Jaja, "The Enugu Colliery Massacre in Retrospect: An Episode in British Administration of Nigeria," *Journal of the Historical Society of Nigeria* 11, nos. 3–4 (1982–1983): 86–106.
38. Martin Luther King, Jr., *Stride toward Freedom: The Montgomery Story* (New York: Harper and Row, 1958), 44.
39. King, "Letter from Birmingham Jail."
40. Gaines, *African Americans in Ghana*, 81. Ebere Nwaubani has made a similar argument that African Americans deployed the new (independent) Africa in the late 1950s and 1960s as a weapon in their fight for freedom in America. See Ebere Nwaubani, *The United States and Decolonization in West Africa, 1950–1960* (Rochester, NY: University of Rochester Press, 2001), 236.
41. King, "Letter from Birmingham Jail."
42. See, for instance, Paniel E. Joseph, "The Black Power Movement: A State of the Field," *Journal of American History* 96, no. 3 (2009): 751–76.
43. Malcolm X, "Travels to Africa," transcript of a radio show in New York, Dec. 27, 1964.
44. See for instance Bodil Folke Frederiksen, "Print, Newspapers and Audience in Colonial Kenya: African and Indian Improvement, Protest and Connections," *Africa* 81, no. 1 (2011): 155–72; Stephanie Newell, "New Spaces, New Writers: The First World War and Print Culture in Colonial Ghana," *Research in African Literature* 40, no. 2 (2009): 1–15; and Frederick O. Kumolalo, "The Anglo-West African Press and African American Struggle for Equality during the Eisenhower Administration: A Case Study of the Ghanaian and Nigerian Press," *Journal of the Historical Society of Nigeria* 21 (2012): 154–70.
45. For a study of Azikiwe's American education and his political activism, see Patrick J. Furlong, "Azikiwe and the National Church of Nigeria and the Cameroons: A Case Study of the Political Use of Religion in African Nationalism," *African Affairs* 91, no. 364 (1992): 433–52. Azikiwe further studied at Storer College, Harvard University, and the University of Pennsylvania.
46. *West African Pilot*, Lagos, May 21, 1954.
47. The states were Cameroon, Togo, Madagascar, the Democratic Republic of the Congo, Somalia, Benin, Niger, Burkina Faso, Ivory Coast, Chad, the Central African Republic, the Republic of Congo, Gabon, Senegal, Mali, Nigeria, and Mauritania. Most were part of the fast-dying French Empire.

48. Martin Luther King, Jr., "Give Us the Ballot," address delivered at the Lincoln Memorial, Washington, DC, May 17, 1957.

49. Ibid.

50. Martin Luther King, Jr., "I Have a Dream," address delivered in Washington, DC, Aug. 25, 1963.

51. Frederick Olumide Kumolalo, "Gazing At, Cheering On: The Anglo-West African Press and the American Civil Rights Movement in the Camelot Years, 1960–1963," *Journal of the Historical Society of Nigeria* 23 (2014): 19–47, here 19.

52. Ibid., 20.

53. *West African Pilot*, Lagos, May 22, 1954: 2.

54. *Daily Times*, Lagos, Jan. 18, 1958: 4.

55. *Daily Times*, Lagos, Sept. 25, 1957: 13.

56. Letter from Jackie Robinson to President Eisenhower, May 13, 1958, Records as President, Official File, Box 614, Eisenhower Library.

57. Press release containing speech on radio and television by President Eisenhower, Sept. 24, 1957, Kevin McCann Collection of Press and Radio Conferences and Press Releases, Box 20, Eisenhower Library. See also Thomas Borstelmann, *The Cold War and the Color Line: American Race Relations in the Global Arena* (Cambridge, MA: Harvard University Press, 2001), 102–04.

58. Letter from President Eisenhower to Jackie Robinson, June 4, 1958, Records as President, Official File, Box 614, Eisenhower Library.

59. *Daily Times*, Lagos, Sept. 2, 1957: 13.

60. *Daily Times*, Lagos, Oct. 2, 1957: 13.

61. *Daily Times*, Lagos, Oct. 4, 1957: 13.

62. See Odd Arne Westad, *The Global Cold War: Third World Interventions and the Making of Our Times* (New York: Cambridge University Press, 2007), 135.

63. *Ashanti Pioneer*, Accra, April 27, 1961.

64. For Kennedy's Speech, see J. F. Kennedy/Special Speech to Joint Session of the Congress of the United States, May 25, 1961, The Miller Center, University of Virginia.

65. *Ethiopian Herald*, Addis Ababa, May 29, 1961.

66. *Nigerian Morning Post*, Lagos, Oct. 6, 1962.

67. *West African Pilot*, Lagos, Jan. 26, 1963.

68. *Daily Express*, Lagos, March 1, 1963: 1, 5.

69. *Ghanaian Times*, Accra, April 15, 1963.

70. *Ghanaian Times*, Accra, May 9, 1963: 1.

71. *Ghanaian Times*, Accra, May 10, 1963: 1.

72. *Ghanaian Times*, Accra, May 20, 1963: 12.

73. *Cameroonian Times*, Yaoundé, May 21, 1963.

74. *Daily Express*, Lagos, May 24, 1963: 6.

75. *Ghanaian Times*, Accra, July 2, 1963: 8. For a compelling insight on this, see Kumolalo, "Gazing At, Cheering On," 35–36.

76. *Daily Express*, Lagos, June 13, 1963: 1.

77. *West African Pilot*, Lagos, Aug. 26, 1963: 2.

78. Nnamdi Azikiwe, address to the NAACP Convention on the organization's fiftieth anniversary, New York City, July 19, 1959.
79. Patrice Lumumba, "African Unity and National Independence," speech delivered at the closing session of the International Seminar organized by the Congress for the Freedom of Culture, University of Ibaḍan, Nigeria, March 22, 1959.
80. *Ghanaian Times*, Accra, May 24, 1963: 3.
81. *Ghanaian Times*, Accra, July 9, 1963: 4.
82. *Ethiopian Herald*, Addis Ababa, October 3, 1963.
83. *Cameroonian Times*, Yaoundé, May 21, 1963.
84. *West African Pilot*, Lagos, Aug. 27, 1963: 2.
85. Du Bois to Nkrumah, cited in Mark Stafford and John Davenport, *W. E. B. Du Bois: Scholar and Activist* (Philadelphia: Chelsea House, 2015), 99.
86. Malcolm X, speech at Ford Auditorium, Detroit, Feb. 14, 1965. This address was Malcolm's last public speech before his assassination by rival Black Muslims on Feb. 21, 1965, in Washington Heights, New York City.

10. THE COLD WAR

1. Michael Wesley, "Interpreting the Cold War," in *Power and International Relations: Essays in Honour of Coral Bell*, ed. Desmond Ball and Sharyn Lee (Canberra: ANU Press, 2014), 79–91, here 82.
2. Ashley Jackson, *The British Empire and the Second World War* (London: Hambledon Continuum, 2006), 171.
3. Alexander Moorhead, *The Desert War: The Classic Trilogy on the North African Campaign, 1940–1943* (London: Aurum Press, 2017).
4. Alan Taylor, "World War II: The North African Campaign," *The Atlantic*, Boston, Sept. 4, 2011.
5. For a detailed study of West African material and manpower contributions during the Second World War, see David Killingray, "Military and Labour Recruitment in the Gold Coast during the Second World War," *Journal of African History* 23, no. 1 (1982): 83–95.
6. Chima J. Korieh, *For King and County* (forthcoming from Cambridge University Press), 1–2.
7. Nigerian National Archives Calabar (NNAC), Calprof 3/1/2353, Loyalty to the King and Government, 1939.
8. Ibid.
9. NNAC, Calprof 3/1/2353. It might be remembered that palm oil and kernel were essential to the Germans and that their factories were located in Calabar before the First World War. See Calprof, 5/4/410, NA/E—German Factories at Calabar, 1914. For detailed work on this, see A. Olorunfemi, "West Africa and Anglo-German Trade Rivalry, 1898–1914," *Journal of the Historical Society of Nigeria* 11, nos. 1–2 (1981–1982): 21–35.
10. See Nigerian National Archives Ibadan (NNAI), Ijebu Prof. 1/2562, Memorandum on Instructions and Directives on War Information; and *Daily Service*, Lagos, June 21,

1945. Names of the sponsoring town, such as Ijebu, Kano, and Nsukka, were pub-lished in the *Daily Service* and other national newspapers.

11. *Gold Coast Times*, Accra, March 13, 1939: 1.
12. *West African Pilot*, Lagos, Sept. 4, 1939: 3.
13. *West African Pilot*, Lagos, Feb. 12, 1942: 1.
14. *Nigerian Daily Times*, Lagos, April 1, 1939: 1.
15. *New York Amsterdam News*, "Germans Adopt U.S. Jim Crow: Hitler's Paper Outlines New Drive on Jews," Dec. 31, 1938: 1.
16. Ibid.
17. The campaign was launched by the publication, in the *Courier Journal*, of a letter to the editor from James Q. Thompson, "Should I Sacrifice to Live 'Half American'?" *Pittsburgh Courier*, Jan. 31, 1942: 3.
18. Vice President Henry Wallace, speech to union workers in Detroit, MI, July 25, 1943.
19. John R. Williams, "Epochal Radio Speeches Reflect Courier Journal's 'Double V' Theme: 50,000 Hear Wallace," *Pittsburgh Courier Journal*, July 31, 1943: 1, 4 (col. 5). See also Alex Ross, "How American Racism Influenced Hitler," *New Yorker*, April 30, 2018; and James O. Whiteman, "Hitler's American Model: The United States and the Making of Nazi Race Laws," *The Atlantic*, November 2017.
20. See National Archives Kew (NAK), CO875/11/1, "Colonial Propaganda: Aims and Policy," memorandum by Edmett, Aug. 6, 1941. See also NNAI, Commissioner for Colonies Papers, Comcol 601/59, "British War Aims, 1943."
21. Bonny Ibhawoh, "Second World War Propaganda, Imperial Idealism, and Anti-Colonial Nationalism in British West Africa," *Nordic Journal of African Studies* 16, no. 2 (2007): 234.
22. See Report of the Commission of *Rapporteurs*, League of Nations (LN) Council DOC, B7/21/68/106 (1921), "The Right of Nations to Self-Determination," Aug. 14, 1941. In the document, President Franklin D. Roosevelt and Prime Minister Winston Churchill pledged to "respect the right of all peoples to choose the form of govern-ment under which they will live" and declared their "wish to see sovereign rights and self-determination restored to those who have been forcibly deprived of them."
23. For this description, see NLN, *Ellesmere Guardian*, "Morocco: Rich African Region, of French Empire," Canterbury, NZ: Stronghold March 10, 1942: 6.
24. Correspondent Report, "New Sultan Proclaimed: Deposed Sultan's Uncle," Aug. 20, 1953.
25. For an insightful study of the performance of Moroccan servicemen in the war, see Moshe Gersovich, "Collaboration and Pacification: French Conquest, Moroccan Combatants, and the Transformation of the Middle Atlas," *Comparative Studies of South Asia, Africa and the Middle East* 24, no. 1 (2004): 141–48.
26. For a recent discussion of Truman's action, see DeNeen L. Brown, "They Thought Black Soldiers Couldn't Fight," *Washington Post*, July 24, 2018. Other episodes of violence profoundly troubled Truman. In 1946, in Georgia, a mob shot and killed two Black men and their wives. No one ever stood trial for the crime. In South Carolina, police pulled a young African American soldier from a bus and beat him blind.

27. Executive Order 9808, Dec. 5, 1946, as reproduced in Steven F. Lawson, *To Secure These Rights* (Boston, MA: Bedford/St. Martin's, 2004), 45.

28. President Truman cited in Carl T. Rowan, "Harry Truman and the Negro: Was He Our Greatest Civil Rights Hero?" *Ebony* 15, no. 1 (November 1959): 45.

29. Memorandum from President Harry S. Truman to Attorney General Tom C. Clark (Cc: David K. Niles, Administrative Assistant to the President), Sept. 20, 1946, as reprinted in Dennis Merrill, ed., *Documentary History of the Truman Presidency*, vol. 11: *The Report of the Committee on Civil Rights and President Truman's Message to Congress of February 2* (Bethesda, MD: University Publications of America, 1996), Document 43, p. 124.

30. The phrase "Truman Doctrine" came from the text of a speech delivered by President Truman before a joint session of Congress on March 12, 1947. Secretary of State George C. Marshall elaborated on the Truman Doctrine in what is now called the "Marshall Plan Speech," delivered in July 1948.

31. NAACP Papers, Group II, Series A, General Office File (1940s–1955) box 637, file "United Nations Petition" (NAACP, October 1947).

32. See Michael L. Krenn, *The African American Voice in U.S. Foreign Policy since World War II* (New York: Garland Publishing, 1999), 76.

33. Dwight D. Eisenhower, Inaugural Address, Washington, DC, Jan. 20, 1953.

34. Letitia Lawson, "U.S. African Policy since the Cold War," *Strategic Insights* 7, no. 1 (2007): 1–15.

35. President Truman presented his plan to a joint session of Congress on March 12, 1947. The doctrine of containment also included a recommendation for financial assistance to Greece and Turkey after the British government informed the United States that it would no longer be able to provide financial aid to both countries. See Address of the President of United States, Document no. 171, 80th Congress, 1st Session, House of Representatives, March 12, 1947.

36. President Harry Truman, Joint Session of Congress, March 12, 1947. See also George C. Marshall, speech at Harvard, June 5, 1947.

37. Dwight D. Eisenhower, Inaugural Address.

38. Manning Marable, *Race, Reform, and Rebellion: The Second Reconstruction in Black America, 1945–1982* (Jackson: University Press of Mississippi, 1984), 18.

39. Emperor Haile Selassie, Appeal to the League of Nations, Address by Emperor Haile Selassie, Geneva, Switzerland, June 30, 1936.

40. Thomas J. Noer, "New Frontier and Old Priorities in Africa," in *Kennedy's Quest for Victory: American Foreign Policy, 1961–63*, ed. Thomas G. Paterson (New York: Oxford University Press, 1989), 254.

41. *Democrat and Chronicle*, Rochester, NY, April 2, 1960: 1; *Independent*, Long Beach, CA, April 12, 1960: 7; and *Daily News-Record*, Harrisonburg, VA, April 12, 1960.

42. Alan P. Dodson and Steve Marsh, *U.S. Foreign Policy since 1945*, 2nd ed. (New York: Routledge, 2001), 117; Stephen Metz, "American Attitudes towards Decolonization in Africa," *Political Science Quarterly* 99, no. 3 (1984): 518, 521; and Eric Kaku Quaidoo, "The United States and Overthrow of Kwame Nkrumah" (M.A. thesis, Fort Hays State University, 2010), 10.

43. Thomas J. Noer, "New Frontiers and Old Priorities in Africa," in *Kennedy's Quest for Victory in Foreign Policy, 1961–1963*, ed. Thomas G. Paterson (Oxford: Oxford University Press, 1989), 253–81, here 260.

44. All quotes from Dwight D. Eisenhower, "Message to the People of Ghana on the Occasion of Its Independence," Accra, Ghana, March 6, 1957, The American Presidency Project, http://www.presidency.ucsb.edu/ws/?pid=10988.

45. Eisenhower, "Inaugural Address."

46. For the text of President Eisenhower's invitation to him, dated March 4, 1958, and his reply, see *Public Papers of the Presidents of the United States: Dwight D. Eisenhower, 1958* (Washington, DC: Government Printing Office, 1959), 211–13.

47. Memorandum of Conversation, No. 294, Prime Minister Nkrumah's Talk with the President, July 23, 1958, Eisenhower Library, Whitman File, International File, Secret, Drafted by Deputy Assistant Secretary of State for African Affairs Joseph Palmer 2d.

48. See Department of State, Central Files, 033.45J11/7-2458, A Memorandum of a Conversation with Under Secretary of State Herter concerning Ghana's Economic Aims, Conference Files, Lot 63, D 123, Nkrumah Visit.

49. For insight on this project, see Central Intelligence Agency, Office of National Estimates, Staff Memorandum No. 85–63, Dec. 19, 1963, 10.

50. Kevin K. Gaines, *African Americans in Ghana: Black Expatriates and the Civil Rights Era* (Chapel Hill: University of North Carolina Press, 2006), esp. chap. 3, p. 81. See also Lalbila Yoda, "The Influence of the USA on the Political Ideas of Kwame Nkrumah," *Round Table* [Great Britain] 326 (April 1993): 187.

51. Kwame Nkrumah, *Ghana: The Autobiography of Kwame Nkrumah* (London: Nelson, 1957), 48. See also David Lamb, *The Africans* (New York: Vintage Books, 1987), 286; and Yekutiel Gershoni, *Africans on African Americans: The Creation and Uses of an African-American Myth* (London: Macmillan, 1997), 142.

52. All quotes in Dwight D. Eisenhower, Address before the 15th General Assembly of the United Nations, New York, Sept. 22, 1960.

53. For a history of events that ended with the coup, see U.S. Department of State, Foreign Relations of the United States, 1961–1963, vol. 21 (Washington, DC: Government Printing Office, 1995), 341–49.

54. John Pradoes, *Safe for Democracy: The Secret Wars of the CIA* (Chicago: Ivan R. Dee, 2007), 328–29.

55. See John L. Adedeji, "The Legacy of J. J. Rawlings in Ghanaian Politics, 1979–2000," *African Studies Quarterly* 5, no. 2 (2001): 2–27.

56. See Paul Nugent, "Nkrumah and Rawlings: Political Lives in Parallel?" *Transactions of the Historical Society of Ghana* 12 (2009–2010): 35–56; and Eboe Hutchful, "New Elements in Militarism: Ethiopia, Ghana, and Burkina," *International Journal* 41, no. 4 (1986): 802–30.

57. Koojo S. Lewis, *How America Toppled Nkrumah* (Winneba, Ghana: Victoria Press, 1967), 4. See also William Blum, *Killing Hope: U.S. Military and CIA Interventions since World War II* (Monroe, ME: Common Courage Press, 2004), 198–200; and John Stockwell, *In Search of Enemies: A CIA Story* (New York: W. W. Norton & Company, 1974), 10–15.

58. David Rooney, *Kwame Nkrumah: Vision and Tragedy* (Legon, Accra: Sub-Saharan Publishers, 2007), 13.

59. Central Intelligence Agency, Office of National Estimates, Staff Memorandum No. 85–63 (Revised), Dec. 19, 1963, 5.

60. For a classic insight into this thought, see Kwame Nkrumah, *Neocolonialism: The Last Stage of Imperialism* (London: Thomas Nelson, 1965).

61. Patrice Lumumba, Speech at Africa, Accra, Ghana, Dec. 11, 1958.

62. Colin Legum, ed., *Zambia: Independence and Beyond: The Speeches of Kenneth Kaunda* (London: Nelson, 1966), 16; Max Addo, *Ghana's Foreign Policy in Retrospect* (Accra: Waterville, 1967), 29–30; and Bruce Oudes, "U.S.-African Relations: Kaunda's Diplomatic Offensive," *Africa Report* (New York) 20, no. 3 (1975): 41.

63. Tim Weiner, *Legacy of Ashes: The History of the CIA* (New York: Doubleday, 2007), xvii, 162.

64. See Ludo de Witte, *The Assassination of Patrice Lumumba* (London: Verso, 2001), esp. 1–27. Arguably, de Witte provided the most detailed account of the collaboration between Belgian forces and the U.S. Green Berets in Katanga in an operation code-named Operation Barracuda by the CIA.

65. See Patrice Lumumba, National Radio Address, 1960, in Jean Van Lierde, ed., *Lumumba Speaks: The Speeches and Writings of Patrice Lumumba, 1958–1961* (Boston: Little, Brown, and Company, 1972). In the address, Lumumba had cited the actions of Belgian troops in Katanga, where he noted that they started shooting at Belgian troops as soon as they landed. He went on to appeal to Tshombe to stop actions and return to a united Congo nation.

66. Special National Intelligence Estimate (SNIE) 65–2–61, Jan. 10, 1961, FRUS, 1961–63, vol. 20: Congo Crisis, Washington, DC, Dec. 7, 1961.

67. FRUS, 1864–1968, vol. 23, Congo, 1960–1968, No. 14, Telegram from the Central Intelligence Agency to the Station in the Congo, Dir 47587 (Out 62966), Washington, Aug. 27, 1960. See also Weiner, *Legacy of Ashes*, 187–88, emphasis in original.

68. FRUS, 1864–1968, vol. 23, Congo, 1960–1968, No. 14, Telegram from the Central Intelligence Agency to the Station in the Congo, Dir 47587 (Out 62966), Washington, Aug. 27, 1960. See also Central Intelligence Agency Files, Job 79–00149A, DDO/IMS Files, Box 23, Folder 1, African Division, Senate Select Committee, Volume II, Secret.

69. Treaty Document 102–1, Treaty with the People's Republic of the Congo Concerning the Reciprocal Encouragement and Protection of Investments, Washington, DC, Feb. 12, 1990.

70. See Jean-Michel Mabeko Tali, *Disidencias e poder de estado. O MPLA perante si proprio (1962–1977)* (Luanda: Editorial Nzila, 2001), chaps. 1–3 for an account of the origins of the MPLA. See also Carlos Pacheco, *MPLA, um nascimento polemico (as falsficaçoes da historia)* (Lisbon: Vega, 1997).

71. Archivo Carlos Medina Gallego/Carlos Medina Gallego Archives (ACMG), Movimento Popular de Libertação de Angola/Popular Movement for the Liberation of Angola (MPLA), *Historia de Angola* (Oporto: Ediçoes Afrontamento, 1975); MPLA, *Angola: Documentos do MPLA* (Lisbon: n.p., 1977); and Don Barnett and Ron Harvey,

The Revolution in Angola: MPLA, Life Stories, and Documents (Indianapolis and New York: Bobbs-Merrill, 1972).

72. Sanford J. Ungar, "Jonas Savimbi: Big Welcome for a Bad Start," *Washington Post*, Jan. 26, 1986; and Terry Atlas, "Angolan Rebel to Lobby Washington," *Chicago Tribune*, Jan. 28, 1986.

73. See for instance David Keen, *The Privatization of War: A Political Economy of Conflict in Sierra Leone* (London: James Currey, 1997); Mark Bradbury, *Rebels without a Cause* (London: CARE, 1995); Mats Berdal and David M. Malone, eds., *Greed and Grievance: Economic Agendas in Civil Wars* (Boulder, CO: Lynne Rienner Publishers, 2000); and Stephen J. Stedman, "Spoilers Problems in Peace Processes," *International Security* 22, no. 2 (Fall 1997): 5–53.

74. See Robin Luckham with Ismail Ahmed, Robert Muggah and Sarah White, "Conflict and Poverty in Sub-Saharan Africa: An Assessment of the Issues and Evidence," Working Paper 128, Institute of Development Studies.

75. Howard W. French, "From Old Files, a New Story of U.S. Role in Angola War," *New York Times*, March 31, 2002. See the original CIA report, marked "Confidential," NI-1589–77, June 23, 1977, approved for release on 01/01/2006 and identified as M 77–015C, "Cuban Involvement in Angola."

76. Both quotes are found in Andrew Buncombe, "CIA Angola Lies Exposed 25 Years Later," *The Independent*, London, April 5, 2002. For the original work, see Piero Gleijeses, *Conflicting Missions, Havana, Washington and Africa, 1959–1976* (Chapel Hill: University of North Carolina Press, 2002), 271.

77. Both quotes in French, "From Old Files."

78. Gerald Horne, *From the Barrel of a Gun: The United States and the War against Zimbabwe* (Chapel Hill: University of North Carolina Press, 2001).

79. John Goshko, "Rhodesia Lobby under Scrutiny by Justice Department," *Washington Post*, March 29, 1977. The Southern Rhodesia lobby office was opened in February 1966, three months after its November 1965 declaration of independence from Britain. Before that, the minority government of Ian Smith had kept a diplomatic presence in Washington that was officially part of the British embassy.

80. All quotes in FRUS, 1958–1960, Africa, Vol. 17, No. 6, Memorandum of Discussion at the 137th Meeting of the National Security Council, Aug. 7, 1958. See also *U.S. Policy toward Africa South of the Sahara Prior to Calendar Year 1960*, NSC5719/1; and Memos for NSC from Executive Secretary, same subject, July 29 and Aug. 5 and 6, 1958.

81. An overview of the history of French nuclear policy can be found in J. Doise and M. Vaisse, *Politique étrangère de la France: Diplomatie et outil militaire, 1871–1991* (Paris: Seuil, 1992), chap. 1; and Alain Peyrefitte, *C'était de Gaulle*, 3 vols. (Paris: De Fallois/Fayard, 1994–2000), esp. vol. 1, pp. 419–20.

82. Julius Holmes: Memorandum to Secretary of State Dulles, Feb. 6, 1958, in FRUS, 1958–60, vol. 16: Africa (Washington, DC: Government Printing Office, 1992). See also M. Vaisse, *La grandeur: Politique étrangère du général de Gaulle, 1958–1969* (Paris: Fayard, 1999), 128–30.

83. Tawia Adamafio, "French Nuclear Tests in the Sahara," speech delivered by Hon. Tawia Adamafio, general secretary of the Convention People's Party, at the Palla-

dium, Accra, Sept. 1, 1960, on the French plan to hold another nuclear test in the Sahara.

84. See Jean-Marc Regnault, "France's Search for Nuclear Test Sites, 1957–1963," *Journal of Military History* 67, no. 4 (2003): 1232.

85. Adamafio, "French Nuclear Tests in the Sahara."

86. File 9, 13 R 132 contains a report from General Ailleret dated Jan. 12, 1959. Cited in Regnault, "France's Search for Nuclear Test Sites, 1957–1963," 2230 fn.

87. Adamafio, "French Nuclear Tests in the Sahara."

88. See Tunde Adeniran, "Nuclear Proliferation and Black Africa: The Coming Crisis of Choice," *Third World Quarterly* 3, no. 4 (1981): 673–83, here 676.

89. Adamafio, "French Nuclear Tests in the Sahara."

90. Ibid.

91. "Quand les appelés du contingent servaient de cobayes," *Le Parisien*, Paris, Feb. 16, 2010. See also "France Exposed Troops to Radiation," *The Independent*, London, Feb. 17, 2010; and "France Used Troops as Nuclear 'Guinea Pigs,'" *Reuters*, Feb. 16, 2010.

92. Jean Louis Valatx, "Conséquences sur la santé des essais nucléaires français — Résultats sur 1800 questionnaires" [Health Consequences of French Nuclear Tests — Results of 1800 Questionnaires], website of the Association des Vétérans des Essais Nucléaires (AVEN), www.aven.org/aven-acceuil-actions-medicales-enquete-sante).

93. Michel Verger cited in "*Gerboise Bleue* on 3 February 1960 — The First French Nuclear Test Conducted in the Algerian Desert" (accessed on Dec. 21. 2018 at https://www.ctbto.org/specials/testing-times/13-february-1960-the-first-french-nuclear-test).

94. Kathum El-Abodi cited in "Algerians Used by France for Nuclear Tests: Report," *Al Arabiya News*, Oct. 17, 2010, http://www.alarabiya.net/articles/2010/02/18/100704.html.

95. Ibid.

96. *Middle Eastern Report and Information Project* (MERIP), "Class Roots of Sadat Regime: Reflections of an Egyptian Leftist," *Reports* 56 (April 1977): 3–7.

11. AFRICAN-BORN IMMIGRANTS IN THE UNITED STATES

1. Basil Davidson, *The Blackman's Burden: Africa and the Curse of the Nation* (London: John Curry, 1992), 75.

2. See for instance Ronald Labonte, *The African Brian Drain: Managing the Drain Working with the Diaspora* (Accra: Association of African Universities, 2018); and Jonathan Crush, ed., *The Brain Drain of Health Professionals from Sub-Saharan Africa to Canada* (Idasa, South Africa: Southern African Migration Project, 2006), esp. 33–40.

3. President George H. W. Bush (1989–1993) signed the Immigration Act of 1990 — Pub. L. 101-649, 104 Sta. 4978 into law in November 1990. The majority of Africans began to avail themselves of the opportunity from 2000.

4. Monica Anderson, "African Immigrant Population in the U.S. Steadily Climbs," Pew Research Center, Feb. 14, 2017. See also Monica Anderson and Gustavo Lopez, "Key Facts about Black Immigrants in the U.S.," Pew Research Center, Jan. 24, 2018.

5. John A. Arthur, *Invisible Sojourners: African Immigrant Diasporas in the U.S.* (Westport, CT: Praeger, 2000); and April Gordon, "The New Diaspora—African Immigration to the United States," *Journal of Third World Studies* 15, no. 1 (1998): 79–103.

6. Pew Research Center, "African Immigrant Population in the U.S. Steadily Climbs," Feb. 14, 2017.

7. See for instance A. Adepoju, "Leading Issues in International Migration in Sub-Saharan Africa," in C. Cross, D. Gelderblom, N. Roux, and J. Mafukidze, eds., *Views on Migration in Sub-Saharan Africa: Proceedings of an African Alliance Migration Workshop* (Cape Town: HSRC Press, 2006); K. Hoggart and C. Mendoza, "African Immigrant Workers in Spanish Agriculture," *Sociologia ruralia* 39, no. 4 (1999): 538–62; and Thomas Y. Owusu, "Residential Patterns and Housing Choices of Ghanaian Immigrants in Toronto, Canada," *Housing Studies* 14, no. 1 (1999): 77–97.

8. Rachael R. Reynolds, "An African Brian Drain: Igbo Decisions to Immigrate to the U.S.," *Review of African Political Economy* 29, no. 92 (2002): 273–84; and A. Hagopian, A. Ofosu, A. Fatusi, R. Biritwum, A. Essel, L. Gary Hart, and C. Watts, "The Flight of Physicians from West Africa: Views of African Physicians and Implications for Policy," *Social Science and Medicine* 61, no. 8 (2005): 1750–60.

9. Kevin J. A. Thomas, "What Explains the Increasing Trend in African Emigration to the U.S.?" *International Migration Review* 45, no. 1 (2011): 3–28.

10. Figures from U.S. Census Bureau, "Historical Census Statistics on Foreign-Born Population of the United States: 1850 to 2000," Population Division, Working Paper No. 81, compiled by Campbell Gibson and Kay Jung, Washington, DC, February 2006. See for instance Kwado Konadu-Agyemang and Baffour K. Takyi, "An Overview of African Immigration to US and Canada," in *The African Diaspora in North Africa: Trends, Community Building, and Adaptation*, ed. Kwado Konadu-Agyemang, Baffour K. Takyi, and John A. Arthur (Lanham, MD: Lexington Books, 2006), 189–289.

11. Walter L. Williams, "Ethnic Relations of African Students in the United States, with Black Americans, 1870–1900," *Journal of Negro History* 65, no. 3 (1980): 228–49.

12. U.S. Immigration and Naturalization Service, *Statistical Yearbook of the Immigration and Naturalization Service, 1997* (Washington, DC: Government Printing Office, 1999), 25; and Campbell Gibson and Emily Lenon, "Historical Census Statistics on Foreign-Born Population of the United States: 1850–1990," U.S. Census Bureau, Working Paper No. 29, Washington, DC, Feb. 1999.

13. Williams, "Ethnic Relations of African Students in the United States," 229.

14. Gustavo Lopez and Jynnah Radford, "Facts on U.S. Immigrants, 2015: Statistical Portrait of the Foreign-Born Population in the United States," Pew Research Center, Washington, DC, May 3, 2017. See also U.S. Census Bureau, "Historical Census Statistics on Foreign-Born Population," Washington, DC, February 2006.

15. U.S. Census Bureau, *The Foreign-Born Population 2000: Census 2000 Brief*, December 2003 (accessed on Aug. 14, 2018 at https://www.census.gov/prod/2003pubs/c2kbr-34.pdf).

16. Mary Medeiros Kent, "Immigration and America's Black Population," *Population Bulletin* 62 (2007): 3–16; and Gordon, "The New Diaspora—African Immigration to

the United States." See also Konadu-Agyemang, Takyi, and Arthur, *The New African Diaspora in North Africa*.

17. U.S. Immigration and Naturalization Service, *Statistical Yearbook of the Immigration and Naturalization Service, 1997* (Washington, DC: Government Printing Office, 1999). See also U.S. Census Bureau, *The Foreign-Born Population*, December 2003.

18. See Konadu-Agyemang, Takyi, and Arthur, *The New African Diaspora in North America*, 119. U.S. Census Bureau, *The Foreign-Born Population*. For an analysis of this report, see John R. Logan and Glenn Dean, *Black Diversity in Metropolitan America* (Albany, NY: Urban and Regional Research, University of Albany, 2003). Lewis and Dean concluded that overall the number of African Americans with roots in Africa tripled in the 1990s.

19. See U.S. Census Bureau, *The Foreign-Born Population*. See also Logan and Deane, *Black Diversity in Metropolitan America*.

20. Raphael Chijioke Njoku, "Current Debates in Contemporary African Studies," in *Africa and the Wider World*, ed. H. Tijani, R. Njoku, and T. Jones (New York: Pearson, 2010), 343–62.

21. See, for instance, Stephen Castles, "Development and Migration—Migration and Development: What Comes First? Global Perspective and African Experiences," *Theoria: A Journal of Social and Political Theory* 56, no. 121 (2009): 1–31; and Gordon F. De Jong, Aphichat Chamratrithirong, and Quynh-Giang Tran, "For Better, for Worse: Life Satisfaction Consequences of Migration," *International Migration Review* 36, no. 3 (2002): 838–63.

22. Jill H. Wilson and Shelly Habecker, "The Lure of the Capital City: An Anthro-Geographical Analysis of Recent African Immigration to Washington, D.C.," *Population, Space, and Place* 14 (2008): 433–48.

23. Amy Hagopian, Matthew J. Thompson, Meredith Fordyce, Karin E. Johnson, and L. Gary Hart, "The Migration of Physicians from Sub-Saharan Africa to the United States of America: Measures of the African Brain Drain," *Human Resources for Health* 2, no. 17 (2014), https://human-resources-health.biomedcentral.com/articles/10.1186/1478-4491-2-17.

24. William J. Carrington and Enrica Detragiache, "How Extensive Is the Brain Drain?" *Finance and Development* 36, no. 2 (1999): 46–49.

25. Monica Anderson and Philip Connor, "Sub-Saharan African Immigrants in the U.S. Often More Educated than Those in Top European Destinations," Pew Research Center, Washington, DC, April 24, 2018. See also JBHE Foundation, "African Immigrants in the United States Are the Nation's Most Highly Educated Group," *Journal of Blacks in Higher Education* 26 (1999–2000): 60–61.

26. Immanuel Wallerstein, *The Modern World System*, vol. 1: *Capitalist Agriculture and the Origins of the European World Economy in the Sixteenth Century* (New York: Academic Press, 1974), and *The Modern World System*, vol. 2: *Mercantilism and the Consolidation of the European World-Economy, 1600–1750* (New York: Academic Press, 1980). Douglas S. Massey, Joaquin Arango, Graeme Hugo, Ali Kouaouci, Adela Pellegrino, and J. Edward Taylor, *Worlds in Motion: Understanding International*

Migration at the End of the Millennium (New York: Oxford University Press, 1998). See also Xavier Thierry, "Recent Immigration in France and Elements for a Comparison with the United Kingdom," *Population* 59, no. 5 (2004): 635–72.

27. Monica Boyd, "Family and Personal Networks in International Migration: Recent Developments and New Agendas," *International Migration Review* 23, no. 3 (1989): 638–70.

28. A. R. Zolberg, "The Next Waves: Migration Theory for a Changing World," *International Migration Review* 23, no. 3 (1989): 403–30; and A. R. Zolberg, "Matters of State: Theorizing Immigration Policy," in C. Hirschman, P. Kasinitz, and J. Dewind, eds., *The Handbook of International Migration: The American Experience* (New York: Russell Sage Foundation, 1999), 71–93.

29. See Tajudeen Adewumi Adebisi, "The Visa Lottery versus Brain Drain: The Impact of the African Diaspora on Vocational Artisanship," in *The New African Diaspora in the United States*, ed. Toyin Falola and Adebayo Oyebade (New York: Routledge, 2017), 155–64.

30. Barbara Dietz, "Ethnic German Migration from Eastern Europe and the Former Soviet Union to Germany: The Effects of Migrant Networks," Discussion Paper No. 68, IZA, Bonn, Germany, 1999.

31. The Quardu-Gboni Mandingo Association (QGMAA) in the Americas, By-Laws and Constitution, Submitted by the Constitution Review Committee, May 28, 2007.

32. Ghana Association of Houston, Inc., Constitution of the Ghana Association, Houston, TX (1999), http://ghanaassociationofhouston.org/ (accessed on Oct. 10, 2018).

33. QGMAA in the Americas, By-Laws and Constitution Review, May 28, 2007.

34. QGMAA, "Black and Red Valentine Party," Saturday, Feb. 17–18, Newark, NJ, 2012.

35. Congo Town Hall, "Ten Years, One Life at a Time," Notes from a Town Hall Event at the Museum of Tolerance, Los Angeles, May 14, 2014.

36. UCLA African Studies Center, "The Congolese Community of Southern California Presents an Evening of Healing and Hope" (accessed on Oct. 10, 2018 at http://international.ucla.edu/africa/event/3010).

37. Peter P. Ekeh, "Colonialism and the Two Publics in Africa: A Theoretical Statement," *Comparative Studies in Society and History* 17 (1975): 91–112.

38. Austin M. Ahanaotu, "The Role of Ethnic Unions in the Development of Southern Nigeria, 1916–66," in Boniface I. Obichere, ed., *Studies in Southern Nigerian History: A Festschrift for Joseph Christopher O. Anene* (London: Frank Cass, 1982), 153–74, here 156. See also Nigerian National Archives Enugu (NNAE), 4715, CALPROF 7, 1/2424, "National Independence Party" (1953–1954); and Ruth Chapman Audrey, "Political Development in Eastern Nigeria: The Role of the Ethnic Unions" (M.A. thesis, Columbia University, 1967).

39. Christopher Fyfe, *Africanus Horton: West African Scientist and Patriot, 1835–1883* (London: Oxford University Press, 1972), 45–50, 79–80; and Ahanaotu, "The Role of Ethnic Unions," 171.

40. Adiele E. Afigbo, *Ropes: Studies in Igbo History and Culture* (Nsukka, Nigeria: University Press in association with Oxford University Press, 1981), 345–46; and Ikenna Nzimiro, *Studies in Igbo Political Systems: Chieftaincy and Politics in Four*

Niger States (London: Frank Cass, 1972), 106. See also Elizabeth Isichei, *The Ibo People and the Europeans: The Genesis of a Relationship to 1906* (London: Faber and Faber, 1973), 153, 179, 217–21; S. N. Nwabara, *Iboland: A Century of Contact with Britain, 1860–1960s* (Atlantic Highlands, NJ: Humanities Press, 1978), 224–25; Eghosa E. Osaghae, *Trends in Migrant Political Organizations in Nigeria: The Igbo Union in Kano* (Ibadan: IFRA, 1994); and Audrey C. Smock, *Ibo Politics: The Role of Ethnic Unions in Eastern Nigeria* (Cambridge, MA: Harvard University Press, 1971).

41. These associations persist today as cultural associations and continue to sponsor village- and town-based projects in diverse forms.

42. *Afikpo Town Welfare Association Constitution*, March 20, 1950, Afikpo, 1952, 14–15.

43. Association of Nigerians in the Capital District (hereafter ANCD) of New York, Constitution, New Albany, NY, April 2003.

44. Ibid.

45. Ibid.

46. ANCD Constitution.

47. For an engaging study of this, see Ayokunle Olumuyiwa Omobowale, Mofeyisara Oluwatoyin Omobowale, and Olawale Olufolaban Ajani, "Emigration and Social Value of Remittance in Nigeria," in Emmanuel Yewah and 'Dimeji Togunde, eds., *Across the Atlantic: African Immigrants in the United States* (New York: Common Grounds, 2010), 127–36.

48. Yinka Adegoke, "Moving Cash within Africa Is the Untapped Opportunity for Money Transfer Firms," *Quartz Africa*, March 7, 2018; Elizabeth Adegbesan, "Nigeria Tops Remittances to Sub-Saharan Africa with $22bn—World Bank," *Vanguard*, Lagos, April 24, 2018.

49. Jocelyne Sambira, "African Remittances Reduce Poverty," *Sierra Leone Telegraph*, Freetown, Sept. 17, 2013.

50. Adams Bodorro, "African Diaspora Remittances Are Better than Foreign Aid Funds," *World Economics*, October 2013: 21–29.

51. Clifford Geertz, *Interpretation of Cultures: Selected Essays by Clifford Geertz* (New York: Basic Books, 1965), 89–91.

52. Max Weber, *The Protestant Ethic and the Spirit of Capitalism* (New York: Scribner, 1958).

53. See Emmanuel K. Twesigye, "Religious Institutions: Mode of Adaptation for African Immigrants in the U.S.A.," in *Across the Atlantic: African Immigrants in the United States*, ed. Emmanuel Yewah and 'Dimeji Togunde (New York: Common Grounds, 2010), 137–48.

54. Antonio Olivo, "African Immigrants Hope for a Chicago Community of Their Own," *Chicago Tribune*, Jan. 14, 2013.

55. Wesley Granberg-Michaelson, "The Hidden Immigration Impact on American Churches," *Washington Post*, Sept. 23, 2013.

56. Adebayo Oyebade, "African Immigrants and Their Churches," in *The New African Diaspora in the United States*, ed. Toyin Falola and Adebayo Oyebade (New York: Routledge, 2016), 18.

57. Afe Adogame, *The African Christian Diaspora: New Currents and Emerging Trends in World Christianity* (London: Bloomsbury, 2013), 27.

58. Peter Beinart, "Breaking Faith: The Culture War over Religious Morality Has Faded; In Its Place Is Something Much Worse," *The Atlantic*, April 2017.

59. Granberg-Michaelson, "The Hidden Immigration Impact on American Churches."

60. Ibigbolade Aderibigbe, "African Initiated Churches and African Immigrants in the United States: A Model in the Redeemed Christian Church of God, North America (RCCGNA)," *Contemporary Perspectives on Religions in Africa and the African Diaspora* 1, no. 1 (2015): 241–58.

61. Oyebade, "African Immigrants and Their Churches," 18.

62. Afe Adogame, "Raising Champions, Taking Territories: African Churches and the Mapping of New Religious Landscapes in the Diaspora," in Theodore Louis Trost, ed., *The African Diaspora and the Study of Religion* (New York: Palgrave Macmillan, 2007), 17–34, here 23. See also Afe Adogame, "Reconfiguring the Global Religious Economy: The Role of African Pentecostalism," in Donald E. Miller, Kimon S. Sargeant, and Richard Flory, eds., *Spirit and Power: The Growth and Global Impact of Pentecostalism* (Oxford: Oxford University Press, 2013), 185–203, here 191.

63. Adogame, "Raising Champions, Taking Territories," 22–23.

64. Shelly Habecker, "Becoming African American: African Immigrant Youth in the United States and Hybrid Assimilation," *Africology: The Journal of Pan African Studies* 10, no. 1 (2017): 55–75.

65. Joseph Conteh, "How African Americans and African Immigrants Differ," *Globalist*, Nov. 16, 2013.

66. Antonio Olivo, "African Immigrants Hope for a Chicago Community of Their Own," *Chicago Tribune*, Jan. 14, 2013.

67. "Nigerian Community in U.S. to Float Community Bank," *The Sun*, Lagos, Aug. 22, 2018.

68. See https://peopleofcolorintech.com/interview/pocit-59-makinde-adeagbo/. Njoku, one of the authors, knows the Adeagbo family in person and shared a home with his parents in Louisville, KY, in 2003, when young Makinde was graduating from high school.

12. U.S. PRESSURES

1. President Barack Obama addresses the Ghanaian Parliament in Accra, Ghana, July 11, 2009. See also Barack H. Obama, "The Key to Success: U.S. President Obama, on Good Governance in Africa," in *The Report: Nigeria 2010* (Oxford: Oxford Business Group, 2010), 26; and Richard Joseph, "The American Presidency and Democracy Promotion in Africa," *Brookings Bulletin*, Aug. 23, 2012.

2. David Smith, "Power Struggle in Burkina Faso after Blaise Compaoré Resigns as President," *The Guardian*, London, Nov. 1, 2014. See also Lila Chouli, "The Popular Uprising in Burkina Faso and the Transition," *Review of African Political Economy* 42, no. 144 (2015): 325–33.

3. The White House, Office of the Press Secretary, "Remarks by President Obama to the People of Africa," Mandela Hall, African Union Headquarters, Addis Ababa, Ethiopia, July 18, 2015.

4. Human Rights Watch, *Burundi: World Report 2018*. See also "Burundi Votes in a Referendum over President's 2034 'Power Grab,'" *The Guardian*, London, May 16, 2018.

5. The General Peace Agreement consists of five protocols: (a) the nature of the conflict; (b) democracy and good governance (constitution and transitional arrangements); (c) questions of peace and security (defense and security force reform and a permanent ceasefire); (d) reconstruction and development (economic matters); (e) guarantees on implementation of the agreement. See "Arusha Peace Agreement for Burundi," *United Nations Peacemaker*, Nairobi, Aug. 28, 2000.

6. See Aislinn Laing, "Burundi Coup: General Announces Overthrow of President Nkurunziza," *The Telegraph*, London, May 13, 2015.

7. White House, Office of the Press Secretary, "Fact Sheet: Burundi Executive Order," Nov. 23, 2016.

8. "Burundi's President Is Now Supreme Eternal Guide: Retirement Out," *The Economist*, May 19, 2015. See also Human Rights Watch, *Burundi: World Report 2018*.

9. James Munyaneza, "Kagame Wins Rwanda Poll by a Landslide," *The New Times*, Kigali, Aug. 5, 2017; Clement Uwiringiyimana, "Rwanda's Kagame Wins Third Presidential Term by Landslide," *Reuters*, Aug. 4, 2017.

10. Cono Gaffey, "Congo's Denis Sassou Nguesso Extends 32-Year Rule," *Newsweek*, March 24, 2016. During the election mired in fraud, the president ordered a communications blackout to prevent all mobile and internet communications.

11. "Why Kabila's Bid to Remain in Power Is Bad News for the Democratic Republic of the Congo," *The Conversation*, Aug. 31, 2017.

12. AFP, "Joseph Kabila Maintains Suspense over Election Plans," *The East African*, Nairobi, July 20, 2018, https://www.theeastafrican.co.ke/news/africa/DR-Congo-Joseph -Kabila-maintains-suspense-over-plans/4552902-4672640-ua7kmnz/index.html.

13. Mo Ibrahim Foundation, 2015 *Ibrahim Index of African Governance — Index Report*, 2015, 4; and Mo Ibrahim Foundation, 2017 *Ibrahim Index of African Governance — Index Report*, 2017, 13, 21, 28.

14. IDA Documents NS D-8846, Institute for Defense Analyses (IDA), *U.S.-African Partnerships: Advancing Common Interests*, December 2017.

15. "Disquiet Grows over How Gaddafi Met His End," *InterAksyon.com*, Oct. 22, 2011.

16. George Charamba quoted by Josh Kron, "Many in Sub-Saharan Africa Mourn Qaddafi's Death," *New York Times*, Oct. 22, 2011.

17. "2002 Ikeja Cantonment Bomb Blast: I Was Busy Helping Others Not Knowing My Two Children Had Died," *Punch Newspaper*, Lagos, Jan. 28, 2002.

18. Francisca U. Uzodinma, Personal Communication, Jan. 28, 2002. For more on the consequences of the blast in which 600 people lost their lives, see M. Olowopeju, "Years after Victims of Ikeja Bomb Blast Compensated," *Vanguard*, Lagos, April 26, 2014.

19. "Bombings in Lagos Jolt Nigeria's Relations with U.S.," *New York Times*, Jan. 19, 1997.

20. Ibid.

21. S/RES/687 Security Council Resolution (UNSCR) No. 687, Iraq/Kuwait April 3, 1991; and Council on Foreign Relations, "Iraq: Weapons Inspection: 1991–1998," Feb. 3, 2005. For more on that attack, see Special Report, "U.S. and British Forces Attack Iraq," *The Guardian*, London, Feb. 16, 2001.

22. See Raphael Chijioke Njoku, "Deconstructing Abacha: Demilitarization and Democratic Consolidation in Nigeria after the Abacha Era," *Government and Opposition* 36, no. 1 (2001): 71–96, here 83; and Reuben Abati, "The Nation versus Abacha," *The Guardian*, Lagos, May 1, 1998: 20.

23. Paul Tiyambe Zeleza, "The Struggle for Human Rights in Africa," *Canadian Journal of African Studies* 41, no. 3 (2007): 474–506, here 474.

24. See Mark T. Berger, "The End of the 'Third World'?" *Third World Quarterly* 15 (1994): 257–75; Mark T. Berger, "After the Third World? History, Destiny and the Fate of Third Worldism," *Third World Quarterly* 25 (2004): 9–39; and Arif Dirlik, "Specters of the Third World: Global Modernity and the End of the Three Worlds," *Third World Quarterly* 25 (2004): 131–48.

25. Nigel Harris, *The End of the Third World: Newly Industrializing Countries and the Decline of an Ideology* (London: Penguin, 1987), 7. See also Hans-Henrik Holm, "The End of the Third World?" *Journal of Peace Research* 27 (1990): 1–7; and Fouad Makki, "The Empire of Capital and the Remaking of Centre-Periphery Relations," *Third World Quarterly* 25 (2004): 149–68.

26. UNE (01)/R3 UN, ECA, Conference of Ministers, 1990.

27. Michael Bratton and Robert Mattes, "Support for Democracy in Africa: Intrinsic and Instrumental?" *British Journal of Political Science* 31, no. 3 (2001): 447–74.

28. Joel D. Barkan and Njuguna Ng'ethe, "Kenya Tries Again," *Journal of Democracy* 9 (1998): 32–49. See also Joel Samoff, "Pluralism and Conflict in Africa: Ethnicity, Institutions and Class in Tanzania," *Civilization* 3233, nos. 1–2 (1982–1983): 97–134, here 98.

29. Jean-François Bayart, Stephen Ellis, and Beatrice Hibou, *The Criminalization of the State in Africa* (Bloomington: Indiana University Press, 1999), esp. 25–26.

30. It is intriguing that President Sarkozy, who was in power from May 16, 2007, to May 15, 2012, initiated the vicious air bombardments against Gaddafi in Libya in 2011. Angelique Chrisafis, "Nicolas Sarkozy in Police Custody over Gaddafi Allegations," *The Guardian*, London, March 20, 2018; and Rebecca Perring, "Nicolas Sarkozy 'Arrested': Former French President in Custody in Police Probe," *Express*, London, March 20, 2018.

31. Paul Collier and Anke Hoeffler, "Greed and Grievance in Civil Wars," *Oxford Economic Papers* 56, no. 4 (2004): 563–95. See also Anke Hoeffler, "'Greed' versus 'Grievance': A Useful Conceptual Distinction in the Study of Civil Wars?" *Studies in Ethnicity and Nationalism* 11, no. 2 (2011): 272–84.

32. Paul Richards, "The Political Economy of Internal Conflict in Sierra Leone," Working Paper 21 (The Hague: Netherlands Institute of International Relations "Clingendael," August 2003), esp. 20–22.

33. Brandon Valeriano, "Power Politics and Interstate War in Africa," *African Security* 4 no. 3 (2011): 195–221.

34. Matia K., cited by Agendia Aloysius, "France, La Francophonie, French and African Dictators," published Oct. 29, 2008, http://agendia.jigsy.com/entries/africa/france-la -francophonie-french-and-african-dictators-2.

35. Robert Neuwirth, "African Monetary Union Stirs Criticism of France: Former Colonies Use a Franc Tied to the Euro," *Bloomberg*, April 17, 2014.

36. Stephen Ryan, "The Voice of Sanity Getting Hoarse? Destructive Processes in Violent Ethnic Conflict," in Edwin N. Wilmsen and Patrick McAllister, eds., *The Politics of Difference: Ethnic Premises in a World of Power* (Chicago: University of Chicago Press, 1996), 155.

37. E. E. Azar, *The Management of Protracted Social Conflict* (Aldershot, UK: Dartmouth, 1990), 16.

38. See "Human Rights in Africa: The Debate Continues," *West Africa*, Nov. 4–10, 1991.

39. Jack Donnelly, *Universal Human Rights in Theory and Practice* (Ithaca, NY: Cornell University Press, 1989), 46–47, 71. Rhoda E. Howard, *Human Rights in Commonwealth Africa* (Totowa, NJ: Rowman and Littlefield), 23–28, 39–40.

40. Donnelly, *Universal Human Rights*, 104.

41. Timothy Fernyhough, "Human Rights and Pre-colonial Africa," in *Human Rights and Governance in Africa*, ed. Ronald Cohen and Goran Hyden (Gainesville, FL: University Press of Florida, 1993), 39–73, here 56, 65. See also Simeon O. Ilesanmi, "Human Rights Discourse in Modern Africa: A Comparative Religious Ethical Perspective," *Journal of Religious Ethics* 23, no. 2 (1995): 293–322.

42. Pieter Boele van Hensbroek, *Political Discourses in African Thought: 1860 to the Present* (Westport, CT, and London: Praeger, 1999), 169–70.

43. J. L. Cohen and A. Arato, "The Contemporary Revival of Civil Society," in J. L. Cohen and A. Arato, *Civil Society and Political Theory* (Cambridge, MA: MIT Press, 1992), 30.

44. New Partnership for Africa's Development (NEPAD), "Consolidated Report of Africa's Regional Economic Communities," NEPAD Planning and Coordination Agency, Midrand, South Africa, January 2015, https://www.nepad.org/file-download/ download/public/14490.

45. Statement of Assistant Secretary Johnnie Carson, Senate Foreign Relations Committee Subcommittee on Africa, April 18, 2012. See also Johnnie Carson, assistant secretary of state for African affairs, remarks to the Harvard University Africa Focus Program, Washington, DC, April 5, 2010.

13. AFRICA AND THE NEW GLOBAL AGE

1. President Roch Kabore of Burkina Faso, "Africa Has Chosen China," *The Sun*, Port Harcourt, Nigeria, Aug. 29, 2018.

2. Center for Strategic and International Studies, "Creating a New U.S. and Africa Partnership," Feb. 23, 2018.

3. "Du Bois, 91, Lauds China," *New York Times*, March 5, 1959.

4. Natural Resource Governance Institute (NRGI), "The Resource Curse: The Political and Economic Challenges of Natural Resource Wealth," 2nd ed., 2014, www.resource governance.org/.

5. These sources are newspapers, official reports, and white papers, as well as published articles and books. Others are images of protests, as well as speeches made in Angola and elsewhere. There is also an interesting body of primary sources related to the Royal Dutch Shell vs. Ogoniland struggle. The website of the U.S. Africa Command (USAAFRICOM or AFRICOM) provides a comprehensive review of the organization's mission and activities; see http://www.africom.mil/AboutAFRICOM .asp.

6. ECOWAS, Protocols, Lomé, Togo, Nov. 5, 1976. These protocols covered a wide range of topics, including member contributions, the exportation of goods within the region, and assessment of loss of revenue.

7. "ECOWAS/CEDECO: Working Towards a Better Economic Political and Cultural Future," *West Africa*, London, July 6, 1987: 1289–92.

8. Ibid., 1291.

9. See, for instance, Edward R. Reid, "After the Oil Glut," *Brookings Bulletin* 18, no. 3–4 (1982): 1079–1101; and Carol Dahl and Meftun Erdogan, "Oil Demands in the Developing World: Lessons from the 1980s Applied to the 1990s," *Energy Journal* 15 (1994): 68–85.

10. "What Was Decided at the Bretton Woods Summit," *The Economist*, July 1, 2014; and Richard C. Duncan, "The Peak of World Oil Production and the Road to the Olduvai Gorge," *Population and Environment* 22, no. 5 (2011): 503–22.

11. See for instance Mohammed E. Ahrari, "OPEC and the Hyperpluralism of the Oil Market in the 1980s," *International Affairs* 61, no. 2 (1985): 265–77; and Roger Owen, "The Arab Economies in the 1970s," *MERIP Reports* 100–101 (1981): 3–13.

12. Howard Schissel, "Mauritania in the Mining Doldrums," *West Africa*, London, Nov. 7, 1983: 2563–64.

13. Eddie Momoh, "Liberian Economy: When the Chips Are Down," *West Africa*, London, Feb. 13, 1984: 317.

14. Ronald Reagan, "Remarks of the President and Head of State Samuel K. Doe of Liberia Following Their Meeting," Aug. 17, 1982. During the speech, Reagan introduced his guest as "Chairman Moe."

15. A/39/211 E/1984/58—UNDP, "Critical Economic Situation in Africa," April 26, 1984.

16. Bakary Darbo cited in "The Enduring Drought," *West Africa*, London, Feb. 13, 1984: 311.

17. A/39/211 E/1984/58—UNDP Critical Economic Situation in Africa, April 26, 1984.

18. Ibid.; "The Enduring Drought." See also "Waking Up to an African Famine," *West Africa*, London, Feb. 13, 1984: 315.

19. "Waking Up to an African Famine."

20. See for instance Charles L. Gladson, "Western Aid to Africa," *Issue: Journal of Opinion* 16, no. 2 (1988): 18–23.

21. "Waking Up to an African Famine."

22. Manzamasso Hodjo and Ram N. Acharya, "Rising Imports and Domestic Rice Production in Togo," paper presented at the Southern Agricultural Economics Association's 2015 Annual Meeting, Atlanta, GA, Jan. 31–Feb. 3, 2015.

23. ECW/HSG/VII/6, Seventh ECOWAS Summit, Final Communique: The Lomé Declaration, Lome, Republic of Togo, Nov. 22–23, 1984, 3–7. See also Adebayo Adedeji, Owodunmi Teriba, and Patrick Bugembe, eds., *The Challenge of African Economic Recovery and Development* (London: Frank Cass, 1991), 142.

24. ECW/HSG/X/3/REV.1, Economic Community of West African States—Authority of Heads of States and Government, Final Communique, Abuja, July 7–9, 1987, 5.

25. ECW/HSG/X/3/REV.1, Economic Community of West African States—Authority of Heads of States and Government, Final Communique, Abuja, July 7–9, 1987, 5–6.

26. Ibid., 6.

27. Owei Lakemfa, "The African Road to China," *Vanguard*, Aug. 24, 2018.

28. Timothy S. Rich and Sterling Recker, "Understanding Sino-African Relations: Neocolonialism or a New Era?" *Journal of International and Area Studies* 20, no. 1 (2013): 61–76; and David Zweig and Bi Jianhai, "China's Global Hunt for Energy," *Foreign Affairs* 84, no. 5 (2005): 25–38.

29. George T. Yu, "Africa in Chinese Foreign Policy," *Asian Survey* 28, no. 8 (1988): 8498; and Owei Lakemfa, "The African Road to China," *Vanguard*, Aug. 24, 2018.

30. Julius Nyerere, "Ujamaa: The Basis of African Socialism" (1963), in Nyerere et al., *Africa's Freedom* (Dar es Salaam: Oxford University Press, 1968), 67–77; and Kwame Nkrumah, "Some Aspects of Socialism in Africa" (1966), in *African Socialism*, ed. William H. Friedland and Carl G. Rosberg (Stanford, CA: Stanford University Press, 1964), 340–41.

31. David Zweig and Jianhai Bi, "China's Global Hunt for Energy," *Foreign Affairs* 84, no. 5 (2005): 25–38.

32. Wei Zhang, "The Allure of the Chinese Model," *International Herald Tribune*, Nov. 1, 2006; and Rich and Recker, "Understanding Sino-African Relations," 61.

33. Liu Hongwu and Mulugeta Gebrehiwot Berhe, *China–Africa Relations 2013: Annual Report* (Stellenbosch, South Africa: Center for Chinese Studies, 2013), 49.

34. Hongming Zhang, "China Policy of Assistance Enjoys Popular Support," *People's Daily*, Peking, June 23, 2006.

35. Anna Katharina Stahl, *EU–China–Africa Trilateral Relations in a Multipolar World: Hic Sunt Dracones* (New York: Palgrave Macmillan, 2017), 2.

36. Anna Katharina Stahl, "Fostering African Development, Governance and Security through Multilateral Cooperation between China and Western Donors: The Case of China–DAC Study Group," in *China–Africa Relations: Governance, Peace and Security*, ed. Mulugeta Gebrehiwot Berhe and Liu Hongwu (Addis Ababa, Ethiopia: Institute of Peace and Security—Addis Ababa University, 2013), 74–96, here 79.

37. Emilian Kavalski, review of Yong Deng, *China's Struggle for Status: The Realignment of International Relations*, *Europe-Asia Studies* 61, no. 8 (2009): 1499–1500.

38. David H. Shinn, "An Opportunistic Ally: China's Increasing Involvement in Africa," *Harvard International Review* 29, no. 2 (2007): 52–56.

39. Jin Sato, Hiroaki Shiga, Takaaki Kobayashi, and Hisahiro Kondoh, "How Do 'Emerging' Donors Differ from 'Traditional' Donors? An Institutional Analysis of Foreign Aid in Cambodia," *JICA Research Institute* 2 (March 2010): 1–47, here 3.

40. Anja Manuel, "China Is Quietly Reshaping the World," *The Atlantic*, Oct. 17, 2017.

41. FOCAC from the website of the Chinese Ministry of Foreign Affairs, http://www.focac.org/eng/; and Shinn, "An Opportunistic Ally," 52–56.

42. Michal Meidan, "China's Africa Policy: Business Now, Politics Later," *Asian Perspective* 30, no. 4 (2006): 69–93, here 70.

43. Shinn, "An Opportunistic Ally," 53.

44. Immanuel Wallerstein, *The Modern World System*, vol. 1: *Capitalist Agriculture and the Origins of the European World Economy in the Sixteenth Century* (New York: Academic Press, 1974), and Wallerstein, *The Modern World System*, vol. 2: *Mercantilism and the Consolidation of the European World-Economy, 1600–1750* (New York: Academic Press, 1980).

45. Richard Drayton, "The Wealth of the West Was Built on Africa's Exploitation," *The Guardian*, London, Aug. 19, 2005.

46. For a reaction to this move among the British audience, see Andrew Meldrum, "Mugabe Land Seizures Force Hundreds of Farm Owners to Flee," *The Guardian*, London, June 2, 2000. The land reform resonates with a similar plan in South Africa in 2018. See John Robertson, "Land Reform Domino Hits South Africa, Inevitably," *The Herald*, Harare, Sept. 2, 2018.

47. Jeremy Youde, "Why Look East? Zimbabwean Foreign Policy and China," *Africa Today* 53, no. 3 (2007): 3–19.

48. "Zimbabwe's President Mnangagwa in First China Visit," *Daily Nation*, Nairobi, April 3, 2018.

49. Charity Manyeruke, Shakespeare Hamauswa, and Aaram Gwiza, "China: A Critical Factor in Zimbabwe's Political Crisis and Its Solution," in *China-African Relations: Governance, Peace and Security*, ed. Gebrehiwot Hongwu and Liu Berhe (Addis Ababa, Ethiopia: Institute for Peace and Security, 2013), 196.

50. "China Backs Zimbabwe Election Result," *East African*, Nairobi, Aug. 3, 2018.

51. "China Releases Funding for Zimbabwe's Largest Power Station Expansion Project," *China Daily*, June 1, 2018. See also Parliament of Zimbabwe, "Ratification of the Loan Agreement between the Government of Zimbabwe and the Export-Import Bank of China Relating to Kariba Hydropower Station," Jan. 23, 2014.

52. Phineas Bbaala, "Emerging Questions on the Shifting Sino-Africa Relations: 'Win-Win' or 'Win-Lose'?" *Africa Development / Afrique et développement* 40, no. 3 (2015): 97–119.

53. Kenneth W. Thompson, "Idealism and Realism: Beyond the Great Debate," *British Journal of International Studies* 3, no. 2 (1977): 199–209. See also Thompson Ayodele and Olusegun Sotola, "China in Africa: An Evaluation of Chinese Investment," *Initiative for Public Policy Analysis*, 2014: 1–20.

54. Ben Dooley, "An 'Old Friend of China': Pres. Xi Jinping Hails Robert Mugabe's Successor Emmerson Mnangagwa," *Hong Kong Free Press*, April 4, 2018.

55. "Zimbabwe's Leader Thanks China's Xi, Pledges to Boost Ties," *Associated Press*, April 3, 2018.

56. "Xi Hails Mugabe's Successor as 'Old Friend of China,'" *Jamaica Observer*, Mona, Jamaica, April 3, 2018.

57. "Government Signs $1.2 billion Tourism Investment Deal," *The Herald*, Harare, April 7, 2018.

58. Sebastian Berger, "Zimbabwe Veto: Britain and U.S. Condemn Russia and China," *The Telegraph*, London, July 12, 2018.

59. Mark A. McDowell, "China in Africa," paper submitted to the faculty of the Naval War College in partial satisfaction of the requirements of the Department of Joint Military Operations, Nov. 2, 2012, 2.

60. Ibid.

61. Ellennor Grace M. Francisco, "Petroleum Politics: China and Its National Oil Companies" (M.A. thesis, European Institute, 2013), 33.

62. Tom Burgis, "Chinese Seek Huge Stake in Nigeria Oil," *Financial Times*, London, Sept. 29, 2009: 9.

63. Zhang Jian, "China's Energy Security: Prospects, Challenges, and Opportunities," Brookings Institute Center for Northeast Asia Policy Studies, July 2011, 32.

64. Olugboyega A. Oyeranti, Adetunji M. Babatunde, and E. Olawale Ogunkola, "The Impact of China–Africa Investment Relations: The Case of Nigeria," AERC Collaborative Research China—Africa Project Policy Brief, no. 8 (November 2010): 1.

65. Lucy Corkin, Christopher Burke, and Martyn Davies, "China's Role in the Development of Africa's Infrastructure," Working Papers in African Studies (Washington, DC: The Johns Hopkins University's Paul H. Nitze School of Advanced International Studies, April 2008), 3.

66. Owei Lakemfa, "The African Road to China," *Vanguard*, Lagos, Aug. 24, 2018.

67. Prince Osuagwu, Emmanuel Elebeke, Tare Youdeowei, and Amarachukwu Nwankwo, "Space Tech: Future of Nigeria's Economy?" *Vanguard*, Lagos, Aug. 30, 2017. See also Prince Osuagwu, "How Nigcomsat-1R Will Impact Nigerian Economy," *Vanguard*, Lagos, Dec. 14, 2011; and McDowell, "China in Africa," 6.

68. Garba Shehu, "Mambila Power: Buhari's Big Bang Project Set to Take Off," *Vanguard*, Aug. 30, 2017; Ediri Ejoh, "FG Approves $5.8bn Power Plant Construction by Chinese Firm," *Vanguard*, Aug. 11, 2017; and McDowell, "China in Africa," 6.

69. "Nigeria, China to Sign $328m Agreement on ICT—Presidency," *Vanguard*, Lagos, Sept. 1, 2018.

70. Dragana Mitrovic, "China's Belt and Road Initiative: Connecting and Transforming Initiative," in *The Belt & Road Initiative in the Global Arena, Chinese and European Perspectives*, ed. Yu Cheng, Lilei Song, and Lihe Huang (New York: Palgrave Macmillan, 2017), 17–35; S. L. Wei, "China's Xi: Trade Between China and Silk Road Nations to Exceed $2.5 trillion," *Reuters*, March 29, 2015. See also Gerald Chan, *Understanding China's New Diplomacy, Silk Roads, and Bullet Trains* (Cheltenham, UK: Edward Elgar Publishing, 2018).

71. Lily Kuo, "Kenya's $3.2 Billion Nairobi–Mombasa Rail Line Opens with Help from China," *Madaraka Express*, Nairobi, June 1, 2017.

72. Ibid.

73. Lakemfa, "The African Road to China."

74. Ibid.

75. We owe immense gratitude to Dr. King Yik, who provided additional insights on these issues related to the skit and Chinese–African relationships. For insight on the growing number of Sub-Saharan African students in China, see Victoria Breeze and Nathan Moore, "China has overtaken the US and UK as top destination for Anglophone African Students," *Quartz Africa*, East Lansing, Michigan State University, June 30, 2017. For statistics on Sub-Saharan African students studying in the United States, see Education USA, *Global Education Guide* (Washington, DC: Published for the Department of State by the Bureau of Education and Cultural Affairs, 2019), 14–21.

76. See Mandy Turner, "Scramble for Africa," *The Guardian*, London, May 1, 2007; and Alan Beattie and Eoin Callan, "China Loans Create 'New Wave of Africa Debt,'" *Financial Times*, London, Dec. 7, 2006.

77. Anja Manuel, "China Is Quietly Reshaping the World," *The Atlantic*, Oct. 17, 2017.

78. Wei Liang, "China's Soft Power in Africa: Is Economic Power Sufficient?" *Asian Perspective* 36, no. 4 (2012): 667–92.

79. World Trade Organization, "Trade Policy Review Report," 4, https://www.wto.org/english/tratop_e/tpr_e/g382_e.pdf.

80. Charles Lindbergh, "America First Speech," Des Moines, IA, Sept. 11, 1941. See also "America First: From Charles Lindbergh to President Trump," *NPR*, Feb. 6, 2017; and Louisa Thomas, "America First, for Charles Lindbergh and Donald Trump," *New Yorker*, July 24, 2016.

81. Donald Trump, "Text of Donald Trump's Speech to the GOP Convention," Cleveland, OH, July 18–21, 2016.

82. Philip Bump and Aaron Blake, "Donald Trump's Dark Speech to the Republican National Convention, Annotated," *Washington Post*, July 21, 2016.

83. Paul Rich, "Reinhold Niebuhr and the Ethics of Realism in International Relations," *History of Political Thought* 13, no. 2 (1992): 281–98; and Bernard Bruneteau, "The Construction of Europe and the Concept of the Nation-State," *Contemporary European History* 9, no. 2 (2000): 245–60.

84. King Yik, Panelist, "U.S. Relations with Asia," 47th Annual Frank Church Symposium on Evolution of U.S. Foreign Policy in the 21st Century, Idaho State University, Pocatello, ID, March 1–2, 2018. I owe Dr. Yik immense gratitude for generously sharing his expert insights and materials on this topic.

85. Office of the United States Trade Representative (USTR), "President Trump Approves Relief for U.S. Washing Machine and Solar Cell Manufacturers," January 2018.

86. Benjamin H. Liebman and Kara M. Reynolds, "Innovation through Protection: Does Safeguard Protection Increase Investment in Research and Development?" *Southern Economic Journal* 80, no. 1 (2013): 205–25.

87. Andualem Sisay Gessesse, "Secretary Tillerson Advises to Be Cautious about Chinese Investments," *New Business Ethiopia: NBE*, Addis Ababa, March 9, 2018. See also "China Builds Ambitiously in Africa, and U.S. Sounds the Alarm," *The Hindu*, Chennai, India, March 9, 2018.

88. See Owei Lakemfa, "Rex Tillerson Came to Africa, Saw and Was Fired," *Vanguard*, Lagos, March 15, 2018.

89. Ibid.
90. Editor, "Kabore: Africa Has Chosen China as Leaders Arrive in Beijing," *Africa Times*, Johannesburg, Aug. 30, 2018; Kabore, "Africa Has Chosen China," *The Sun*, Lagos, Aug. 29, 2018.
91. Editor, "Kabore"; and Kabore, "Africa Has Chosen China."
92. Kabore, "Africa Has Chosen China."
93. Lakemfa, "The African Road to China."
94. Kabore, "Africa Has Chosen China."

14. THE OBAMA PRESIDENCY AND AFRICA

1. These words appeared on a banner in Kogelo, Kenya, celebrating Barack Obama's presidential inauguration on Jan. 20, 2009.
2. Ahmad A. Rahman, *The Regime Change of Kwame Nkrumah: Epic Heroism in Africa and the Diaspora* (New York: Palgrave Macmillan, 2007), 7. For a reflective and sobering analysis of this sentiment, see Jacob F. Ade Ajayi, "Expectations of Independence: A Generation after Independence" *Daedalus* 111, no. 2 (1982): 1–9; and Neil Lazarus, "Great Expectations and After: The Politics of Postcolonialism in African Fiction," *Social Text* 13, no. 14 (1986): 49–63. See also Giacomo Macola, "'It Means as If We Are Excluded from the Good Freedom': Thwarted Expectations of Independence in Luapula Province of Zambia, 1964–6," *Journal of African History* 47, no. 1 (2006): 43–56.
3. James Ferguson, *Expectations of Modernity: Myth and Meanings of Urban Life on the Zambian Copperbelt* (Berkeley: University of California Press, 1999), 13.
4. Karin van Bemmel, "Obama Made in Kenya: Appropriating the American Dream in Kogelo," *Africa Today* 59, no. 4 (2013), 69–90. Bemmel has noted that Obama's extended family in Kenya and indeed individuals and groups across the continent expressed parallel hopes.
5. Nelson Mandela cited in "Mandela Hails Obama after Election Victory," *Mail & Guardian*, Johannesburg, Nov. 5, 2008.
6. Paul Tiyambe Zeleza, *Barack Obama and African Diasporas: Dialogues and Dissensions* (Athens: Ohio University Press, 2009), 5.
7. See the Transatlantic Slave Trade Database, http://www.slavevoyages.org/assessment/estimates. The full extent of time covered is from 1501 to 1866.
8. U.S. Census Bureau, Report No. P60–256, "Income and Poverty in the United States: 2015." For a breakdown on African-born statistics, see David Dixon, "Characteristics of the African Born in the United States," Migration Policy Institute (MPI), Jan. 1, 2006.
9. Ruth Prince, "'Our Son': The U.S. Presidential Election in Western Kenya," *Anthropology Today* 24, no. 6 (2009): 4–7; and Alemayehu G. Mariam, "The Moral Hazard of U.S. Policy in Africa (Part I)," *Ethiopian Review*, March 11, 2011.
10. P. A. Madiega, T. Chantler, G. Jones, and R. Prince, "The U.S. Presidential Election in Western Kenya," *Anthropology Today* 4 (2008): 4–7, here 7; Matthew Carotenuto and Katherine Luongo, *Obama and Kenya: Contested Histories and the Politics of Belonging* (Athens: Ohio University Press, 2016), 98.
11. Carotenuto and Luongo, *Obama and Kenya*, 98.

12. See S. N. Eisenstaedt and René Lemarchand, eds., *Political Clientelism, Patronage and Development* (Beverly Hills, CA: Sage, 1981); Ernest Gellner and John Waterbury, eds., *Patrons and Clients in Mediterranean Societies* (London: Duckworth, 1977); Jonathan Fox, "The Difficult Transition from Clientelism to Citizenship," *World Politics* 46, no. 2, (1994): 151–84; and Steffen Schmidt, James C. Scott, Carl Lande, and Laura Guasti, eds., *Friends, Followers, and Factions: A Reader in Political Clientelism* (Berkeley: University of California Press, 1977).

13. Nicolas van de Walle, "The Democratization of Political Clientelism in Sub-Saharan Africa," paper delivered at the 3rd European Conference on African Studies, Leipzig, Germany, June 4–7, 2009.

14. Michela Wrong, "Kenya Glimpses a New Kind of Hero," *New Statesman*, London, Sept. 11, 2006. See also Bemmel, "Obama Made in Kenya," 74.

15. See Bruce J. Berman, "Ethnicity, Patronage and the African State," *African Affairs* (1998): 97, 305–41; and Horman Chitonge, *Economic Growth and Development in Africa: Understanding Trends and Prospects* (New York: Routledge, 2015), chap. 5. At least, in chapter 5 of his book, Chitonge made this point very strongly. This revelation is contrary to the extant literature inspired by Berman, who once suggested that the client–patron relationship is peculiar to Africa.

16. Raphael Chijioke Njoku, "Consociation: Its Relevance for Nigeria," *Nationalism and Ethnic Politics* 5, no. 2 (1999): 1–35; and Raphael Chijioke Njoku, "Deconstructing Abacha: Demilitarization and Democratic Consolidation in Nigeria after Abacha Era," *Government and Opposition* 36, no. 1 (2001): 71–96.

17. See for instance Claude Ake, *Democracy and Development in Africa* (Washington, DC: Brookings Institution, 1996); Goral Hyden, *Underdevelopment and an Uncaptured Peasantry* (Berkeley: University of California Press, 1980).

18. Ricky Jones, *What Is Wrong with Obamamania? Black America, Black Leadership, and the Death of Political Imagination* (Albany, NY: SUNY Press, 2008). See also Bemmel, "Obama Made in Kenya," 73.

19. Kundai Victor Chirindo, "Barack Obama and the African Idea: Typology, Tropology, and Stasis in Spatial Counter-Narratives" (Ph.D. diss., University of Kansas, 2012), iii.

20. Ann dropped "Stanley," a name given to her by her parents, in 1960 at age 17 for the obvious reason that it is a man's name.

21. Janny Scott, "Obama's Mother No Simple Kansan," *New York Times*, March 14, 2008; Nancy Grape, "A Single Woman Helped Shape Obama," *Maine Women Magazine*, July 25, 2011; and Sarah Watson, "On President Obama's Mother: A Single Woman and Her Egalitarian Spirit," *Pop Matter*, Feb. 7, 2012.

22. Barack Obama, *Dreams from My Father: A Story of Race and Inheritance* (New York: Crown Publishers, 1995).

23. Obama, "Keynote Address at the 2004 Democratic National Convention." See also Barack Obama, "Selma Voting Rights March Commemoration," http://www.barack obama.com/2007/03/04/selma_voting_rights_march_comm.php.

24. Olaudah Equiano, *The Interesting Narrative of the Life of Olaudah Equiano, Or Gustavus Vassa, The African Written By Himself* (London: Published by the author, 1789), chap. 1.

25. Obama, *Dreams from My Father*, 6; also Barack Obama, "How I Am Still Haunted by My Father," *Daily Mail*, Feb. 8, 2008; and Dan P. McAdams, *The Redemptive Self: Stories Americans Live By*, revised and expanded edition (Oxford: Oxford University Press, 2013), 245–46.

26. Joanne F. Price, *Barack Obama: The Voice of an American Leader* (Westport, CT: Greenwood Press, 2008), 14; Jonathan Hart, *From Shakespeare to Obama: A Study of Language, Slavery, and Place* (New York: Palgrave Macmillan, 2013), 170; Janny Scott, "A Free Spirited Wanderer Who Set Obama's Path," *New York Times*, March 14, 2008; and Gary J. Dorrien, *The Obama Question: A Progressive Perspective* (Lanham, MD: Rowman and Littlefield, 2012), 26.

27. "Barack Obama Cancels Meeting after Philippines President Calls Him 'Son of a Whore,'" *The Guardian*, London, Sept. 5, 2016. Duterte was quoted directly by Agence France-Presse.

28. Carol E. Lee, "Obama Nixes Meeting after Rodrigo Duterte Lobs an Insult," *Wall Street Journal Magazine*, New York, Sept. 5, 2016.

29. Janny Scott, *A Singular Woman: The Untold Story of Barack Obama's Mother* (New York: Riverhead Books, 2011); and also Janny Scott, "Obama's Young Mother Abroad," *New York Times*, April 20, 2011.

30. Jeffrey Goldberg, "'The Obama Doctrine': *The Atlantic*'s Exclusive Report on the U.S. President's Foreign Policy Decisions," *The Atlantic*, March 10, 2016; and H. A. Hyller, "Barack Obama's Perspective on Islam Is Mistaken," *The National*, New York, March 17, 2016.

31. Obama, *Dreams from My Father*, 22.

32. Jodi Kantor, "A Candidate, His Minister, and the Search for Faith," *New York Times*, April 30, 2007.

33. Janny Scott, "Obama's Young Mother Abroad," *New York Times*, April 20, 2011. See also Sandra Fluck, review of Janny Scott, *A Singular Woman: The Untold Story of Barack Obama's Mother*, Bookscover2cover, Sept. 17, 2016.

34. Scott, "Obama's Young Mother Abroad."

35. Dan Amira, "President Obama Wanted to Be Prime Minister of Indonesia," *New York Magazine*, April 20, 2011; and Stephanie Condon, "Where Obama 'Learned to Be Cool': Profiling Obama's Mother in Indonesia," *CBS*, April 20, 2011.

36. Kevin Omondi (a.k.a. Dola Kabarry), *Change the World*, 2008 album. Kabarry, whose father's name is also Barrack, met with Obama during his 2008 three-month promotion music tour of the United States. See "Kabarry: I'm Benga's Best," *The Standard*, Nairobi, Oct. 3, 2008.

37. Speaking in proverbs is typical of Luo and a general form of African elders' reaction to historical moments of this nature. Elders react with sayings that capture the essence of the time. See Bemmel, "Obama Made in Kenya," 74.

38. Brian Larkin, "Indian Films and Nigerian Lovers: Media and the Creation of Parallel Modernities," *Africa: Journal of the African International Institute* 67 (1997): 406–40.

39. In its coverage of the visit, *The Telegraph* wrote that "Obama is seeking to lift up the continent of his ancestors." See "Obama Arrives in Ghana on First African Trip," *The Telegraph*, London, July 11, 2009.

40. Maximus Attah, "Ghana Readies Itself for Obama's Visit," *African Voice*, Accra, Ghana, July 2009. Experts on foreign policy issues interjected that Obama chose Ghana as an exemplar of successful democratic politics and to convey a nonconfrontational scolding of the third-term presidents and corrupt dictators who presided elsewhere in Africa. See Drew Hinshaw, "Obama in Africa: Why He Chose Ghana," *Christian Science Monitor*, July 11, 2009.

41. Arjun Appadurai, "Disjuncture and Difference in the Global Cultural Economy," in *The Anthropology of Globalization*, ed. Jonathan Xavier Inda and Renato Rosaldo (Maiden, UK: Blackwell Publishing, 2002), 52.

42. Sehlare Makgetlaneng, "Obama's United States Foreign Policy towards Africa," *Race and History*, March 8, 2008.

43. Jay Newton-Small, "Obama Hosts 51 African Leaders amid Grumbling over His Record," *Time*, Aug. 5, 2014.

44. After the 2009 snub, Nigeria's minister for foreign affairs, Mr. Ojo Maduekwe, summoned the U.S. ambassador to Nigeria to register the country's displeasure with Obama's actions. See Iyorwuese Hagher, *Nigeria: After the Nightmare* (Lanham, MD: University Press of America, 2011), 13; and Heinrich Bergstresser, *A Decade of Nigeria: Politics, Economy and Society, 2004–2016* (Leiden, the Netherlands: Brill, 2016), 136.

45. "Why Obama Snubbed Nigeria," *The Ghanaian Times*, June 2, 2009.

46. Makgetlaneng, "Obama's United States Foreign Policy towards Africa."

47. Barack Obama, Remarks to the Chicago Council on Global Affairs, April 23, 2007, *The American Presidency Project*, http://www.presidency.ucsb.edu/ws/?pid=77043.

48. Jeffrey Gentleman, "Obama Gets a Warm Welcome in Kenya," *New York Times*, Aug. 26, 2006.

49. President Obama, Inaugural Day Address, Jan. 20, 2009. See also Beatrice Gormley, *Barack Obama: Our 44th President: A Real Life Story* (New York: Aladdin, 2015), chap. 15.

50. Frida Ghitis, "Less Change than Some Seek?" *McClatchy Newspapers*, Livonia, MI, Jan. 29, 2009.

51. Schneidman, "Africa: Obama's Three Objectives for Continent." For more on this, see Witney Schneidman, "2015: A Pivotal Year for Obama's Africa Legacy," in *Foresight Africa: Top Priorities for the Continent in 2015*, ed. Jideofor Adibe et al. (Washington, DC: The Brookings Institution, 2015), 42–50.

52. BarackObama.com, "Barack Obama: Fighting HIV/AIDS World Wide," speech in Lake Forest, CA, Dec. 1, 2006 (accessed on July 22, 2018 at https://www.allen-temple.org/images/stories/aidsministry/BarackObamaFightingAIDS.pdf).

53. Ibid.

54. An assessment of this failure is reflected in the USAID report of 2016. See USAID, *Feed the Future Global Performance Evaluation Report* (Washington, DC: United States Agency for International Development, 2016).

55. See U.S. Department of State, "The United States and International Development: Partnering for Growth," Office of the Spokesman, Washington, DC, Aug. 6, 2007.

56. See International Monitoring Fund (IMF), Global Monitoring Report 2004, April 16, 2004, p. ii.

57. See H. Con. Res. 467—Declaring Genocide in Darfur, Sudan, Sponsored by Rep. Payne, Donald M. D-NJ-10 (Introduced 06/24/2004).

58. For the full report on Congolese casualties, see the report by the U.S. Government Accountability Office (GAO), "Testimony before the Congressional Human Rights Caucasus—The Democratic Republic of the Congo: Major Challenges Impede Efforts to Achieve U.S. Policy Objectives; Systematic Assessment of Progress Is Needed," statement by David Gootnick, Director, International Affairs and Trade, released March 6, 2008.

59. For a full study of this, see the original document: "The Comprehensive Agreement between the Government of the Republic of Sudan and the Sudan People's Liberation Movement/Sudan People's Liberation Army," dated Dec. 31, 2004, and signed Jan. 9, 2005. See also Elke Grawert, *After the Comprehensive Agreement in Sudan* (Rochester, NY: Boydell and Brewer, 2010).

60. Mark Bowen, *Black Hawk Down: A Story of Modern War* (New York: Signet Press, 1999), 111; Caleb Carr, "The Consequences of Somalia," *World Policy Journal* 1, no. 4 (1994): 1–4.

61. Ambassador Robert B. Oakley and David Tucker, *Two Perspectives on Interventions and Humanitarian Operations* (Carlisle Barracks, PA: Strategic Studies Institute, U.S. Army War College, July 1, 1997), 16.

62. Kristin Spivey, "The United Nations' Humanitarian Intervention in Somalia and the Just War Theory" (M.A. thesis, Vrije University, Brussels, Belgium, June 2008), 5.

63. For instance, see Eric Schmidt's "U.S. Mission in Somalia: Seeking a Clear Rationale," *New York Times*, Aug. 23, 1993; and Robert D. Warrington, "The Helmets May Be Blue, but the Blood's Still Red: The Dilemma of the U.S. Participation in UN Peace Operations," *Comparative Strategy* 14, no. 1 (January—March 1995): 25.

64. Department of Public Information (hereafter DPI), *United Nations Somalia—UN-OSOM II* (New York: Department of Public Information Printing Office, March 21, 1997), 93. The strict stipulation was that the United States would assume total command of the UNITAF. The mission would remain only until UN peacekeepers were able to resume their duties safely and efficiently. See Ted Galen Carpenter, "Setting a Dangerous Precedent in Somalia," CATO Foreign Policy Briefing No. 20, Dec. 18, 1992, 3.

65. Durant was saved from the crowd by a local militia leader, Yousef Dahir Mo'alim, who planned to ransom him in exchange for the release of imprisoned clan members.

66. Carpenter, "Setting a Dangerous Precedent in Somalia," 312–15, 408.

67. Amnesty International, *AI Report 1997: Somalia* (London: Amnesty International Publications, 1997), 1–2.

68. Bowen, *Black Hawk Down*, 410.

69. Witney W. Schneidman, "Africa: Obama's Three Objectives for Continent," *All Africa*, Sept. 29, 2008, https://allafrica.com/stories/200809291346.html. Schneidman was an adviser on Africa who worked on Obama's election, and he sets out Obama's fundamental policy objectives for Africa. Schneidman was the deputy assistant secretary of state for African affairs during President Clinton's administration. This article is an excerpt from remarks to the Constituency for Africa, 2008 Ronald H. Brown African

Affairs Series forum "U.S. –Africa Policy Agenda and the Next Administration" at the National Press Club in Washington, DC.

70. Andrew Buncombe, "Cameron Didn't Have 'Bromance' with Obama and Thought He Was a Narcissist, Claims Former Adviser," *The Independent*, London, Jan. 8, 2017; and Michael Wolff, *Fire and Fury: Inside the Trump White House* (New York: Henry Holt and Co., 2018).

71. Goldberg, "The Obama Doctrine."

72. Campbell, "Obama in Africa."

73. Patrick Bond, *Looting Africa: The Economics of Exploitation* (London: Zed Books, 2005).

74. James K. Boyce and Léonce Ndikumana, *Africa's Odious Debts: How Foreign Loans and Capital Flight Bled a Continent* (London: Zed Books, 2011).

75. Beatrice Dupuy, "Obama Was a 'Glorified' Senator Who Lacked Experience, MSNBC's Senator Scarborough Says," *Newsweek*, New York, Jan. 10, 2018.

76. John A. Gans, Jr., "The Democratic Primaries," in *The 2008 Presidential Elections: A Story in Four Acts*, ed. Erik Jones and Salvatore Vassallo (New York: Palgrave Macmillan, 2009), 22; Martin Dupuis and Keith Boeckelman, *Barack Obama: The New Face of America* (Westport, CT: Greenwood, 2008), 156; and Dan Balz and Haynes Johnson, *The Battle for America: The Story of an Extraordinary Election* (New York: Penguin Books, 2008).

77. James Ferguson, "Global Disconnect: Abjection and the Aftermath of Modernism," in *The Anthropology of Globalization*, ed. Jonathan Xavier Inda and Renato Rosaldo (Malden, UK: Blackwell Publishing, 2002), 142.

CONCLUSION

1. Frantz Fanon, *The Wretched of the Earth*, trans. Constance Farrington with a preface by Jean-Paul Sartre (New York: Grove Press, 1963), 92–93.

2. See Clement Okafor, "Igbo Cosmology and the Parameters of Individual Accomplishment in *Things Fall Apart*," in *Chinua Achebe's "Things Fall Apart": A Case Book*, ed. Isidore Okpewoh (Oxford: Oxford University Press, 2003), 70; Meki Nzewi and Odyke Nzewi, *A Contemporary Study of Music Arts Informed by African Indigenous Knowledge Systems*, vol. 4: *Illuminations, Reflections, and Explorations* (Pretoria, South Africa: Center for Indigenous Instrumental African Music and Dance, 2007), 89.

3. Martin Luther King, Jr., "Letter from Birmingham Jail" (or "Letter from Birmingham City Jail and the Negro Is Your Brother"), April 16, 1963.

4. John Owen, "How Liberalism Produces Democratic Peace," in *Debating the Democratic Peace*, ed. Michael E. Brown, Sean M. Lynn-Jones, and Steve E. Miller (Cambridge, MA: MIT Press, 1993), 123.

5. Isaiah Berlin, *Four Essays on Liberalism* (London: Oxford University Press, 1969); Michael Doyle, "Liberalism and World Politics," *American Political Science Review* 80, no. 4 (1986): 1151–69; and Stephen Holmes, *The Anatomy of Antiliberalism* (Cambridge, MA: Harvard University Press, 1993), 3–4.

INDEX